STOP!
YOU MAY BE READING THE WRONG WAY!

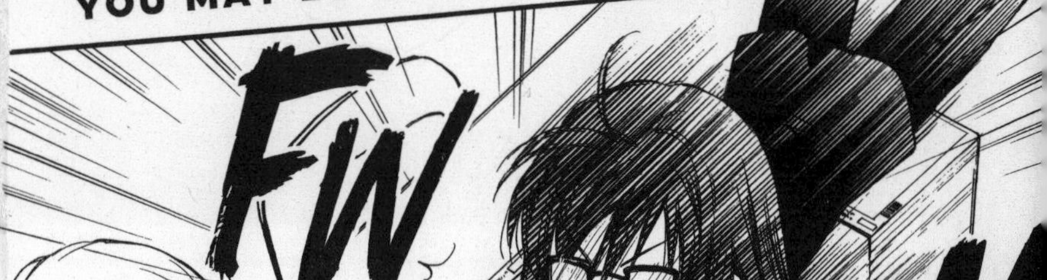
FW
OMP

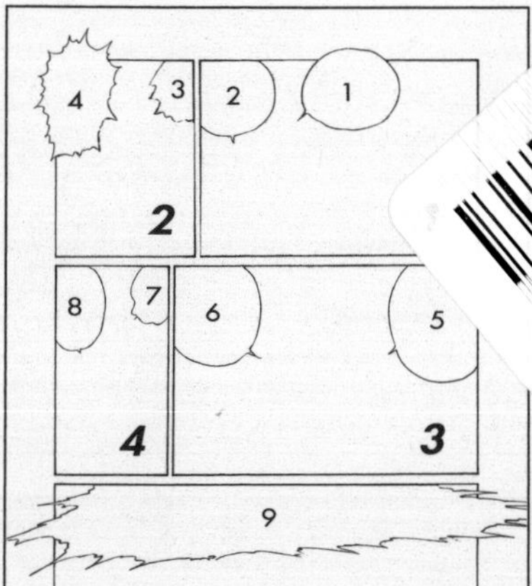
1
2
3
4
2
5
6
7
8
3
4
9
5
142

In keeping with the original Japanese comic format, this book reads from right to left—so action, sound effects and word balloons are completely reversed to preserve the orientation of the original artwork.

Check out the diagram shown here to get the hang of things, and then turn to the other side of the book to get started!

IDOL dreams 2

SHOJO BEAT EDITION

STORY & ART BY **ARINA TANEMURA**

TRANSLATION **Tetsuichiro Miyaki**
TOUCH-UP ART & LETTERING **Inori Fukuda Trant**
DESIGN **Shawn Carrico**
EDITOR **Nancy Thistlethwaite**

Thirty One Idream by Arina Tanemura
© Arina Tanemura 2014
All rights reserved.
First published in Japan in 2014 by HAKUSENSHA, Inc., Tokyo.
English language translation rights arranged with HAKUSENSHA, Inc., Tokyo.

Printed in the U.S.A.

Published by VIZ Media, LLC
P.O. Box 77010
San Francisco, CA 94107

10 9 8 7 6 5 4 3 2 1
First printing, March 2016

www.viz.com

www.shojobeat.com

IDOL dreams

STORY & ART BY

ARINA TANEMURA

2

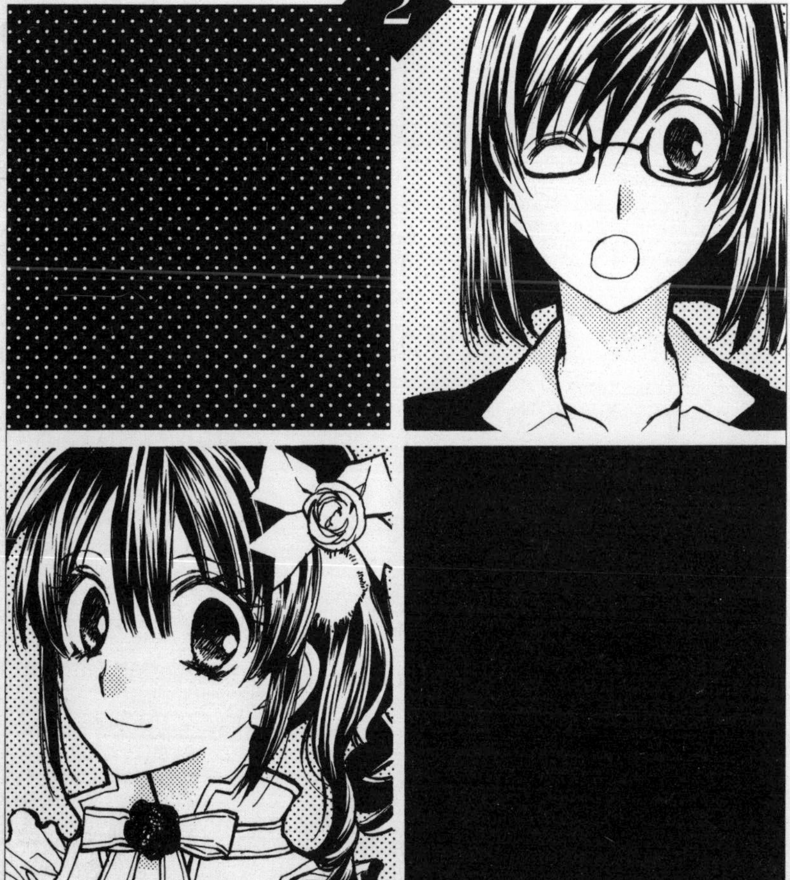

IDOL *dreams* 2

CONTENTS

IDOL dreams

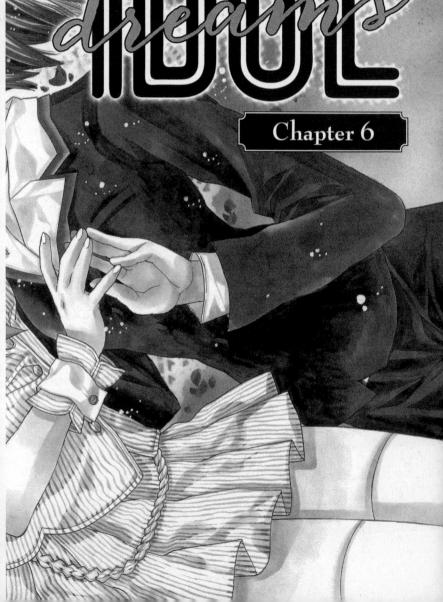

IDOL dreams

Chapter 6

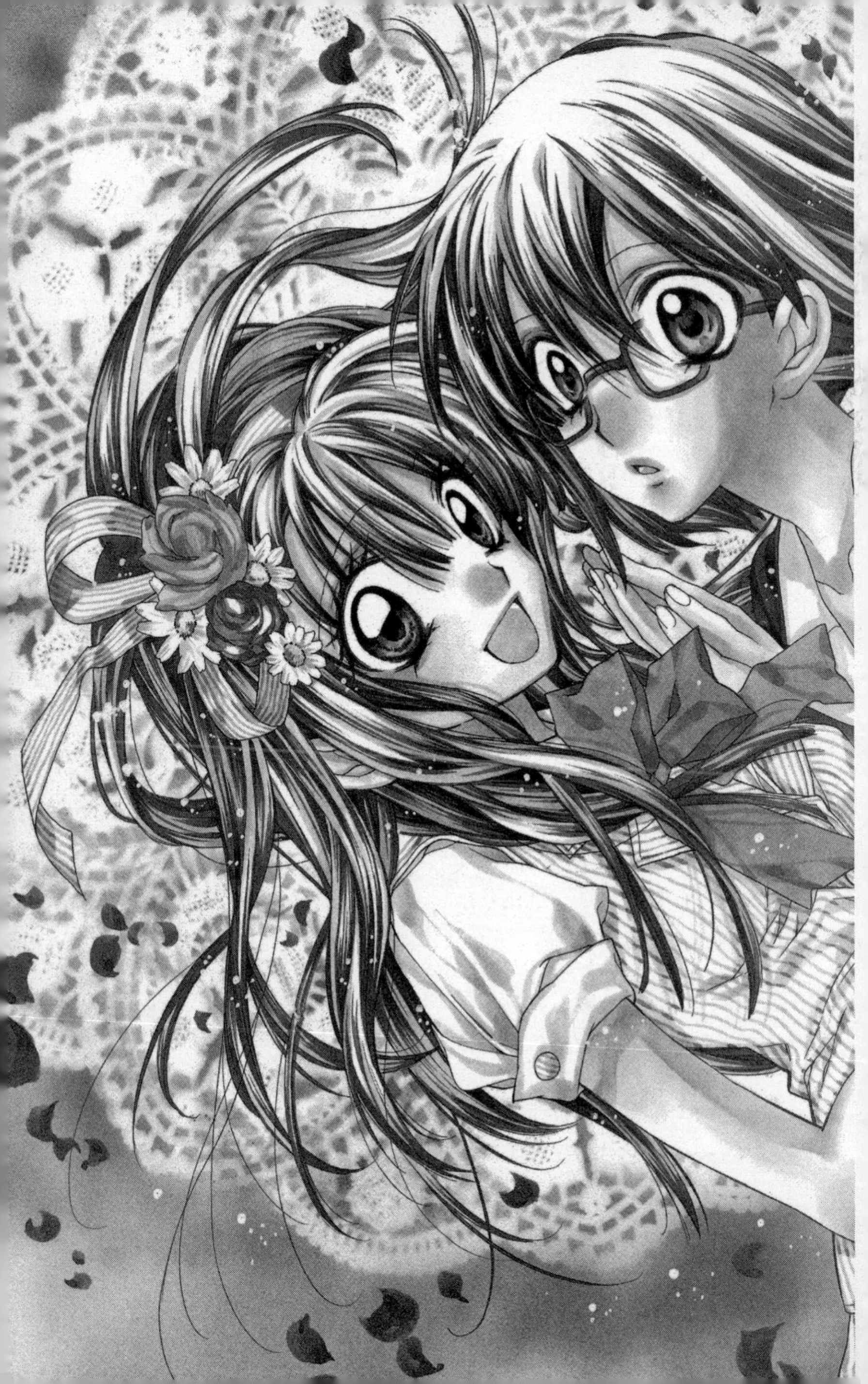

IDOL dreams

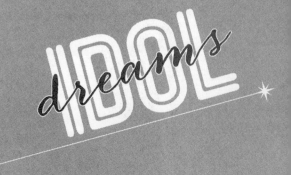

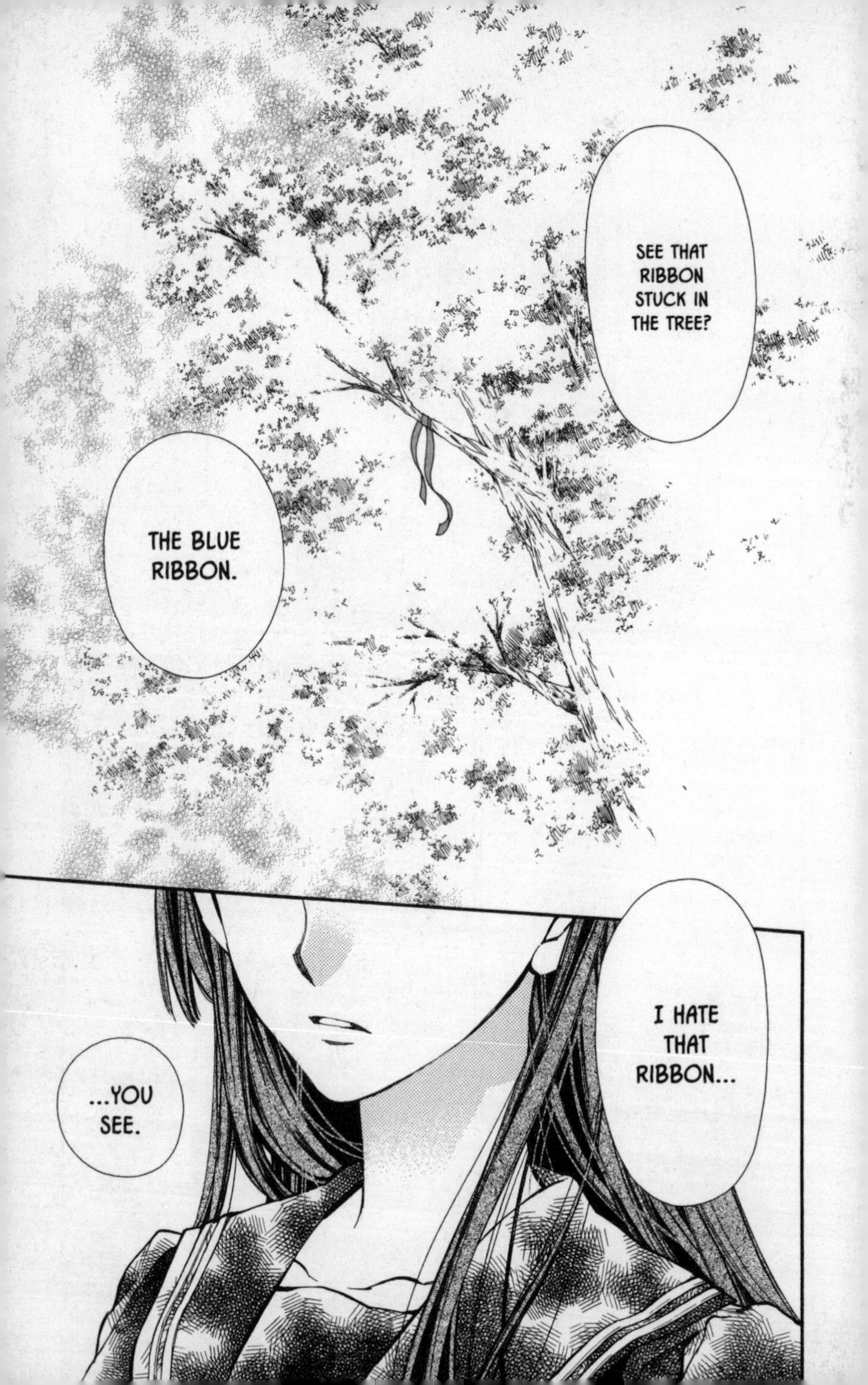
SEE THAT RIBBON STUCK IN THE TREE?
THE BLUE RIBBON.
I HATE THAT RIBBON...
...YOU SEE.

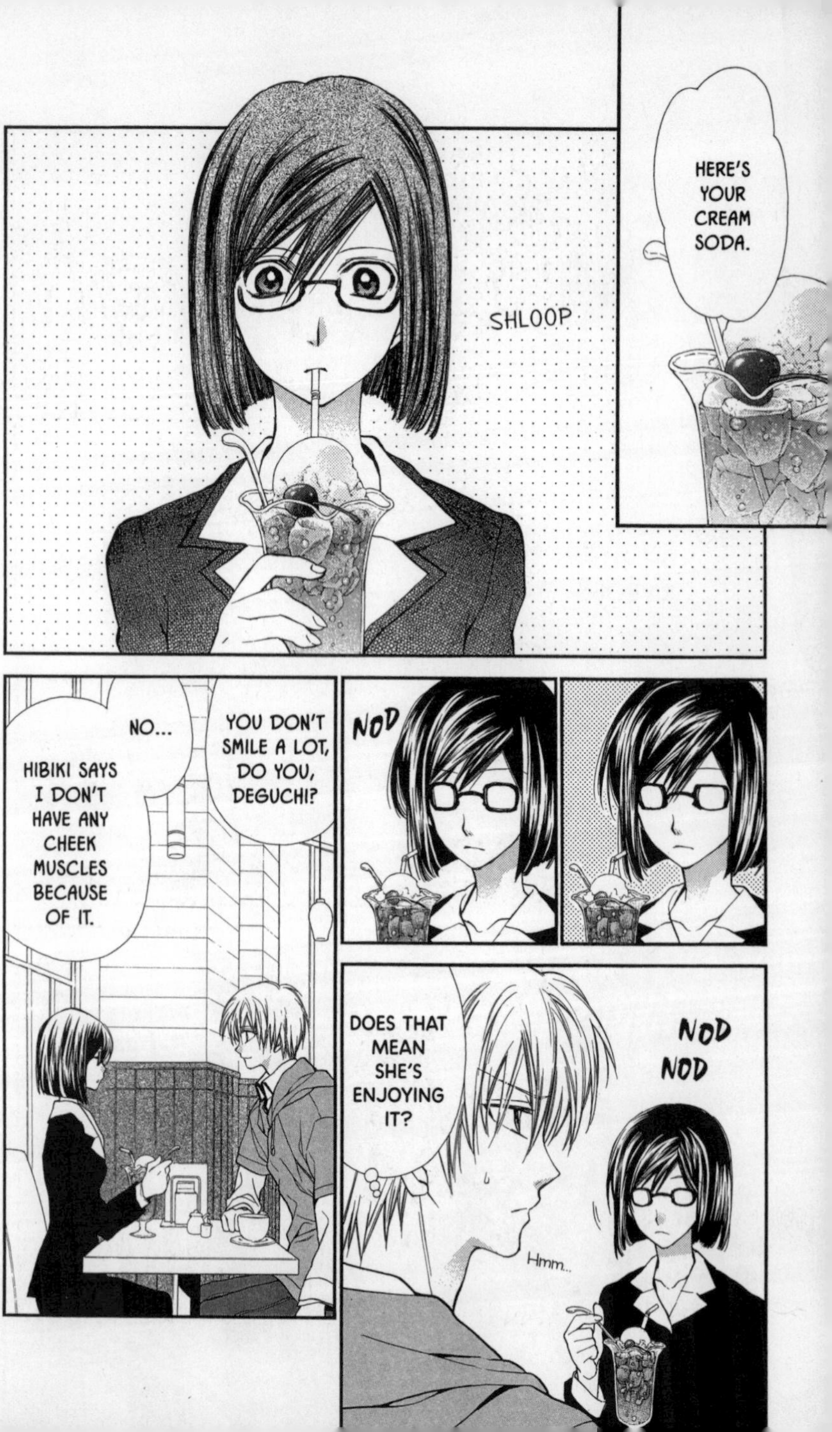
HERE'S YOUR CREAM SODA.
SHLOOP
NOD
DOES THAT MEAN SHE'S ENJOYING IT?
NOD NOD
Hmm..
YOU DON'T SMILE A LOT, DO YOU, DEGUCHI?
NO...
HIBIKI SAYS I DON'T HAVE ANY CHEEK MUSCLES BECAUSE OF IT.

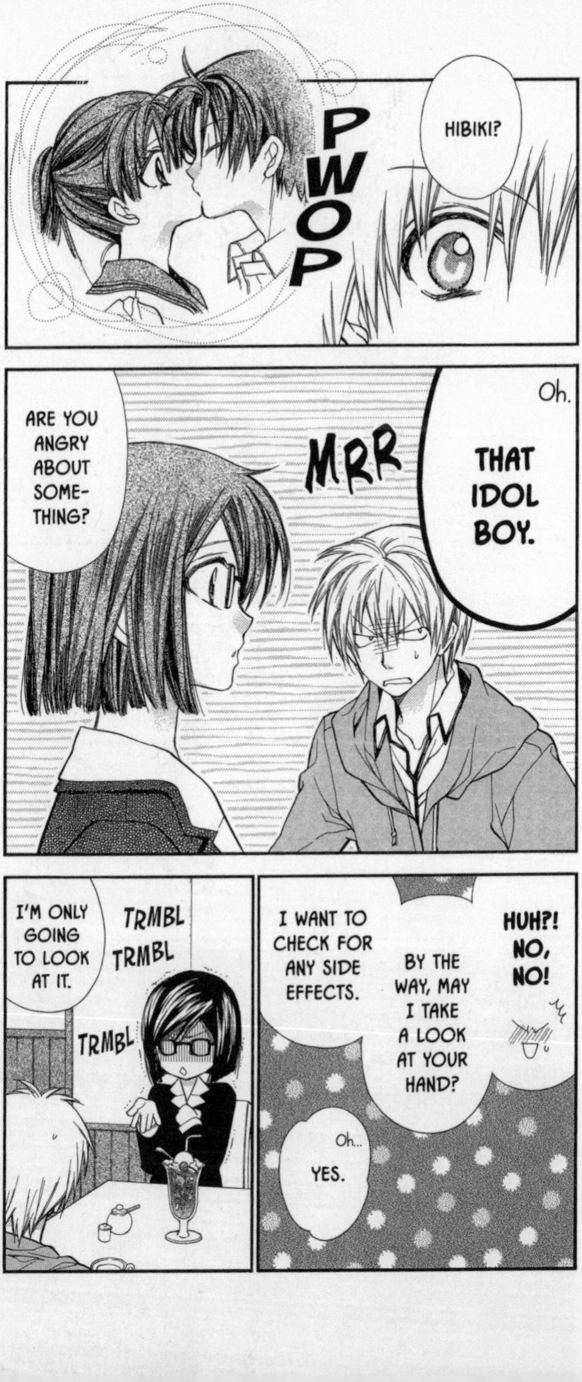
HIBIKI?
PWOP
Oh.
THAT IDOL BOY.
MRR
ARE YOU ANGRY ABOUT SOME-THING?
HUH?! NO, NO!
BY THE WAY, MAY I TAKE A LOOK AT YOUR HAND?
I WANT TO CHECK FOR ANY SIDE EFFECTS.
Oh... YES.
TRMBL
TRMBL
I'M ONLY GOING TO LOOK AT IT.
TRMBL

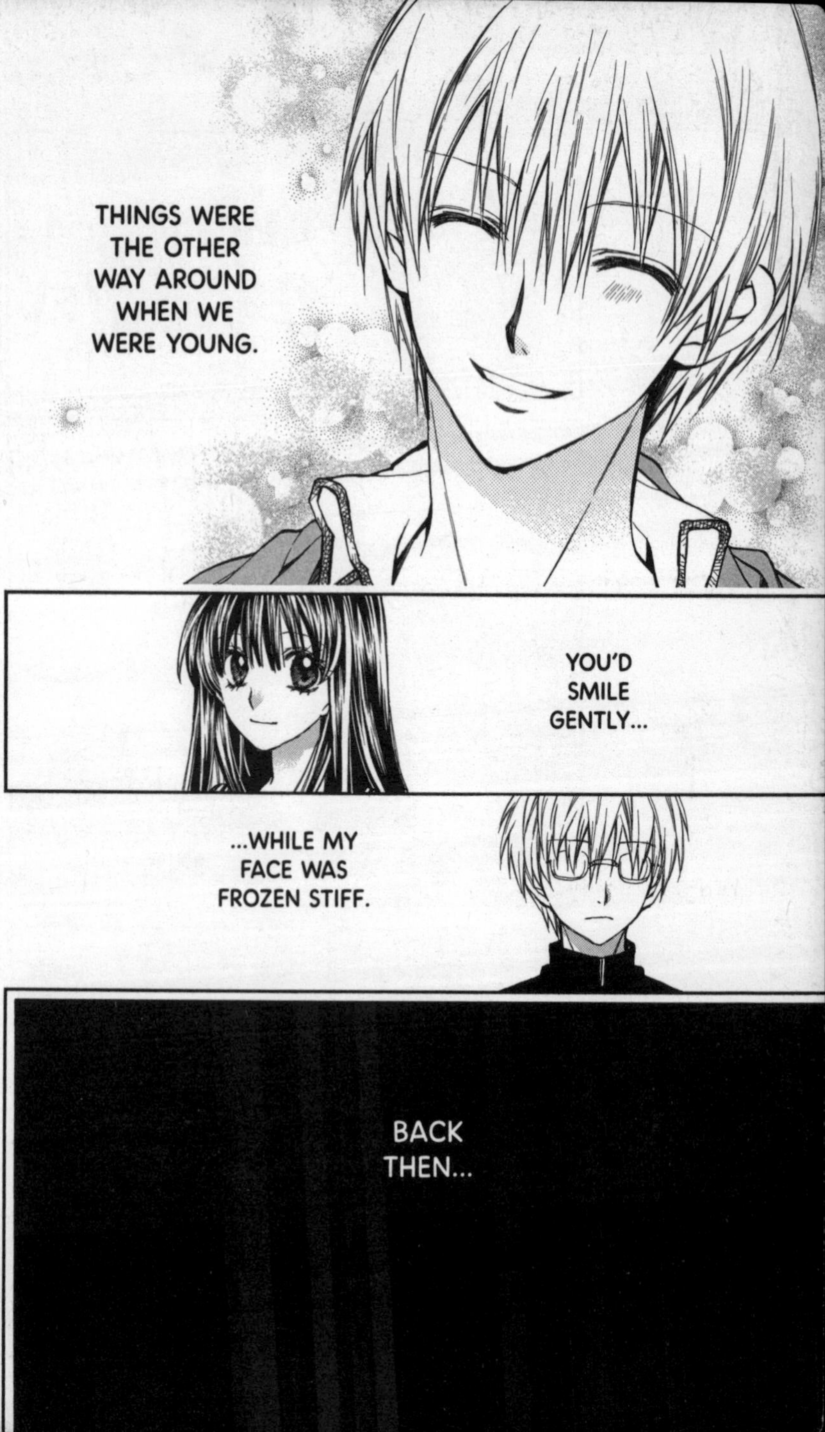
THINGS WERE THE OTHER WAY AROUND WHEN WE WERE YOUNG.
YOU'D SMILE GENTLY...
...WHILE MY FACE WAS FROZEN STIFF.
BACK THEN...

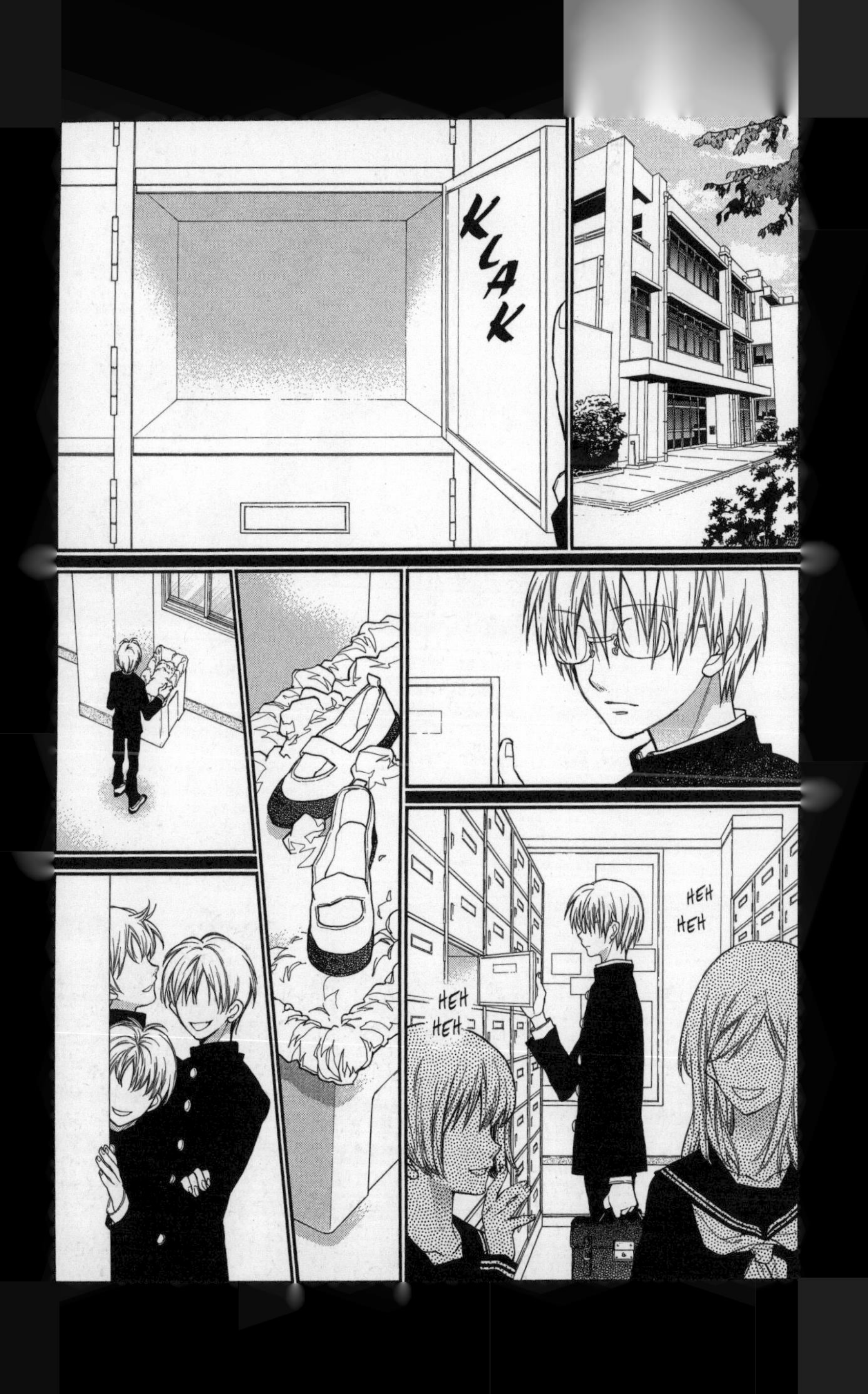
KLAK
HEH HEH
HEH HEH

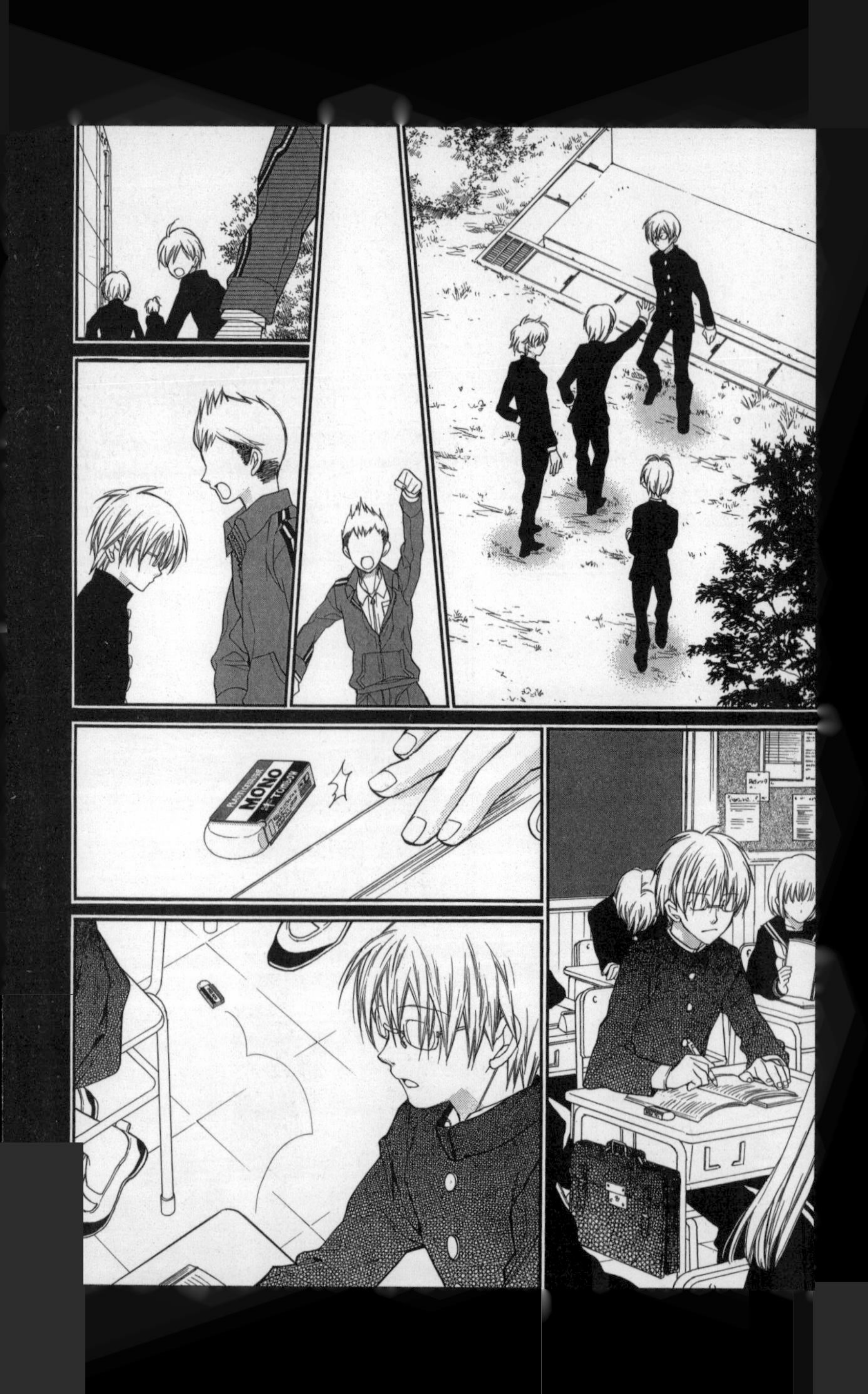
MONO
Tombow

EVERYTHING WAS MEANING-LESS.

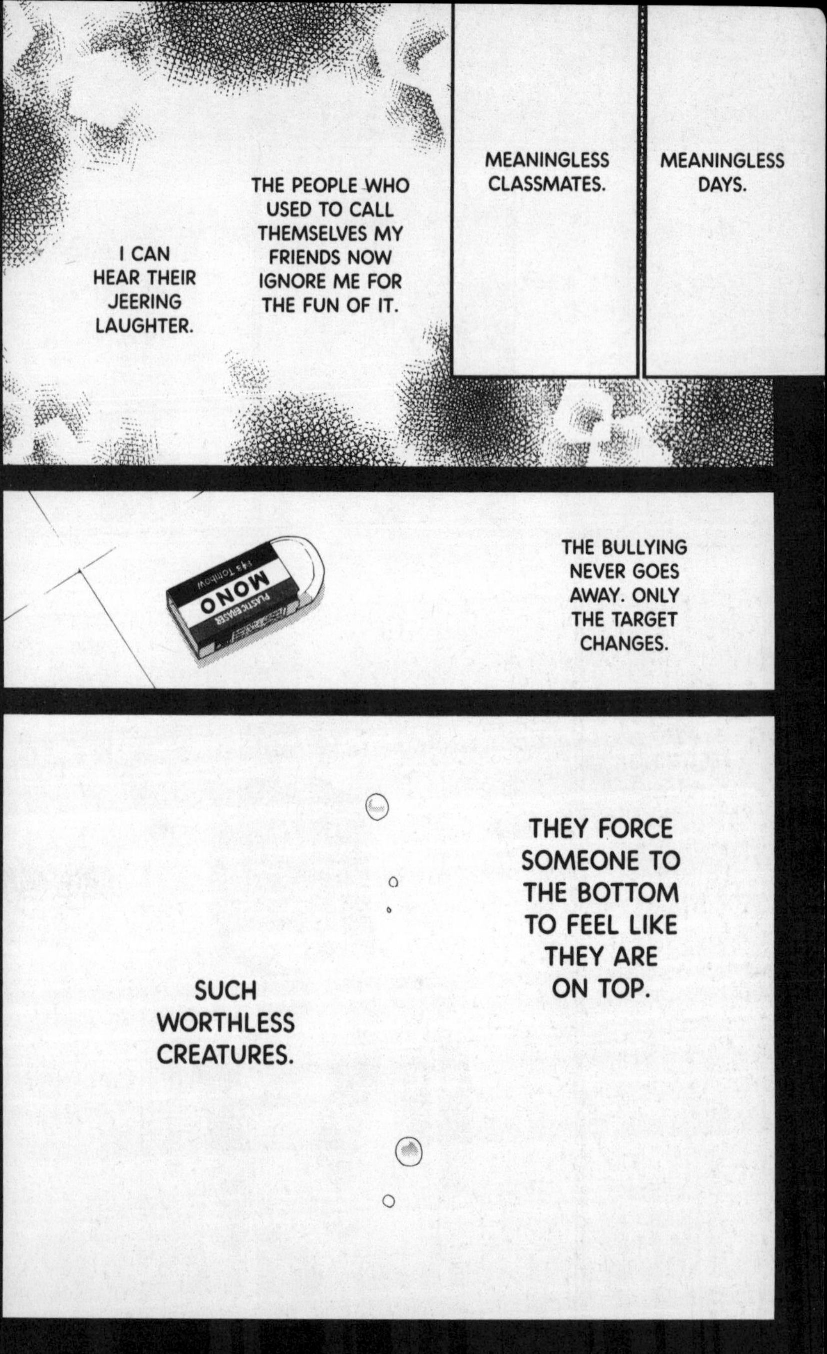
MEANINGLESS DAYS.
MEANINGLESS CLASSMATES.
THE PEOPLE WHO USED TO CALL THEMSELVES MY FRIENDS NOW IGNORE ME FOR THE FUN OF IT.
I CAN HEAR THEIR JEERING LAUGHTER.
THE BULLYING NEVER GOES AWAY. ONLY THE TARGET CHANGES.
MONO
THEY FORCE SOMEONE TO THE BOTTOM TO FEEL LIKE THEY ARE ON TOP.
SUCH WORTHLESS CREATURES.

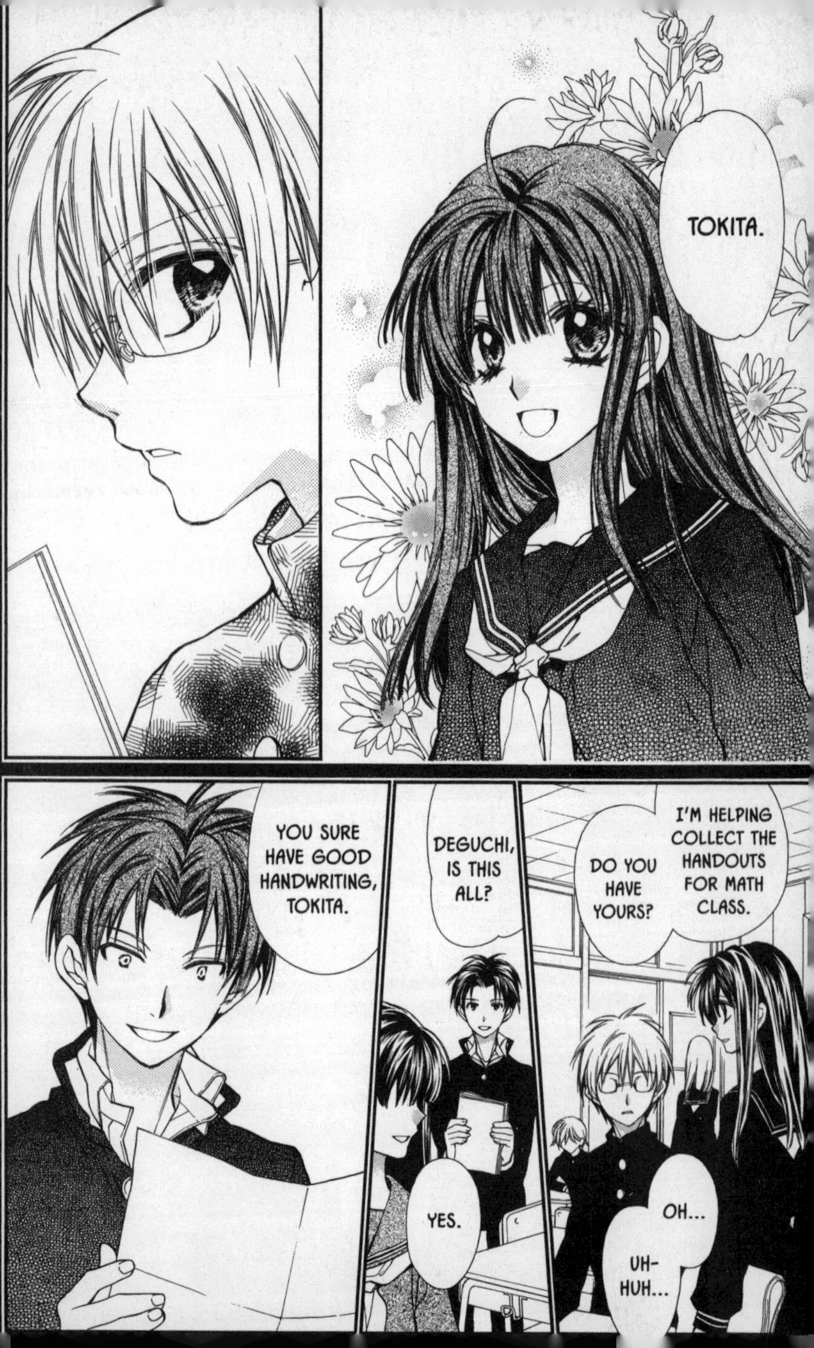
TOKITA.
I'M HELPING COLLECT THE HANDOUTS FOR MATH CLASS.
DO YOU HAVE YOURS?
OH...
UH-HUH...
DEGUCHI, IS THIS ALL?
YES.
YOU SURE HAVE GOOD HANDWRITING, TOKITA.

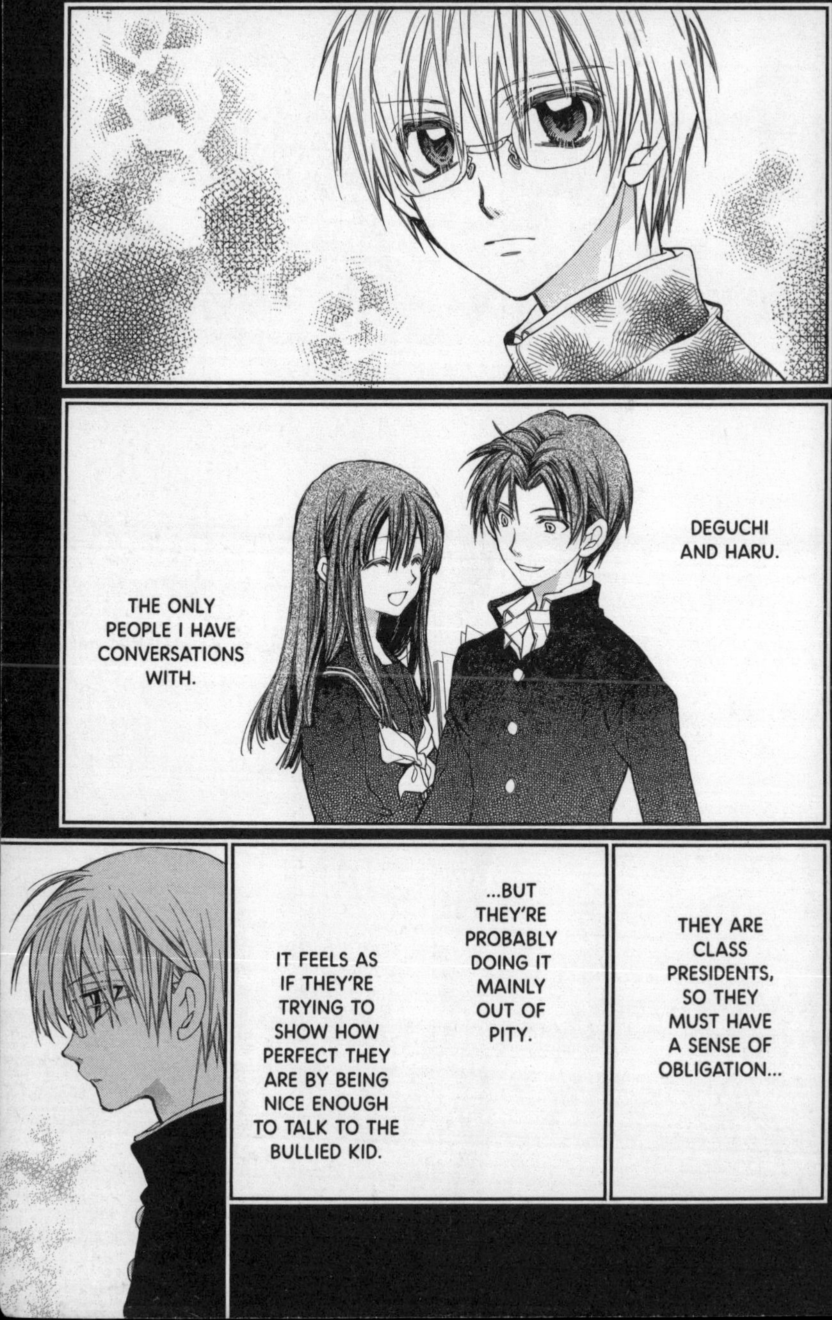
DEGUCHI AND HARU.
THE ONLY PEOPLE I HAVE CONVERSATIONS WITH.
THEY ARE CLASS PRESIDENTS, SO THEY MUST HAVE A SENSE OF OBLIGATION...
...BUT THEY'RE PROBABLY DOING IT MAINLY OUT OF PITY.
IT FEELS AS IF THEY'RE TRYING TO SHOW HOW PERFECT THEY ARE BY BEING NICE ENOUGH TO TALK TO THE BULLIED KID.

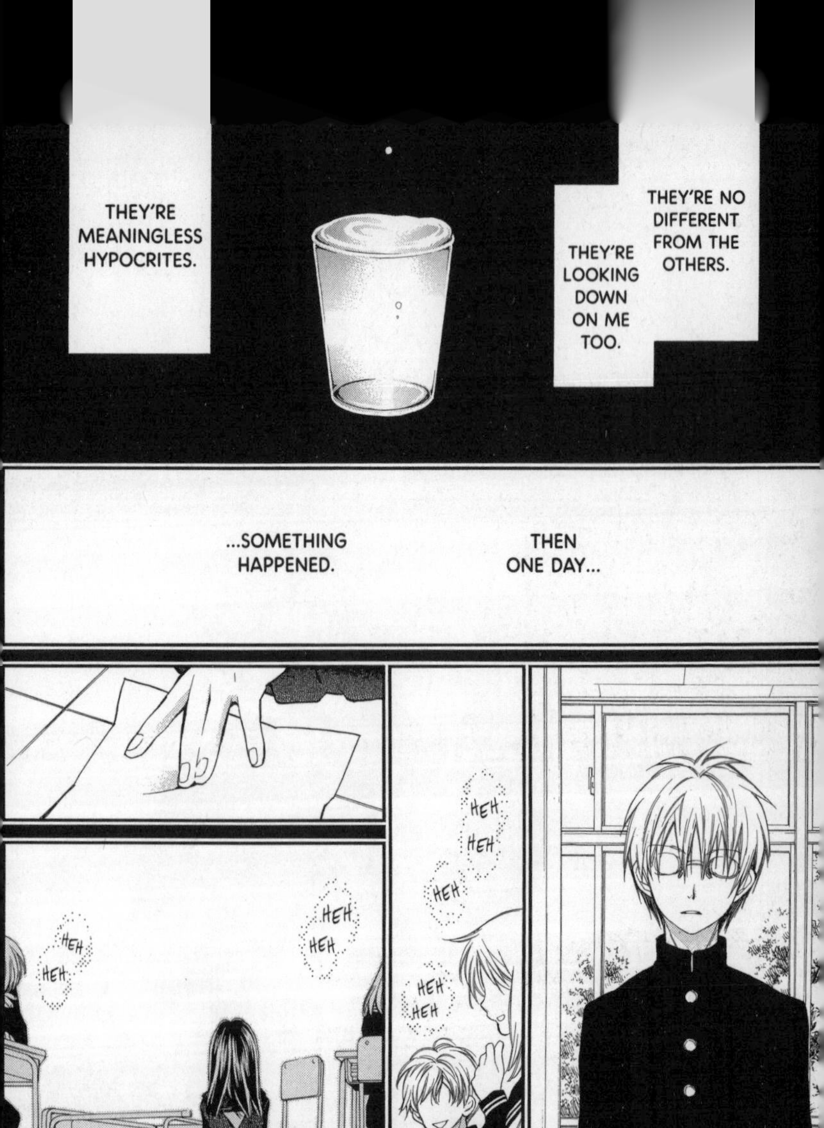
THEY'RE NO DIFFERENT FROM THE OTHERS.
THEY'RE LOOKING DOWN ON ME TOO.
THEY'RE MEANINGLESS HYPOCRITES.
THEN ONE DAY...
...SOMETHING HAPPENED.
HEH HEH
HEH
HEH HEH
HEH HEH
HEH HEH

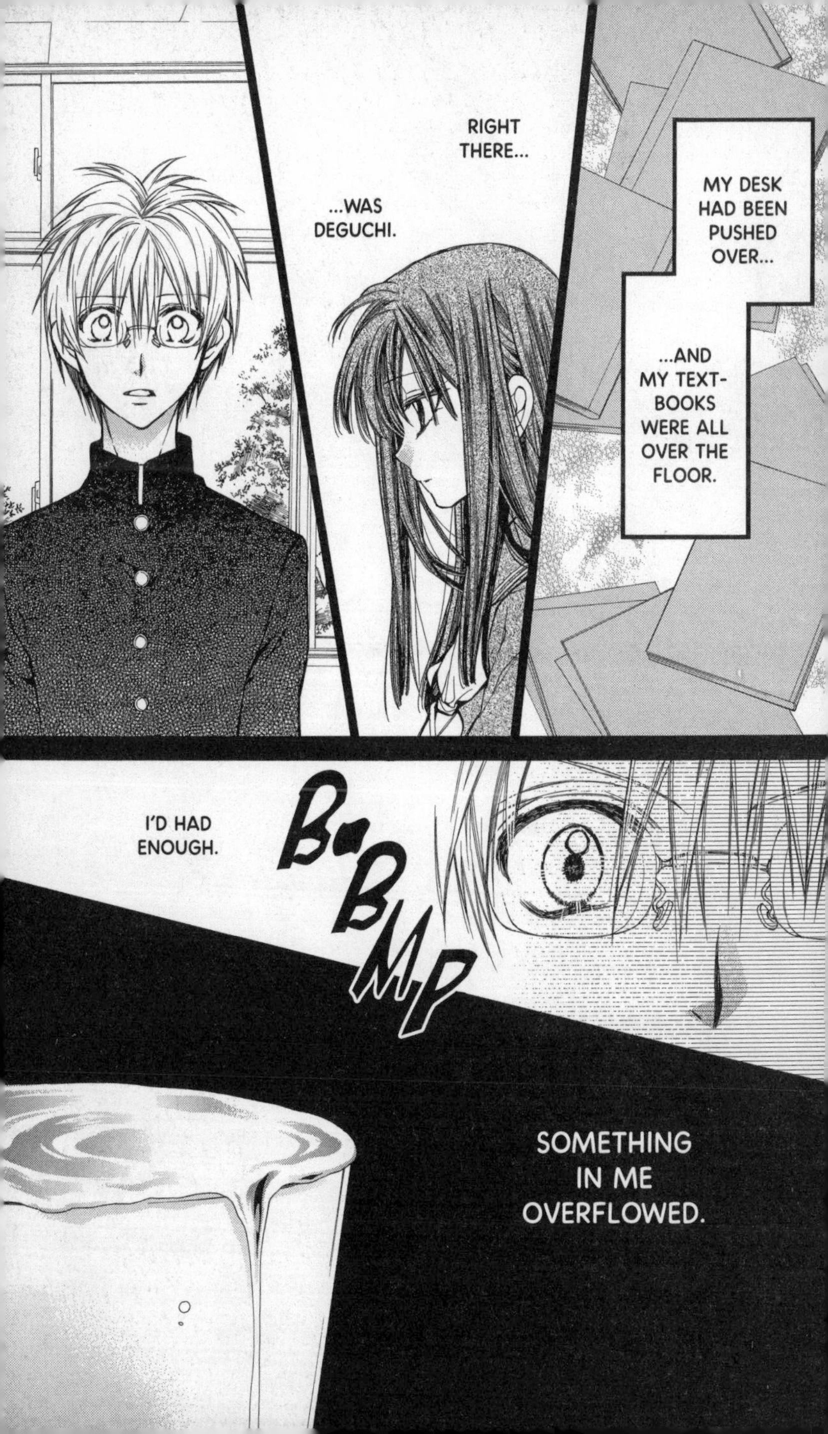
MY DESK HAD BEEN PUSHED OVER...
...AND MY TEXT-BOOKS WERE ALL OVER THE FLOOR.
RIGHT THERE...
...WAS DEGUCHI.
BA-BMP
I'D HAD ENOUGH.
SOMETHING IN ME OVERFLOWED.

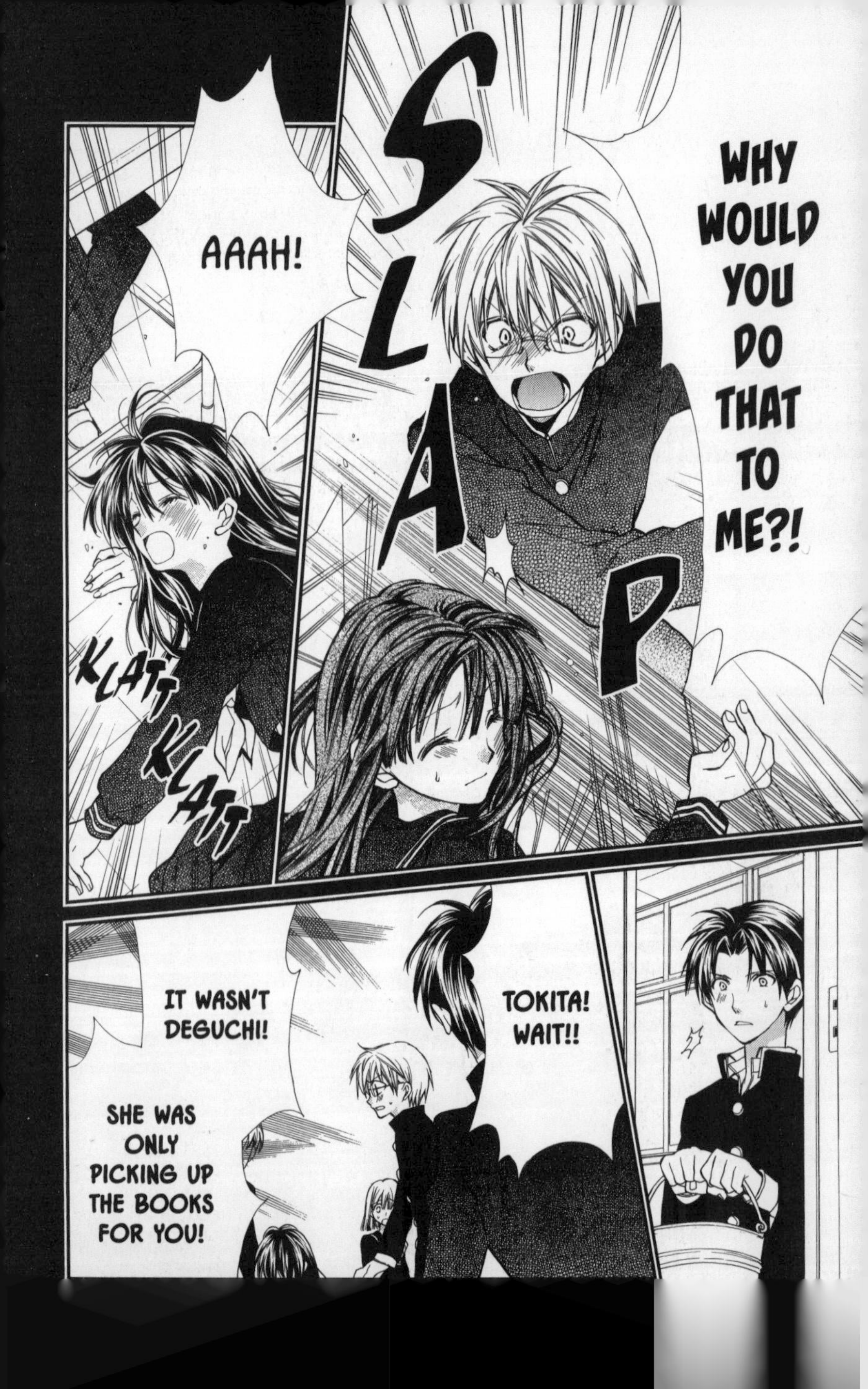
WHY WOULD YOU DO THAT TO ME?!
SLAP
AAAH!
KLATT KLATT
TOKITA! WAIT!!
IT WASN'T DEGUCHI!
SHE WAS ONLY PICKING UP THE BOOKS FOR YOU!

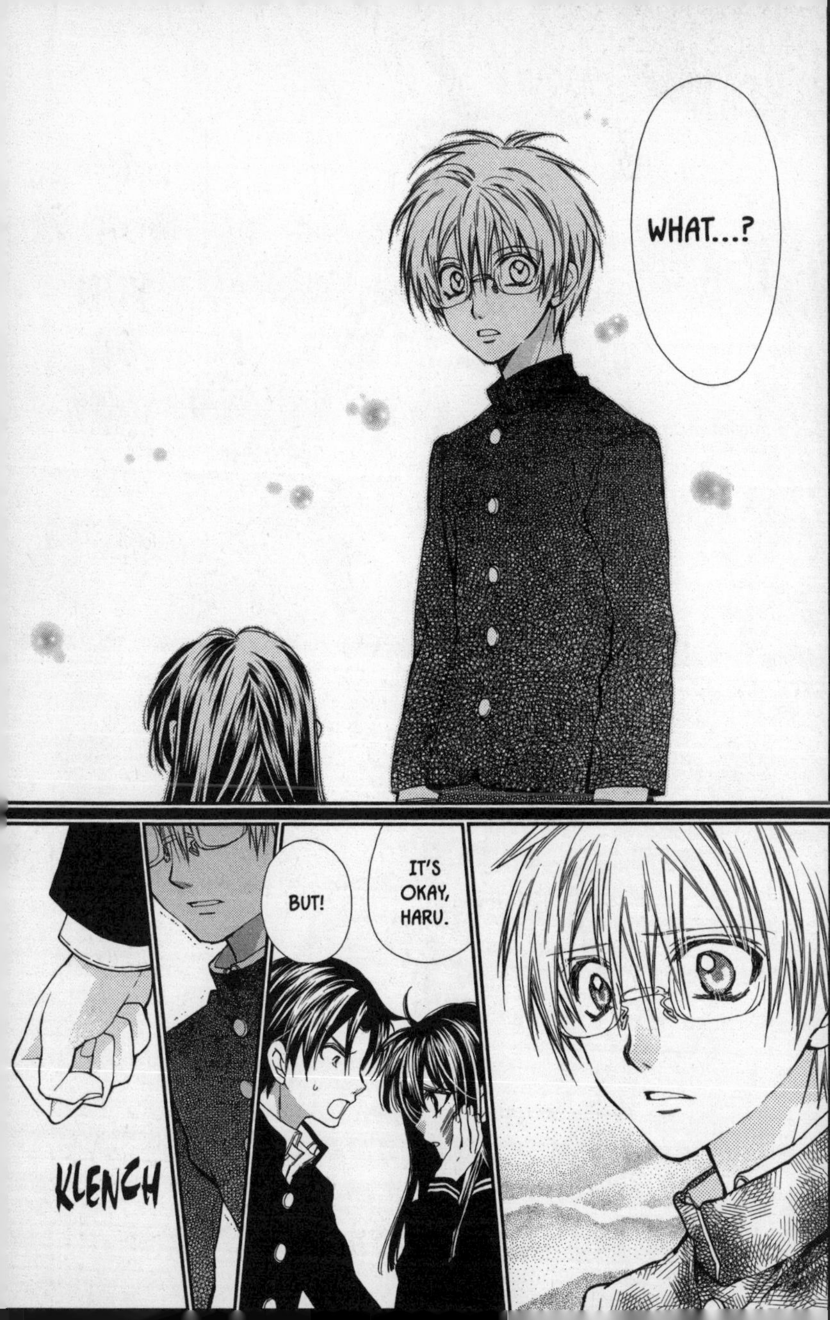
WHAT...?
IT'S OKAY, HARU.
BUT!
KLENCH

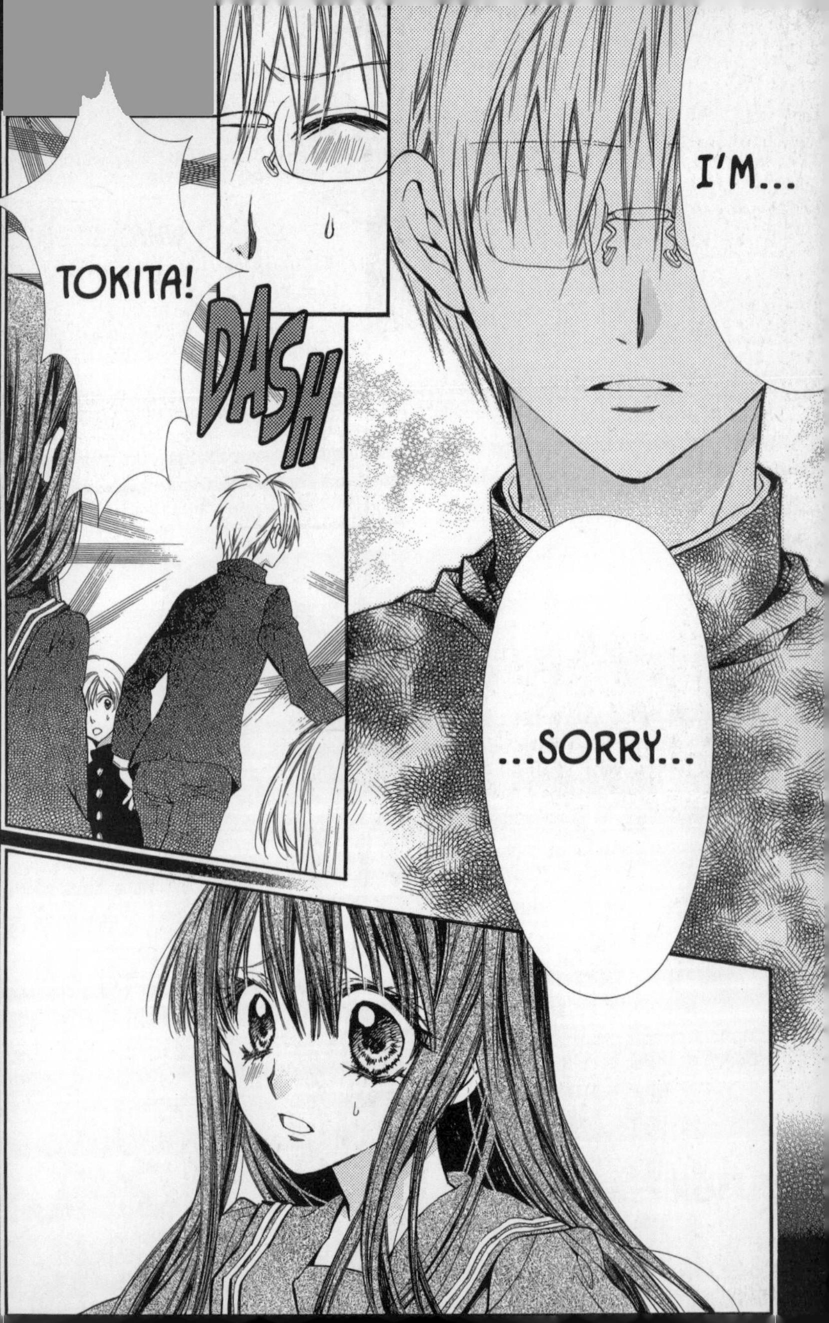
I'M...
...SORRY...
TOKITA!
DASH

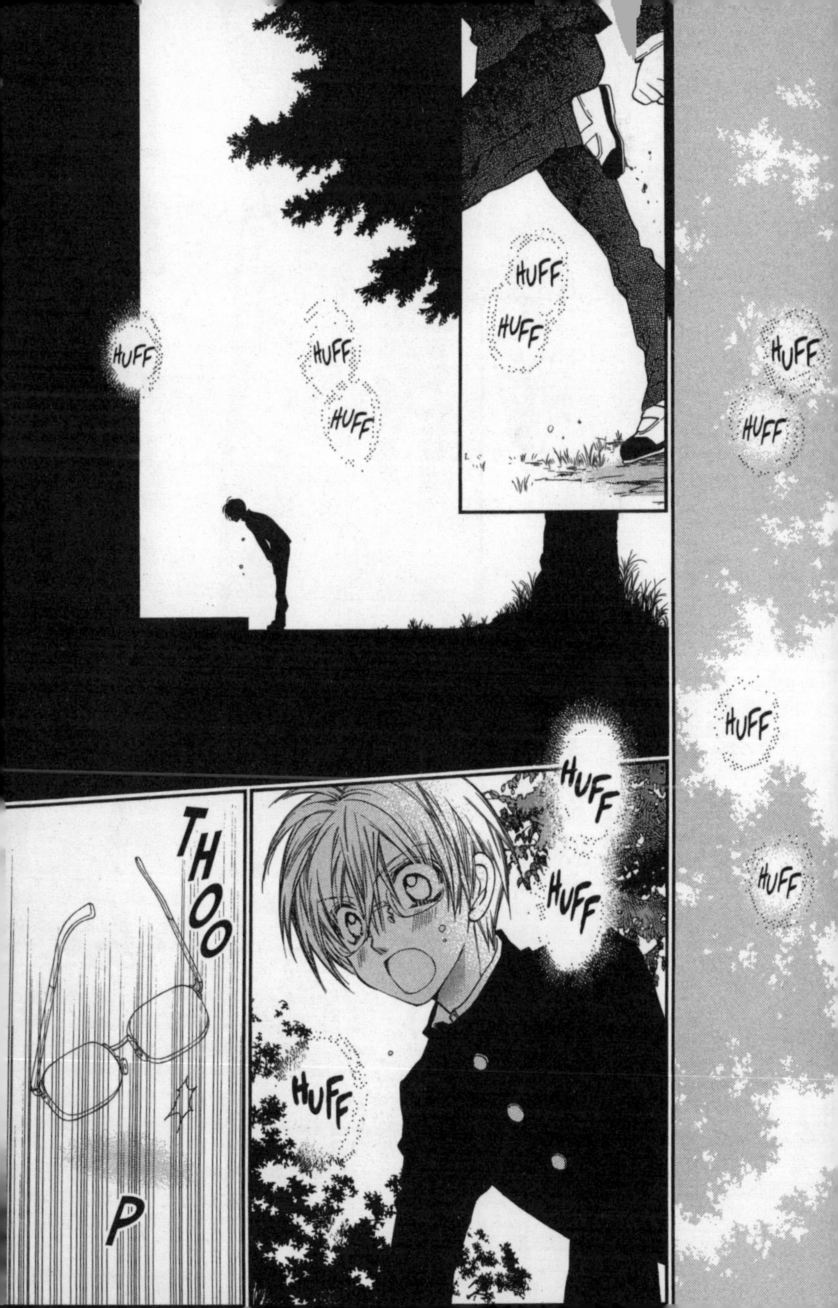
HUFF
HUFF
HUFF
HUFF
HUFF
HUFF
HUFF
HUFF
HUFF
HUFF
HUFF
HUFF
THOOP

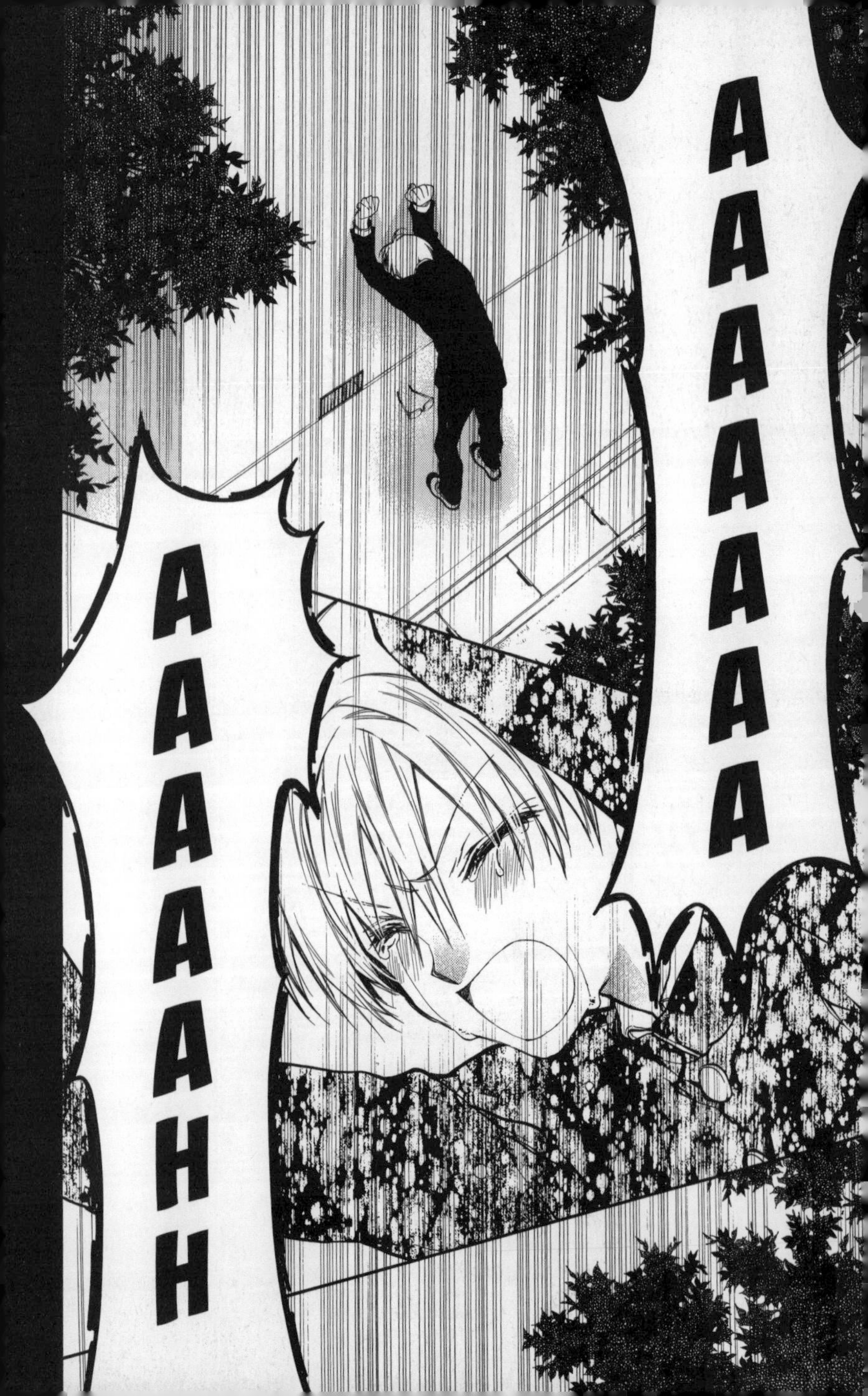
AAAAAAA
AAAAAHH

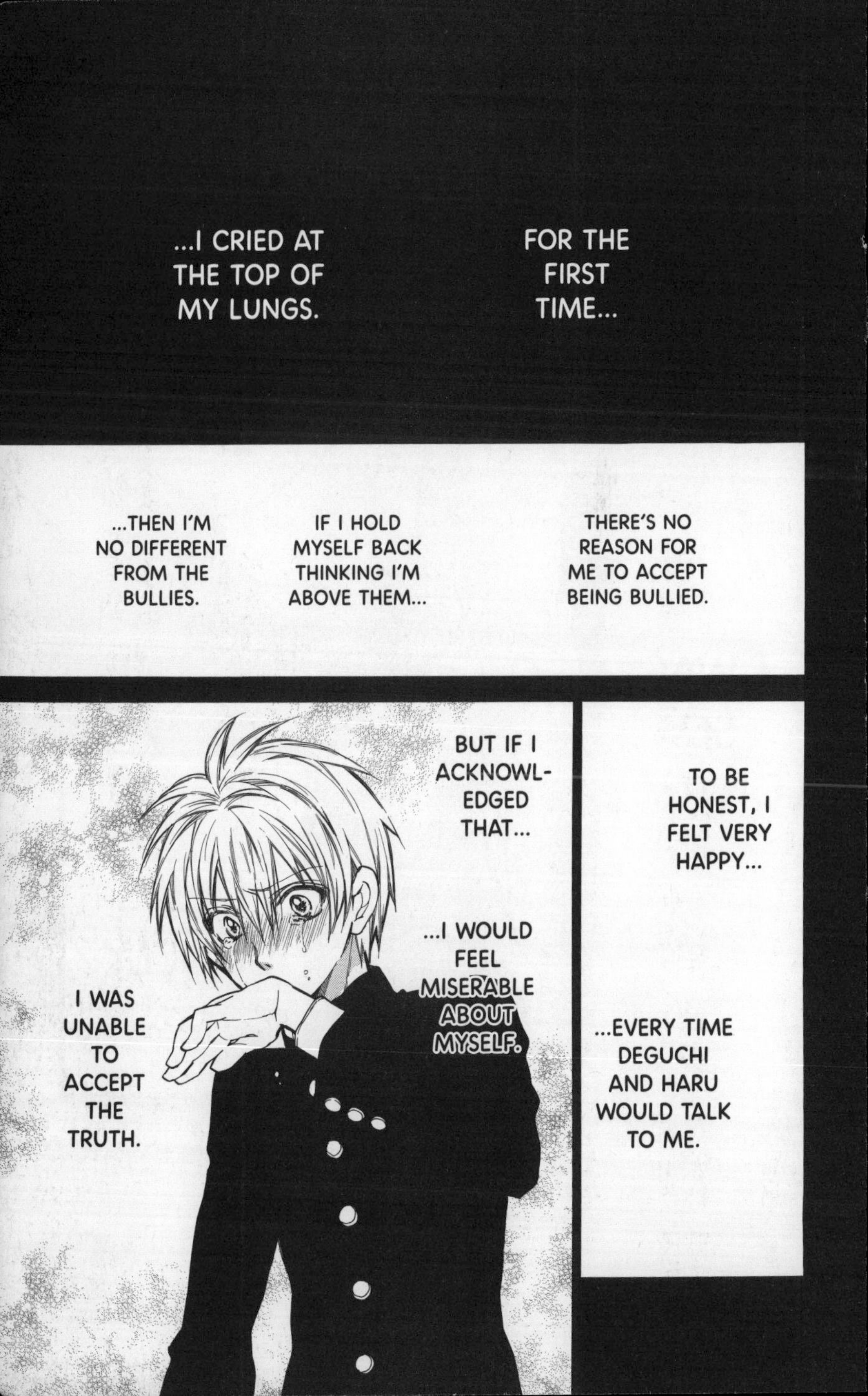
FOR THE FIRST TIME...
...I CRIED AT THE TOP OF MY LUNGS.
THERE'S NO REASON FOR ME TO ACCEPT BEING BULLIED.
IF I HOLD MYSELF BACK THINKING I'M ABOVE THEM...
...THEN I'M NO DIFFERENT FROM THE BULLIES.
TO BE HONEST, I FELT VERY HAPPY...
...EVERY TIME DEGUCHI AND HARU WOULD TALK TO ME.
BUT IF I ACKNOWL-EDGED THAT...
...I WOULD FEEL MISERABLE ABOUT MYSELF.
I WAS UNABLE TO ACCEPT THE TRUTH.

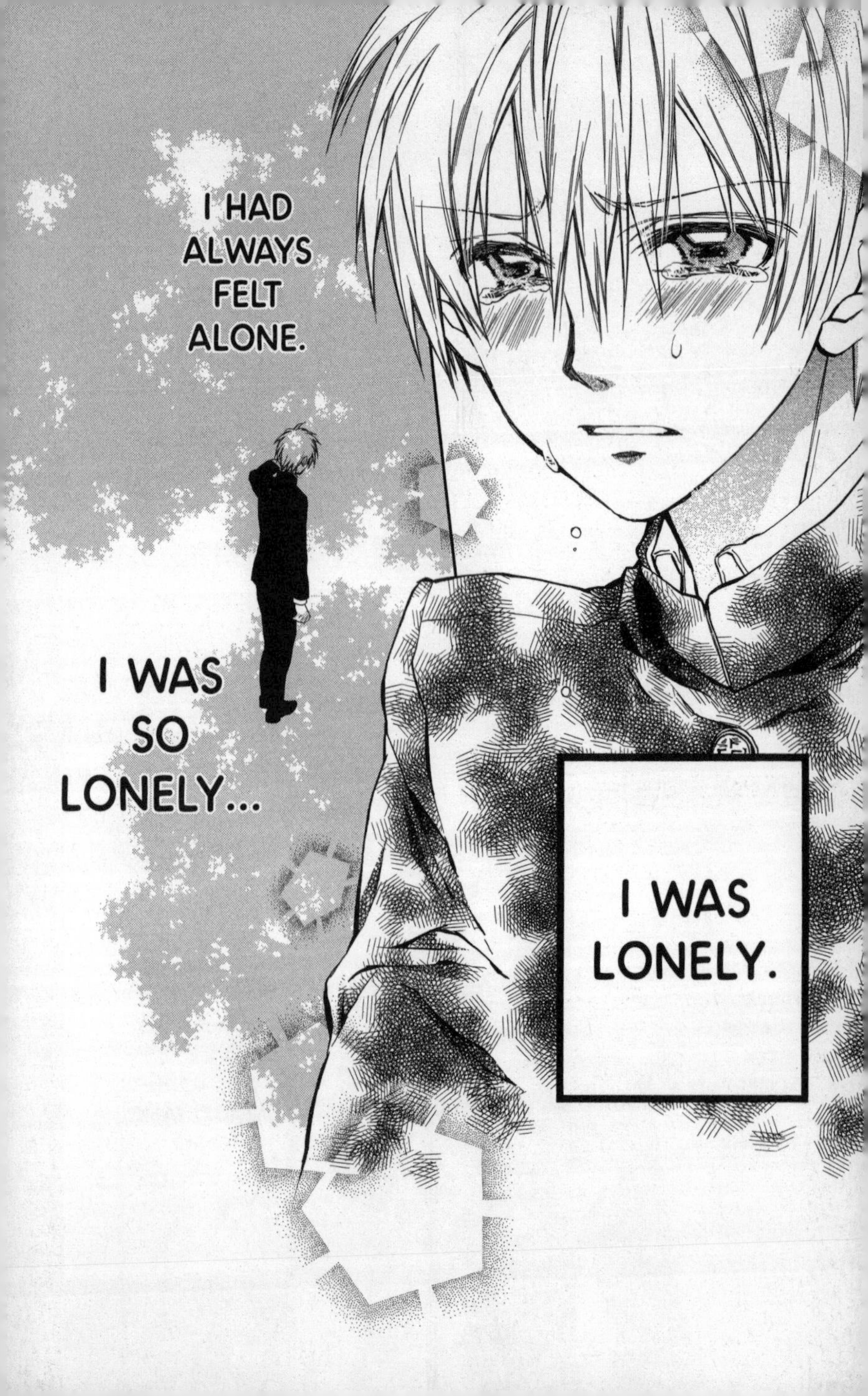
I HAD ALWAYS FELT ALONE.
I WAS SO LONELY...
I WAS LONELY.

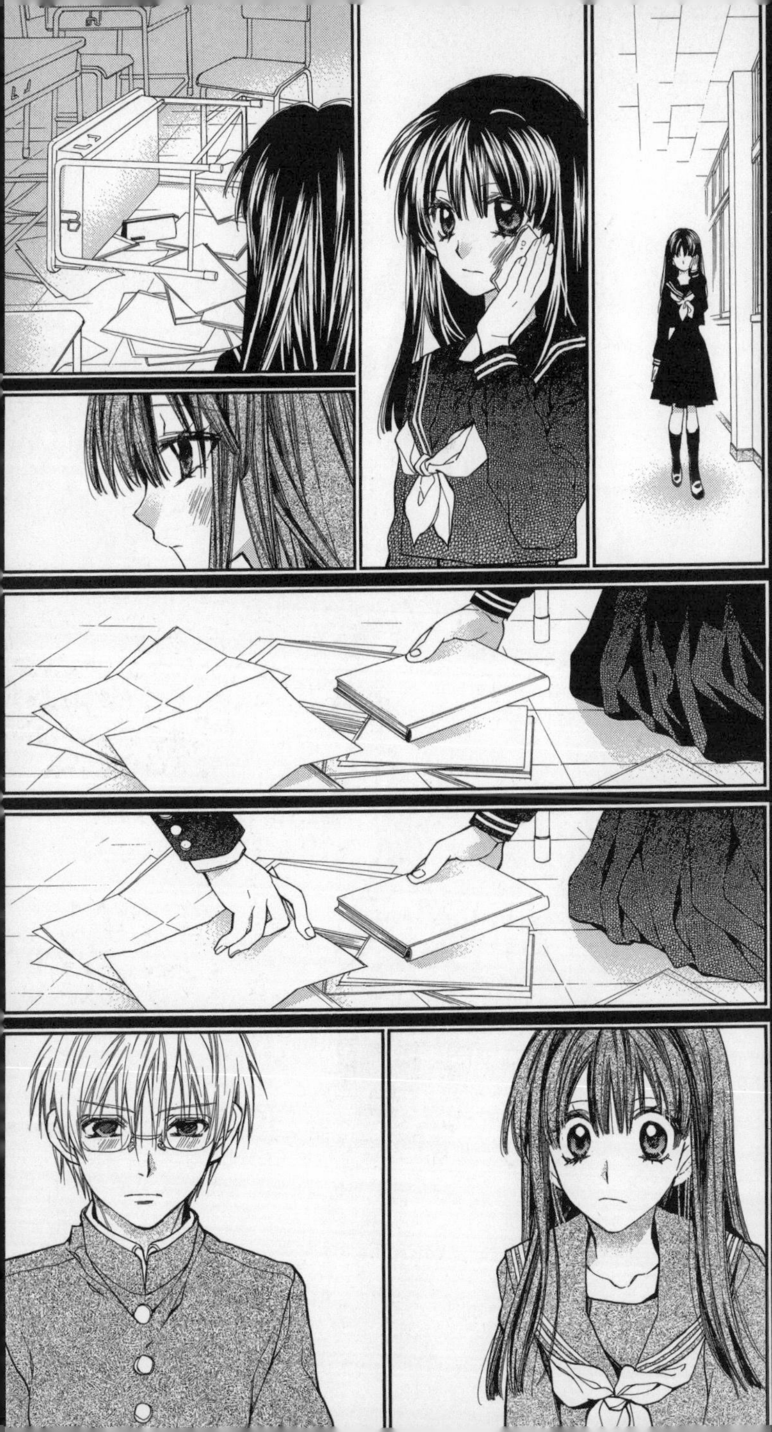

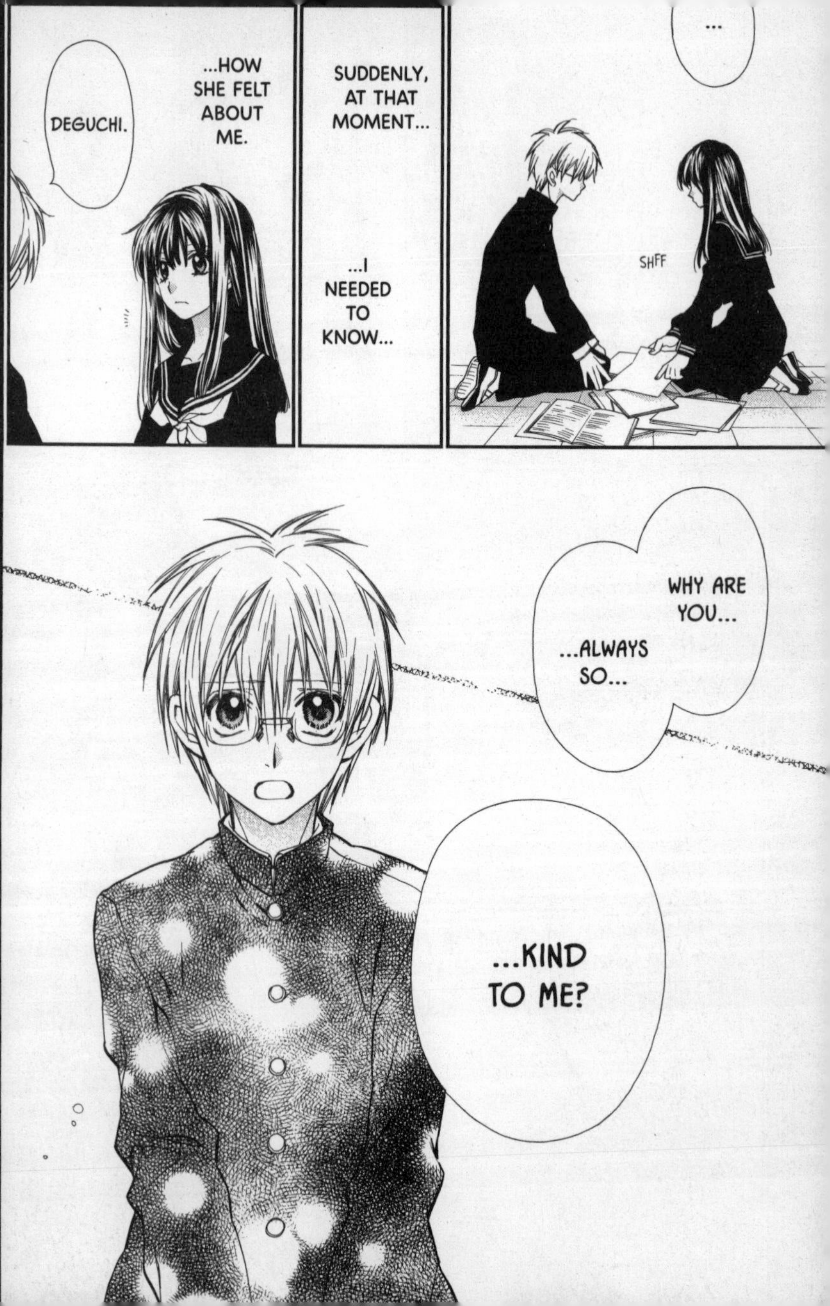
...
SHFF
SUDDENLY, AT THAT MOMENT...
...I NEEDED TO KNOW...
...HOW SHE FELT ABOUT ME.
DEGUCHI.
WHY ARE YOU...
...ALWAYS SO...
...KIND TO ME?

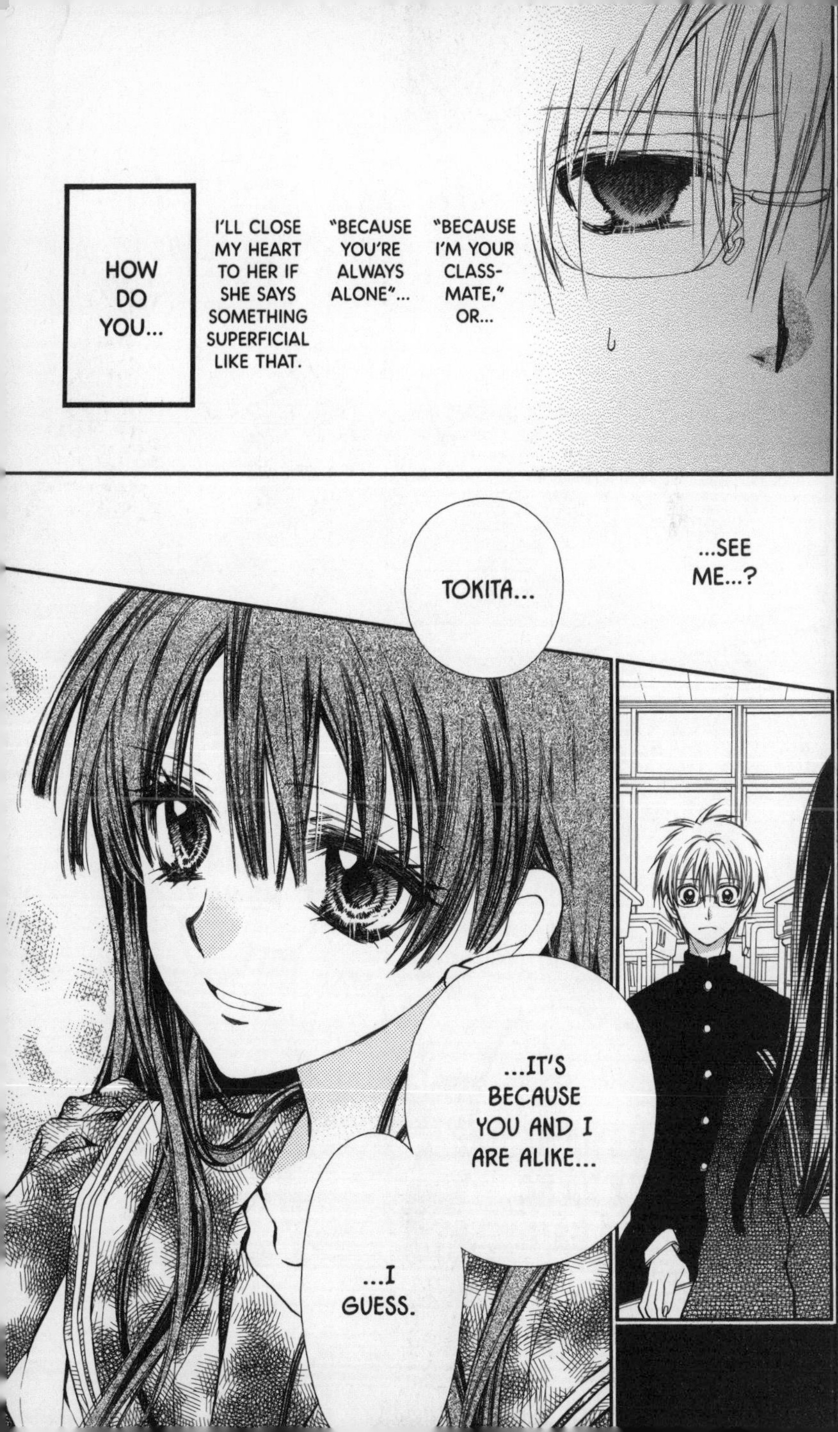
"BECAUSE I'M YOUR CLASSMATE," OR...
"BECAUSE YOU'RE ALWAYS ALONE"...
I'LL CLOSE MY HEART TO HER IF SHE SAYS SOMETHING SUPERFICIAL LIKE THAT.
HOW DO YOU...
...SEE ME...?
TOKITA...
...IT'S BECAUSE YOU AND I ARE ALIKE...
...I GUESS.

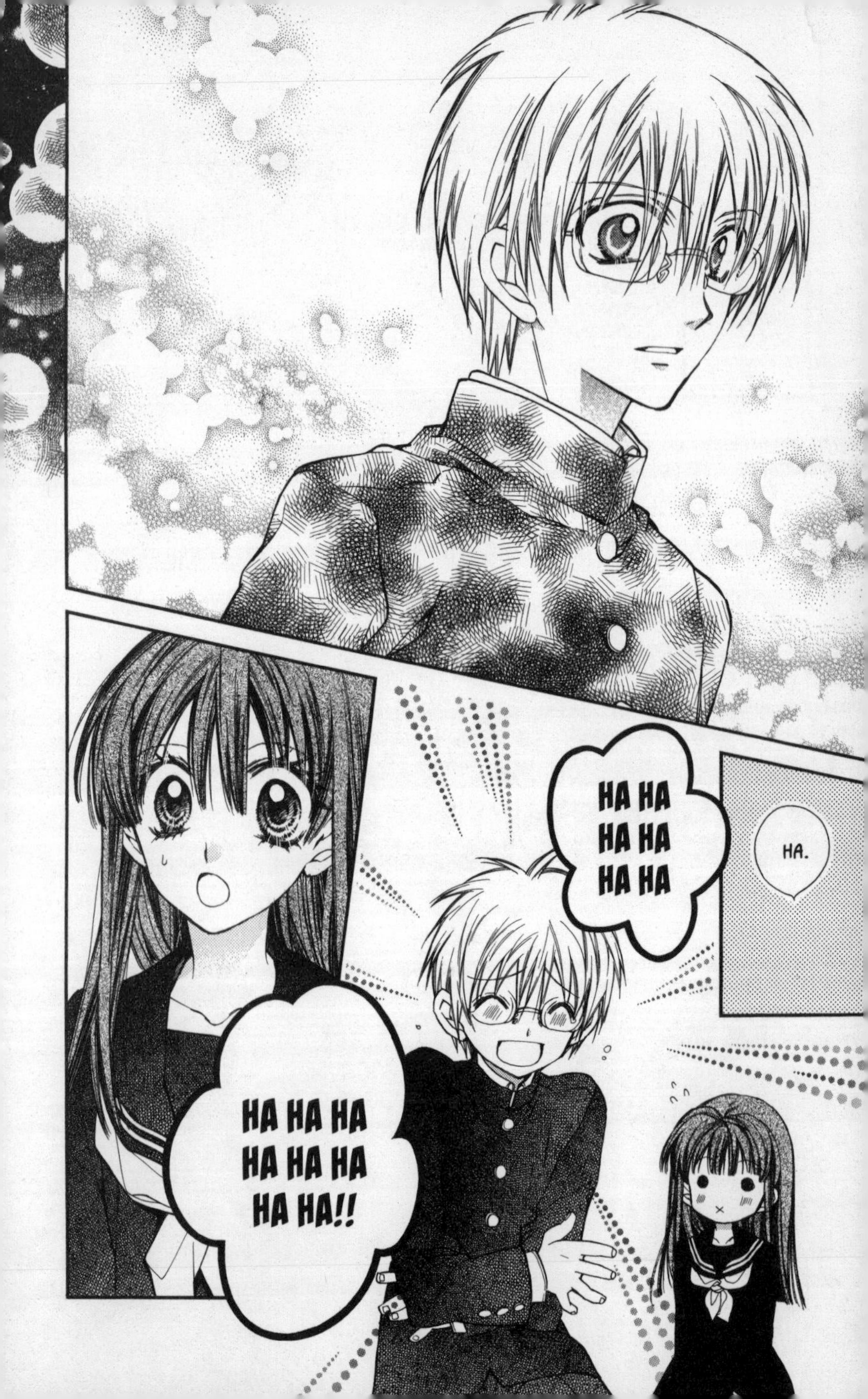
HA.
HA HA HA HA HA HA
HA HA HA HA HA HA HA HA!!

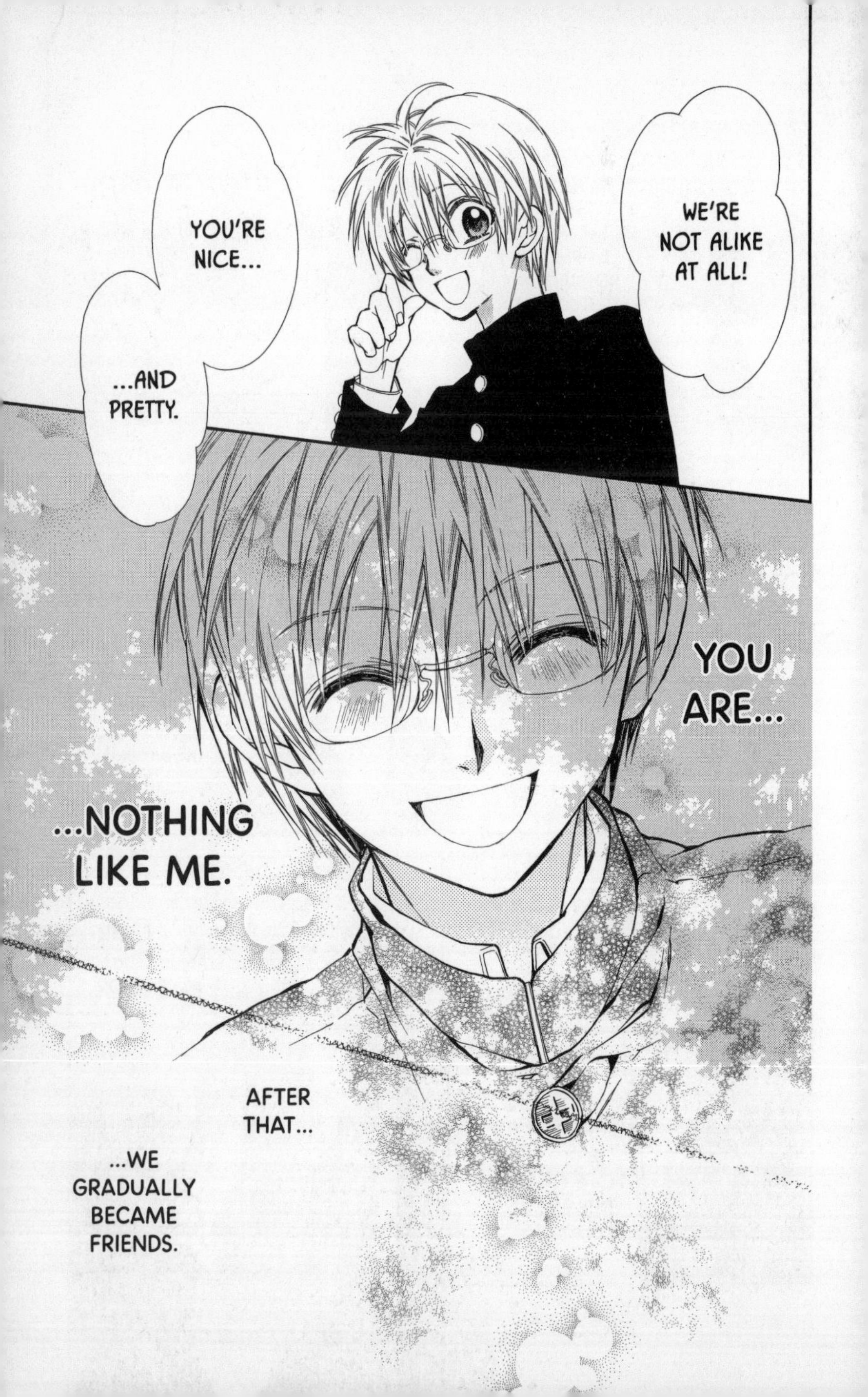
WE'RE NOT ALIKE AT ALL!
YOU'RE NICE...
...AND PRETTY.
YOU ARE...
...NOTHING LIKE ME.
AFTER THAT...
...WE GRADUALLY BECAME FRIENDS.

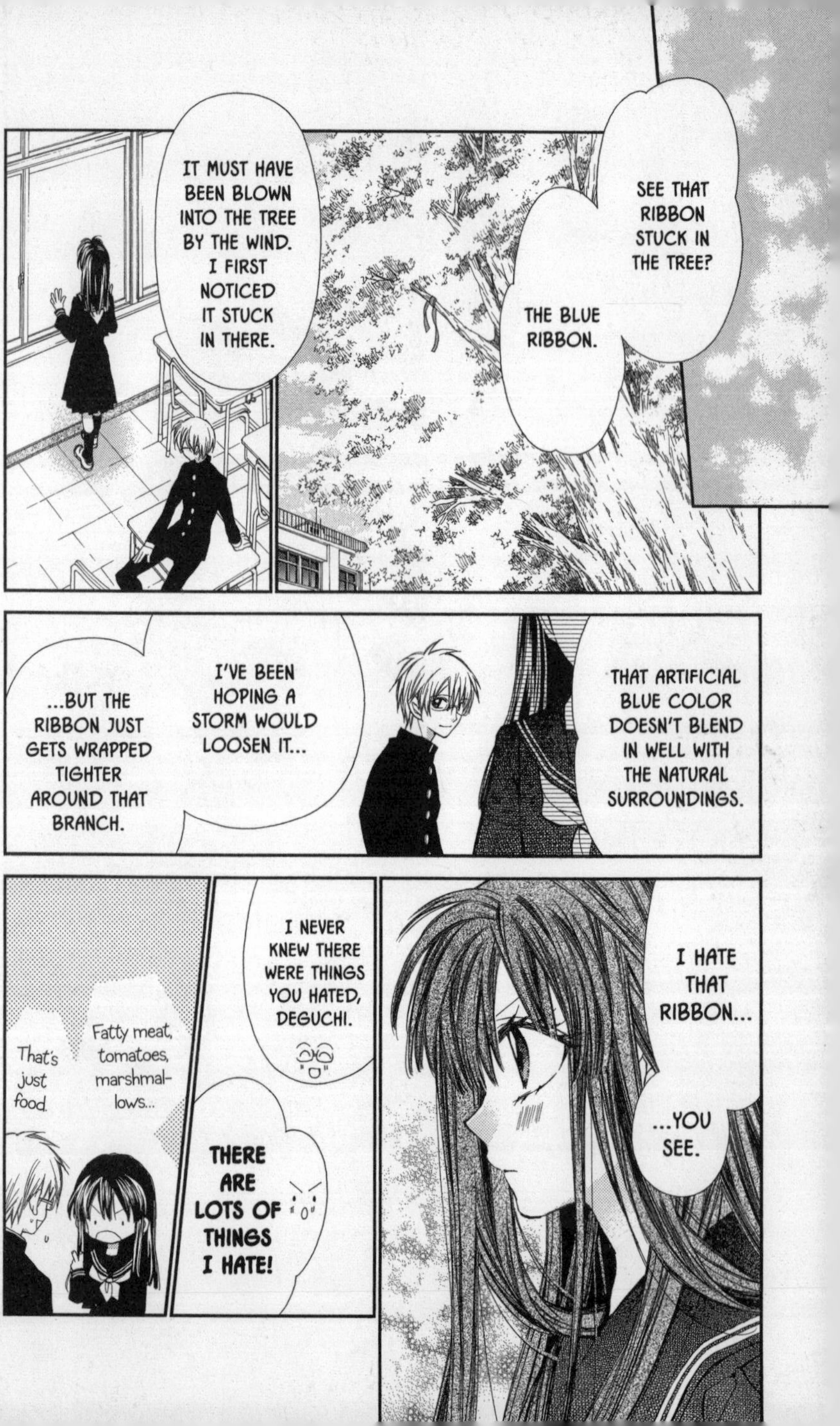
SEE THAT RIBBON STUCK IN THE TREE?
THE BLUE RIBBON.
IT MUST HAVE BEEN BLOWN INTO THE TREE BY THE WIND. I FIRST NOTICED IT STUCK IN THERE.
THAT ARTIFICIAL BLUE COLOR DOESN'T BLEND IN WELL WITH THE NATURAL SURROUNDINGS.
I'VE BEEN HOPING A STORM WOULD LOOSEN IT...
...BUT THE RIBBON JUST GETS WRAPPED TIGHTER AROUND THAT BRANCH.
I HATE THAT RIBBON...
...YOU SEE.
I NEVER KNEW THERE WERE THINGS YOU HATED, DEGUCHI.
THERE ARE LOTS OF THINGS I HATE!
Fatty meat, tomatoes, marshmal-lows...
That's just food.

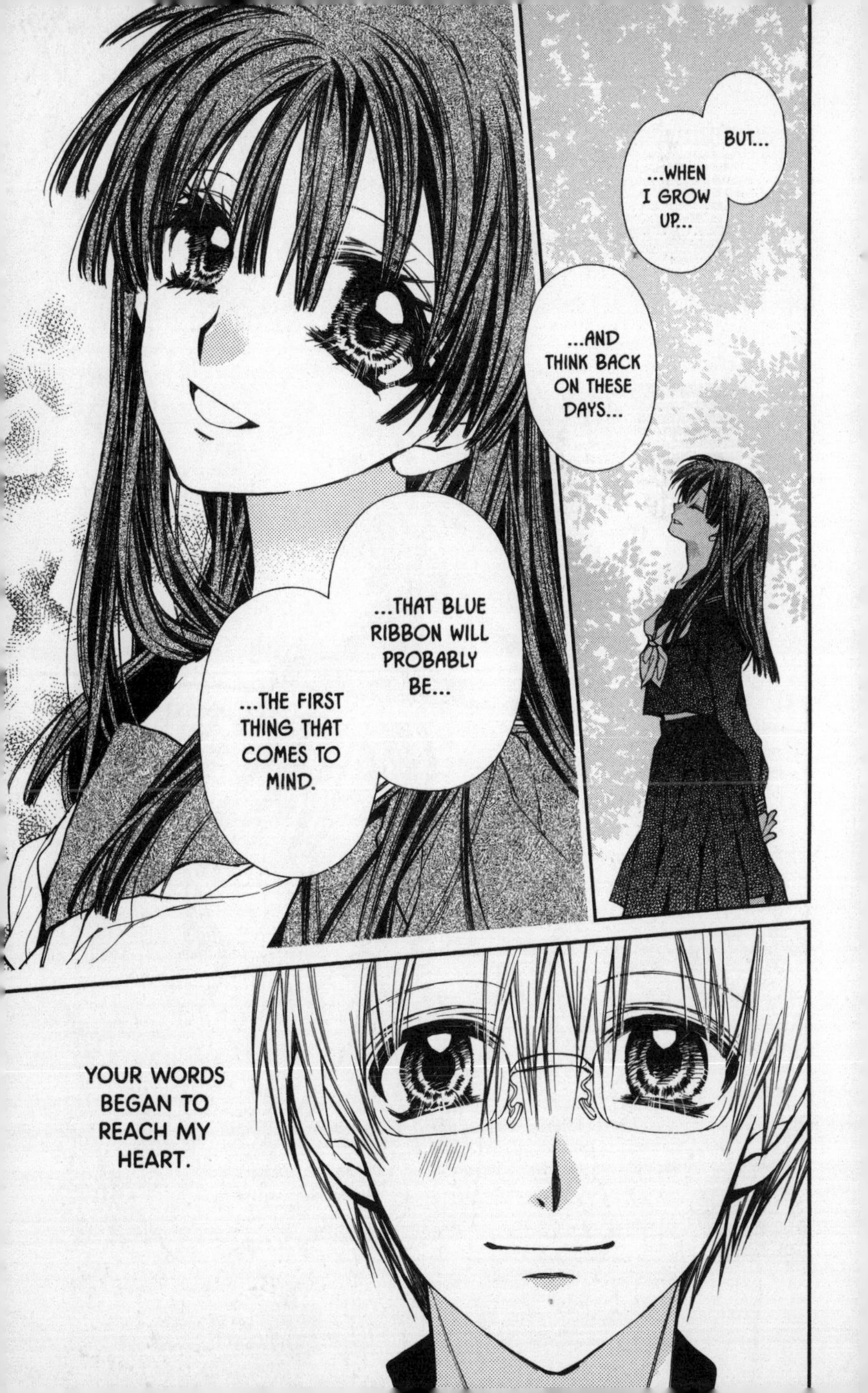
BUT...
...WHEN I GROW UP...
...AND THINK BACK ON THESE DAYS...
...THAT BLUE RIBBON WILL PROBABLY BE...
...THE FIRST THING THAT COMES TO MIND.
YOUR WORDS BEGAN TO REACH MY HEART.

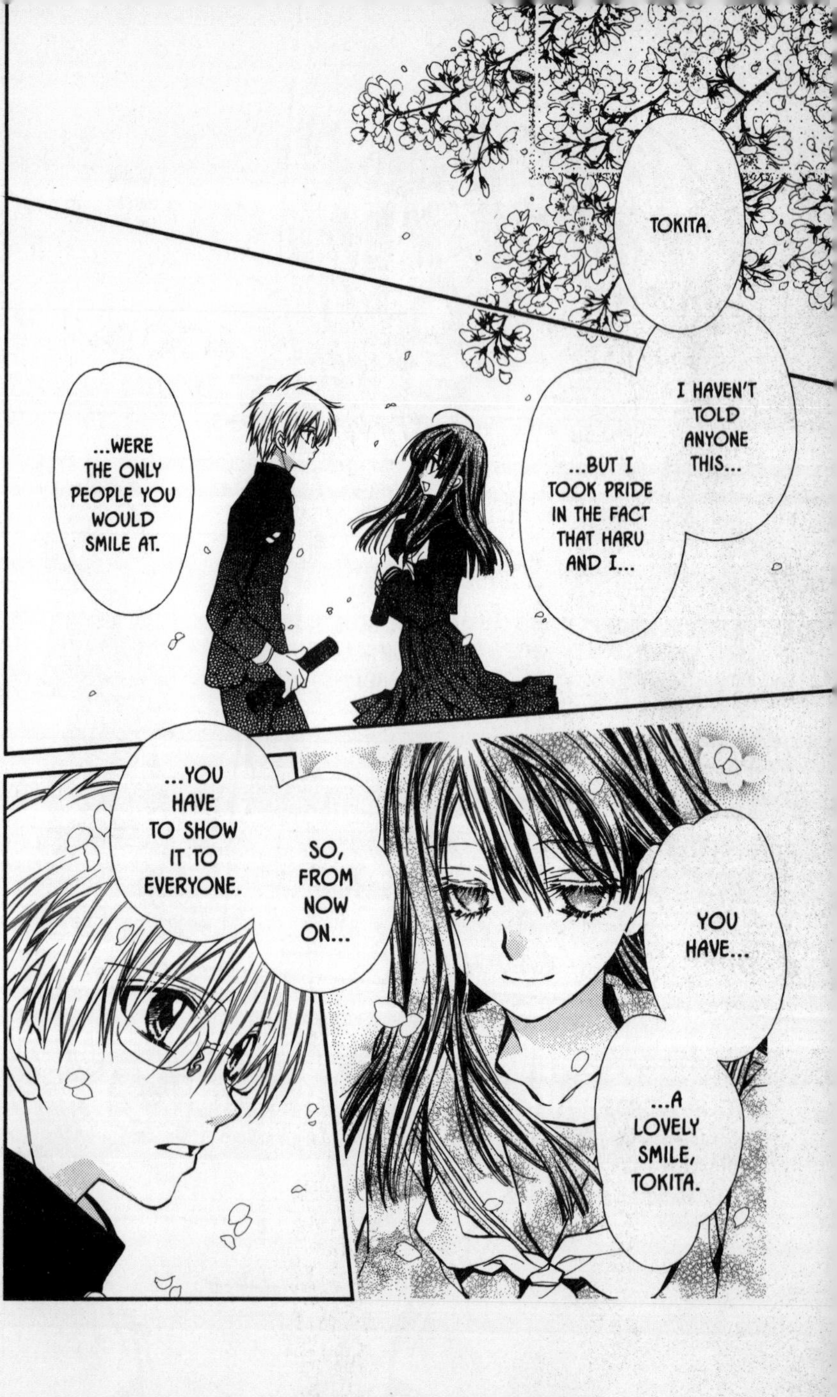
TOKITA.
I HAVEN'T TOLD ANYONE THIS...
...BUT I TOOK PRIDE IN THE FACT THAT HARU AND I...
...WERE THE ONLY PEOPLE YOU WOULD SMILE AT.
YOU HAVE...
...A LOVELY SMILE, TOKITA.
SO, FROM NOW ON...
...YOU HAVE TO SHOW IT TO EVERYONE.

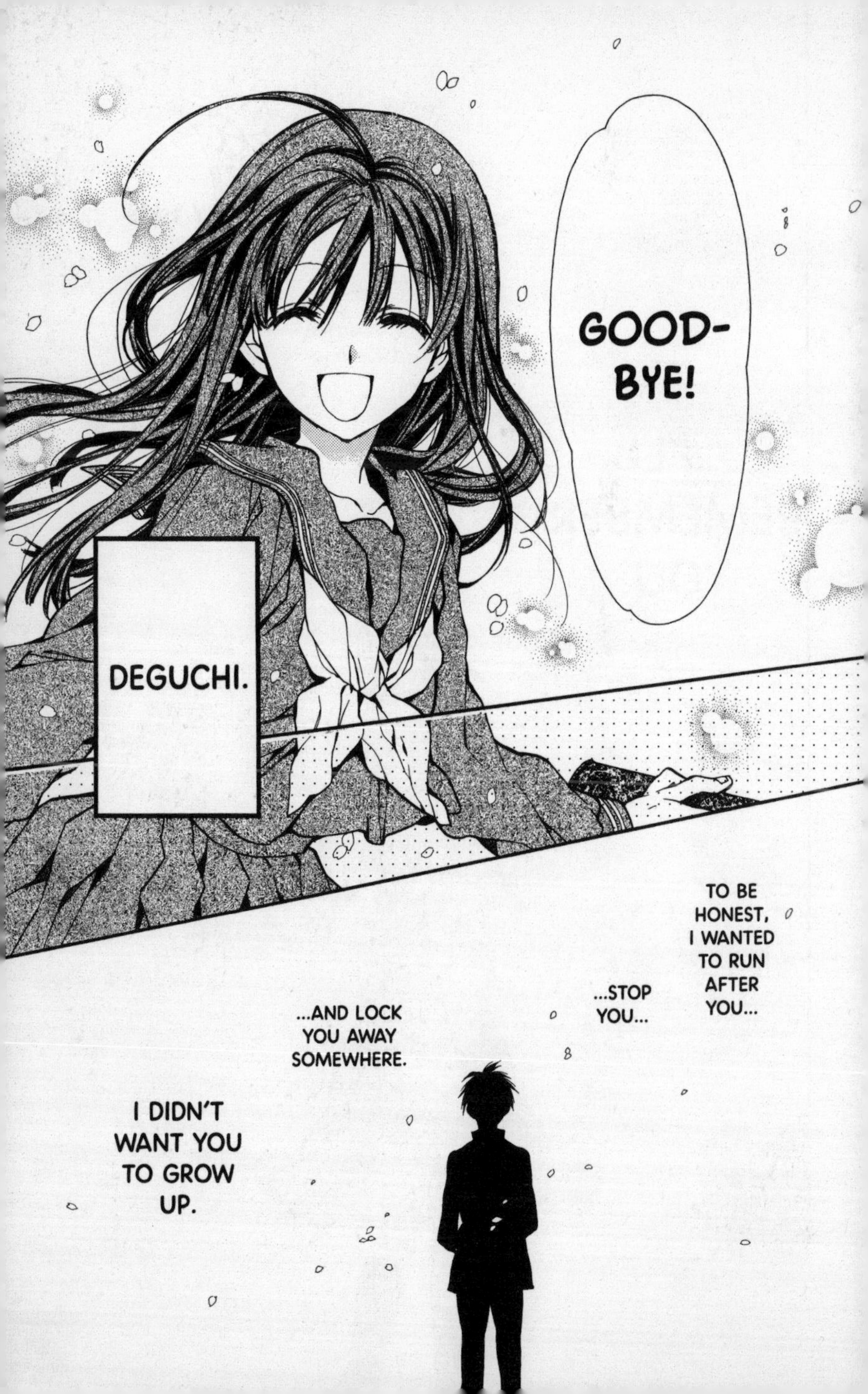
GOOD-BYE!
DEGUCHI.
TO BE HONEST, I WANTED TO RUN AFTER YOU...
...STOP YOU...
...AND LOCK YOU AWAY SOMEWHERE.
I DIDN'T WANT YOU TO GROW UP.

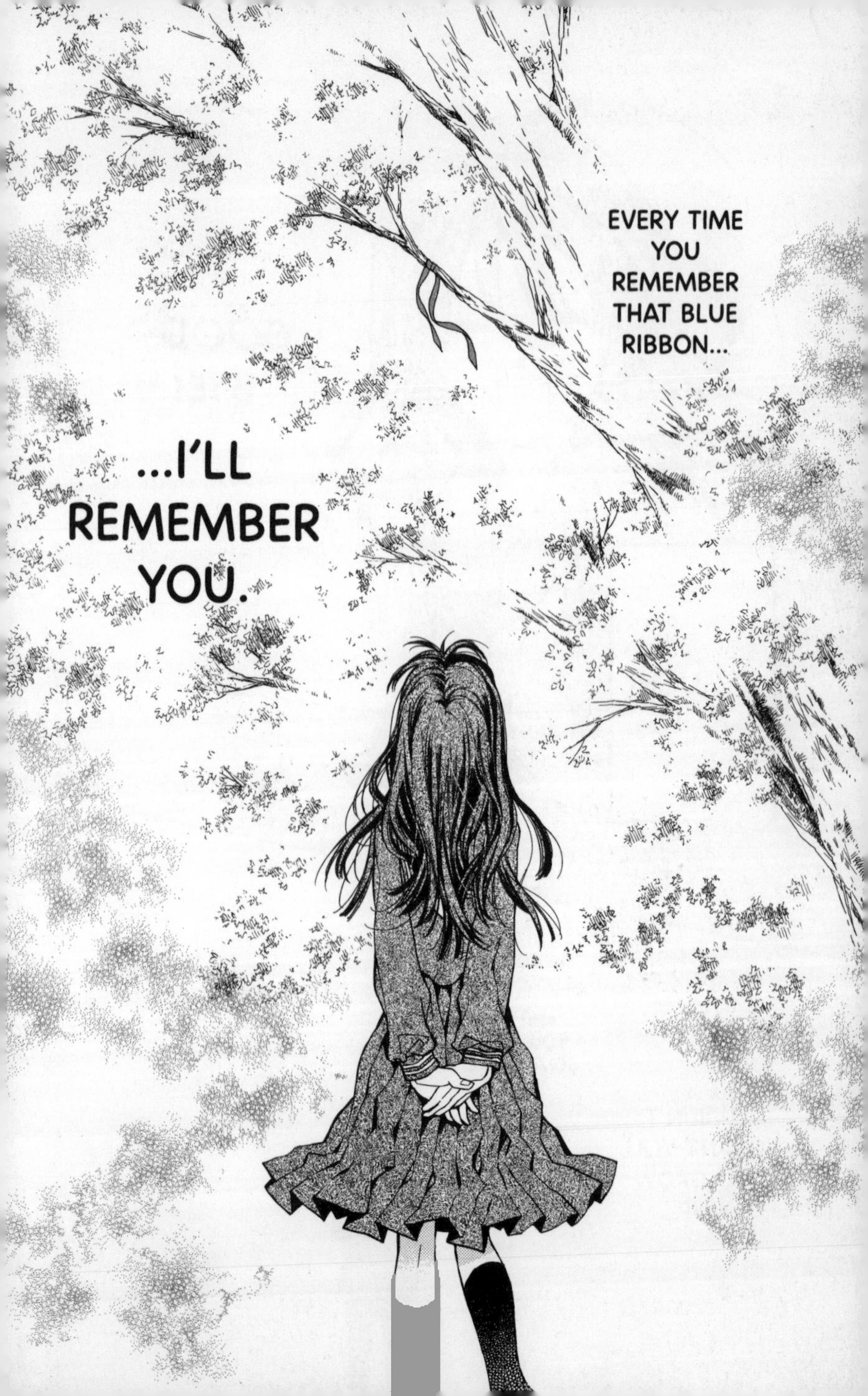
EVERY TIME YOU REMEMBER THAT BLUE RIBBON...
...I'LL REMEMBER YOU.

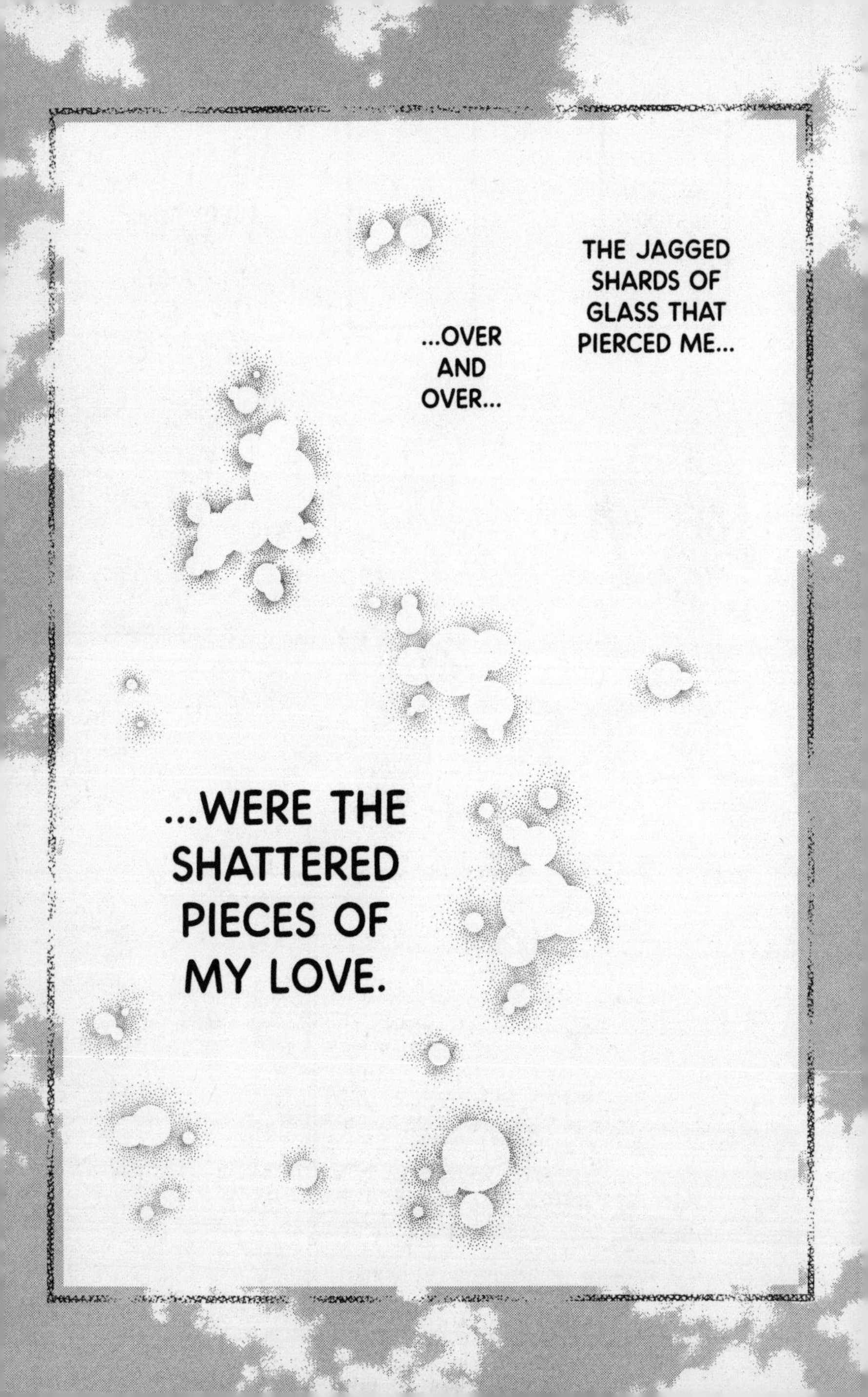
THE JAGGED SHARDS OF GLASS THAT PIERCED ME...
...OVER AND OVER...
...WERE THE SHATTERED PIECES OF MY LOVE.

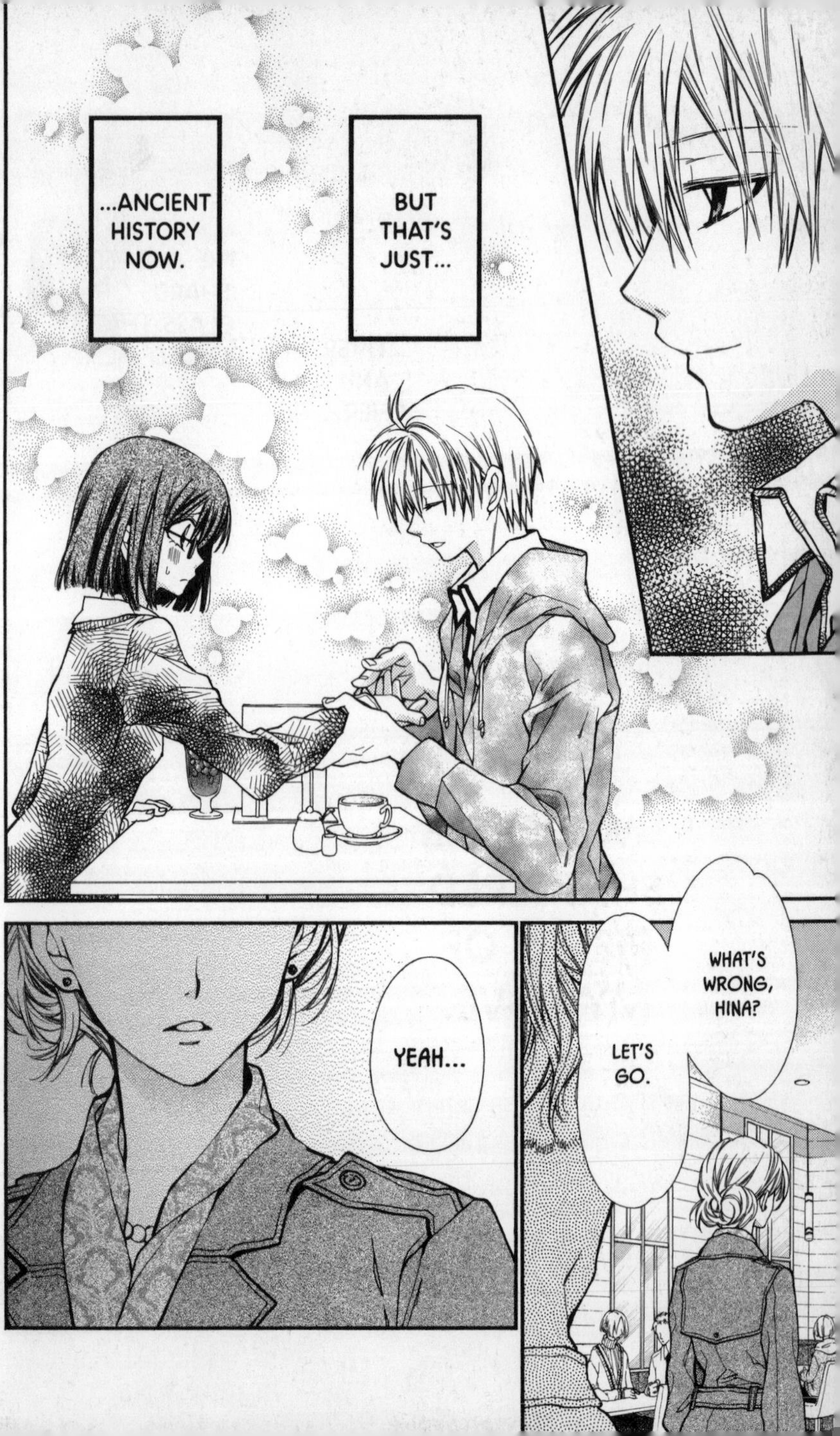

BUT THAT'S JUST...
...ANCIENT HISTORY NOW.
WHAT'S WRONG, HINA?
LET'S GO.
YEAH...

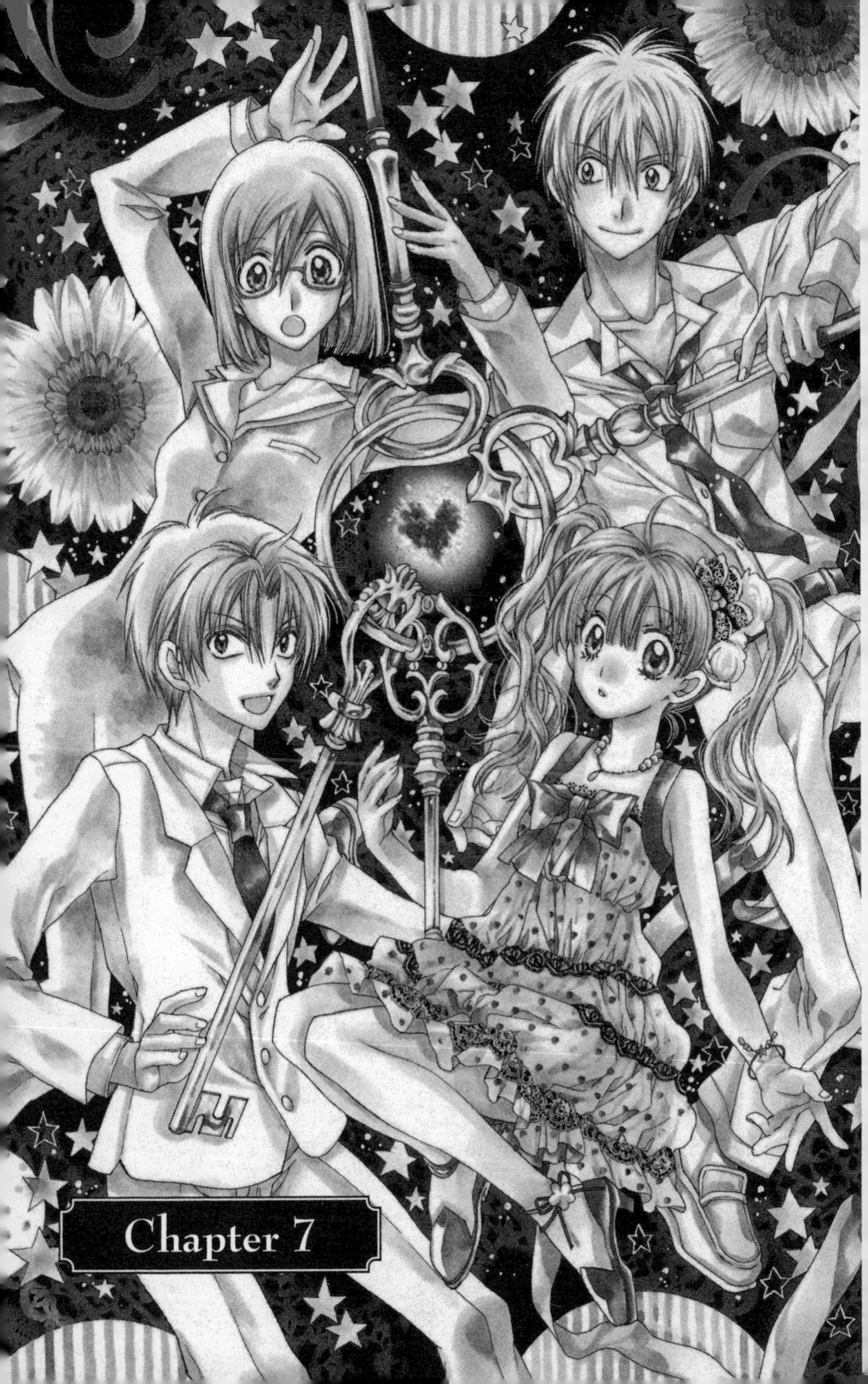

Chapter 7

IDOL dreams

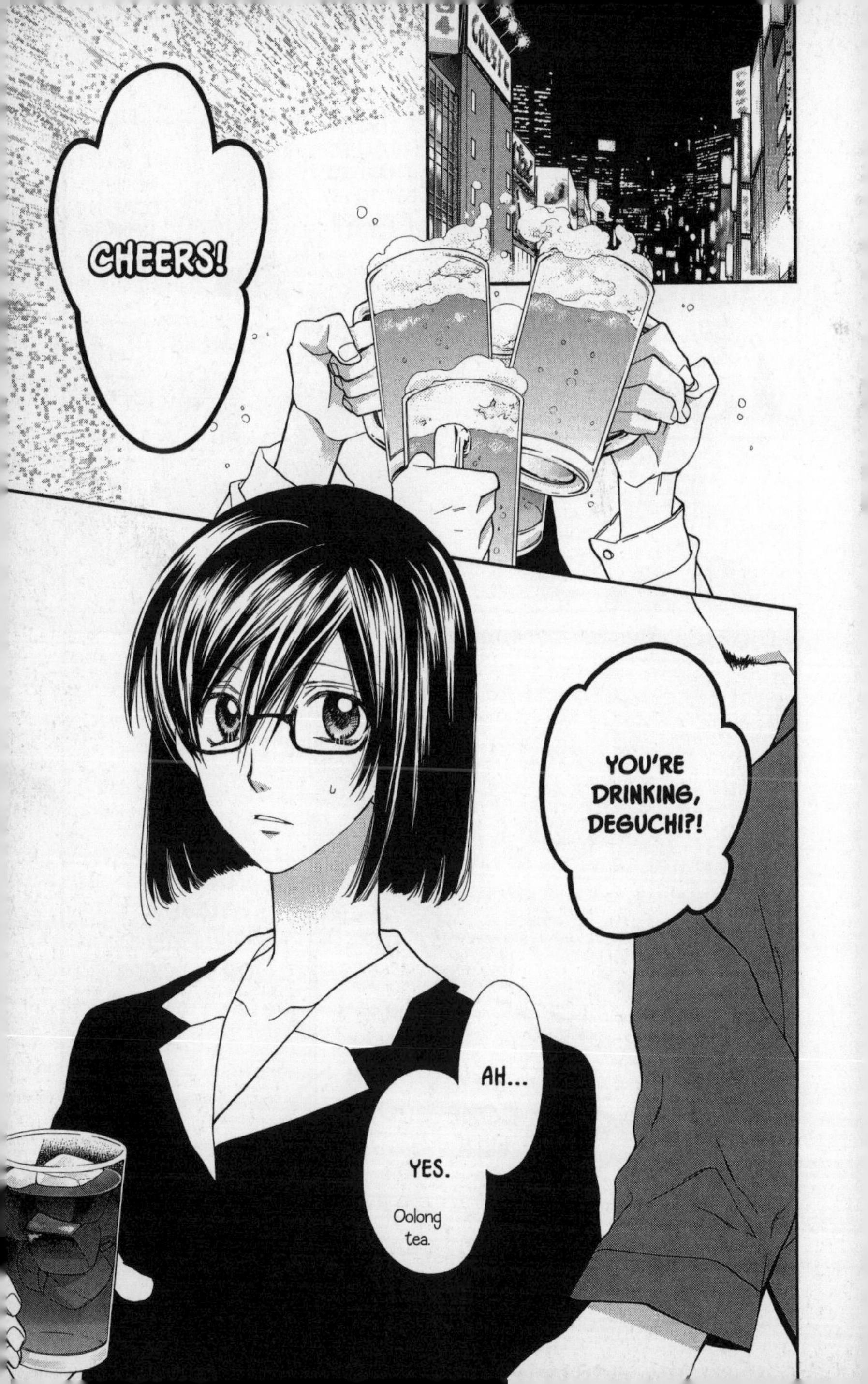
CHEERS!
YOU'RE DRINKING, DEGUCHI?!
AH...
YES.
Oolong tea.

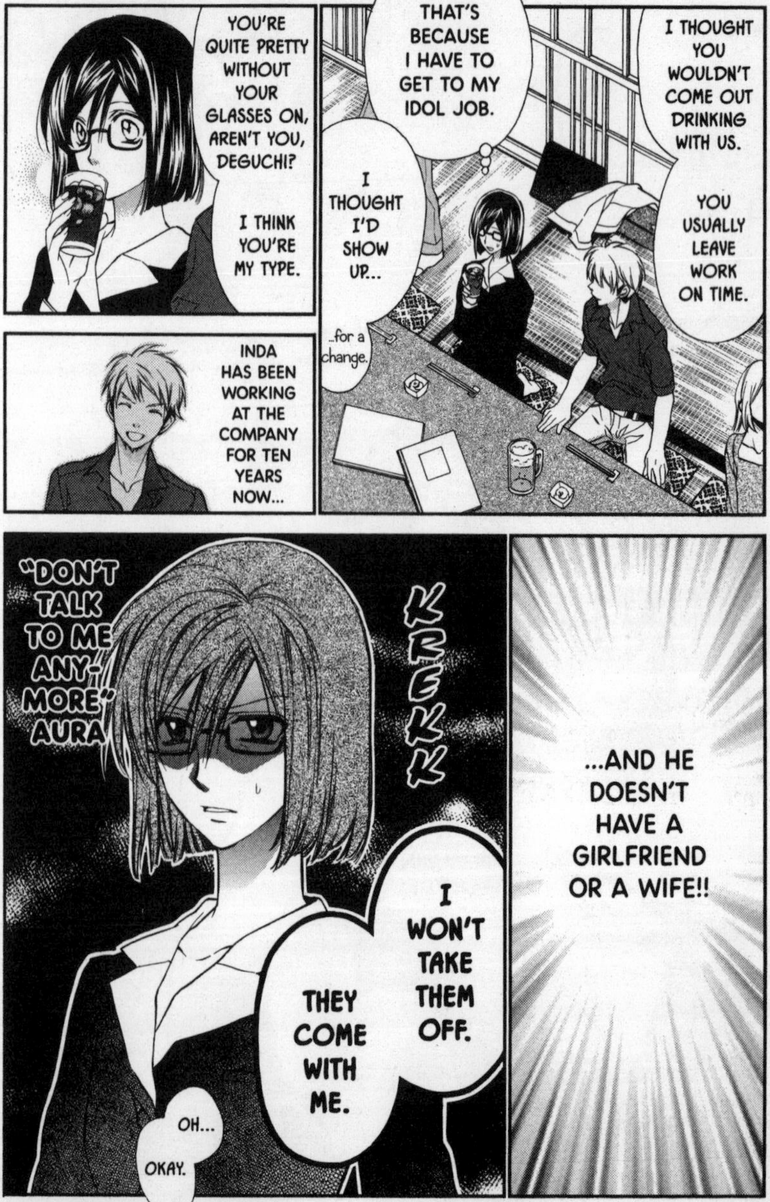
I THOUGHT YOU WOULDN'T COME OUT DRINKING WITH US.
YOU USUALLY LEAVE WORK ON TIME.
THAT'S BECAUSE I HAVE TO GET TO MY IDOL JOB.
I THOUGHT I'D SHOW UP...
...for a change.
YOU'RE QUITE PRETTY WITHOUT YOUR GLASSES ON, AREN'T YOU, DEGUCHI?
I THINK YOU'RE MY TYPE.
INDA HAS BEEN WORKING AT THE COMPANY FOR TEN YEARS NOW...
...AND HE DOESN'T HAVE A GIRLFRIEND OR A WIFE!!
KREKK
"DON'T TALK TO ME ANY-MORE" AURA
I WON'T TAKE THEM OFF.
THEY COME WITH ME.
OH... OKAY.

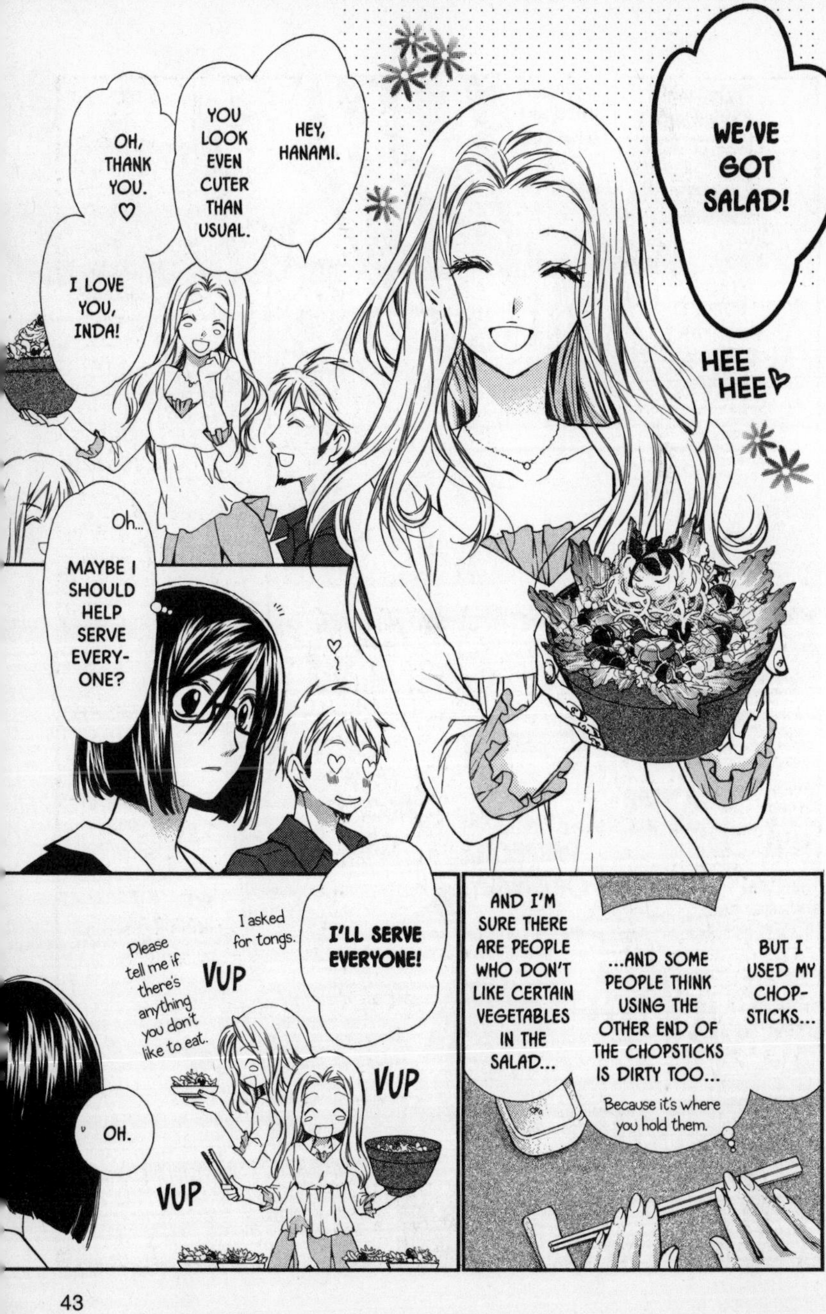
WE'VE GOT SALAD!
HEE HEE♡
HEY, HANAMI.
YOU LOOK EVEN CUTER THAN USUAL.
OH, THANK YOU. ♡
I LOVE YOU, INDA!
Oh...
MAYBE I SHOULD HELP SERVE EVERY-ONE?
BUT I USED MY CHOP-STICKS...
...AND SOME PEOPLE THINK USING THE OTHER END OF THE CHOPSTICKS IS DIRTY TOO...
Because it's where you hold them.
AND I'M SURE THERE ARE PEOPLE WHO DON'T LIKE CERTAIN VEGETABLES IN THE SALAD...
I'LL SERVE EVERYONE!
I asked for tongs.
Please tell me if there's anything you don't like to eat.
VUP
VUP
OH.
VUP

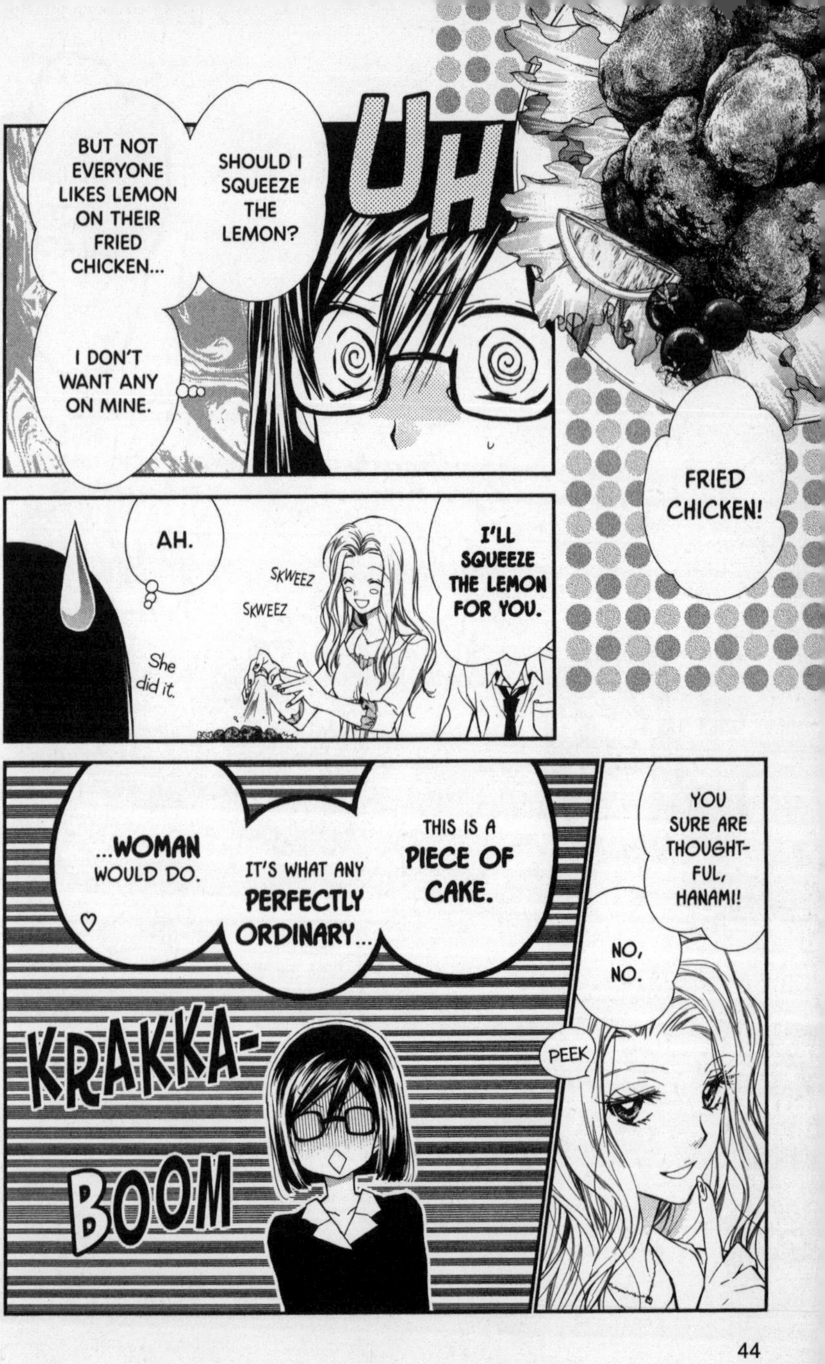
FRIED CHICKEN!
UH
SHOULD I SQUEEZE THE LEMON?
BUT NOT EVERYONE LIKES LEMON ON THEIR FRIED CHICKEN...
I DON'T WANT ANY ON MINE.
I'LL SQUEEZE THE LEMON FOR YOU.
SKWEEZ
SKWEEZ
AH.
She did it.
YOU SURE ARE THOUGHT-FUL, HANAMI!
NO, NO.
PEEK
THIS IS A PIECE OF CAKE.
IT'S WHAT ANY PERFECTLY ORDINARY...
...WOMAN WOULD DO. ♡
KRAKKA-BOOM

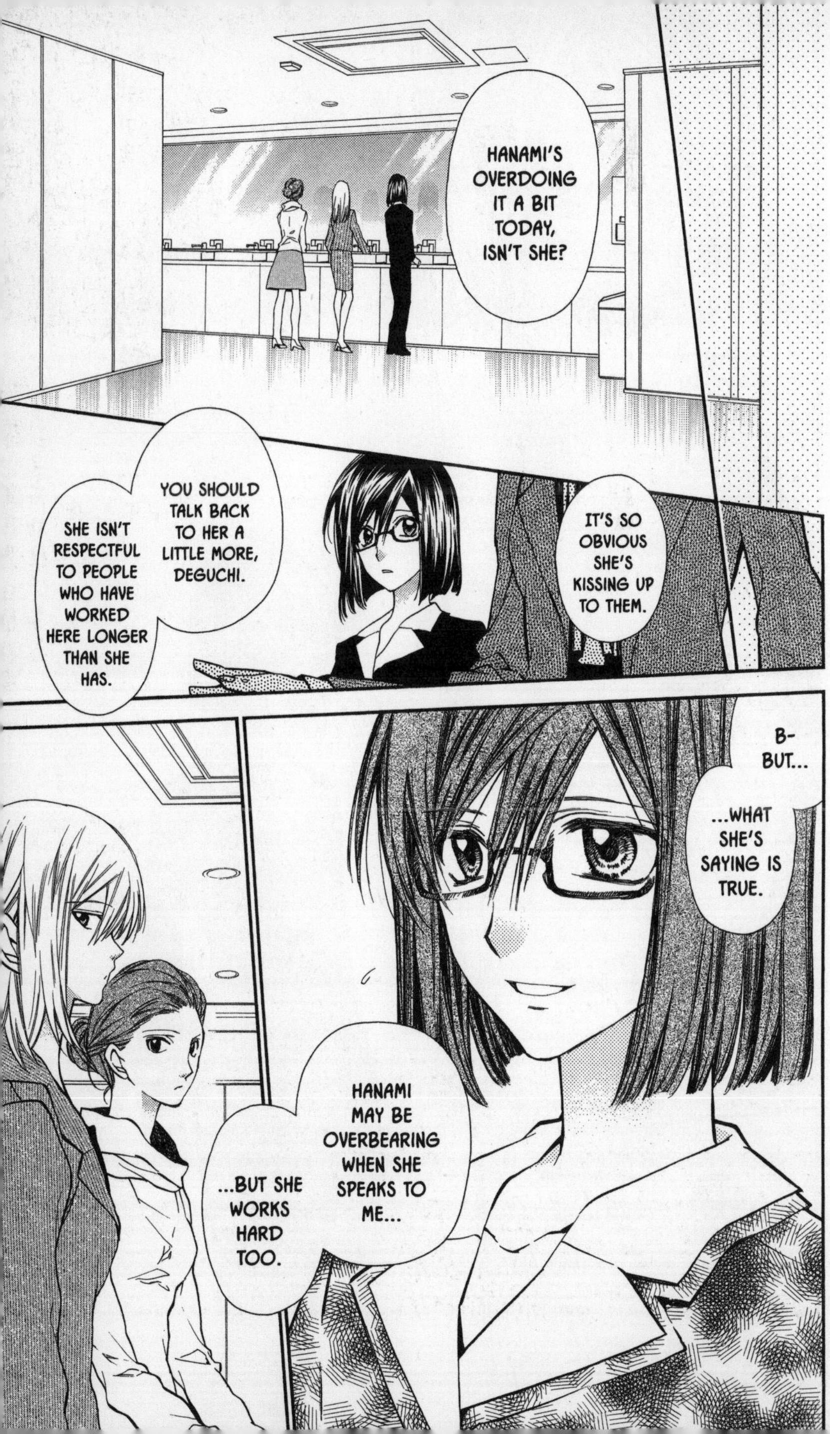
HANAMI'S OVERDOING IT A BIT TODAY, ISN'T SHE?
IT'S SO OBVIOUS SHE'S KISSING UP TO THEM.
YOU SHOULD TALK BACK TO HER A LITTLE MORE, DEGUCHI.
SHE ISN'T RESPECTFUL TO PEOPLE WHO HAVE WORKED HERE LONGER THAN SHE HAS.
B-BUT...
...WHAT SHE'S SAYING IS TRUE.
HANAMI MAY BE OVERBEARING WHEN SHE SPEAKS TO ME...
...BUT SHE WORKS HARD TOO.

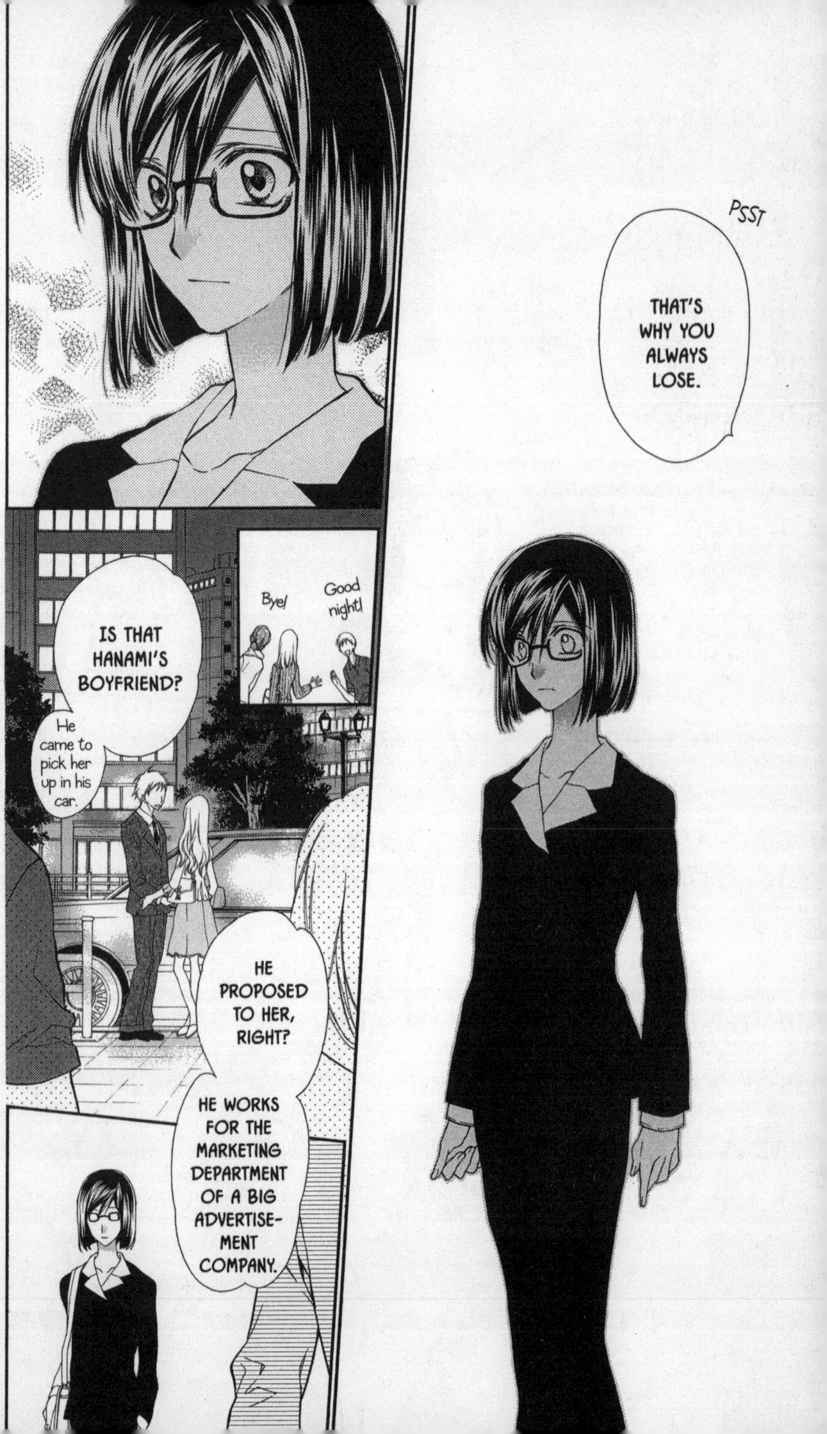
PSST
THAT'S WHY YOU ALWAYS LOSE.
IS THAT HANAMI'S BOYFRIEND?
He came to pick her up in his car.
Good night!
Bye!
HE PROPOSED TO HER, RIGHT?
HE WORKS FOR THE MARKETING DEPARTMENT OF A BIG ADVERTISE-MENT COMPANY.

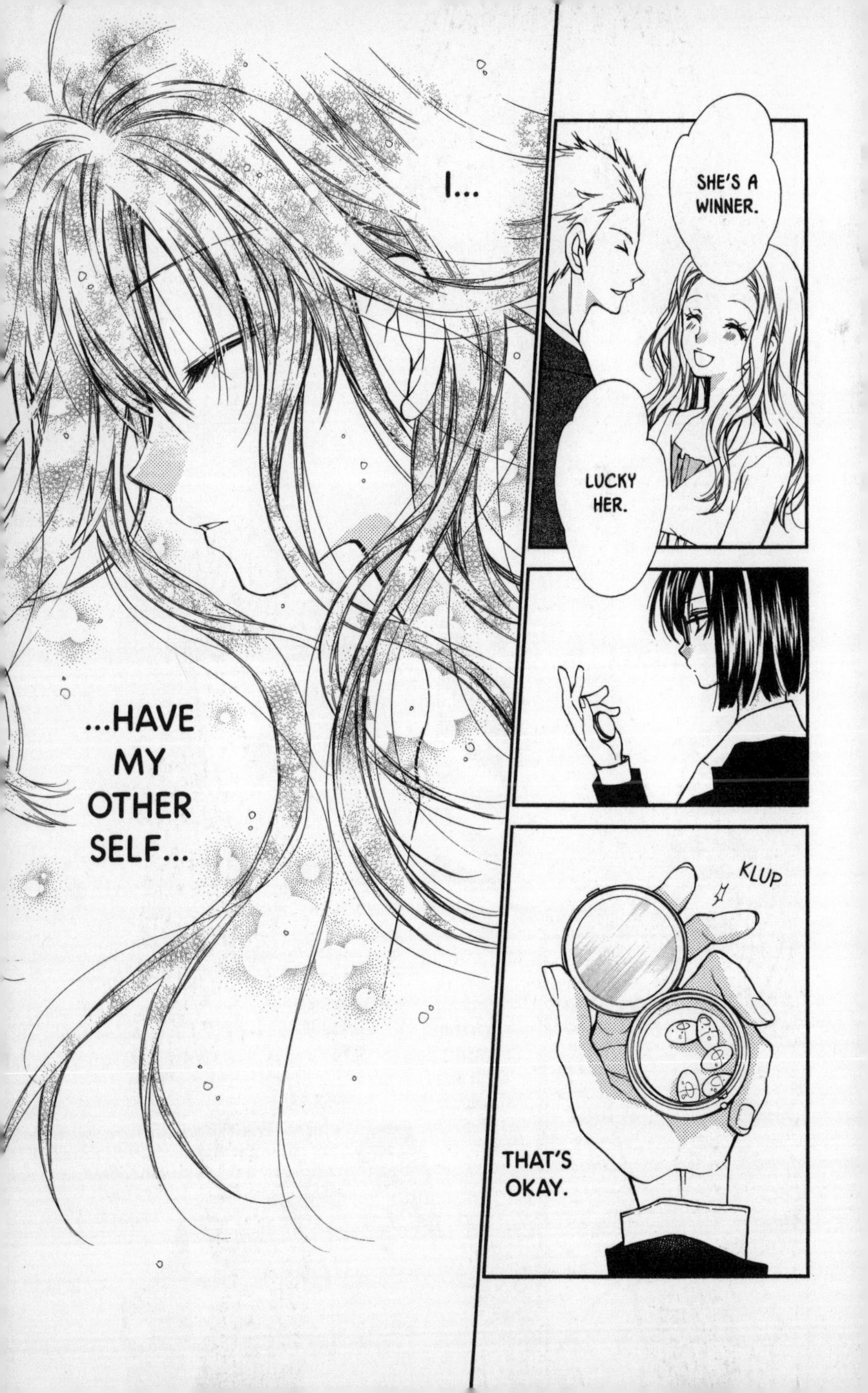
SHE'S A WINNER.
LUCKY HER.
KLUP
THAT'S OKAY.
I...
...HAVE MY OTHER SELF...

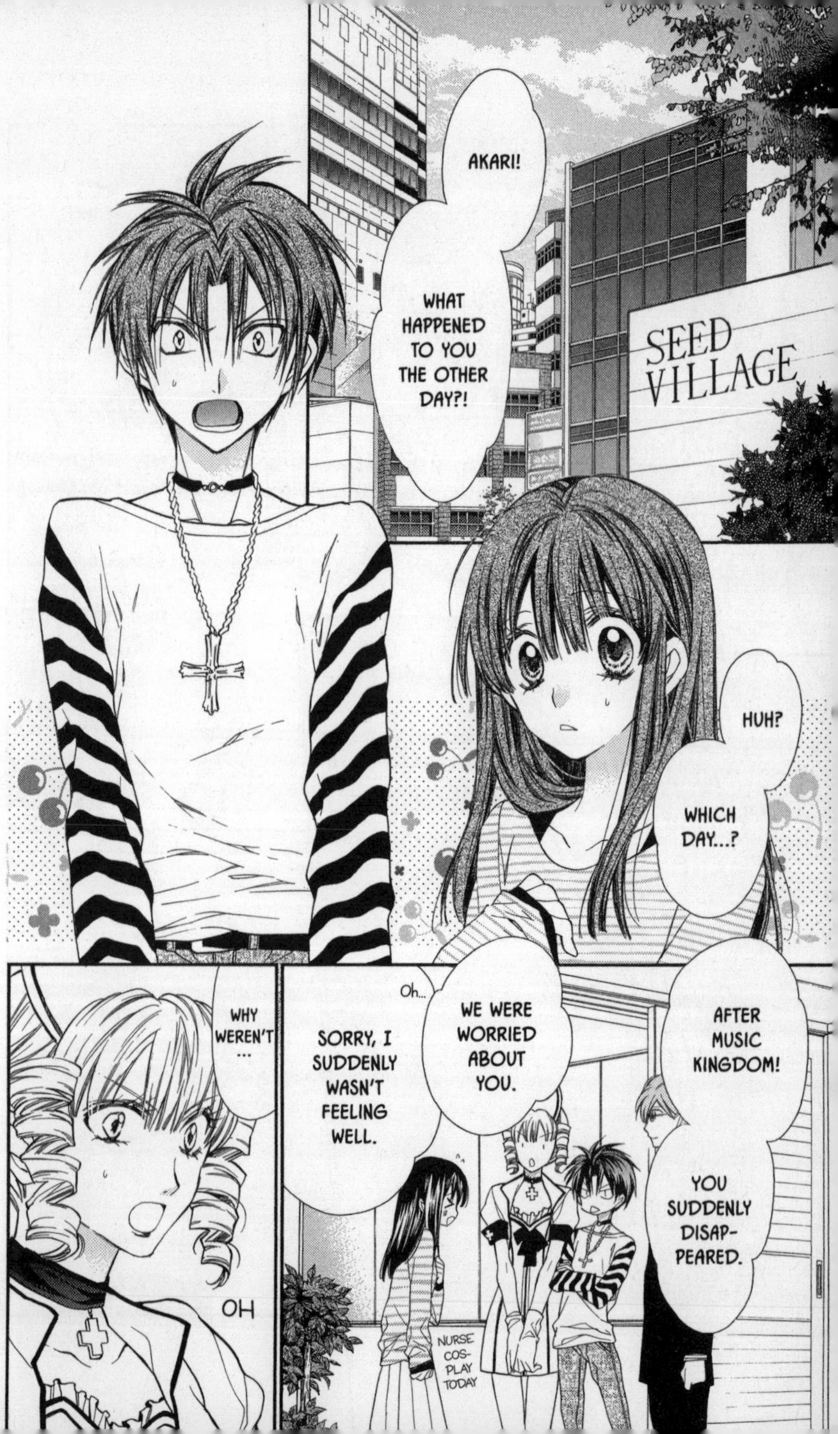
AKARI!
WHAT HAPPENED TO YOU THE OTHER DAY?!
SEED VILLAGE
HUH?
WHICH DAY...?
AFTER MUSIC KINGDOM!
YOU SUDDENLY DISAP-PEARED.
WE WERE WORRIED ABOUT YOU.
Oh...
SORRY, I SUDDENLY WASN'T FEELING WELL.
NURSE COS-PLAY TODAY
WHY WEREN'T ...
OH

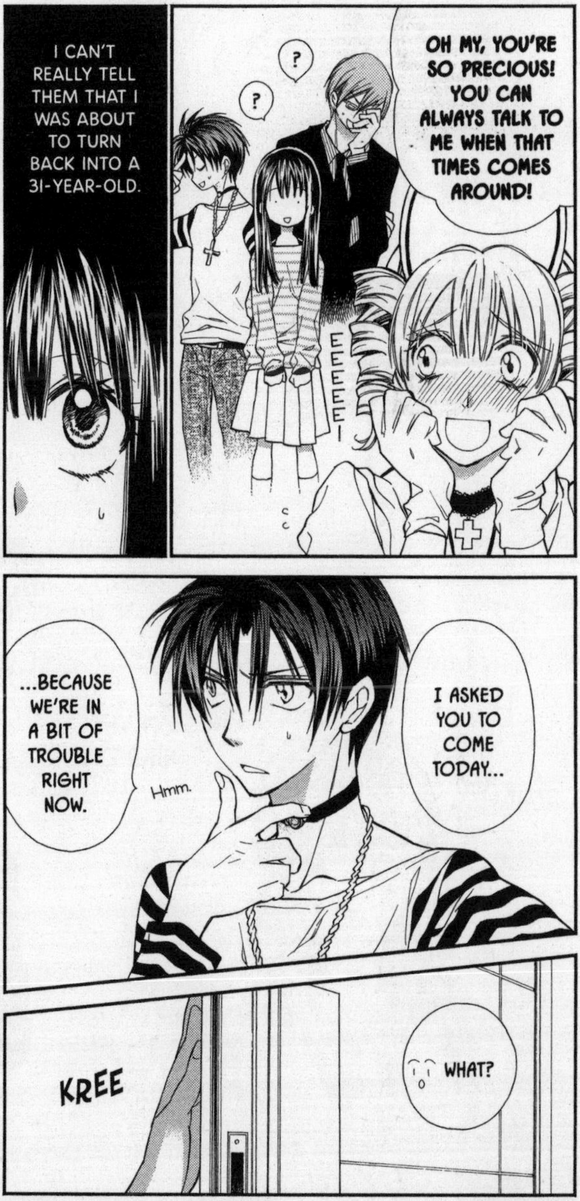

OH MY, YOU'RE SO PRECIOUS! YOU CAN ALWAYS TALK TO ME WHEN THAT TIMES COMES AROUND!
?
?
EEEEE!
I CAN'T REALLY TELL THEM THAT I WAS ABOUT TO TURN BACK INTO A 31-YEAR-OLD.
I ASKED YOU TO COME TODAY...
Hmm.
...BECAUSE WE'RE IN A BIT OF TROUBLE RIGHT NOW.
WHAT?
KREE

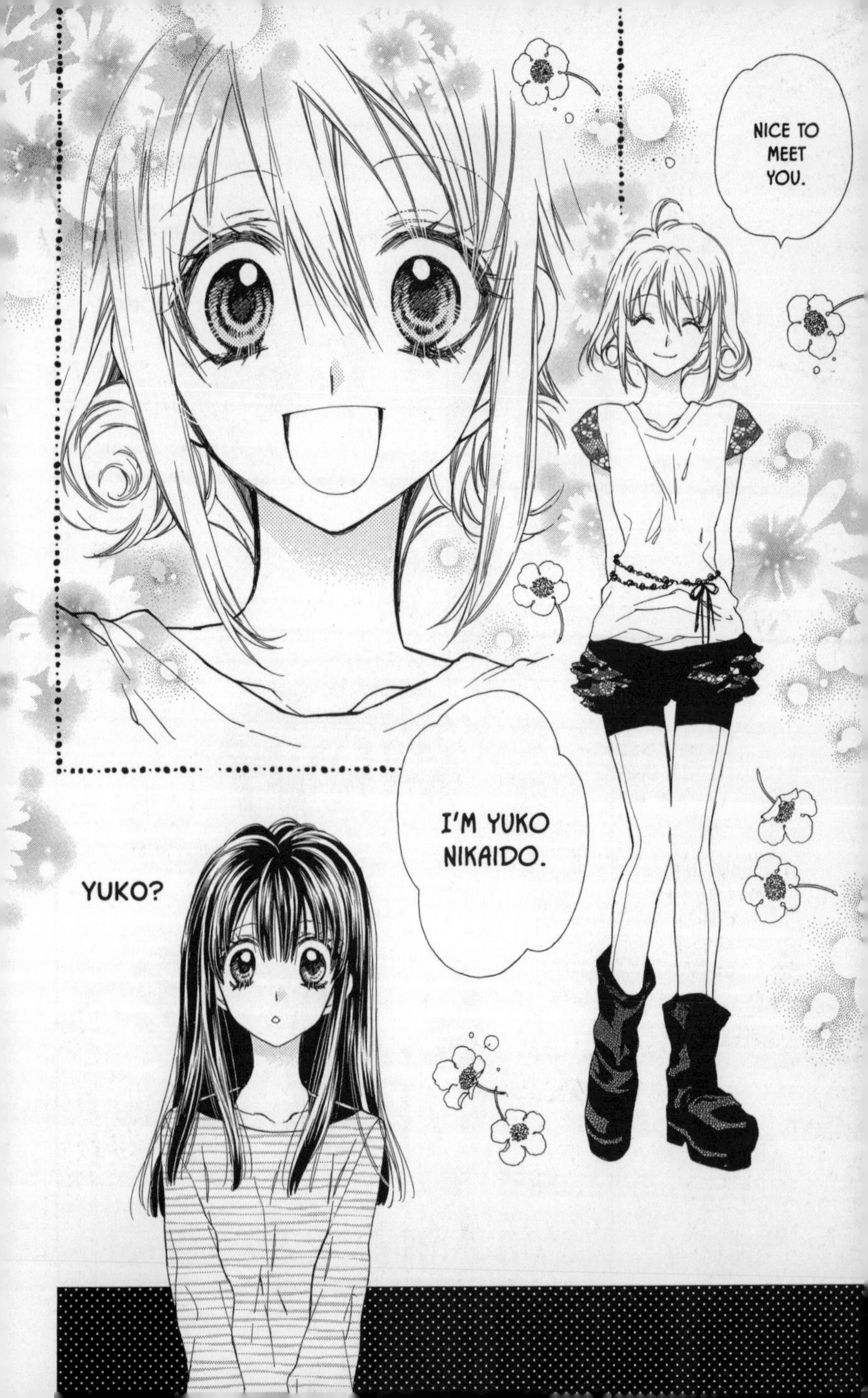
NICE TO MEET YOU.
I'M YUKO NIKAIDO.
YUKO?

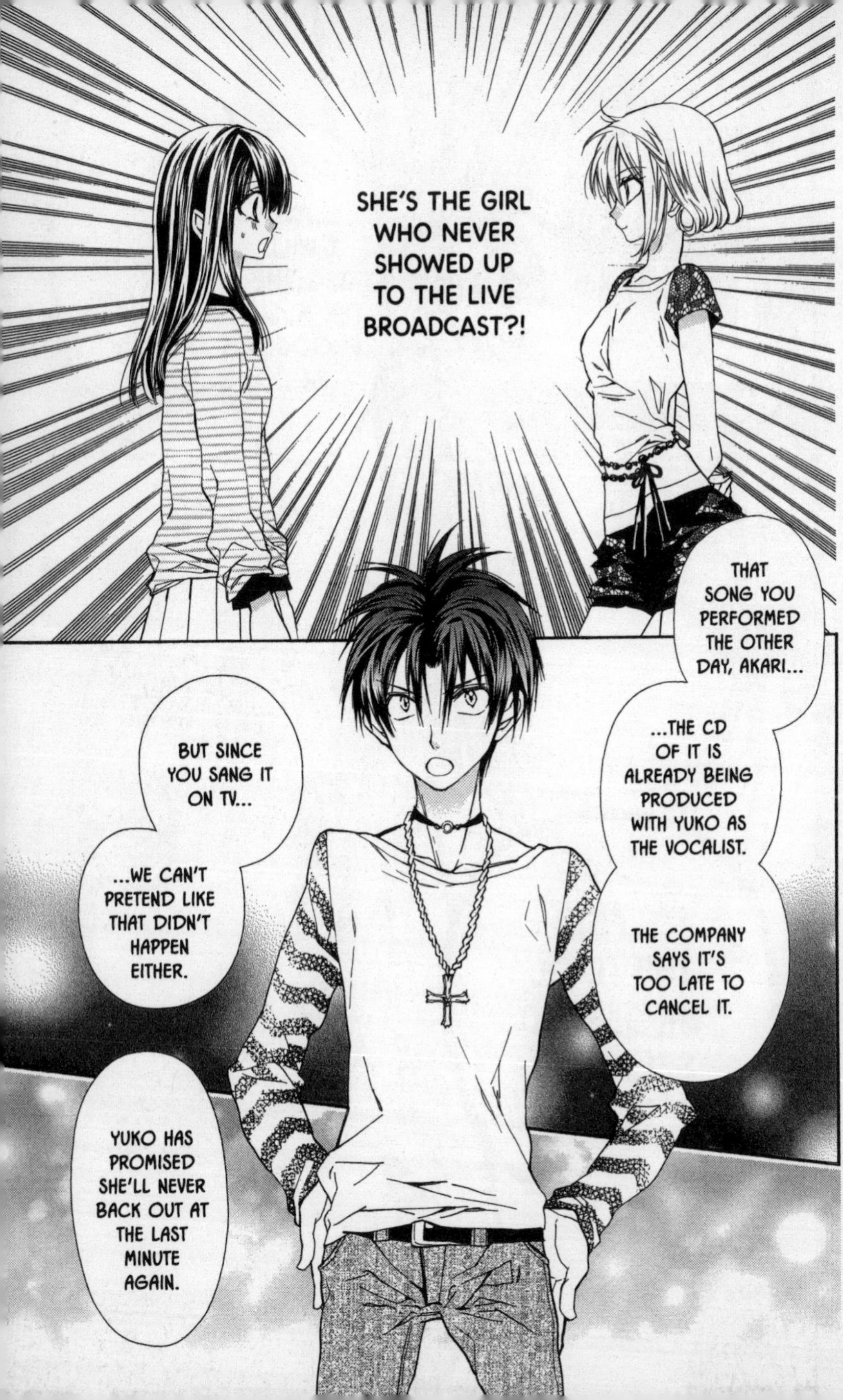
SHE'S THE GIRL WHO NEVER SHOWED UP TO THE LIVE BROADCAST?!
THAT SONG YOU PERFORMED THE OTHER DAY, AKARI...
...THE CD OF IT IS ALREADY BEING PRODUCED WITH YUKO AS THE VOCALIST.
THE COMPANY SAYS IT'S TOO LATE TO CANCEL IT.
BUT SINCE YOU SANG IT ON TV...
...WE CAN'T PRETEND LIKE THAT DIDN'T HAPPEN EITHER.
YUKO HAS PROMISED SHE'LL NEVER BACK OUT AT THE LAST MINUTE AGAIN.

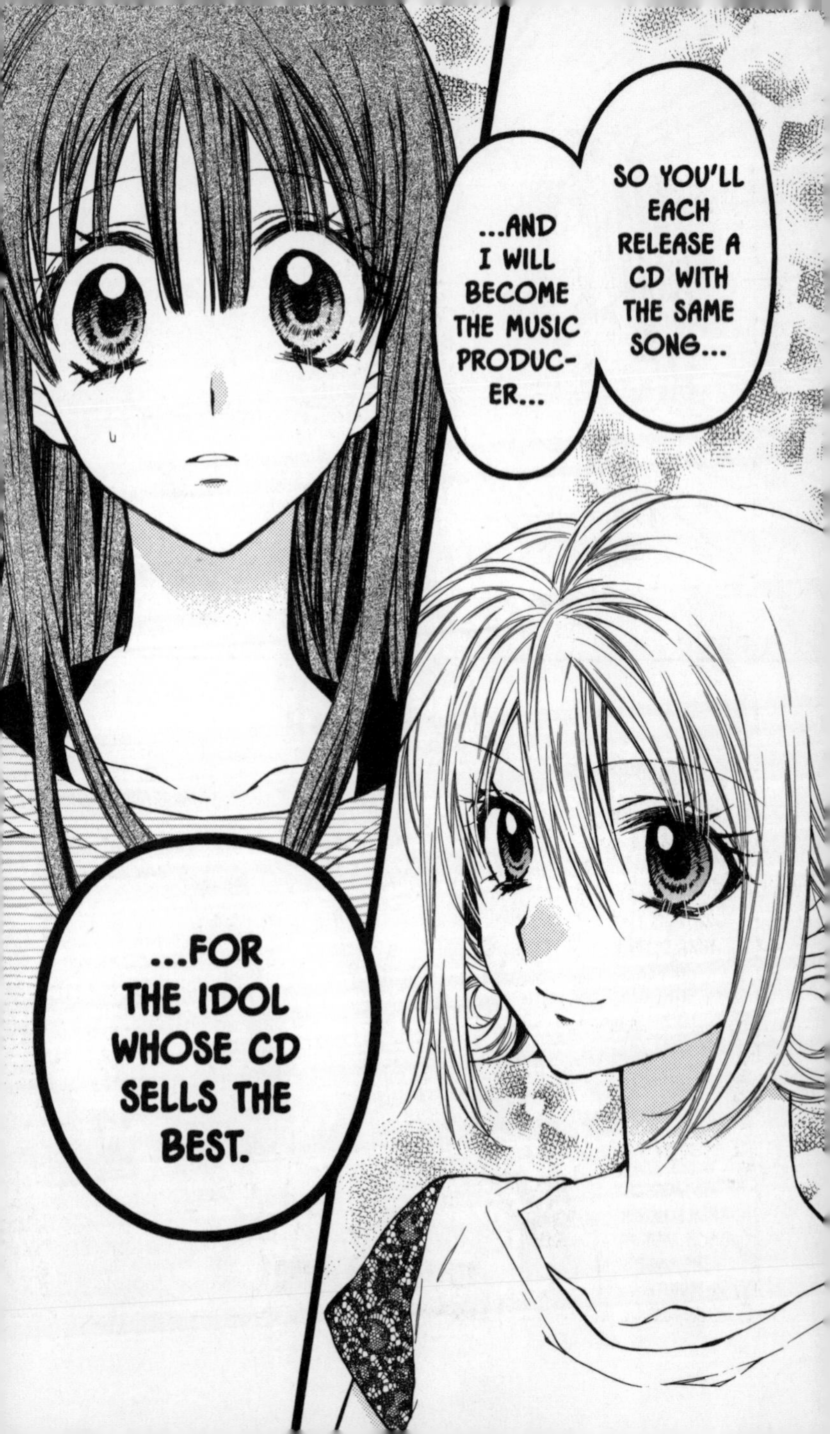
SO YOU'LL EACH RELEASE A CD WITH THE SAME SONG...
...AND I WILL BECOME THE MUSIC PRODUC-ER...
...FOR THE IDOL WHOSE CD SELLS THE BEST.

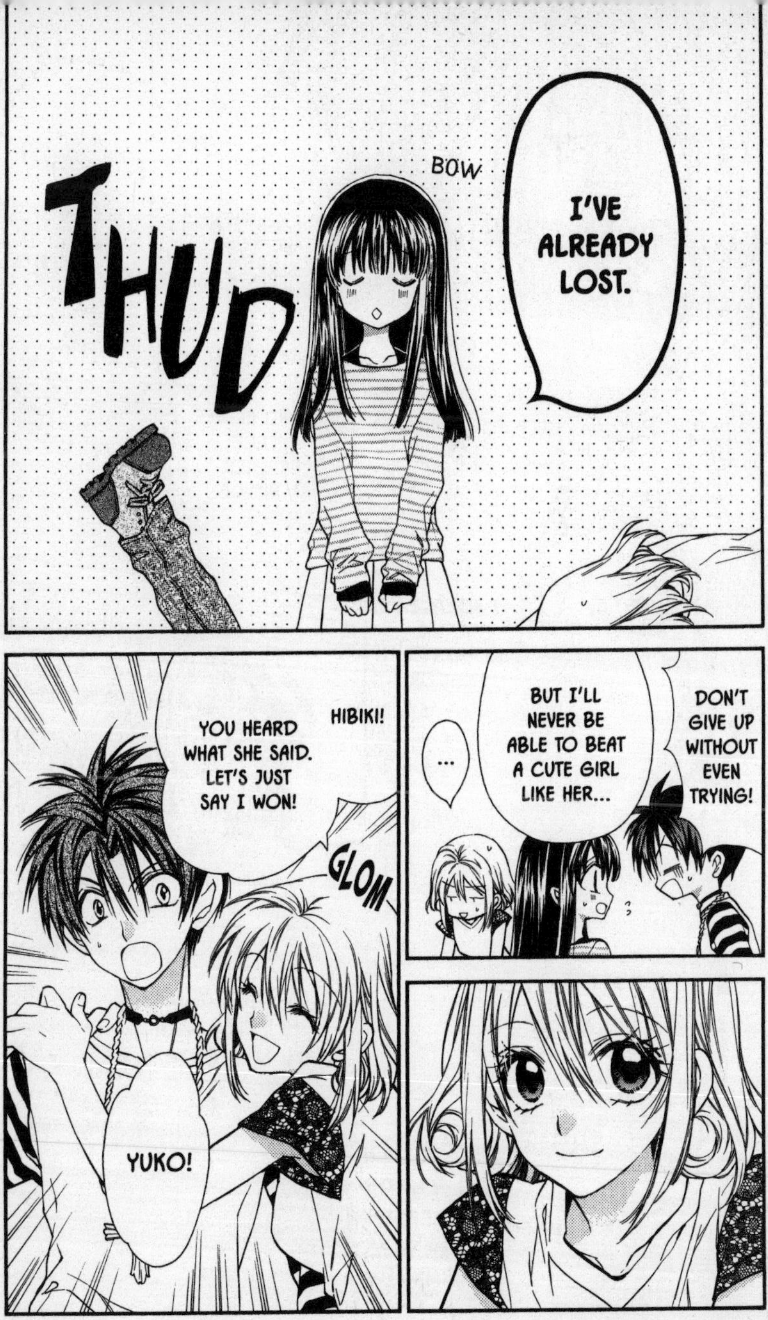
I'VE ALREADY LOST.
BOW
THUD
DON'T GIVE UP WITHOUT EVEN TRYING!
BUT I'LL NEVER BE ABLE TO BEAT A CUTE GIRL LIKE HER...
...
HIBIKI!
YOU HEARD WHAT SHE SAID. LET'S JUST SAY I WON!
GLOM
YUKO!

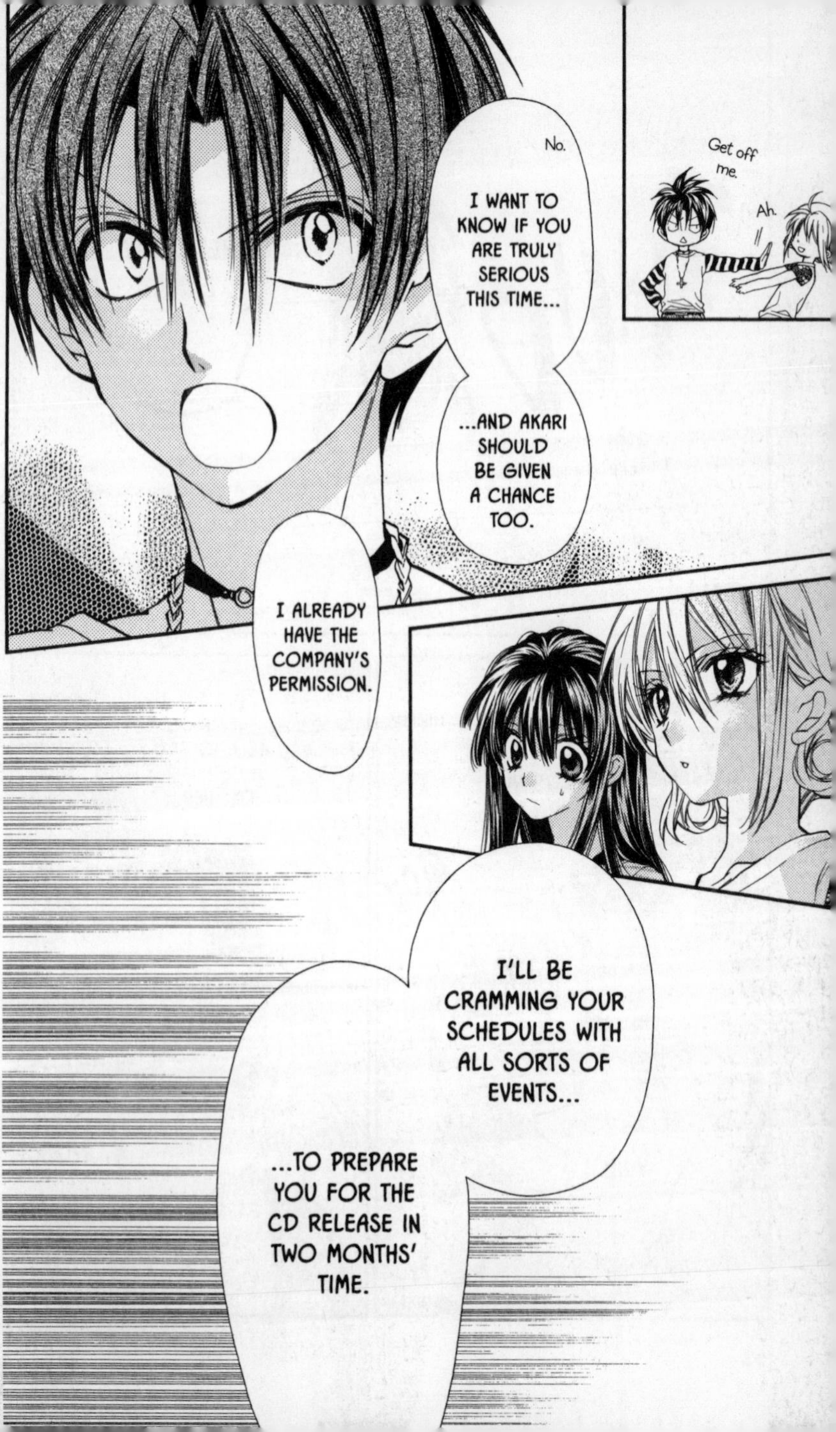
Get off me.
Ah.
No.
I WANT TO KNOW IF YOU ARE TRULY SERIOUS THIS TIME...
...AND AKARI SHOULD BE GIVEN A CHANCE TOO.
I ALREADY HAVE THE COMPANY'S PERMISSION.
I'LL BE CRAMMING YOUR SCHEDULES WITH ALL SORTS OF EVENTS...
...TO PREPARE YOU FOR THE CD RELEASE IN TWO MONTHS' TIME.

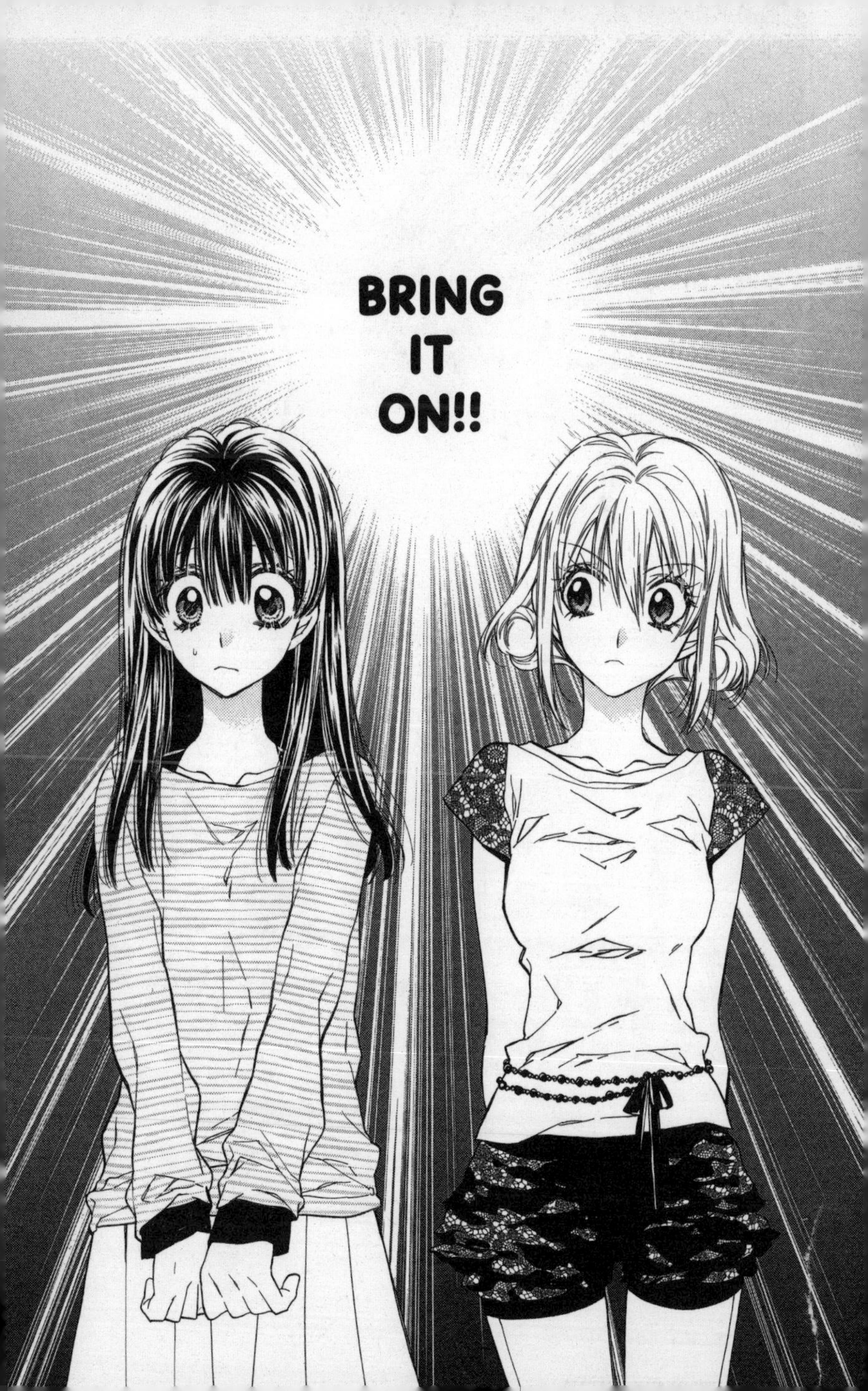
BRING IT ON!!

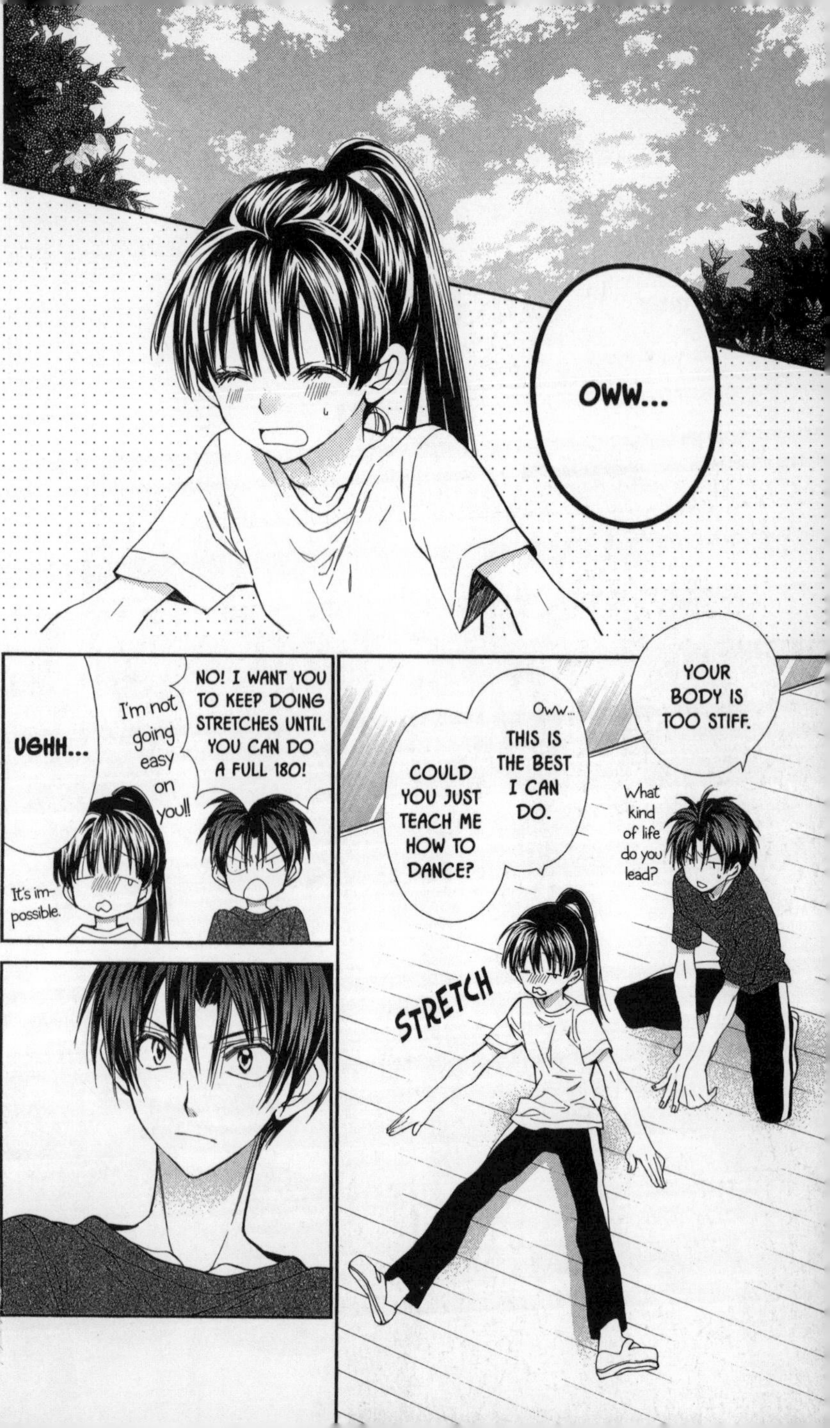
OWW...
YOUR BODY IS TOO STIFF.
What kind of life do you lead?
Oww... THIS IS THE BEST I CAN DO.
COULD YOU JUST TEACH ME HOW TO DANCE?
STRETCH
NO! I WANT YOU TO KEEP DOING STRETCHES UNTIL YOU CAN DO A FULL 180!
I'm not going easy on you!!
UGHH...
It's impossible.

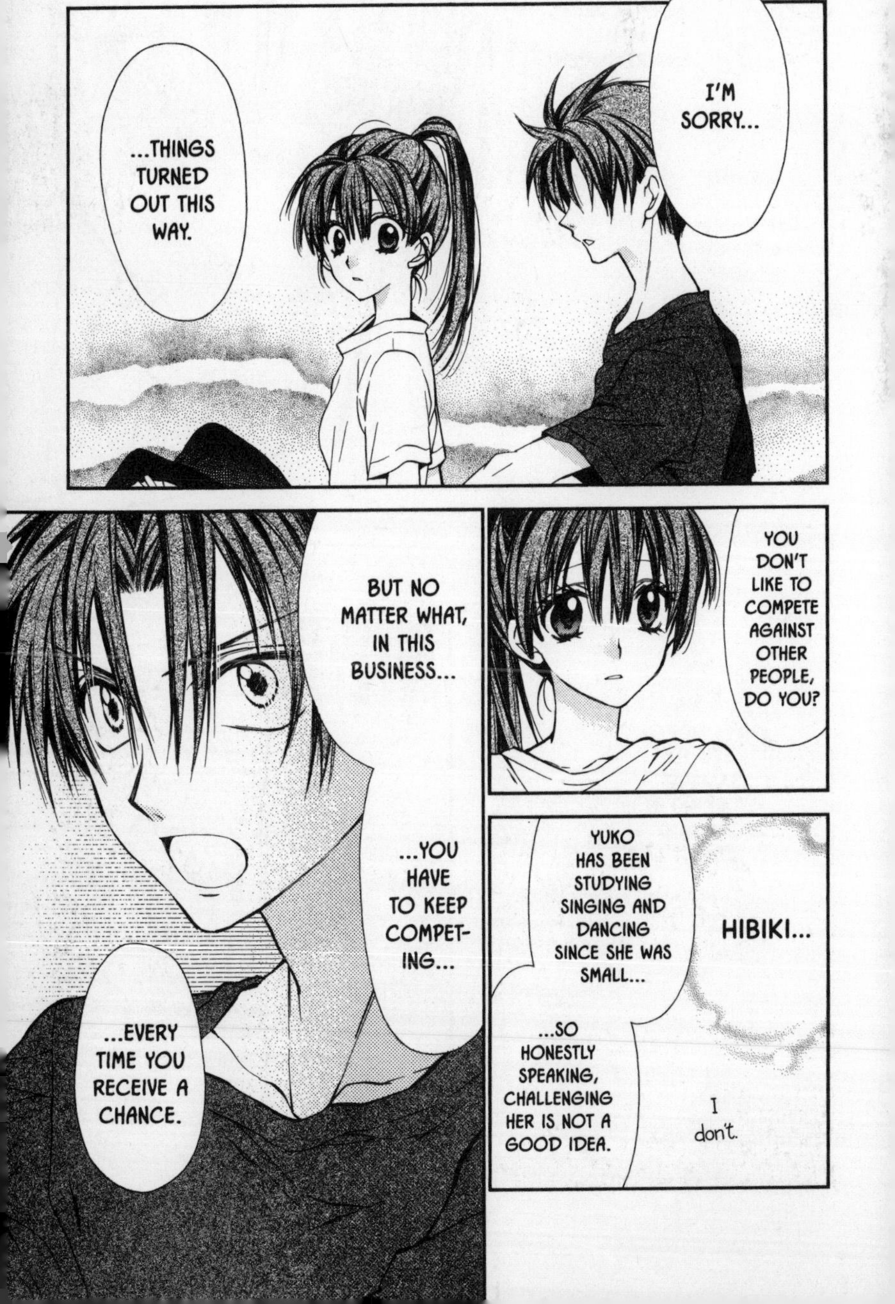
I'M SORRY...
...THINGS TURNED OUT THIS WAY.
YOU DON'T LIKE TO COMPETE AGAINST OTHER PEOPLE, DO YOU?
YUKO HAS BEEN STUDYING SINGING AND DANCING SINCE SHE WAS SMALL...
...SO HONESTLY SPEAKING, CHALLENGING HER IS NOT A GOOD IDEA.
HIBIKI...
I don't.
BUT NO MATTER WHAT, IN THIS BUSINESS...
...YOU HAVE TO KEEP COMPET-ING...
...EVERY TIME YOU RECEIVE A CHANCE.

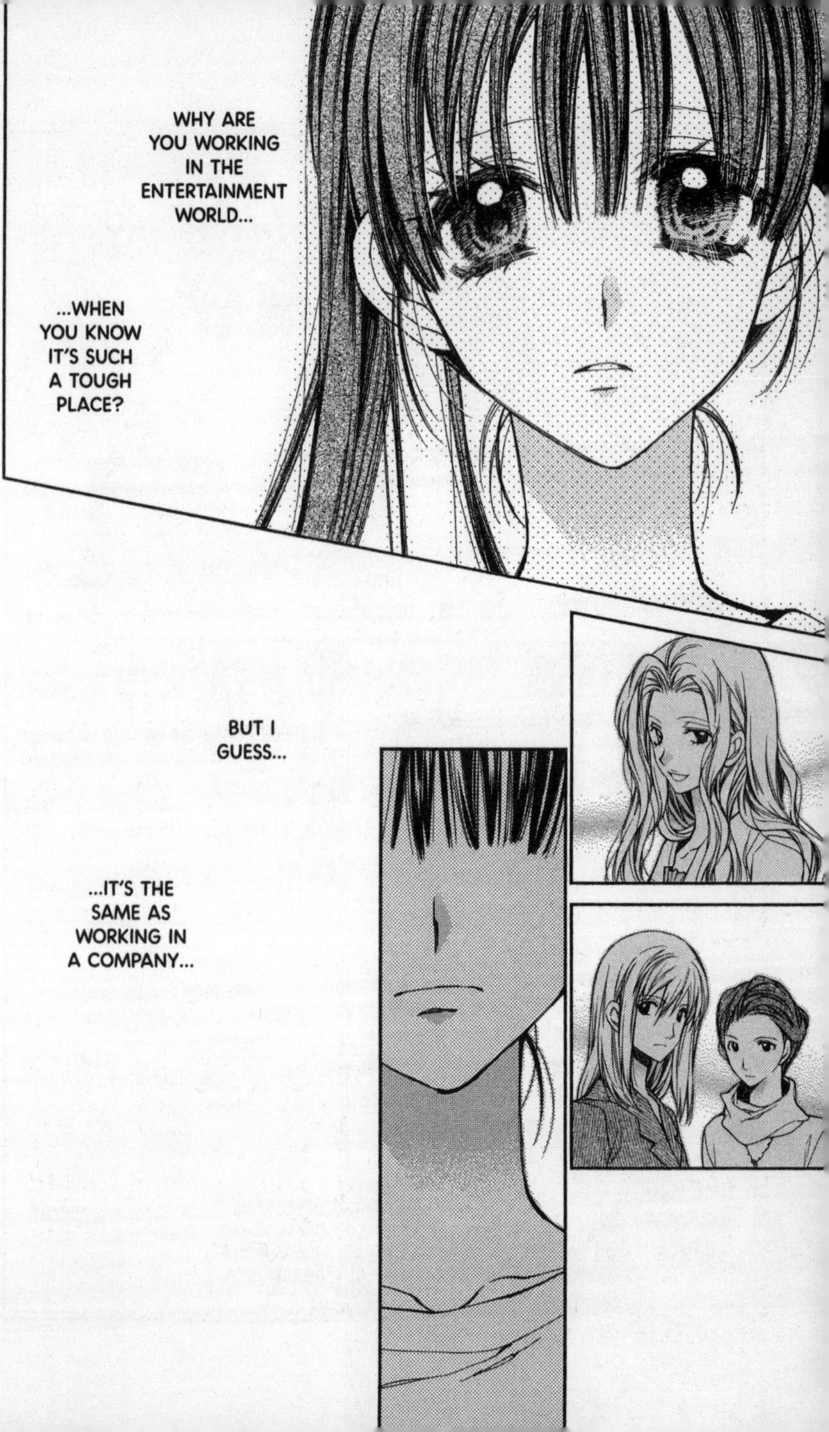
WHY ARE YOU WORKING IN THE ENTERTAINMENT WORLD...
...WHEN YOU KNOW IT'S SUCH A TOUGH PLACE?
BUT I GUESS...
...IT'S THE SAME AS WORKING IN A COMPANY...

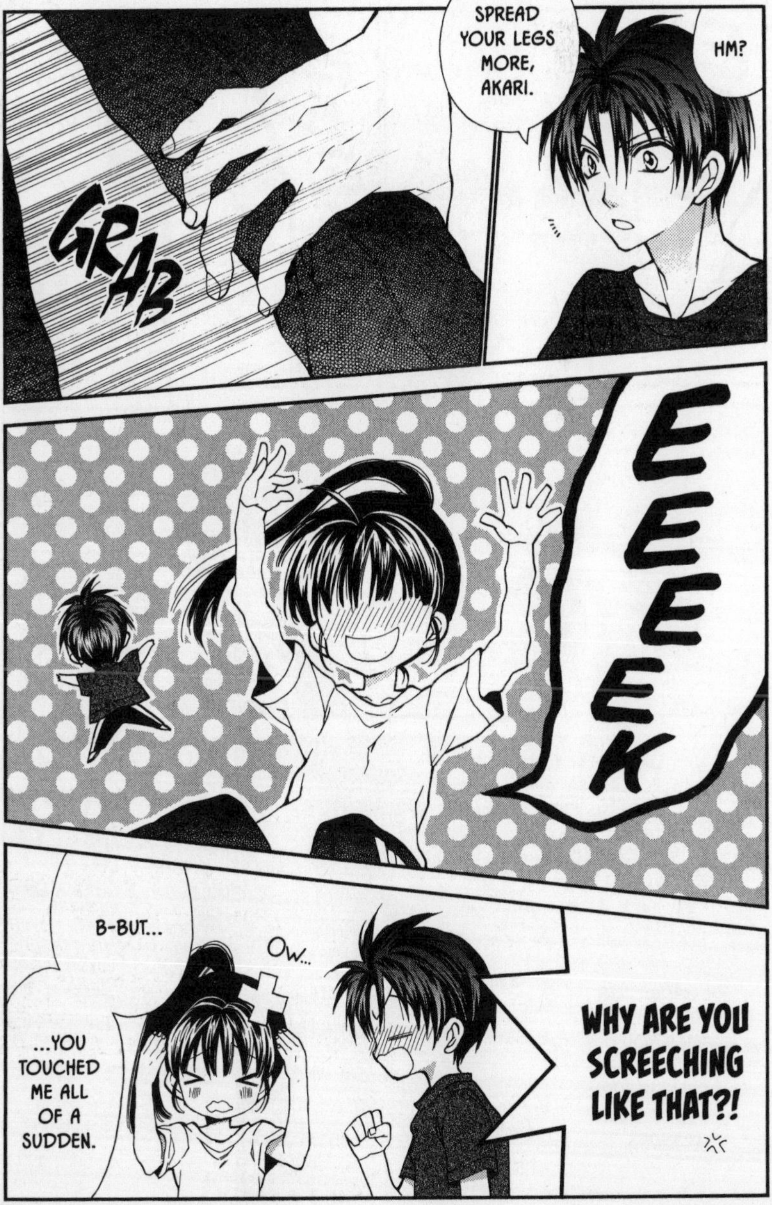
HM?
SPREAD YOUR LEGS MORE, AKARI.
GRAB
EEEEEK
WHY ARE YOU SCREECHING LIKE THAT?!
OW...
B-BUT...
...YOU TOUCHED ME ALL OF A SUDDEN.
BECAUSE SHE'S A 31-YEAR-OLD VIRGIN...

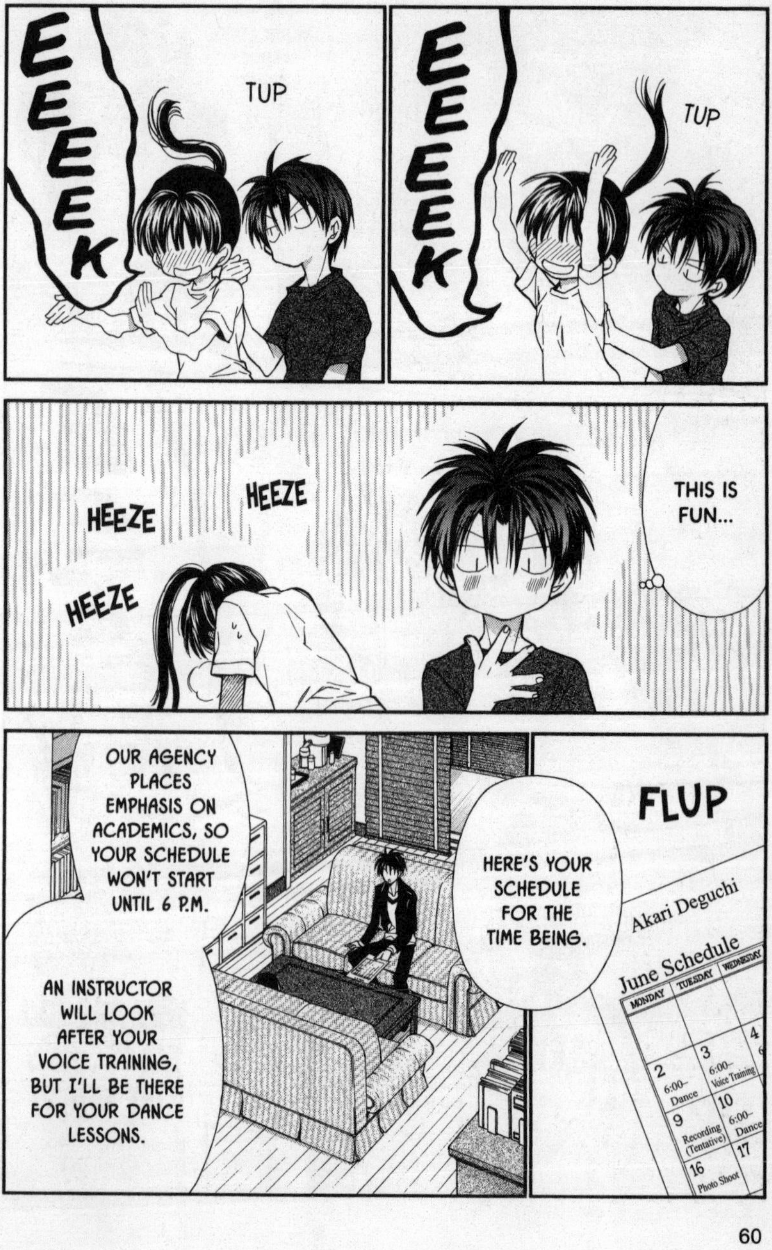
EEEEK
TUP
EEEEK
TUP
THIS IS FUN...
HEEZE
HEEZE
HEEZE
FLUP
Akari Deguchi
June Schedule
MONDAY TUESDAY WEDNESDAY
2 6:00– Dance
3 6:00– Voice Training
4
9 Recording (Tentative)
10 6:00– Dance
16 Photo Shoot
17
HERE'S YOUR SCHEDULE FOR THE TIME BEING.
OUR AGENCY PLACES EMPHASIS ON ACADEMICS, SO YOUR SCHEDULE WON'T START UNTIL 6 P.M.
AN INSTRUCTOR WILL LOOK AFTER YOUR VOICE TRAINING, BUT I'LL BE THERE FOR YOUR DANCE LESSONS.

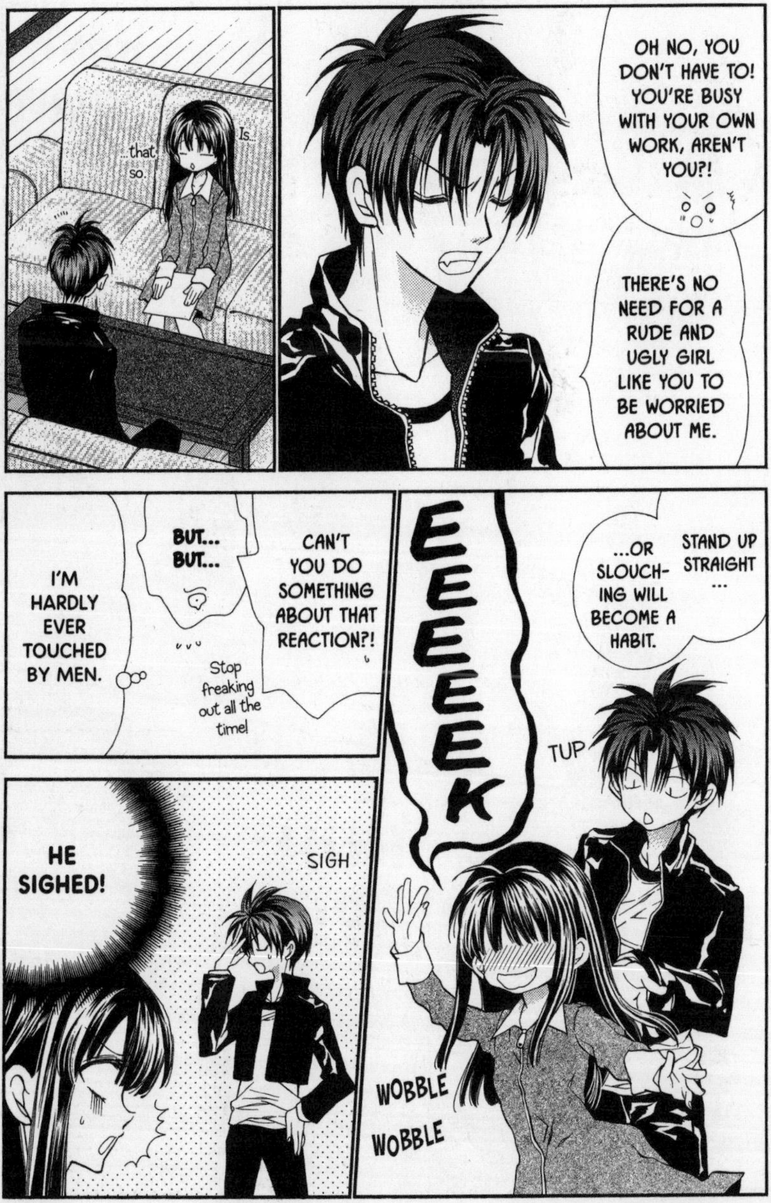
OH NO, YOU DON'T HAVE TO! YOU'RE BUSY WITH YOUR OWN WORK, AREN'T YOU?!
THERE'S NO NEED FOR A RUDE AND UGLY GIRL LIKE YOU TO BE WORRIED ABOUT ME.
Is...
...that so.
STAND UP STRAIGHT...
...OR SLOUCHING WILL BECOME A HABIT.
EEEEEK
TUP
WOBBLE
WOBBLE
CAN'T YOU DO SOMETHING ABOUT THAT REACTION?!
Stop freaking out all the time!
BUT... BUT...
I'M HARDLY EVER TOUCHED BY MEN.
SIGH
HE SIGHED!

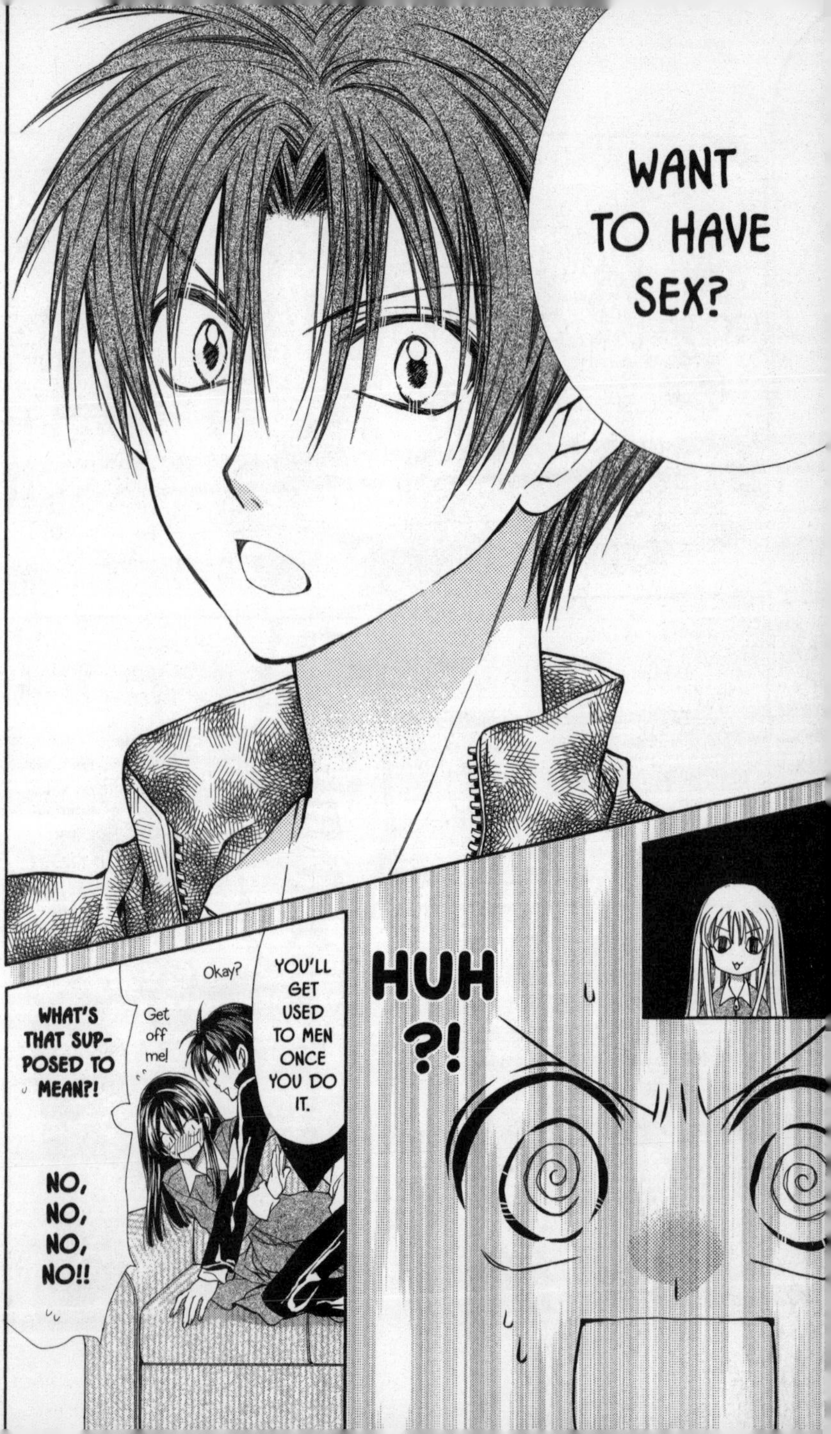
WANT TO HAVE SEX?
HUH ?!
YOU'LL GET USED TO MEN ONCE YOU DO IT.
Okay?
Get off me!
WHAT'S THAT SUP-POSED TO MEAN?!
NO, NO, NO, NO!!

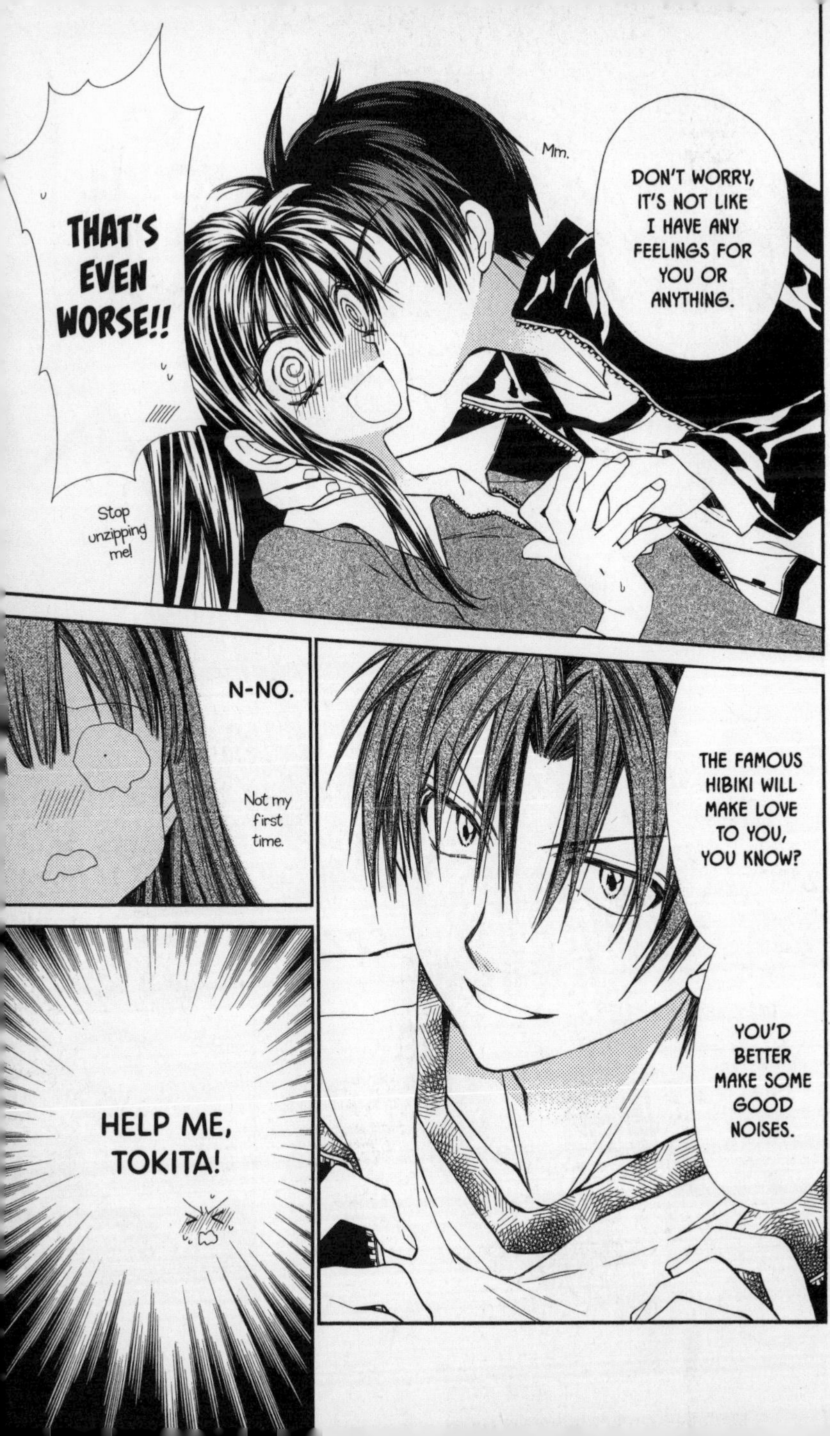
DON'T WORRY, IT'S NOT LIKE I HAVE ANY FEELINGS FOR YOU OR ANYTHING.
Mm.
THAT'S EVEN WORSE!!
Stop unzipping me!
THE FAMOUS HIBIKI WILL MAKE LOVE TO YOU, YOU KNOW?
YOU'D BETTER MAKE SOME GOOD NOISES.
N-NO.
Not my first time.
HELP ME, TOKITA!

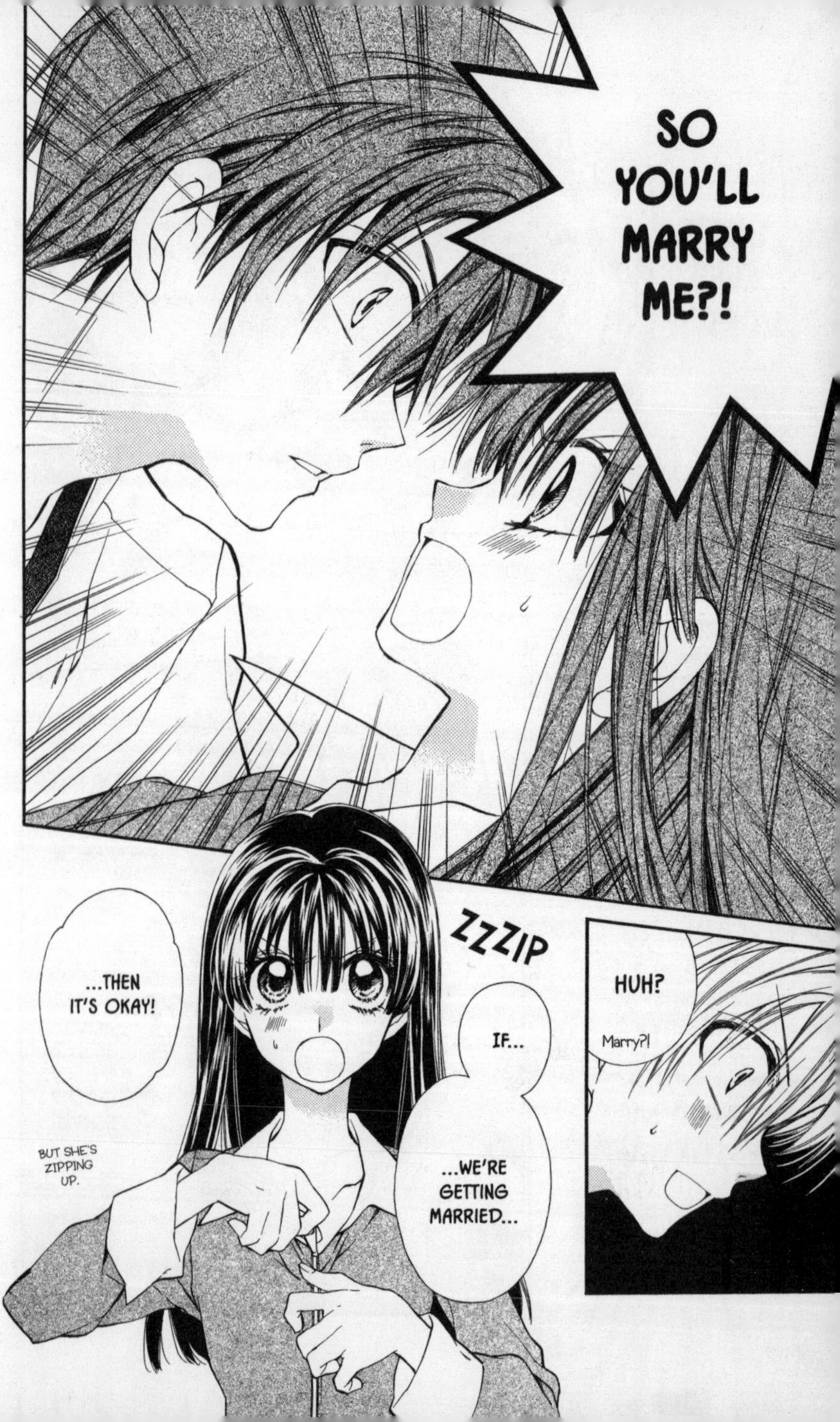
SO YOU'LL MARRY ME?!
HUH?
Marry?!
ZZZIP
IF...
...WE'RE GETTING MARRIED...
...THEN IT'S OKAY!
BUT SHE'S ZIPPING UP.

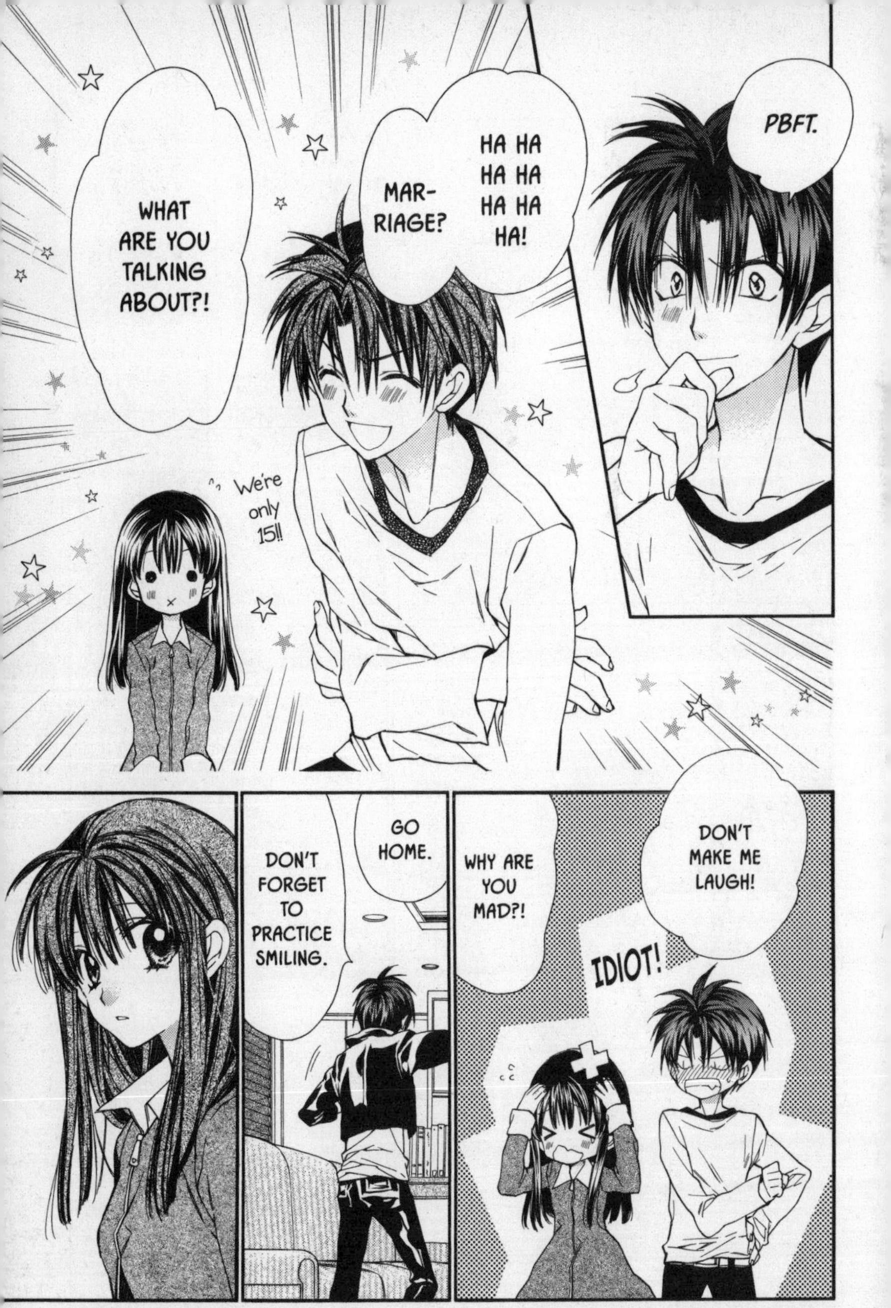
PBFT.
HA HA HA HA HA HA HA!
MAR-RIAGE?
WHAT ARE YOU TALKING ABOUT?!
We're only 15!!
DON'T MAKE ME LAUGH!
IDIOT!
WHY ARE YOU MAD?!
GO HOME.
DON'T FORGET TO PRACTICE SMILING.

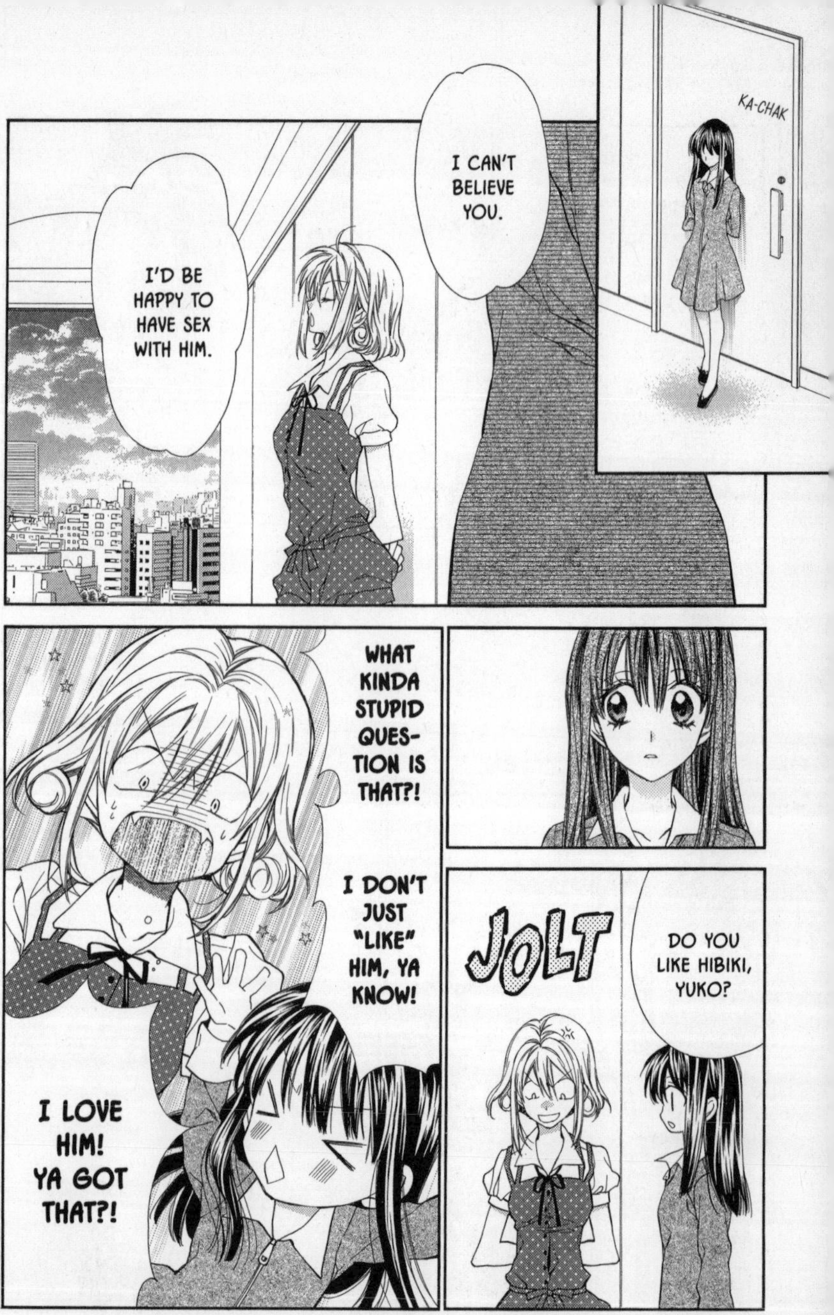
KA-CHAK
I CAN'T BELIEVE YOU.
I'D BE HAPPY TO HAVE SEX WITH HIM.
DO YOU LIKE HIBIKI, YUKO?
JOLT
WHAT KINDA STUPID QUESTION IS THAT?!
I DON'T JUST "LIKE" HIM, YA KNOW!
I LOVE HIM! YA GOT THAT?!

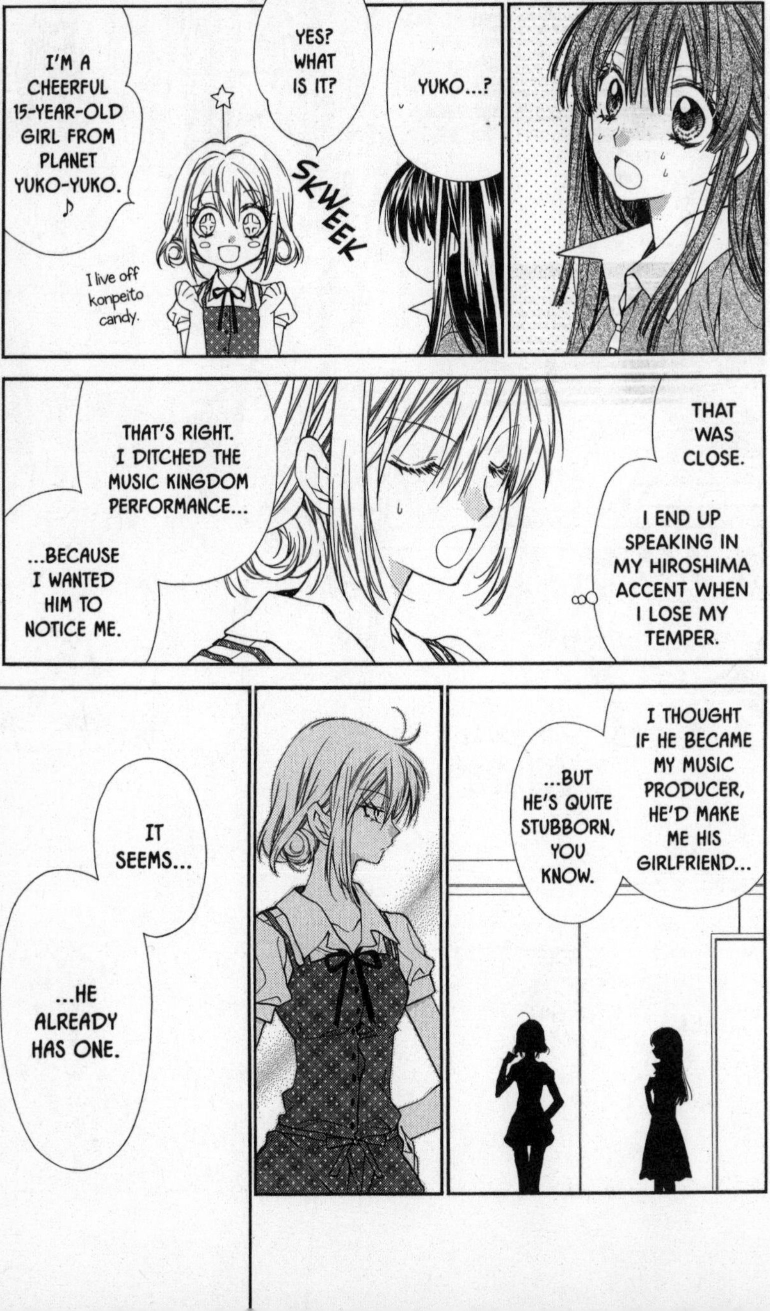
YUKO...?
YES? WHAT IS IT?
SKWEEK
I'M A CHEERFUL 15-YEAR-OLD GIRL FROM PLANET YUKO-YUKO. ♪
I live off konpeito candy.
THAT WAS CLOSE.
I END UP SPEAKING IN MY HIROSHIMA ACCENT WHEN I LOSE MY TEMPER.
THAT'S RIGHT. I DITCHED THE MUSIC KINGDOM PERFORMANCE...
...BECAUSE I WANTED HIM TO NOTICE ME.
I THOUGHT IF HE BECAME MY MUSIC PRODUCER, HE'D MAKE ME HIS GIRLFRIEND...
...BUT HE'S QUITE STUBBORN, YOU KNOW.
IT SEEMS...
...HE ALREADY HAS ONE.

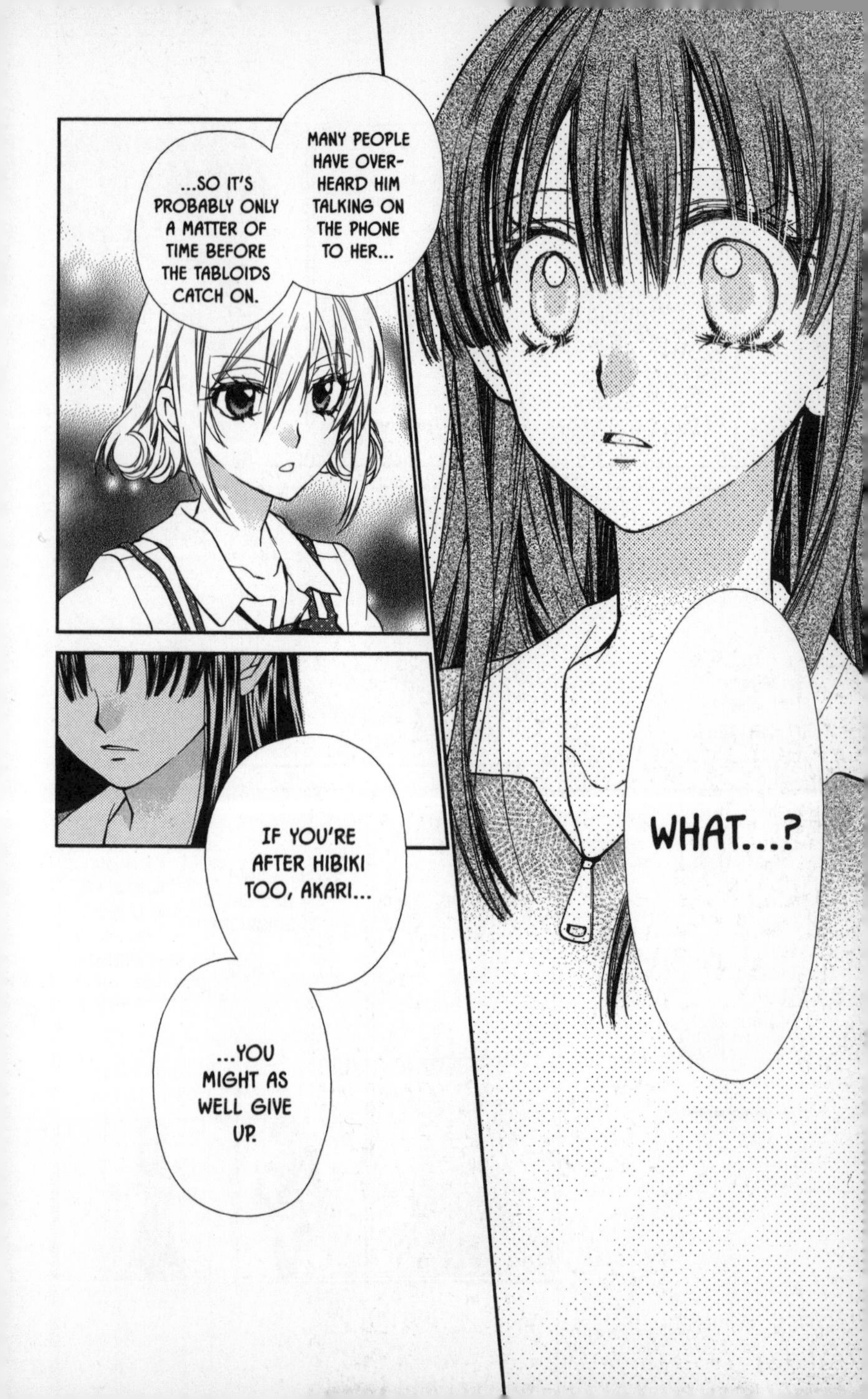

WHAT...?
MANY PEOPLE HAVE OVER-HEARD HIM TALKING ON THE PHONE TO HER...
...SO IT'S PROBABLY ONLY A MATTER OF TIME BEFORE THE TABLOIDS CATCH ON.
IF YOU'RE AFTER HIBIKI TOO, AKARI...
...YOU MIGHT AS WELL GIVE UP.

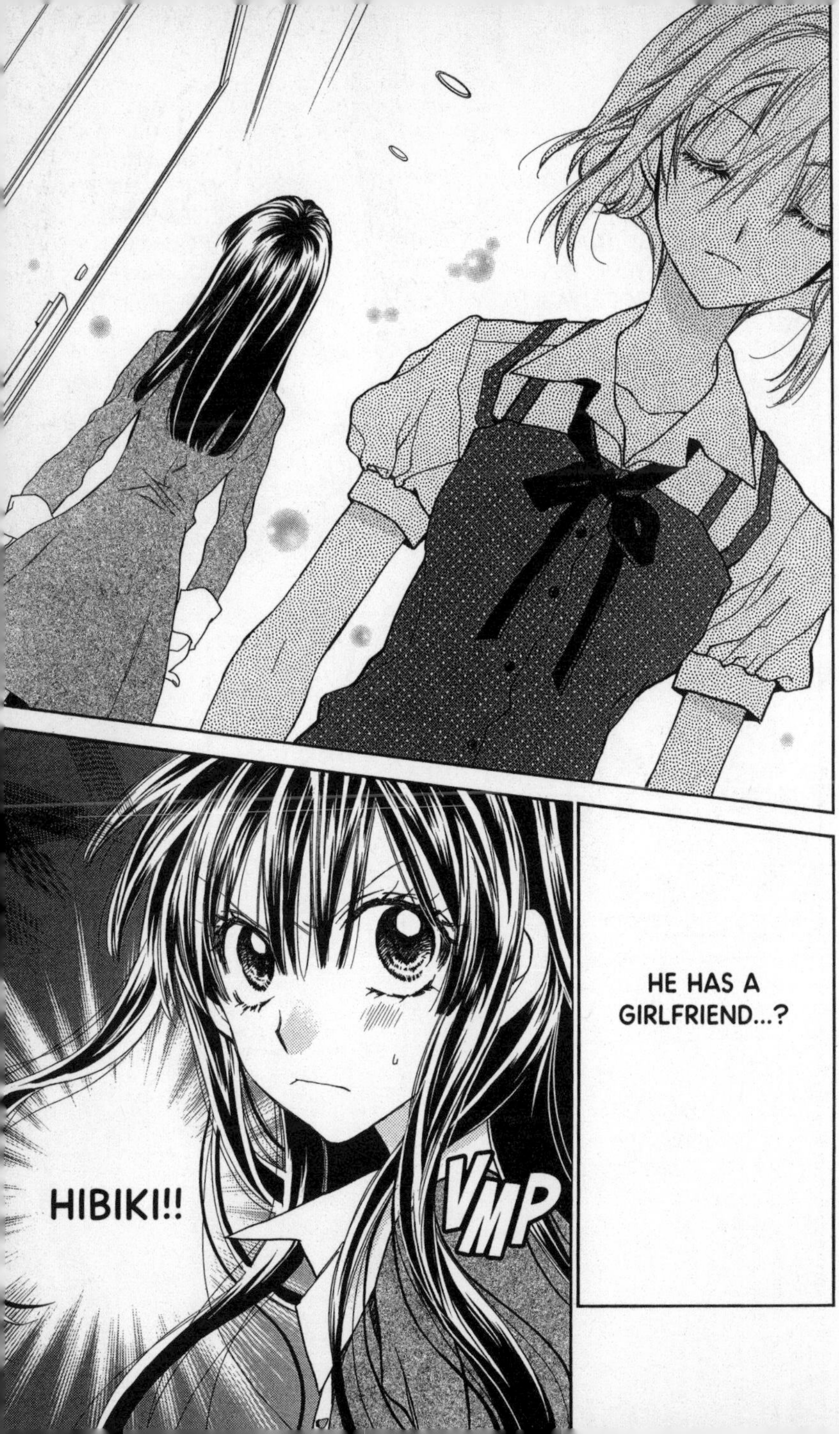
HE HAS A GIRLFRIEND...?
HIBIKI!!
VMP

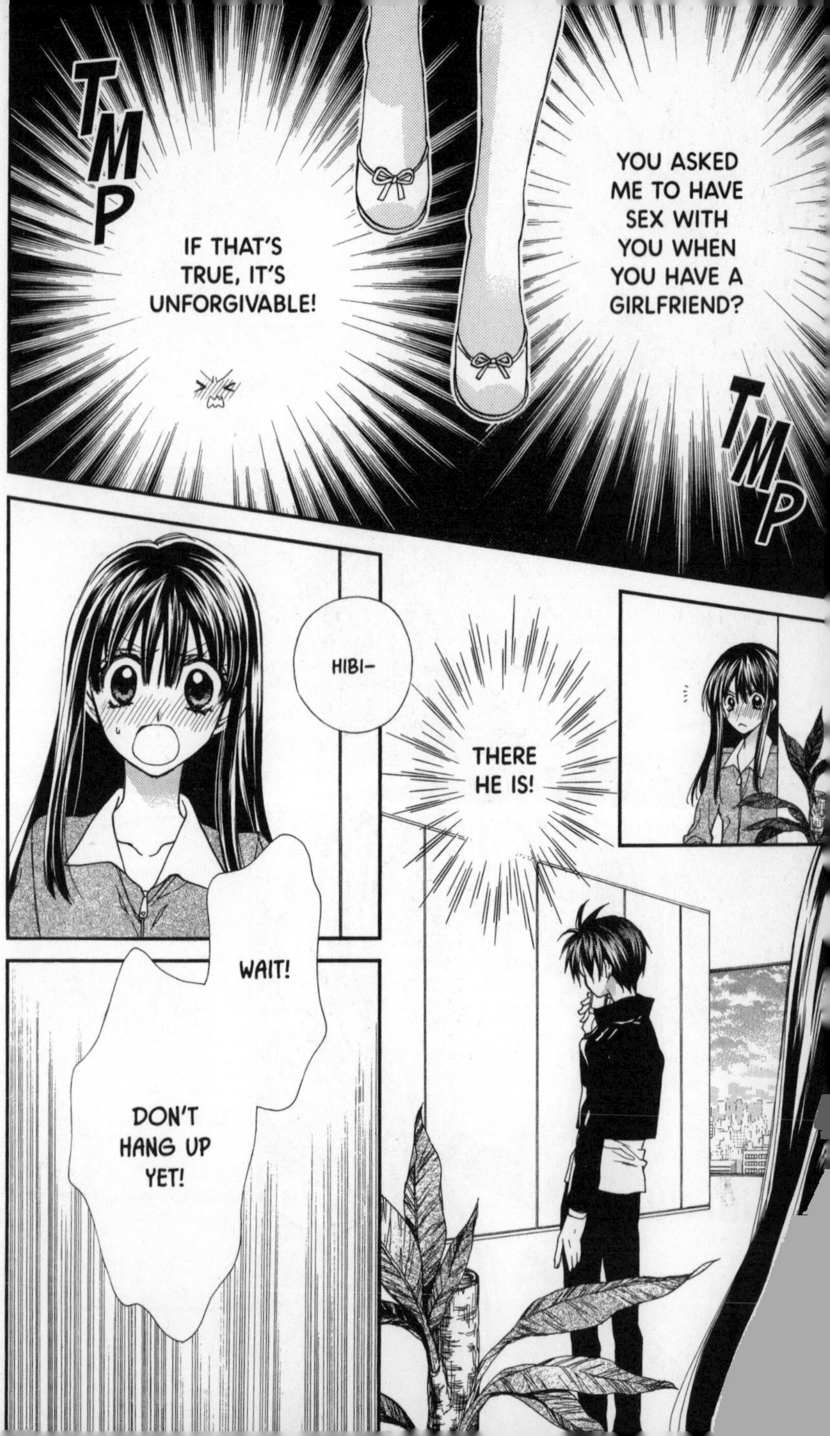
YOU ASKED ME TO HAVE SEX WITH YOU WHEN YOU HAVE A GIRLFRIEND?
TMP
IF THAT'S TRUE, IT'S UNFORGIVABLE!
TMP
THERE HE IS!
HIBI-
WAIT!
DON'T HANG UP YET!

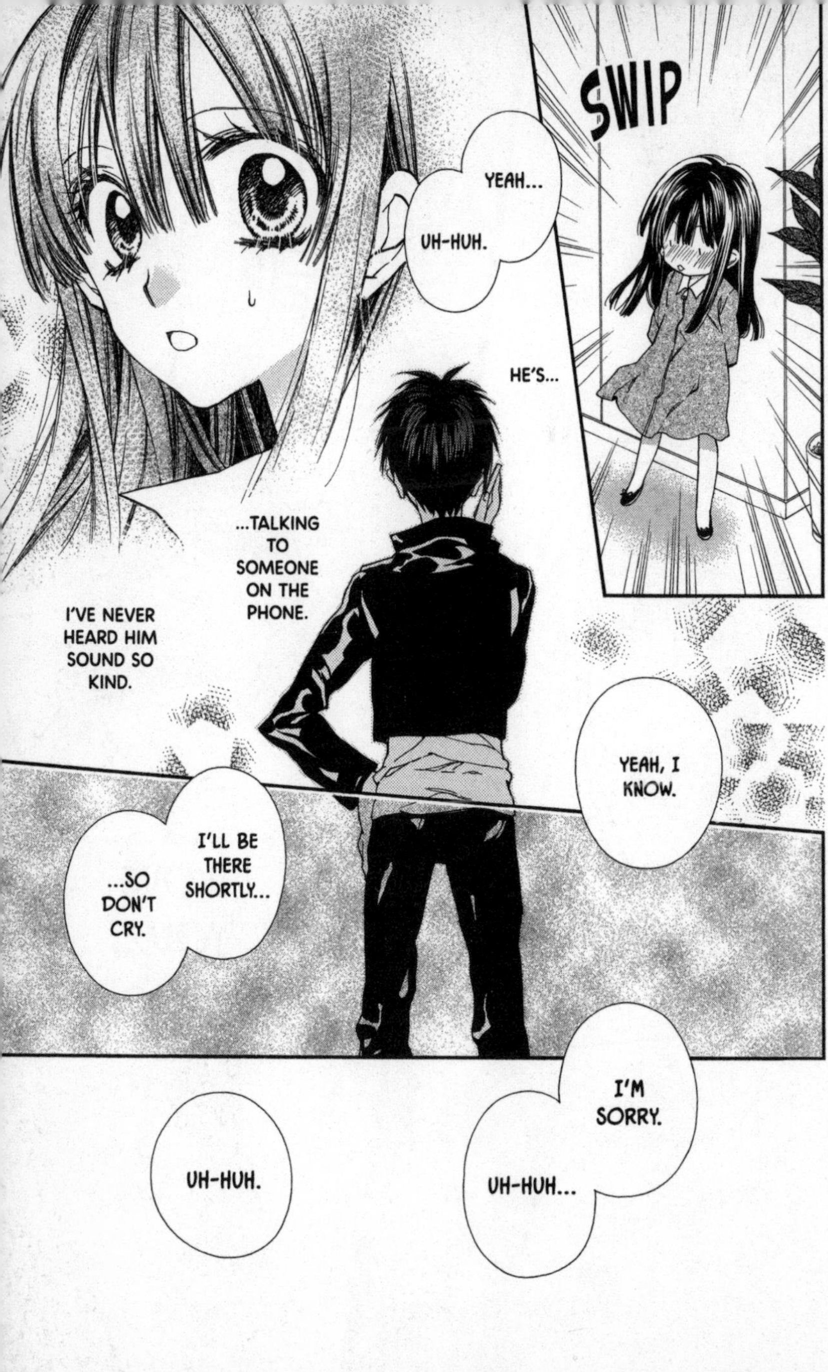
SWIP
YEAH... UH-HUH.
HE'S...
...TALKING TO SOMEONE ON THE PHONE.
I'VE NEVER HEARD HIM SOUND SO KIND.
YEAH, I KNOW.
I'LL BE THERE SHORTLY...
...SO DON'T CRY.
I'M SORRY. UH-HUH...
UH-HUH.

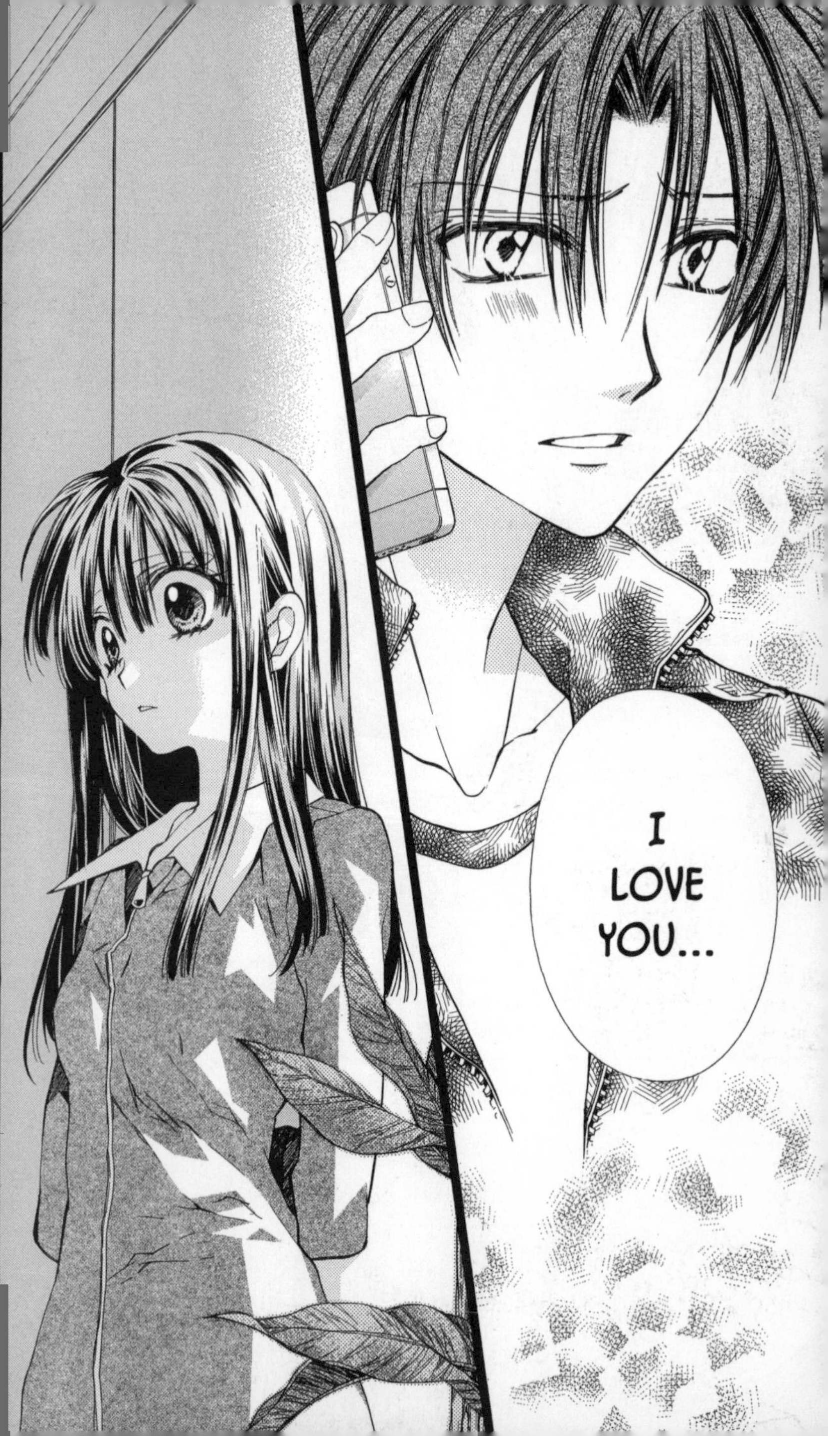
I LOVE YOU...

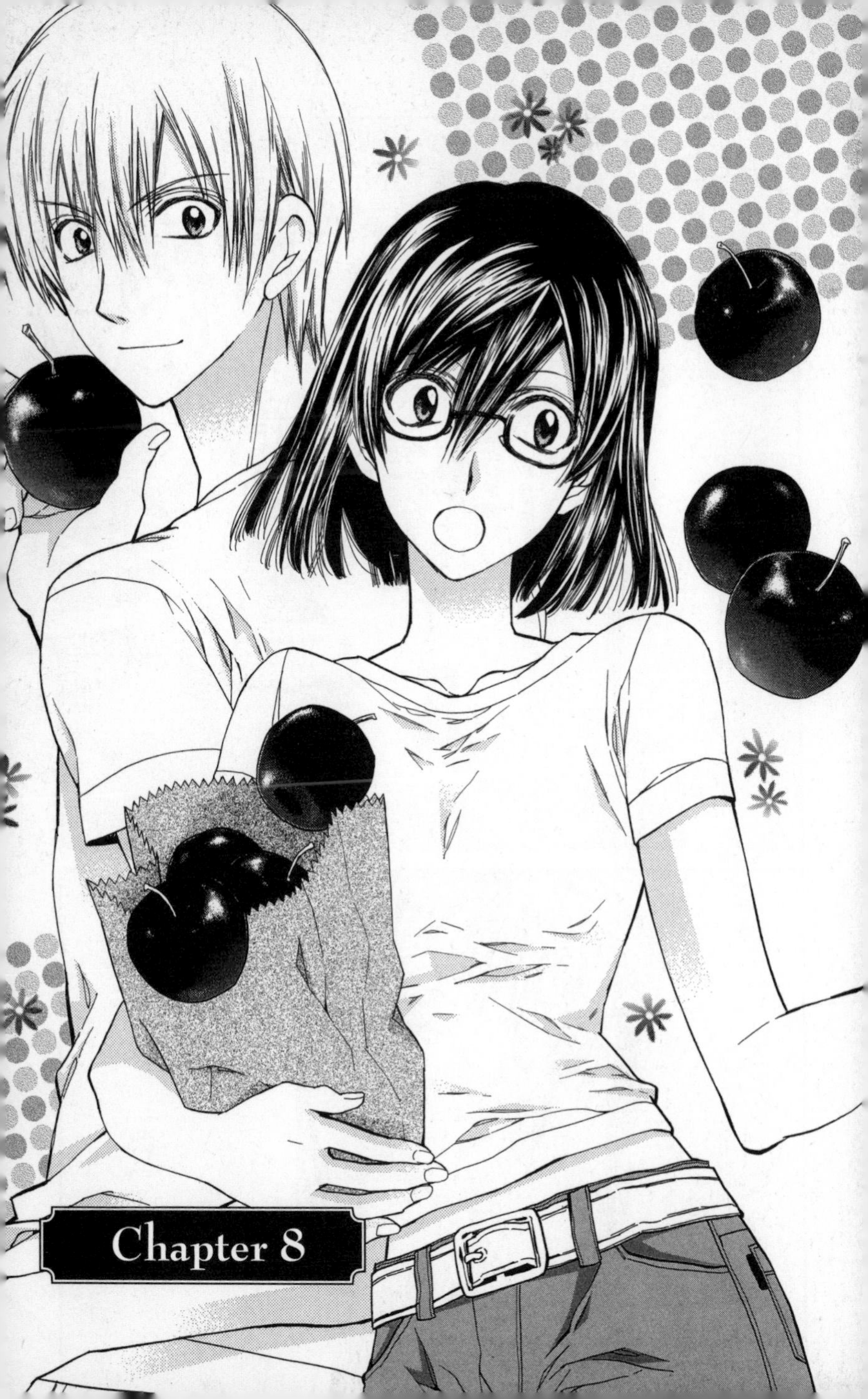
Chapter 8

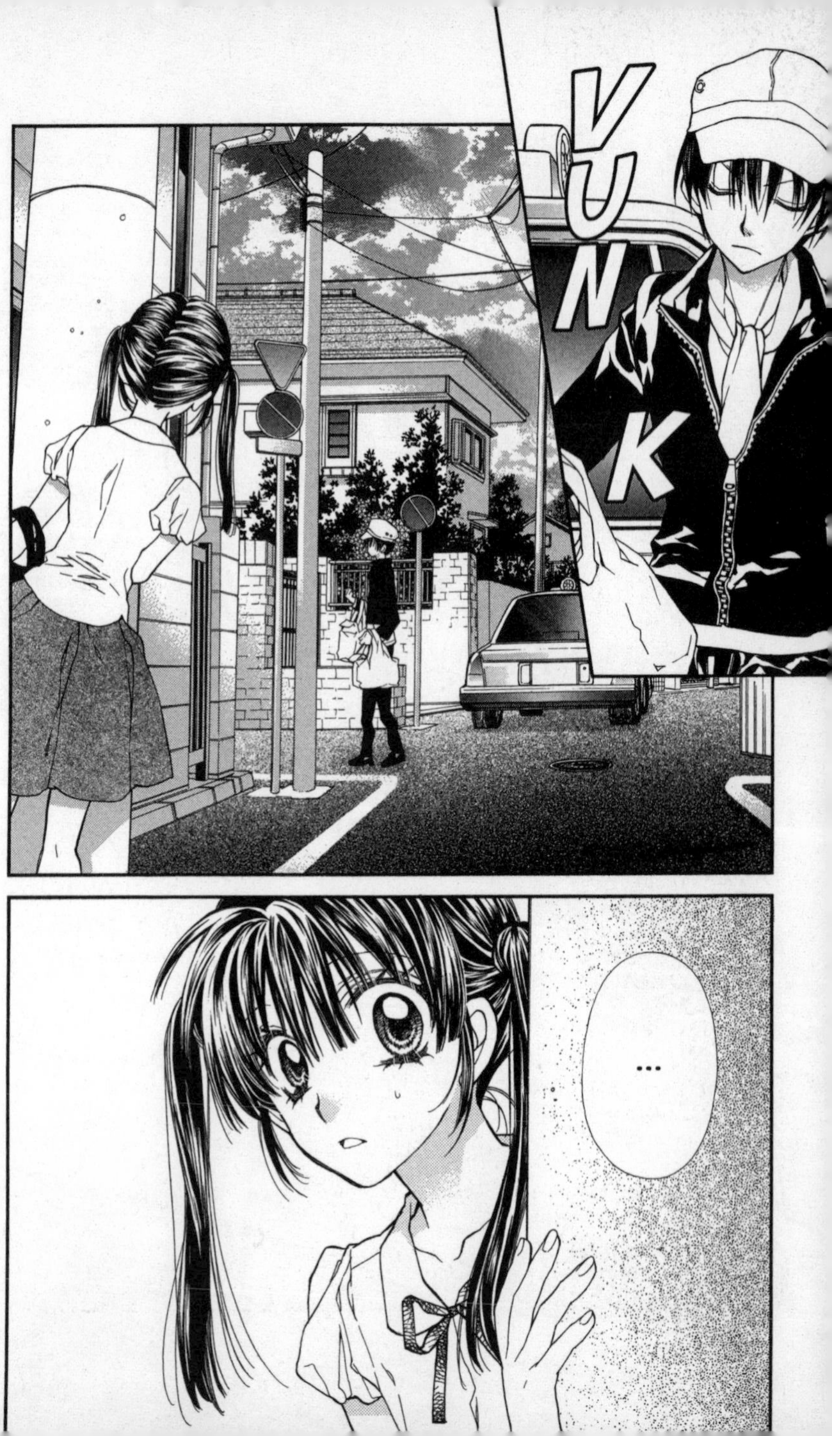
VUNK
...

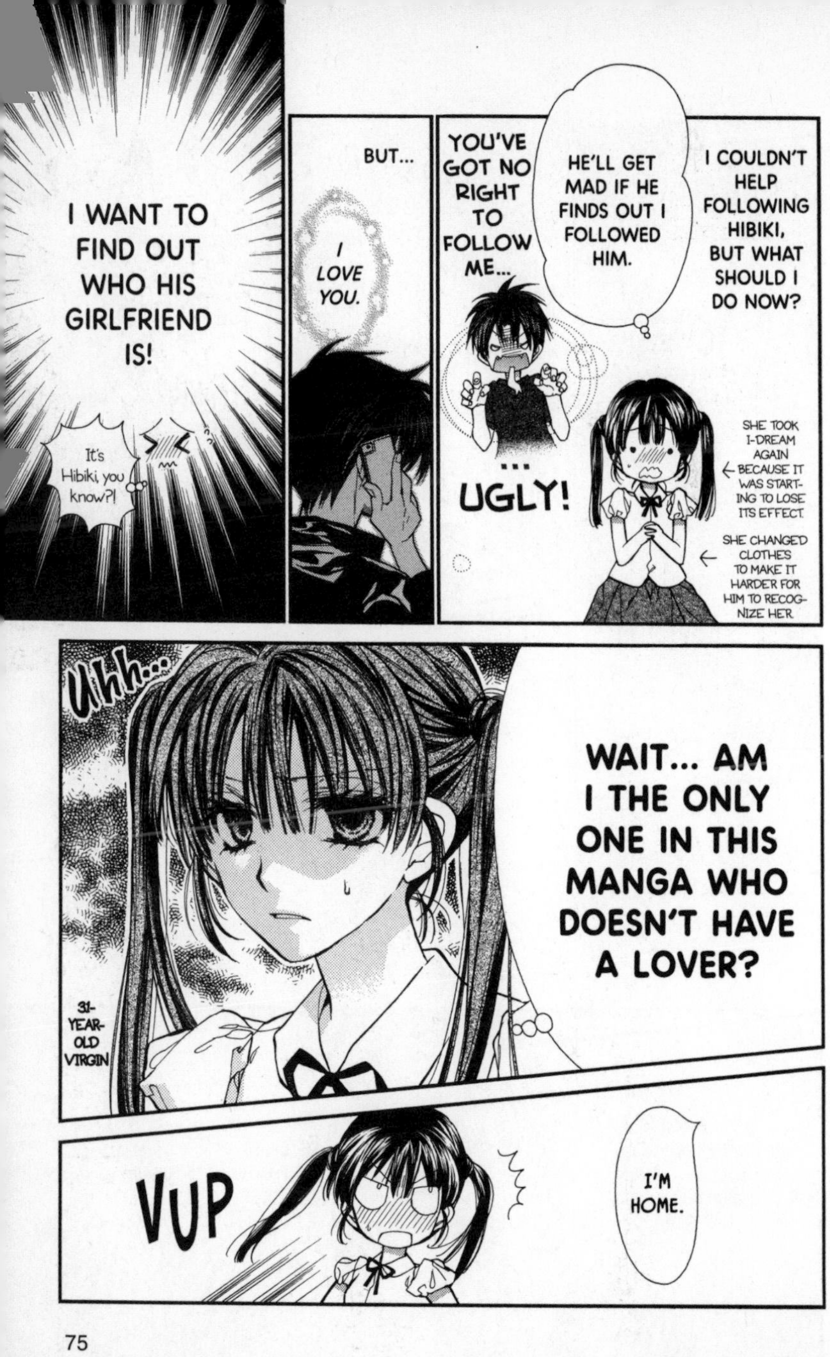
I COULDN'T HELP FOLLOWING HIBIKI, BUT WHAT SHOULD I DO NOW?
HE'LL GET MAD IF HE FINDS OUT I FOLLOWED HIM.
YOU'VE GOT NO RIGHT TO FOLLOW ME...
... UGLY!
SHE TOOK I-DREAM AGAIN BECAUSE IT WAS STARTING TO LOSE ITS EFFECT.
SHE CHANGED CLOTHES TO MAKE IT HARDER FOR HIM TO RECOGNIZE HER.
BUT...
I LOVE YOU.
I WANT TO FIND OUT WHO HIS GIRLFRIEND IS!
It's Hibiki, you know?!
WAIT... AM I THE ONLY ONE IN THIS MANGA WHO DOESN'T HAVE A LOVER?
Uhh...
31-YEAR-OLD VIRGIN
I'M HOME.
VUP

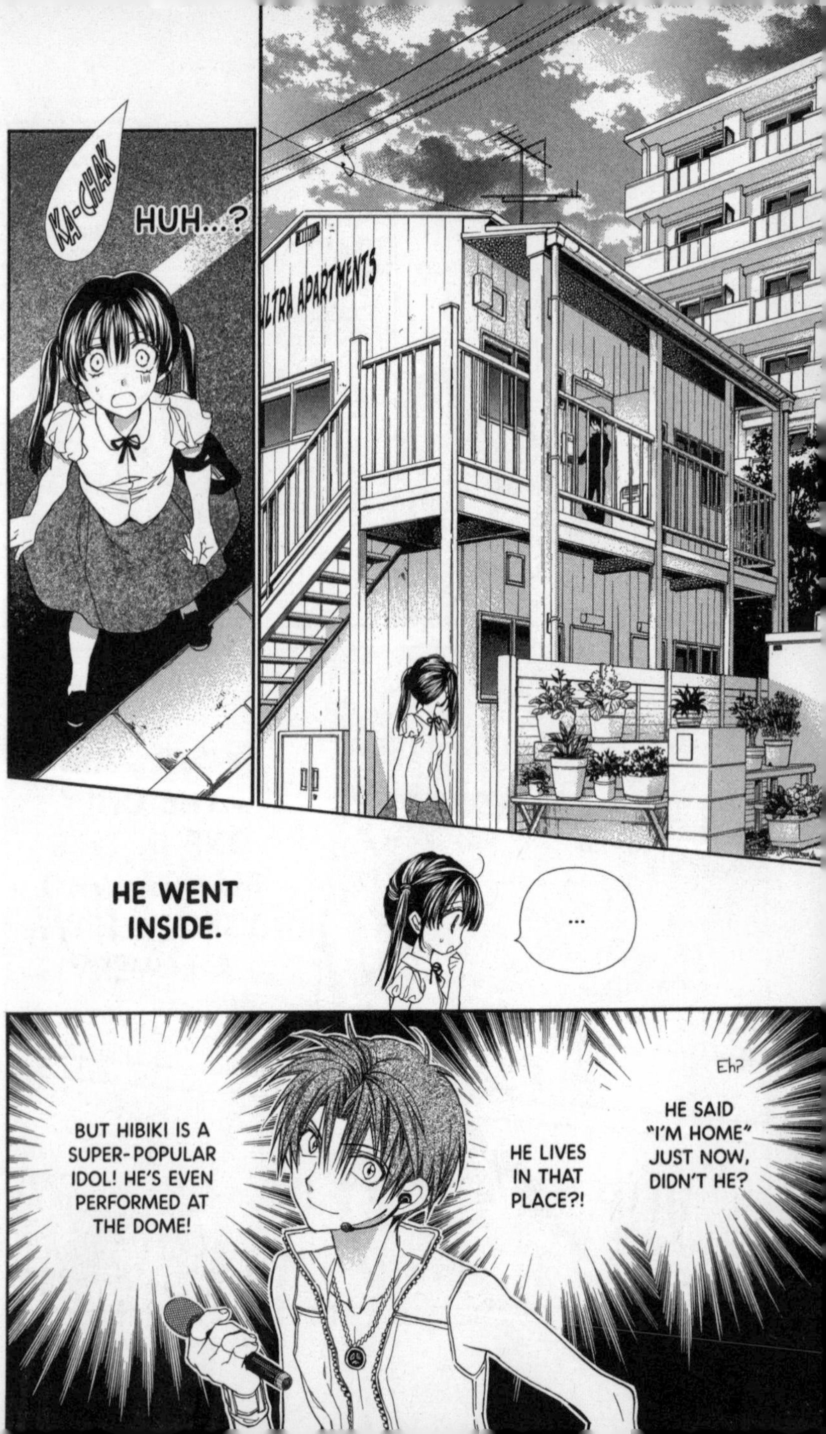
LTRA APARTMENTS
KA-CHAK
HUH...?
...
HE WENT INSIDE.
Eh?
HE SAID "I'M HOME" JUST NOW, DIDN'T HE?
HE LIVES IN THAT PLACE?!
BUT HIBIKI IS A SUPER-POPULAR IDOL! HE'S EVEN PERFORMED AT THE DOME!

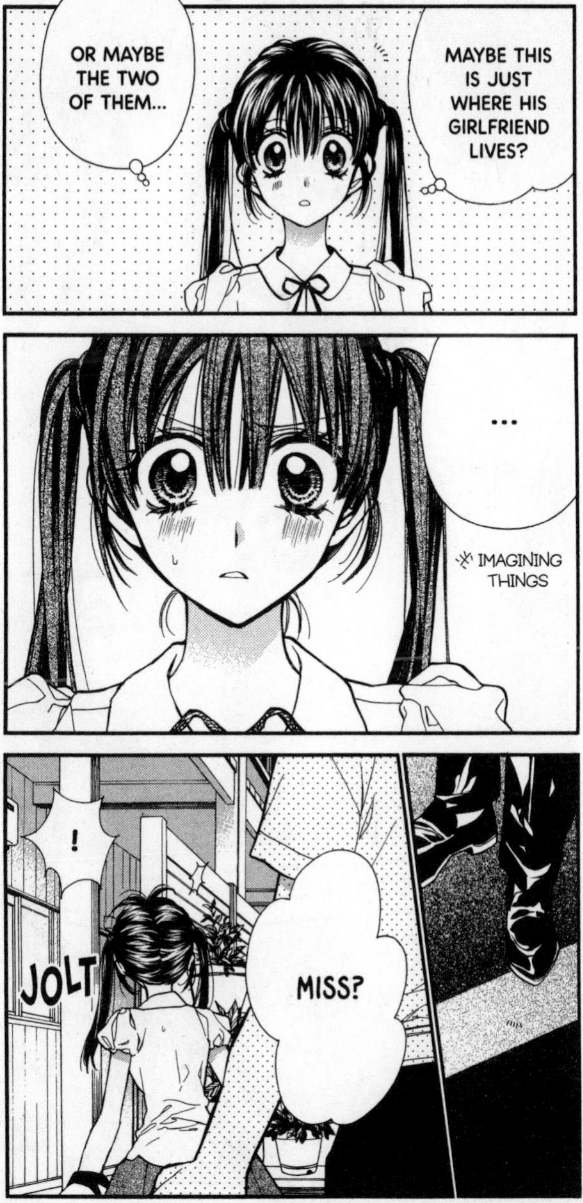
MAYBE THIS IS JUST WHERE HIS GIRLFRIEND LIVES?
OR MAYBE THE TWO OF THEM...
...
※IMAGINING THINGS
MISS?
!
JOLT

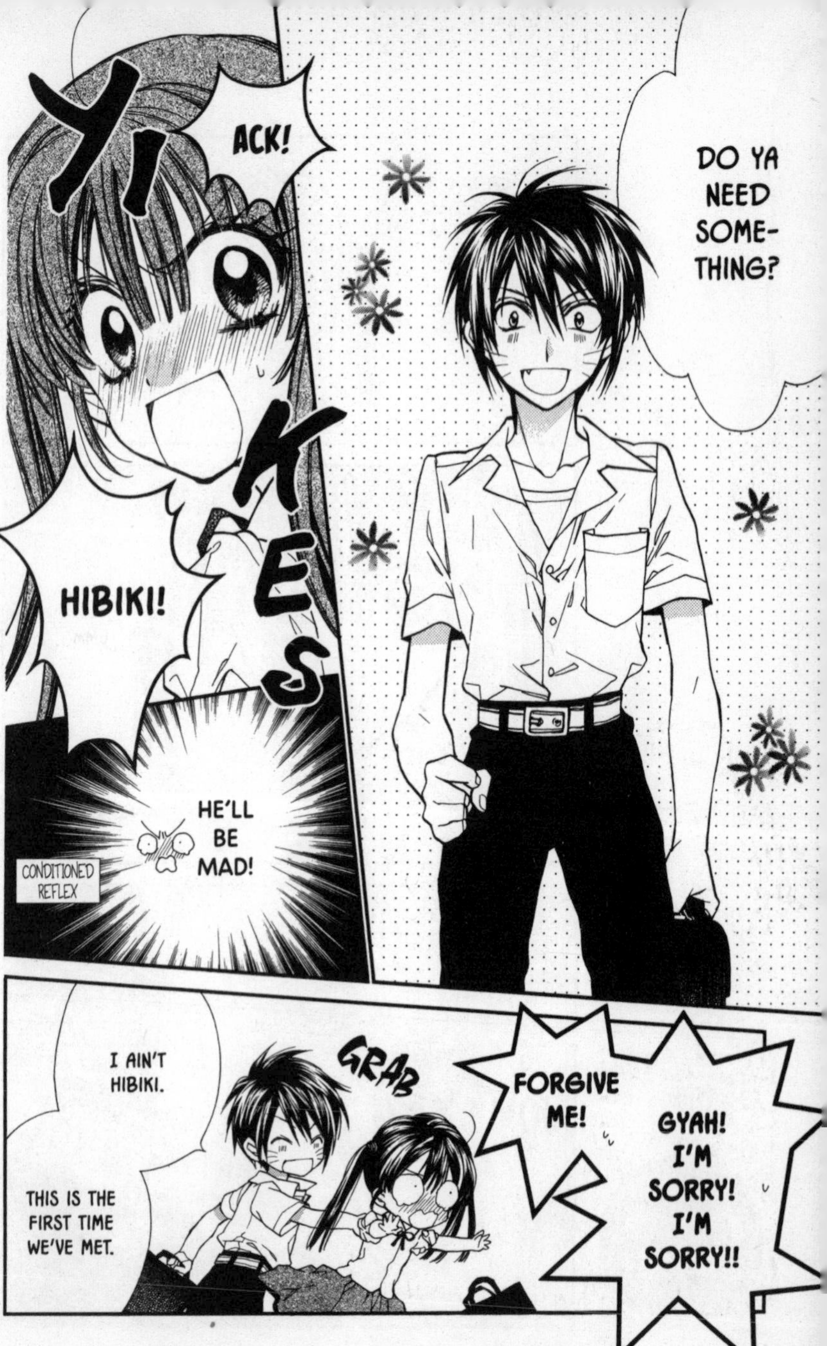

DO YA NEED SOME-THING?
ACK!
YIKES
HIBIKI!
HE'LL BE MAD!
CONDITIONED REFLEX
GYAH! I'M SORRY! I'M SORRY!!
FORGIVE ME!
GRAB
I AIN'T HIBIKI.
THIS IS THE FIRST TIME WE'VE MET.

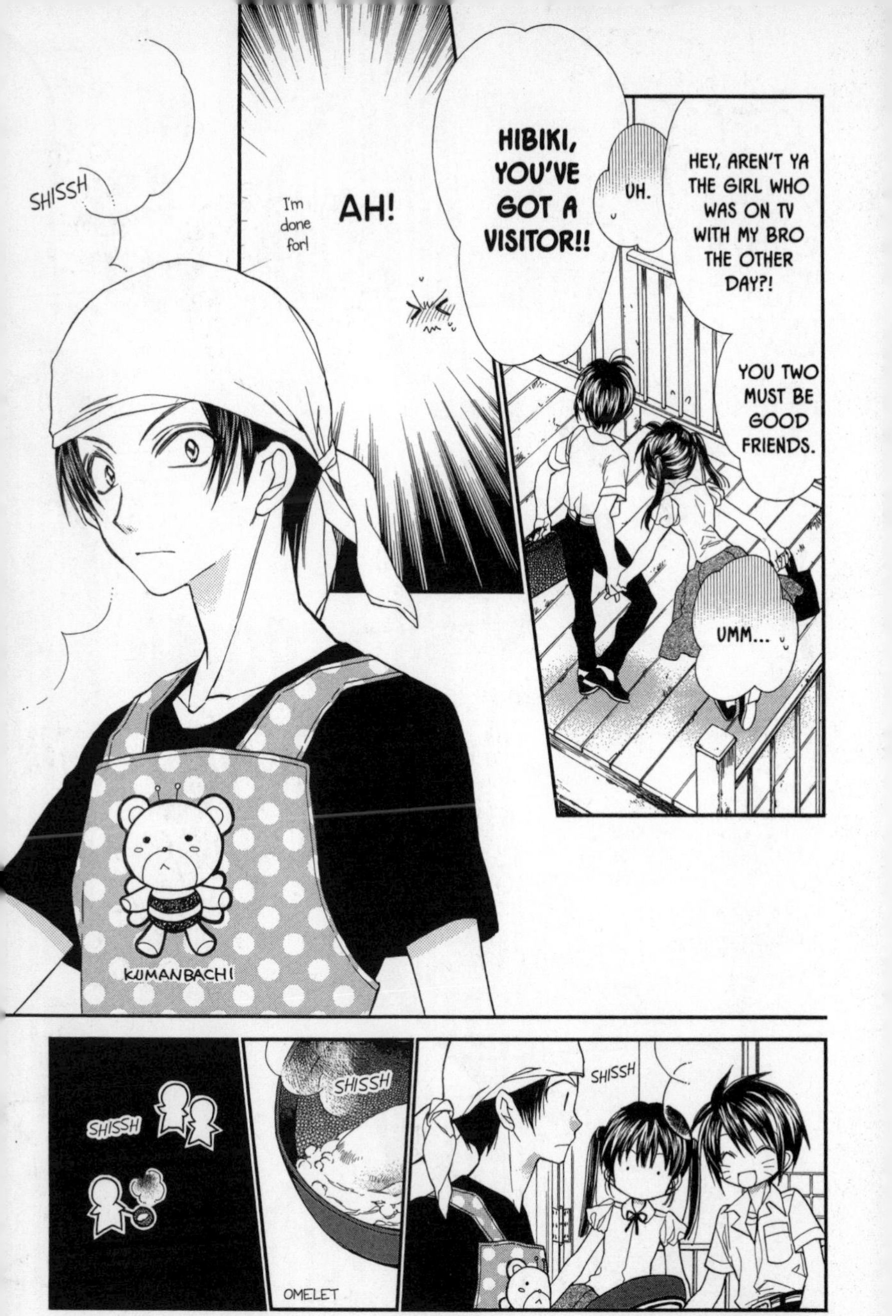
HEY, AREN'T YA THE GIRL WHO WAS ON TV WITH MY BRO THE OTHER DAY?!
UH.
YOU TWO MUST BE GOOD FRIENDS.
UMM...
HIBIKI, YOU'VE GOT A VISITOR!!
AH!
I'm done for!
SHISSH
KUMANBACHI
SHISSH
SHISSH
OMELET
SHISSH

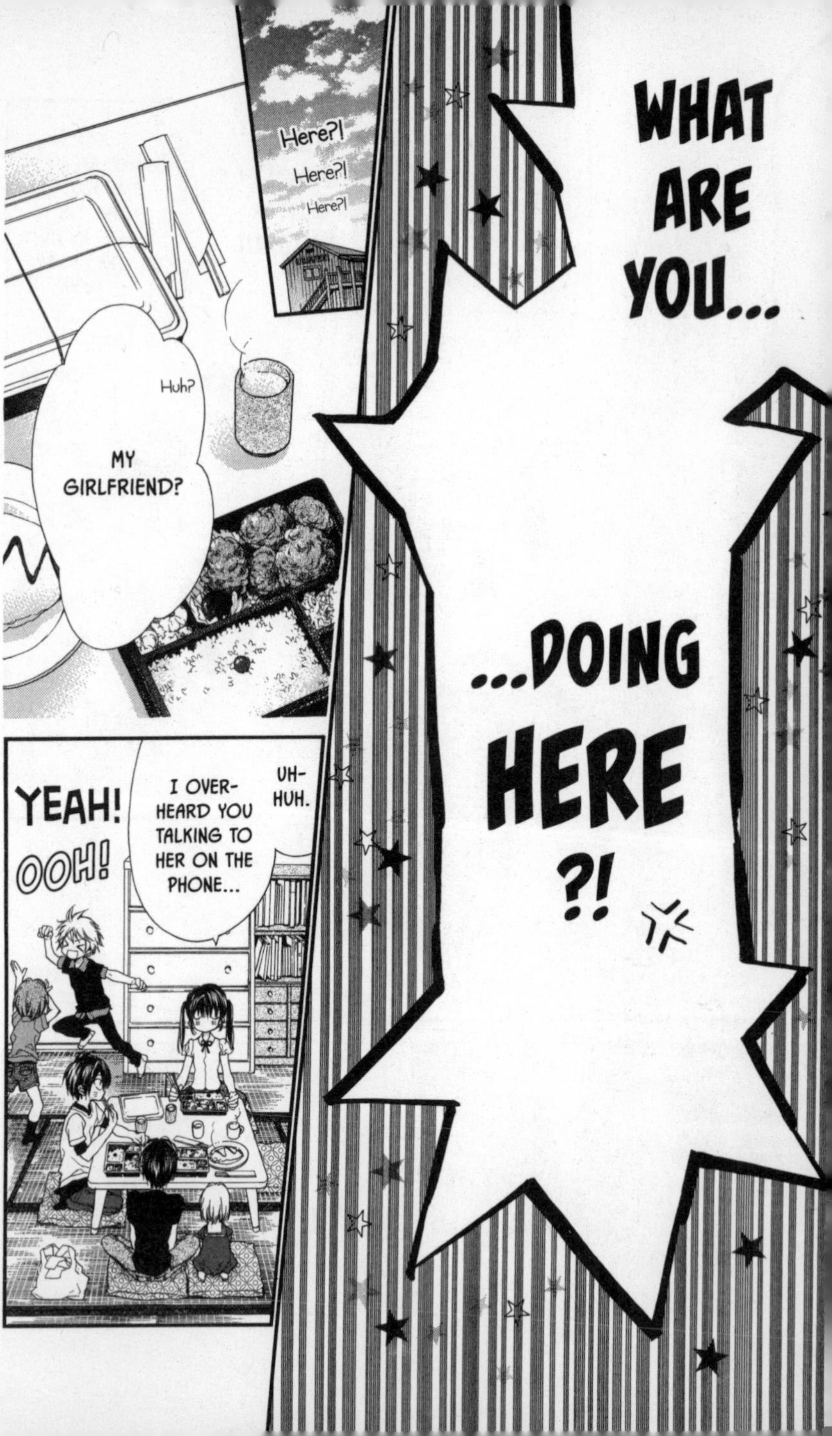
WHAT ARE YOU...
...DOING HERE ?!
Here?!
Here?!
Here?!
Huh?
MY GIRLFRIEND?
UH-HUH.
I OVER-HEARD YOU TALKING TO HER ON THE PHONE...
YEAH!
OOH!

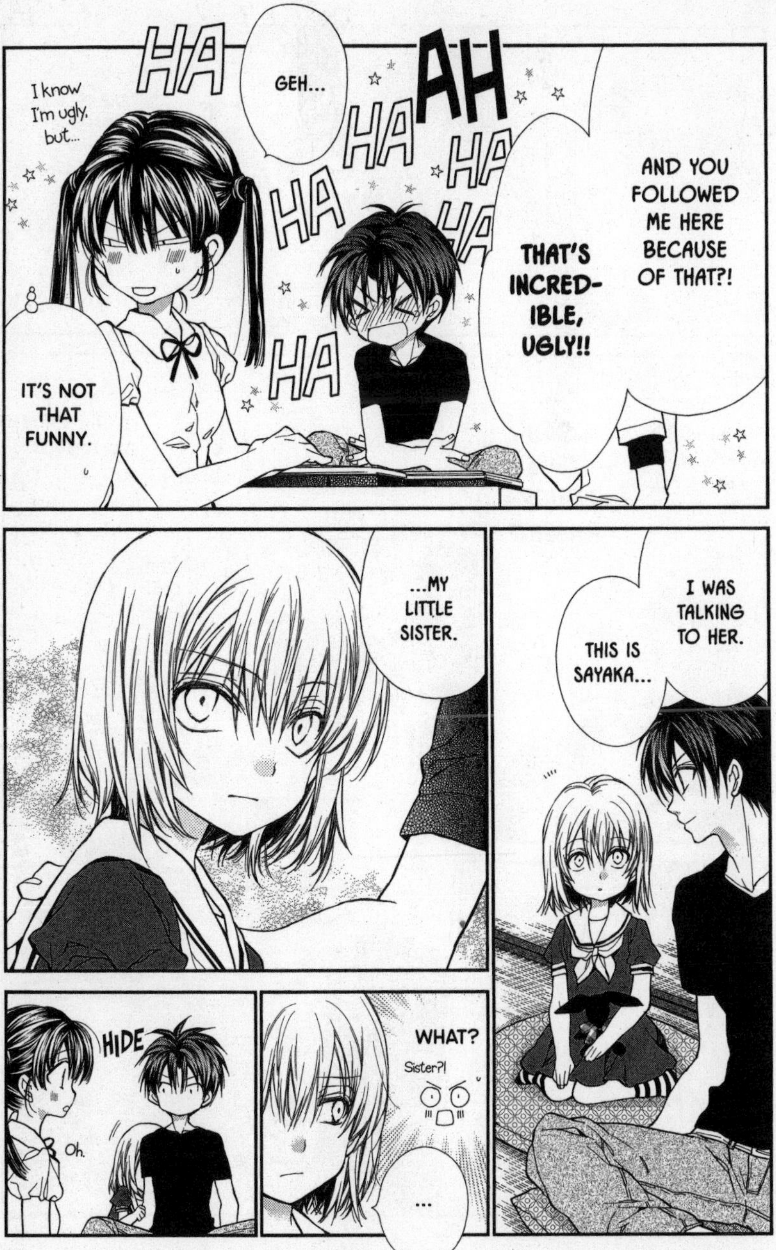
AND YOU FOLLOWED ME HERE BECAUSE OF THAT?!
AH
HA
HA
HA
THAT'S INCRED-IBLE, UGLY!!
HA
GEH...
HA
HA
HA
I know I'm ugly, but...
IT'S NOT THAT FUNNY.
I WAS TALKING TO HER.
THIS IS SAYAKA...
...MY LITTLE SISTER.
WHAT?
Sister?!
...
HIDE
Oh.

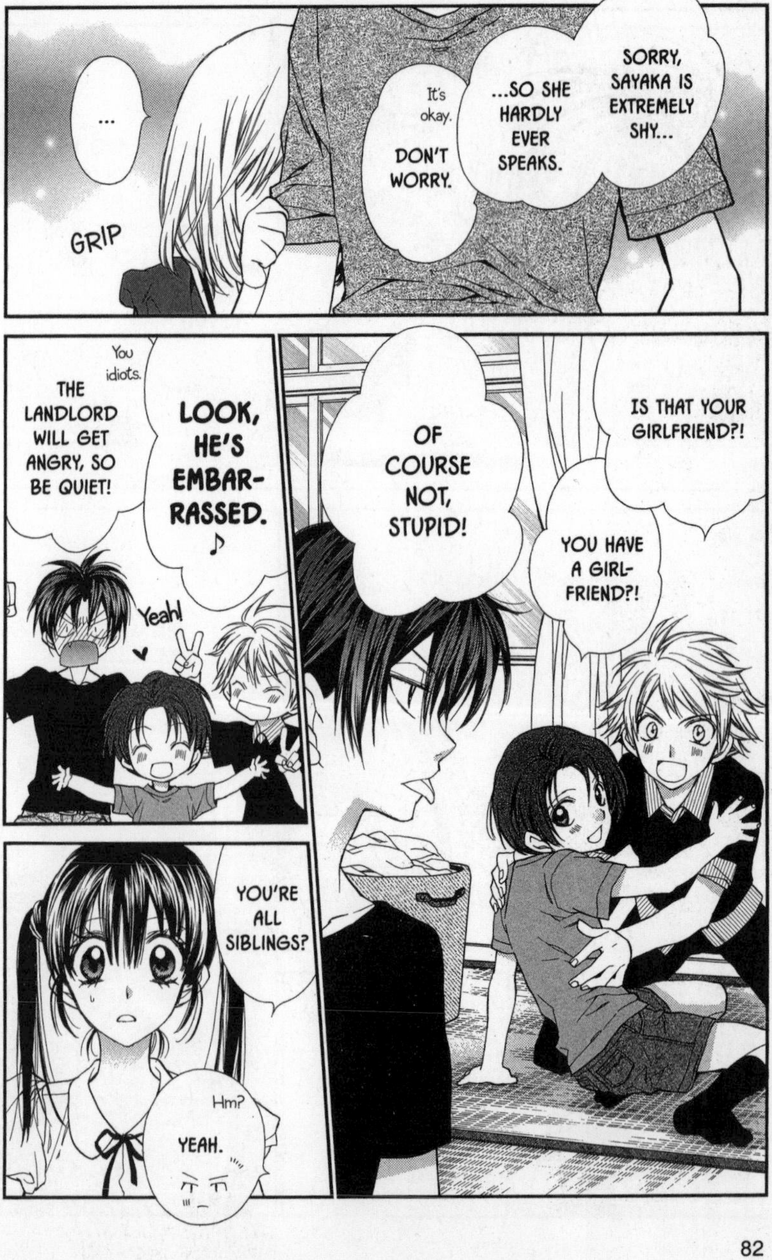
SORRY, SAYAKA IS EXTREMELY SHY...
...SO SHE HARDLY EVER SPEAKS.
It's okay.
DON'T WORRY.
...
GRIP
IS THAT YOUR GIRLFRIEND?!
YOU HAVE A GIRLFRIEND?!
OF COURSE NOT, STUPID!
LOOK, HE'S EMBARRASSED. ♪
You idiots.
THE LANDLORD WILL GET ANGRY, SO BE QUIET!
Yeah!
YOU'RE ALL SIBLINGS?
Hm?
YEAH.

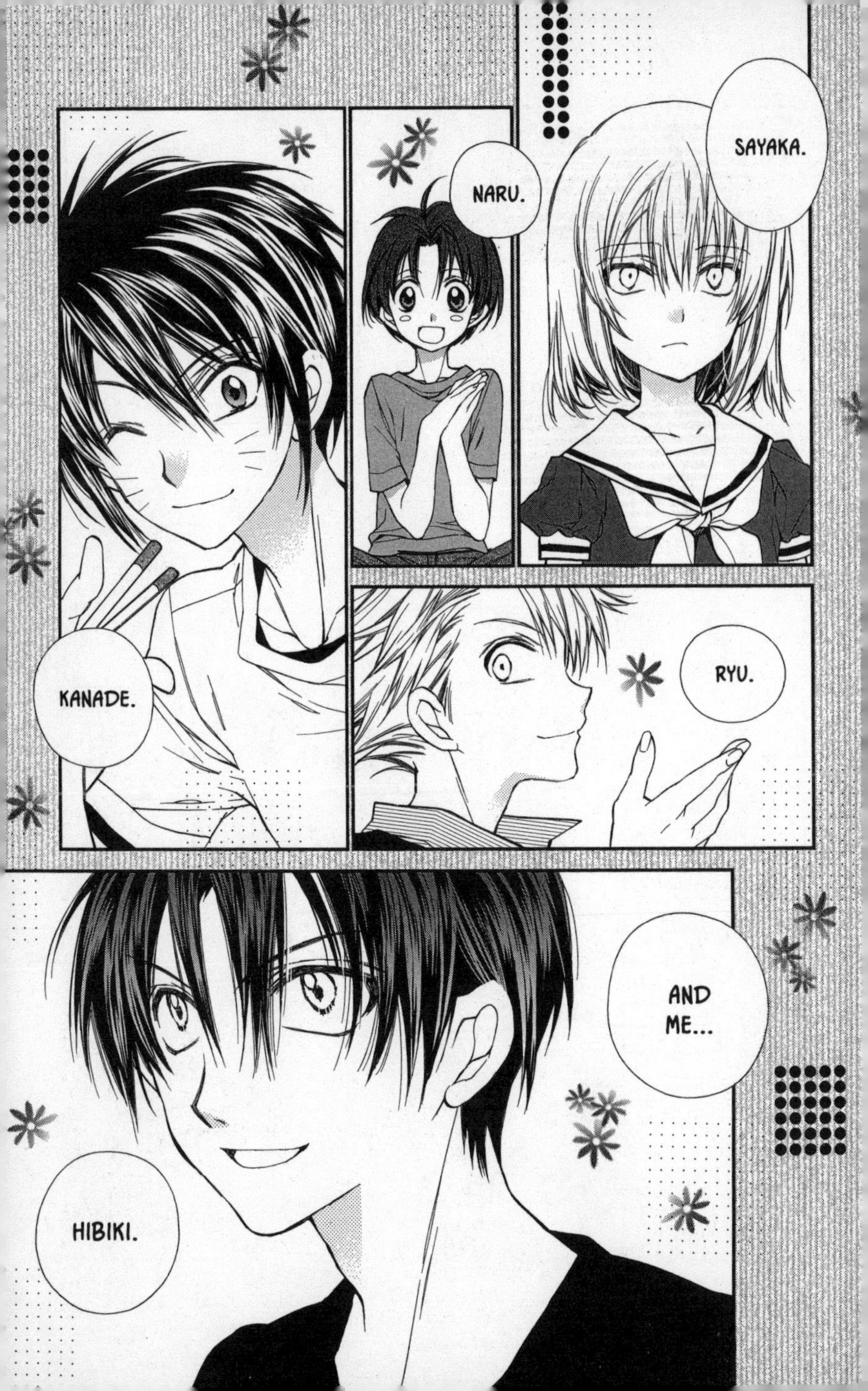

SAYAKA.
NARU.
RYU.
KANADE.
AND ME...
HIBIKI.

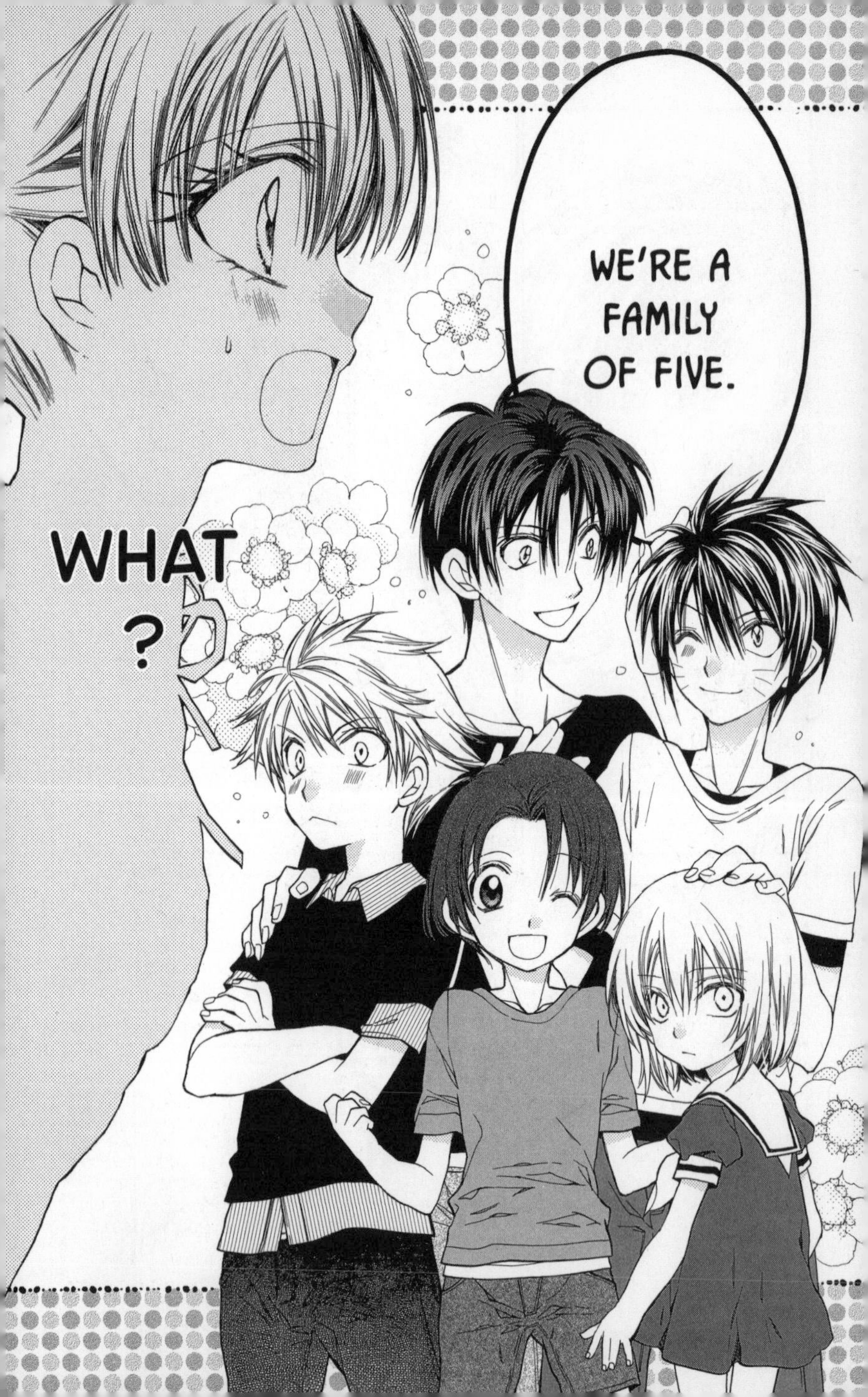
WE'RE A FAMILY OF FIVE.
WHAT?

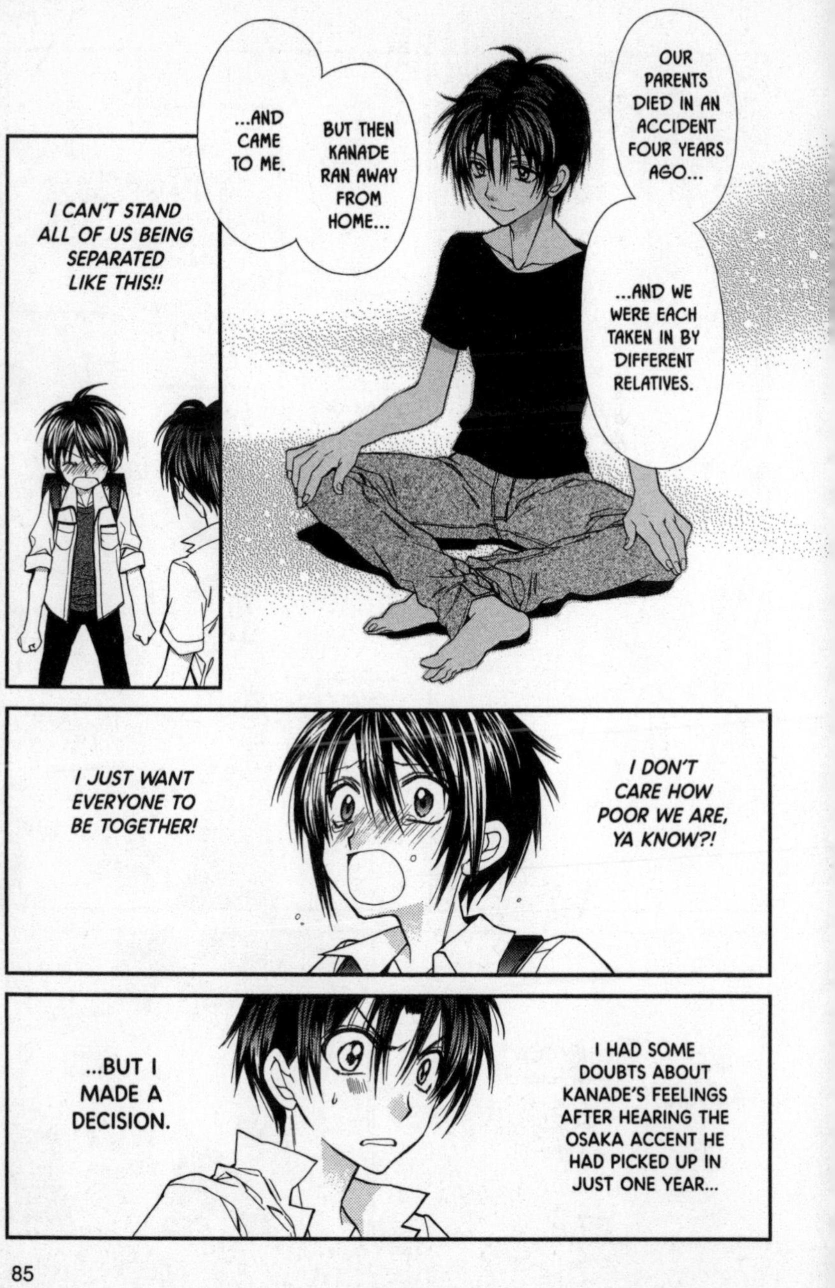
OUR PARENTS DIED IN AN ACCIDENT FOUR YEARS AGO...
...AND WE WERE EACH TAKEN IN BY DIFFERENT RELATIVES.
BUT THEN KANADE RAN AWAY FROM HOME...
...AND CAME TO ME.
I CAN'T STAND ALL OF US BEING SEPARATED LIKE THIS!!
I DON'T CARE HOW POOR WE ARE, YA KNOW?!
I JUST WANT EVERYONE TO BE TOGETHER!
I HAD SOME DOUBTS ABOUT KANADE'S FEELINGS AFTER HEARING THE OSAKA ACCENT HE HAD PICKED UP IN JUST ONE YEAR...
...BUT I MADE A DECISION.

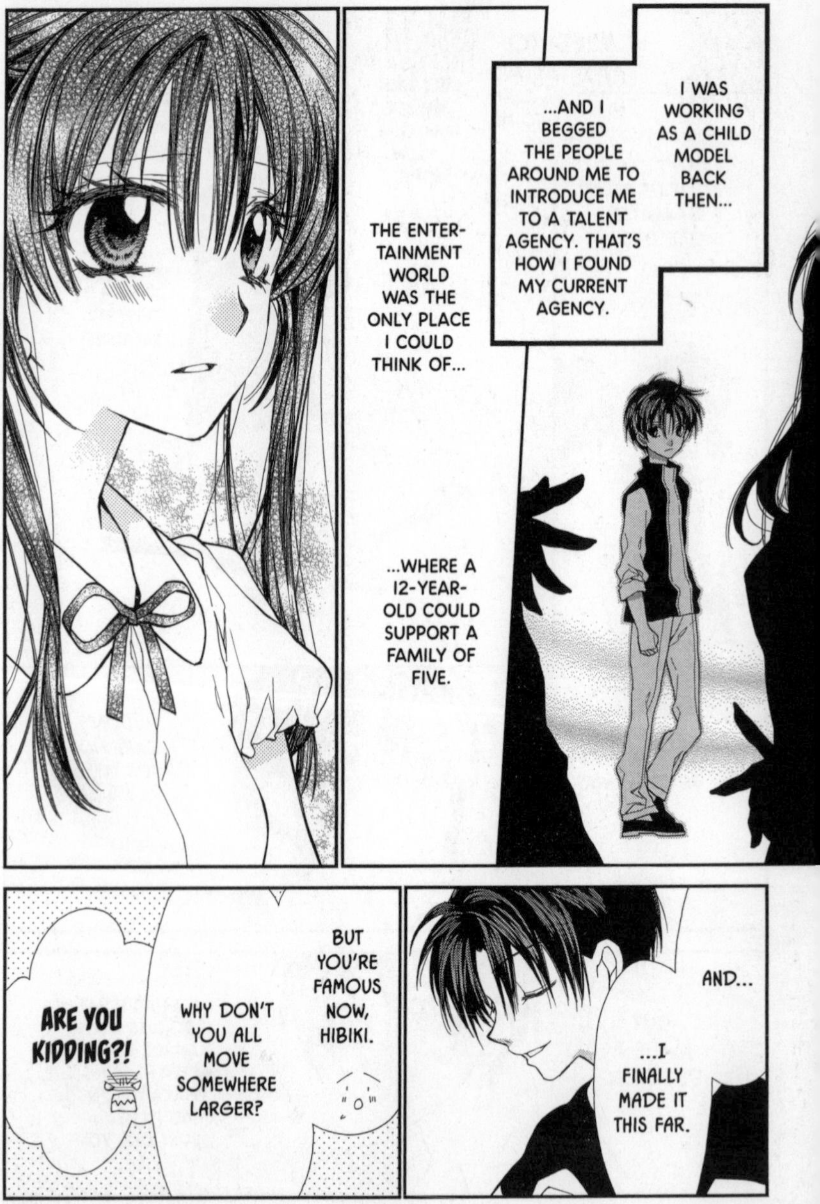
I WAS WORKING AS A CHILD MODEL BACK THEN...
...AND I BEGGED THE PEOPLE AROUND ME TO INTRODUCE ME TO A TALENT AGENCY. THAT'S HOW I FOUND MY CURRENT AGENCY.
THE ENTER-TAINMENT WORLD WAS THE ONLY PLACE I COULD THINK OF...
...WHERE A 12-YEAR-OLD COULD SUPPORT A FAMILY OF FIVE.
AND...
...I FINALLY MADE IT THIS FAR.
BUT YOU'RE FAMOUS NOW, HIBIKI.
WHY DON'T YOU ALL MOVE SOMEWHERE LARGER?
ARE YOU KIDDING?!

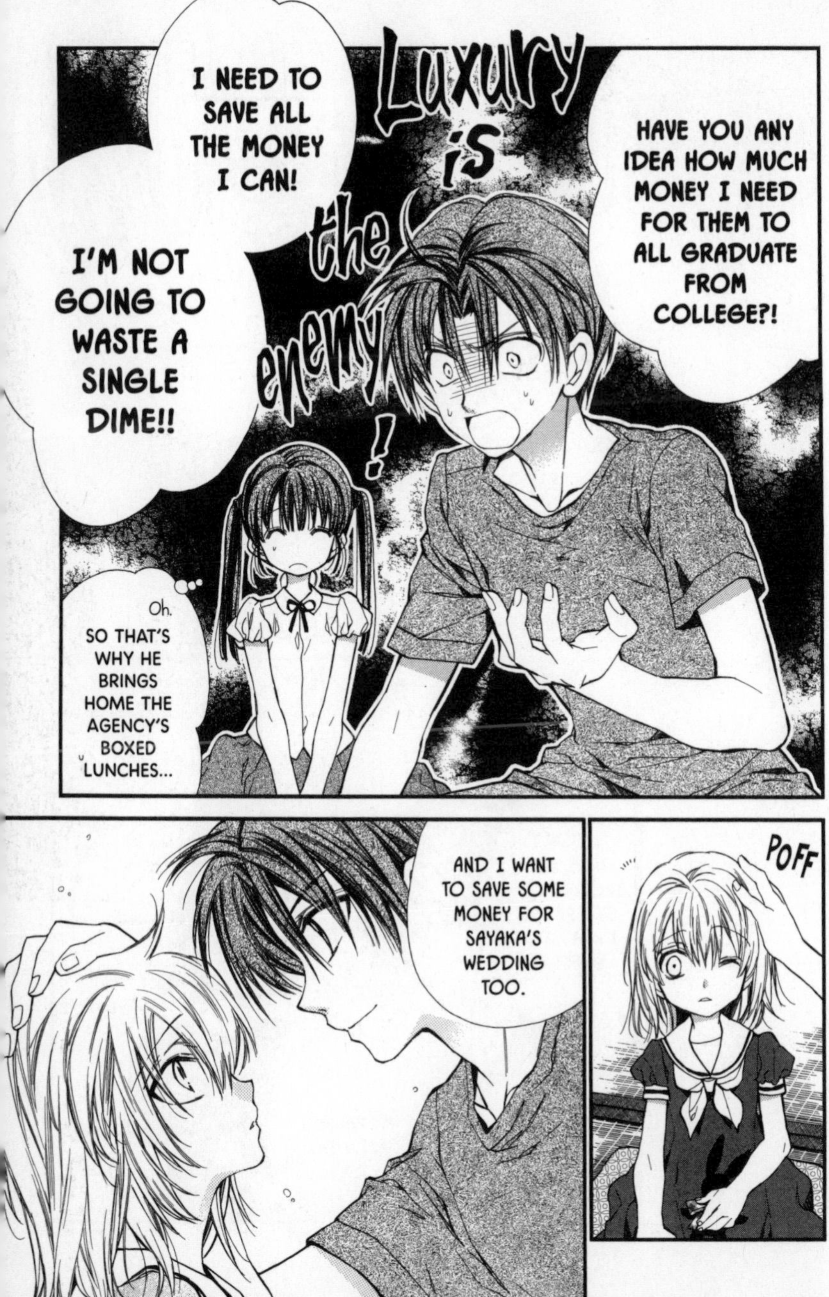
HAVE YOU ANY IDEA HOW MUCH MONEY I NEED FOR THEM TO ALL GRADUATE FROM COLLEGE?!
Luxury is the enemy!
I NEED TO SAVE ALL THE MONEY I CAN!
I'M NOT GOING TO WASTE A SINGLE DIME!!
Oh. SO THAT'S WHY HE BRINGS HOME THE AGENCY'S BOXED LUNCHES...
POFF
AND I WANT TO SAVE SOME MONEY FOR SAYAKA'S WEDDING TOO.

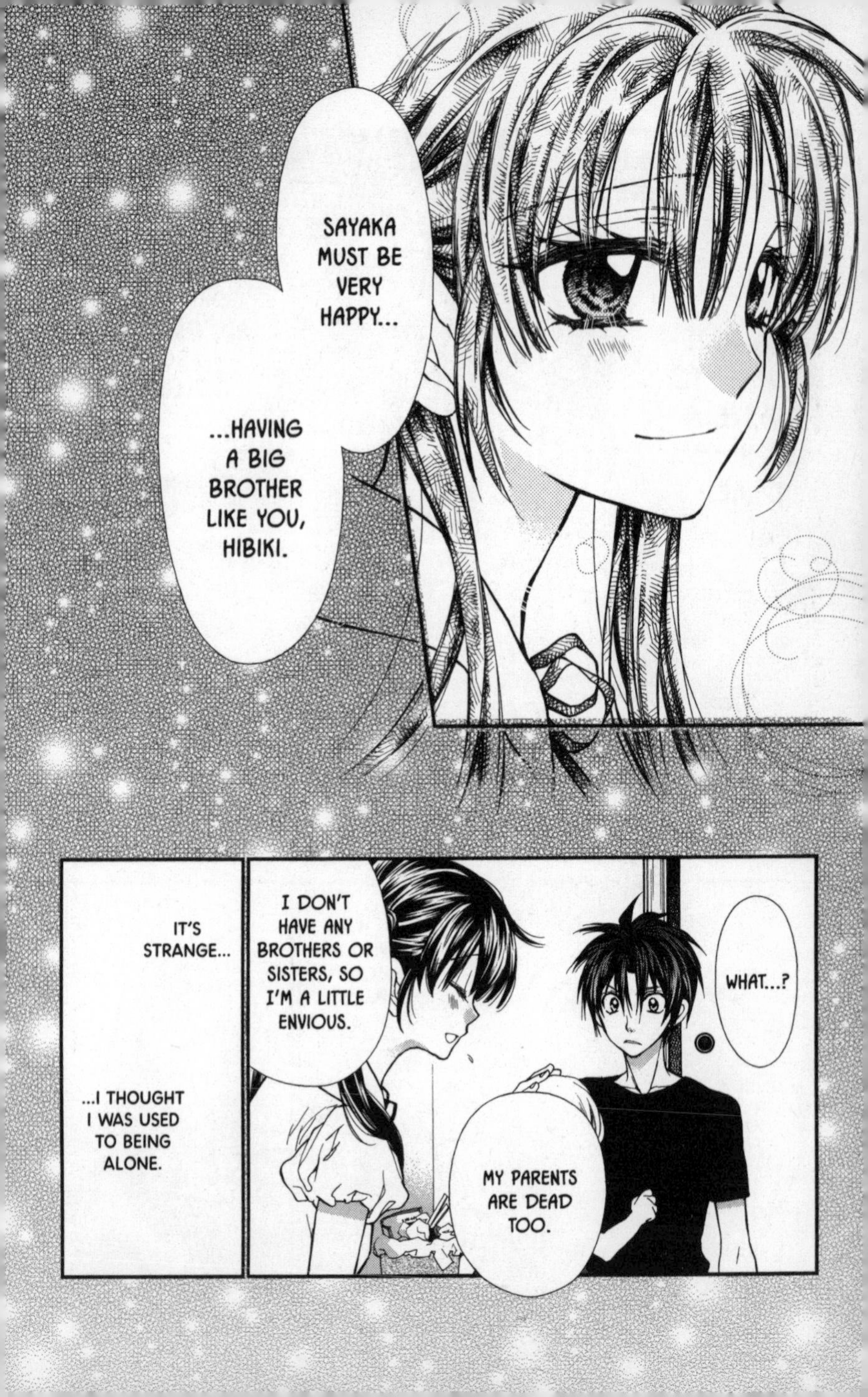
SAYAKA MUST BE VERY HAPPY...
...HAVING A BIG BROTHER LIKE YOU, HIBIKI.
WHAT...?
I DON'T HAVE ANY BROTHERS OR SISTERS, SO I'M A LITTLE ENVIOUS.
MY PARENTS ARE DEAD TOO.
IT'S STRANGE...
...I THOUGHT I WAS USED TO BEING ALONE.

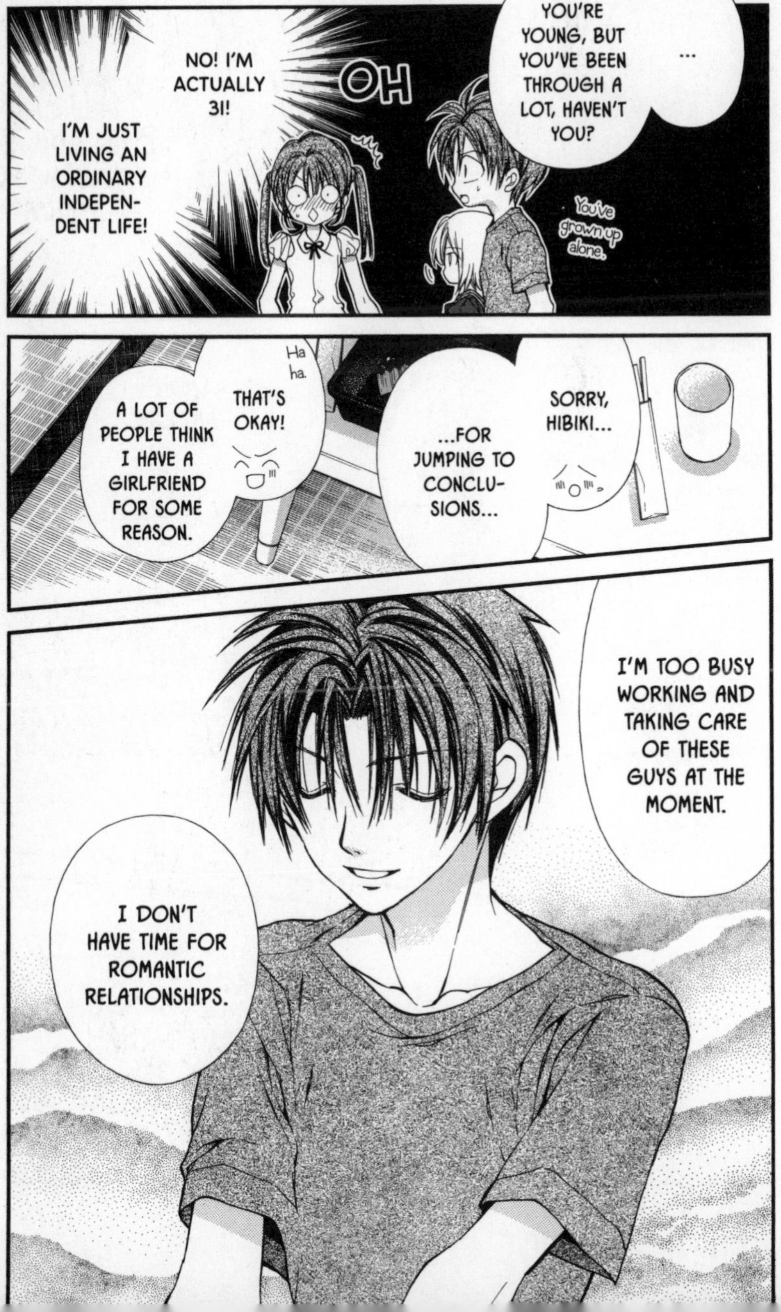
...
YOU'RE YOUNG, BUT YOU'VE BEEN THROUGH A LOT, HAVEN'T YOU?
You've grown up alone.
OH
NO! I'M ACTUALLY 31!
I'M JUST LIVING AN ORDINARY INDEPENDENT LIFE!
SORRY, HIBIKI...
...FOR JUMPING TO CONCLUSIONS...
Ha ha.
THAT'S OKAY!
A LOT OF PEOPLE THINK I HAVE A GIRLFRIEND FOR SOME REASON.
I'M TOO BUSY WORKING AND TAKING CARE OF THESE GUYS AT THE MOMENT.
I DON'T HAVE TIME FOR ROMANTIC RELATIONSHIPS.

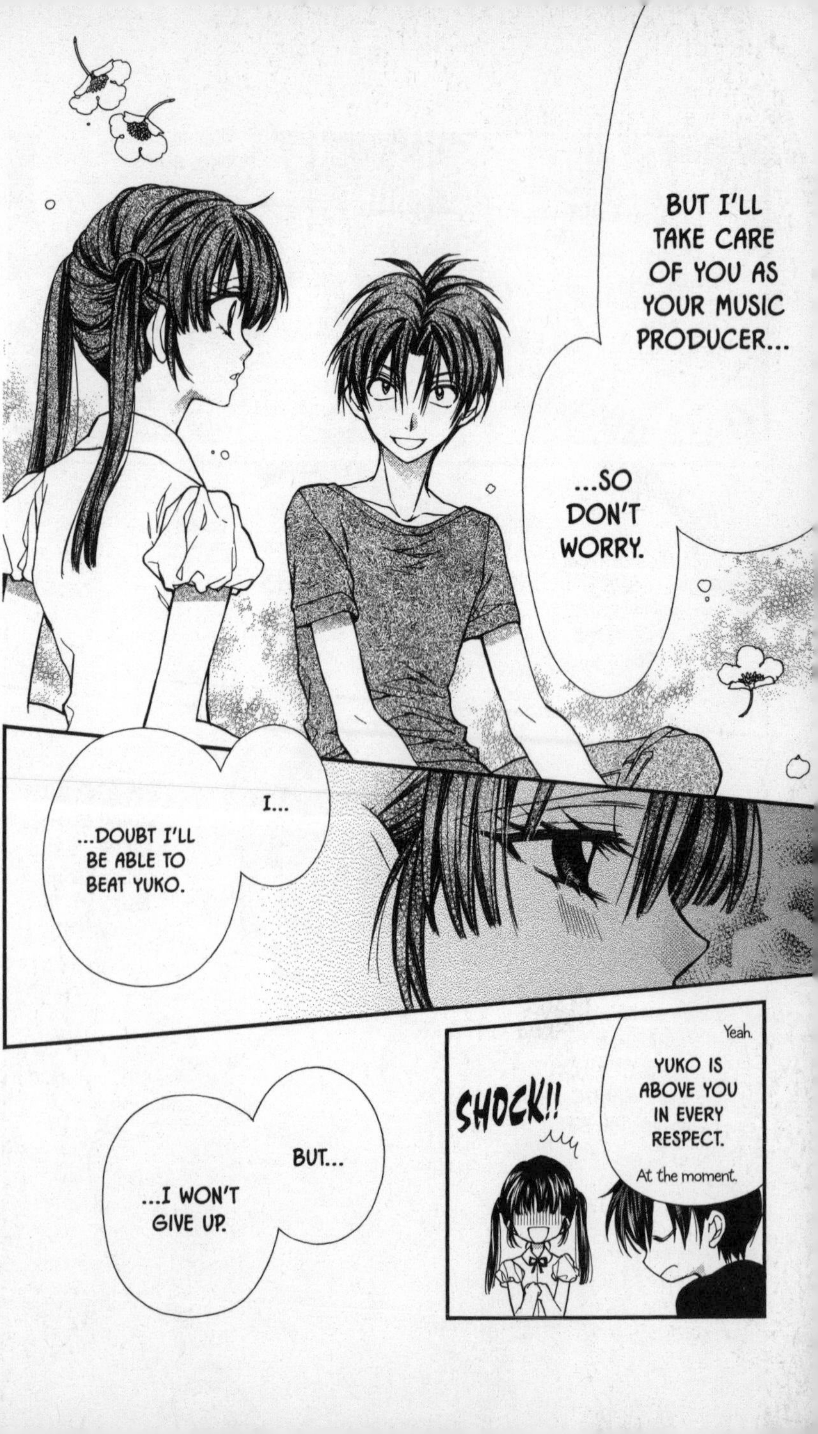
BUT I'LL TAKE CARE OF YOU AS YOUR MUSIC PRODUCER...
...SO DON'T WORRY.
I...
...DOUBT I'LL BE ABLE TO BEAT YUKO.
Yeah.
YUKO IS ABOVE YOU IN EVERY RESPECT.
At the moment.
SHOCK!!
BUT...
...I WON'T GIVE UP.

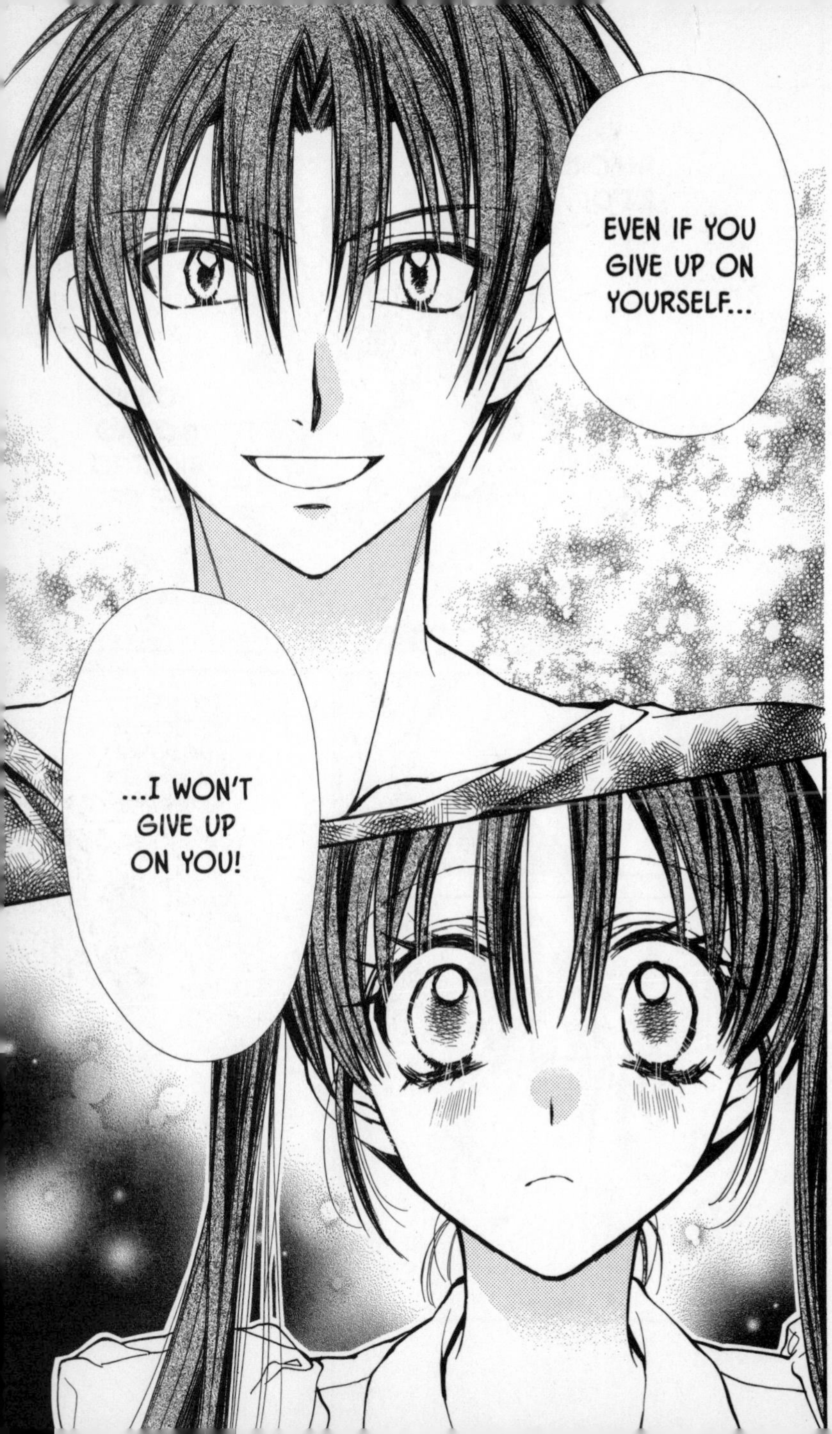
EVEN IF YOU GIVE UP ON YOURSELF...
...I WON'T GIVE UP ON YOU!

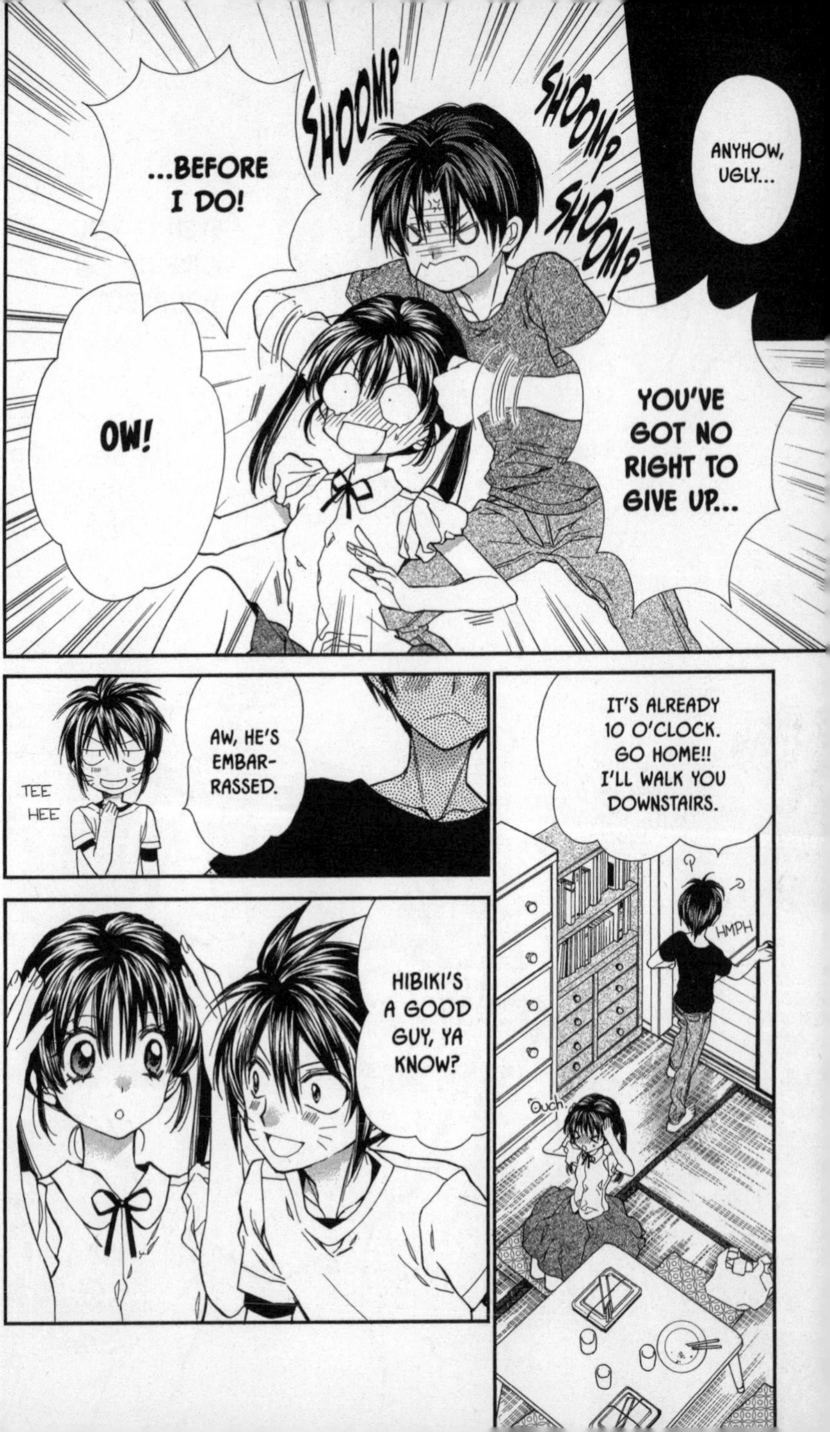
ANYHOW, UGLY...
SHOOMP
SHOOMP
SHOOMP
YOU'VE GOT NO RIGHT TO GIVE UP...
SHOOMP
...BEFORE I DO!
OW!
IT'S ALREADY 10 O'CLOCK. GO HOME!! I'LL WALK YOU DOWNSTAIRS.
HMPH
Ouch!
AW, HE'S EMBAR-RASSED.
TEE HEE
HIBIKI'S A GOOD GUY, YA KNOW?

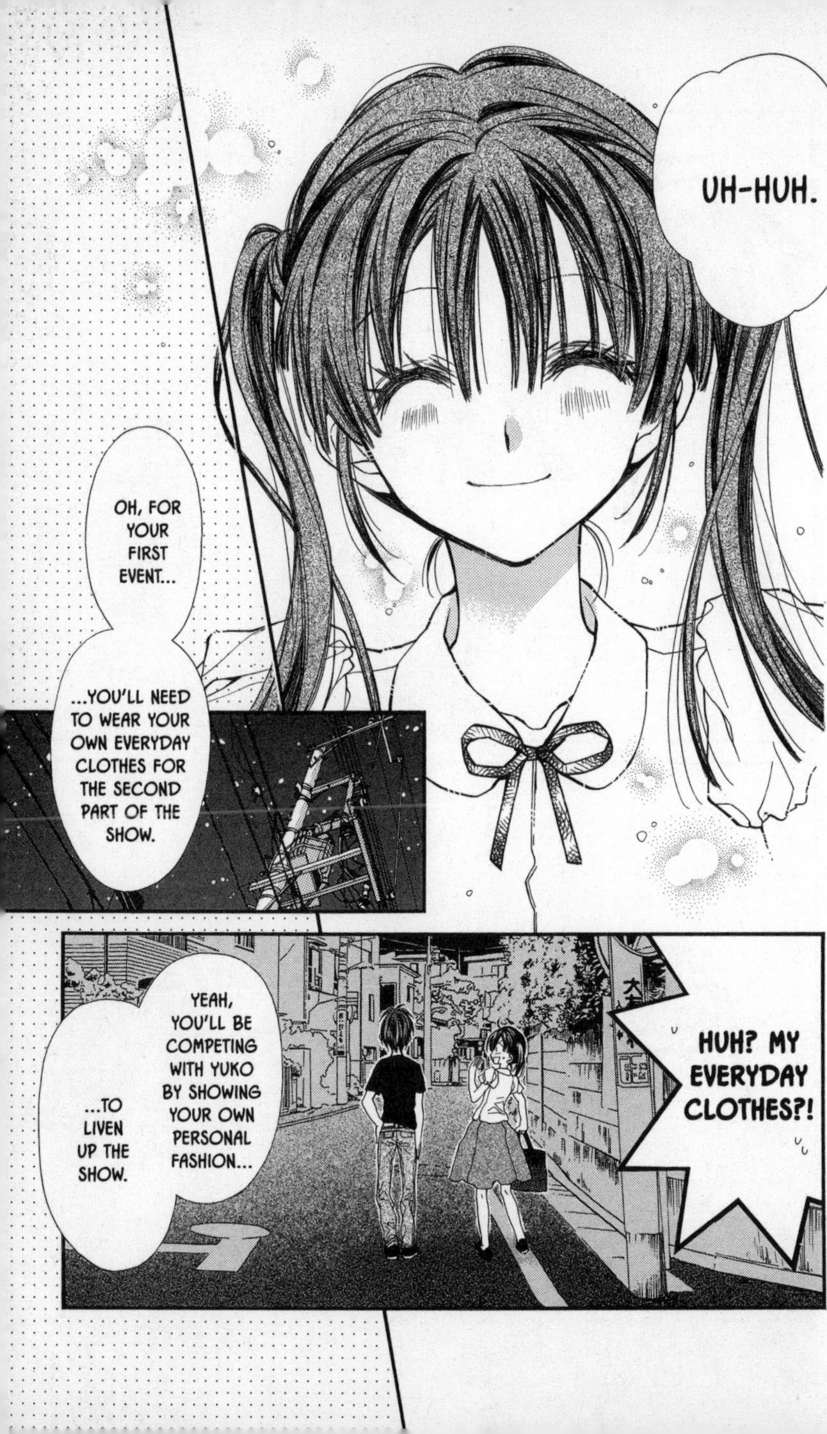
UH-HUH.
OH, FOR YOUR FIRST EVENT...
...YOU'LL NEED TO WEAR YOUR OWN EVERYDAY CLOTHES FOR THE SECOND PART OF THE SHOW.
HUH? MY EVERYDAY CLOTHES?!
YEAH, YOU'LL BE COMPETING WITH YUKO BY SHOWING YOUR OWN PERSONAL FASHION...
...TO LIVEN UP THE SHOW.

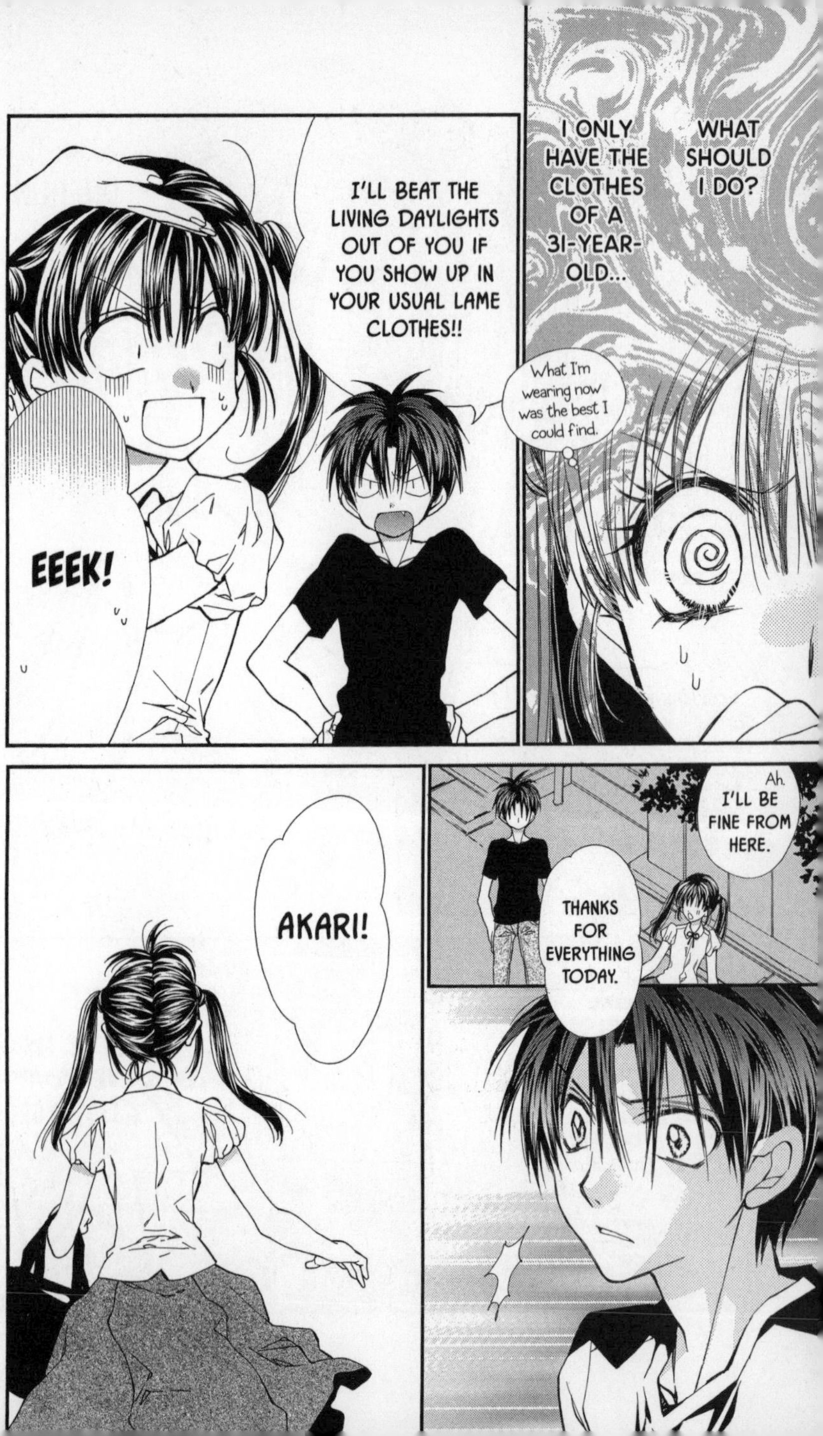
WHAT SHOULD I DO?
I ONLY HAVE THE CLOTHES OF A 31-YEAR-OLD...
What I'm wearing now was the best I could find.
I'LL BEAT THE LIVING DAYLIGHTS OUT OF YOU IF YOU SHOW UP IN YOUR USUAL LAME CLOTHES!!
EEEK!
Ah. I'LL BE FINE FROM HERE.
THANKS FOR EVERYTHING TODAY.
AKARI!

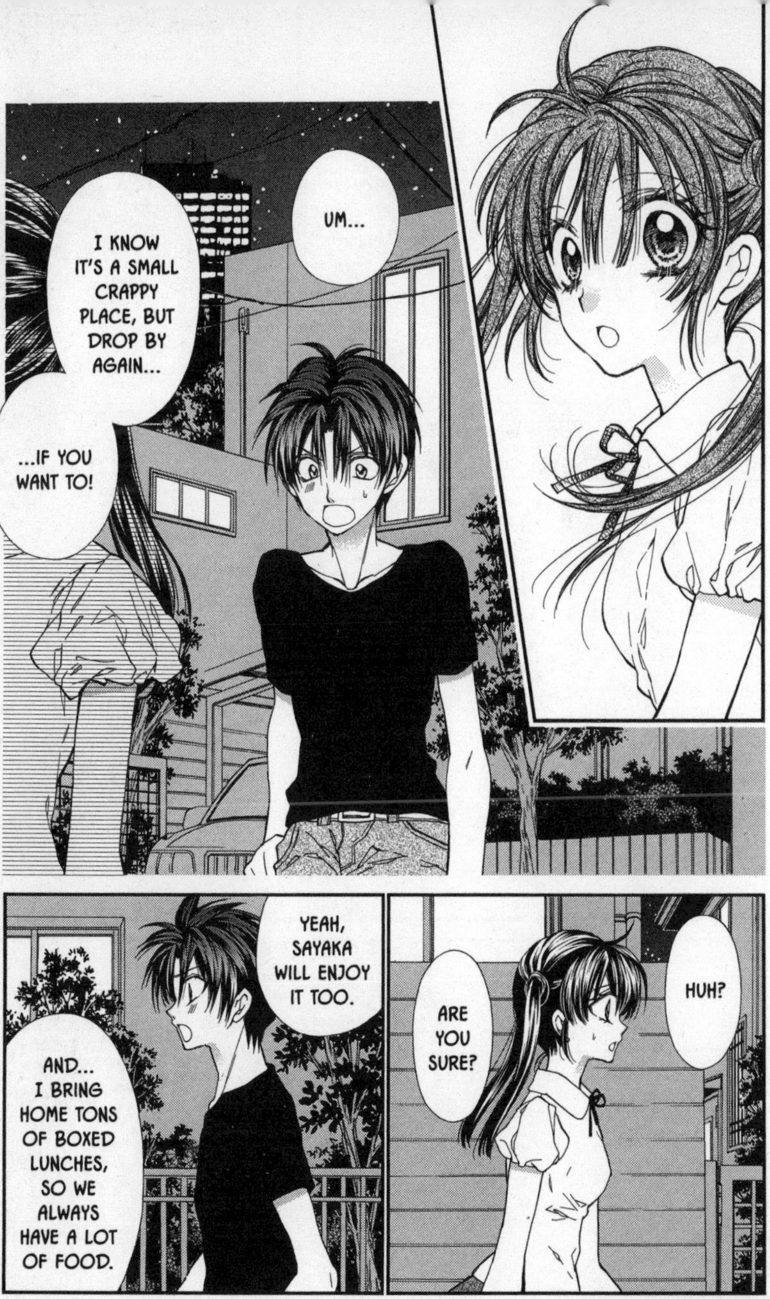
UM...
I KNOW IT'S A SMALL CRAPPY PLACE, BUT DROP BY AGAIN...
...IF YOU WANT TO!
HUH?
ARE YOU SURE?
YEAH, SAYAKA WILL ENJOY IT TOO.
AND... I BRING HOME TONS OF BOXED LUNCHES, SO WE ALWAYS HAVE A LOT OF FOOD.

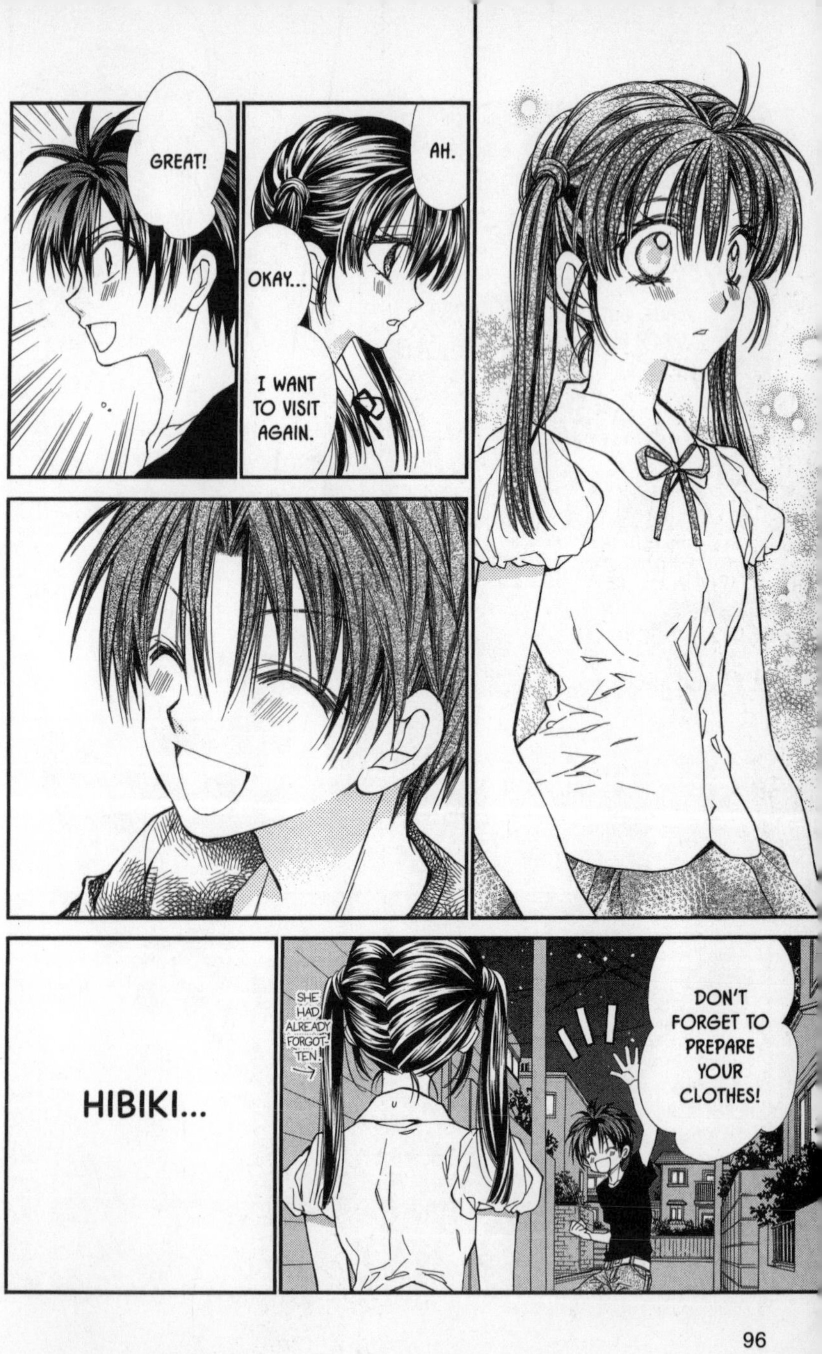
AH.
OKAY...
I WANT TO VISIT AGAIN.
GREAT!
DON'T FORGET TO PREPARE YOUR CLOTHES!
SHE HAD ALREADY FORGOT-TEN.
HIBIKI...

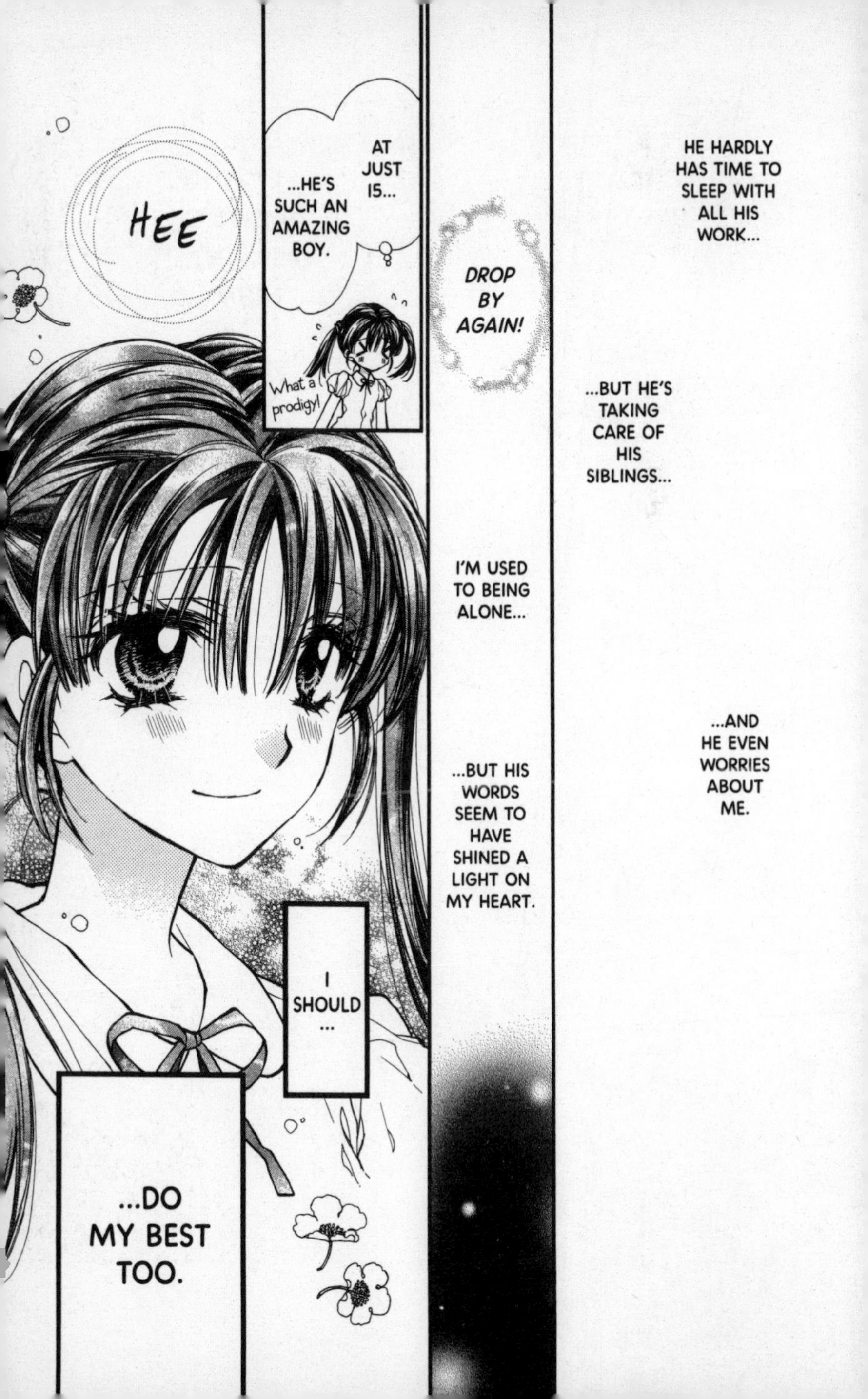
HE HARDLY HAS TIME TO SLEEP WITH ALL HIS WORK...
...BUT HE'S TAKING CARE OF HIS SIBLINGS...
...AND HE EVEN WORRIES ABOUT ME.
DROP BY AGAIN!
I'M USED TO BEING ALONE...
...BUT HIS WORDS SEEM TO HAVE SHINED A LIGHT ON MY HEART.
AT JUST 15...
...HE'S SUCH AN AMAZING BOY.
What a prodigy!
HEE
I SHOULD...
...DO MY BEST TOO.

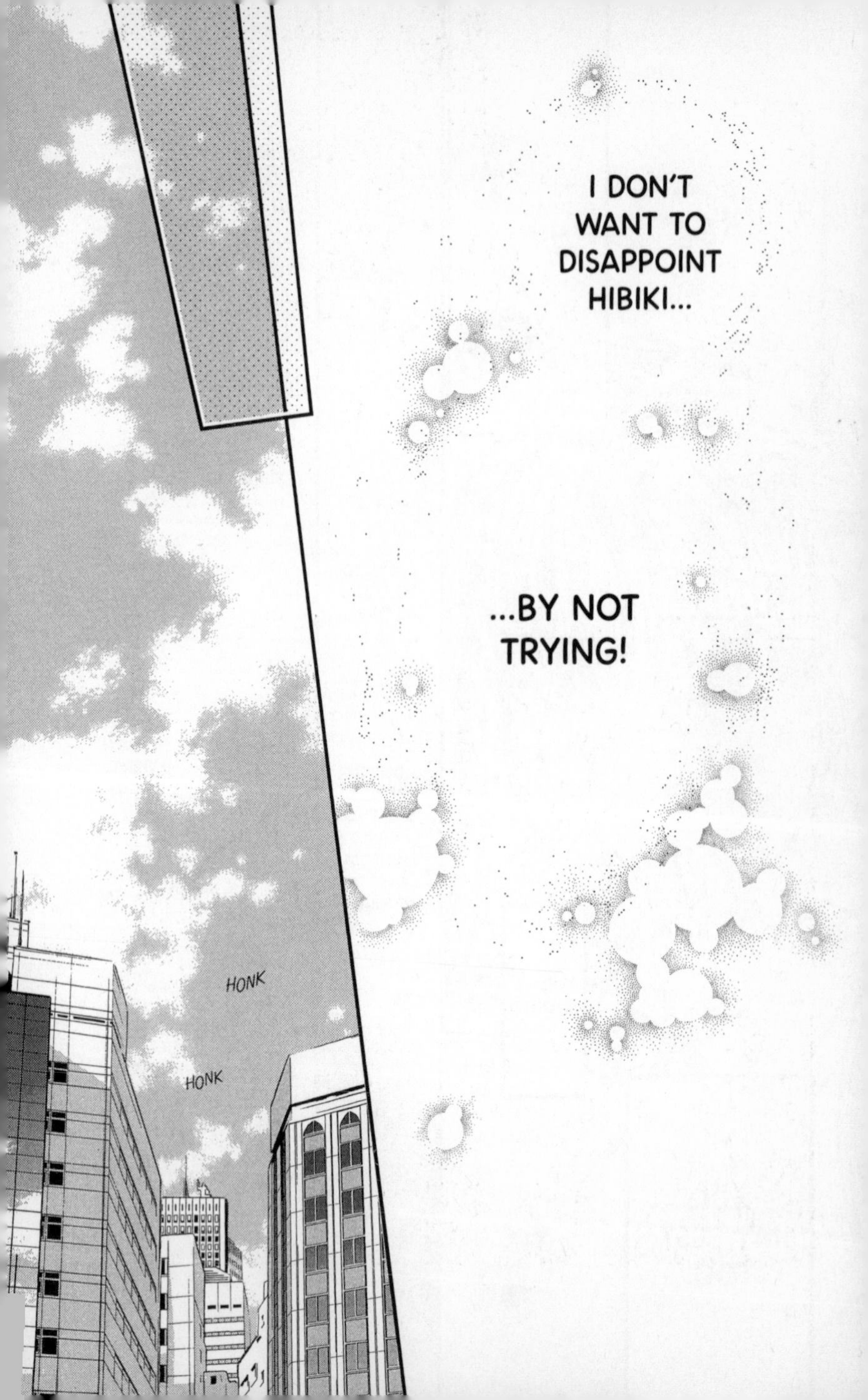
I DON'T WANT TO DISAPPOINT HIBIKI...
...BY NOT TRYING!
HONK
HONK

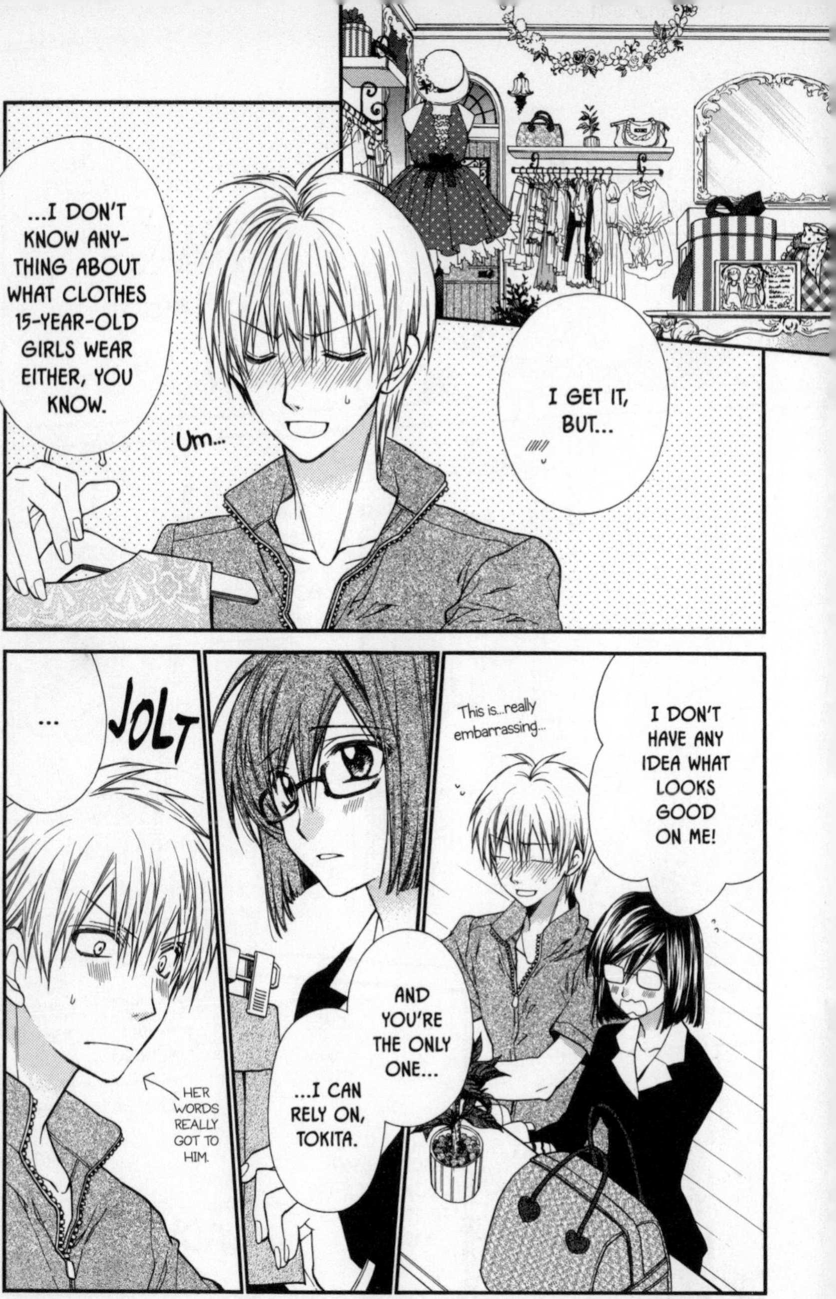
...I DON'T KNOW ANYTHING ABOUT WHAT CLOTHES 15-YEAR-OLD GIRLS WEAR EITHER, YOU KNOW.
Um...
I GET IT, BUT...
I DON'T HAVE ANY IDEA WHAT LOOKS GOOD ON ME!
This is...really embarrassing...
AND YOU'RE THE ONLY ONE...
...I CAN RELY ON, TOKITA.
...
JOLT
HER WORDS REALLY GOT TO HIM.

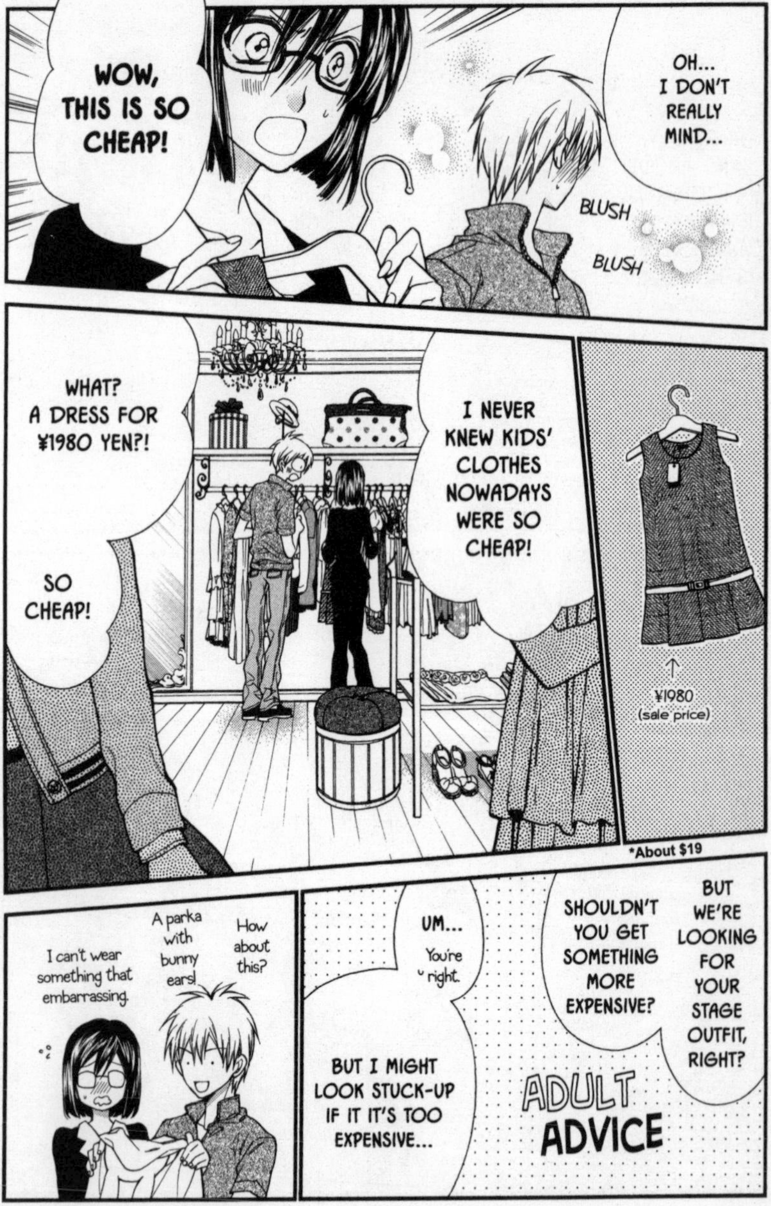
OH... I DON'T REALLY MIND...
BLUSH
BLUSH
WOW, THIS IS SO CHEAP!
¥1980 (sale price)
*About $19
I NEVER KNEW KIDS' CLOTHES NOWADAYS WERE SO CHEAP!
WHAT? A DRESS FOR ¥1980 YEN?!
SO CHEAP!
BUT WE'RE LOOKING FOR YOUR STAGE OUTFIT, RIGHT?
SHOULDN'T YOU GET SOMETHING MORE EXPENSIVE?
UM...
You're right.
ADULT ADVICE
BUT I MIGHT LOOK STUCK-UP IF IT IT'S TOO EXPENSIVE...
How about this?
A parka with bunny ears!
I can't wear something that embarrassing.

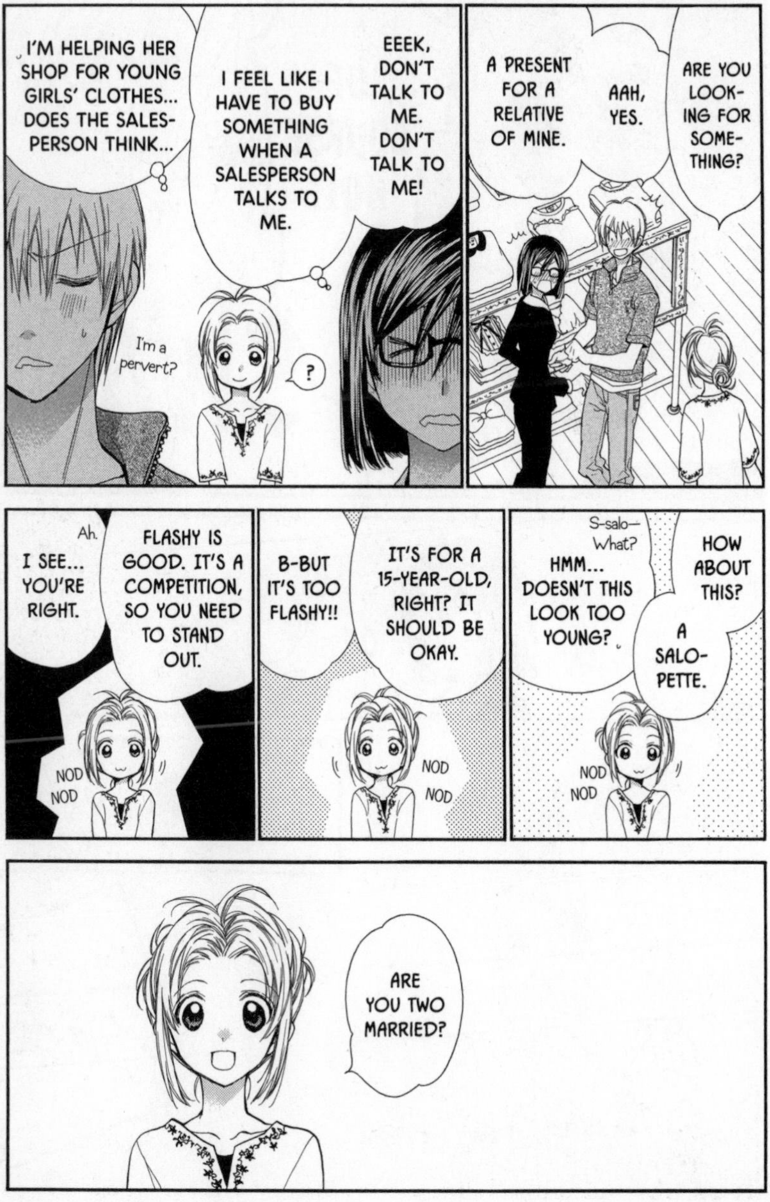
ARE YOU LOOKING FOR SOMETHING?
AAH, YES.
A PRESENT FOR A RELATIVE OF MINE.
EEEK, DON'T TALK TO ME. DON'T TALK TO ME!
I FEEL LIKE I HAVE TO BUY SOMETHING WHEN A SALESPERSON TALKS TO ME.
?
I'M HELPING HER SHOP FOR YOUNG GIRLS' CLOTHES... DOES THE SALESPERSON THINK...
I'm a pervert?
HOW ABOUT THIS?
S-salo— What?
A SALOPETTE.
HMM... DOESN'T THIS LOOK TOO YOUNG?
NOD NOD
IT'S FOR A 15-YEAR-OLD, RIGHT? IT SHOULD BE OKAY.
B-BUT IT'S TOO FLASHY!!
NOD NOD
FLASHY IS GOOD. IT'S A COMPETITION, SO YOU NEED TO STAND OUT.
Ah.
I SEE... YOU'RE RIGHT.
NOD NOD
ARE YOU TWO MARRIED?

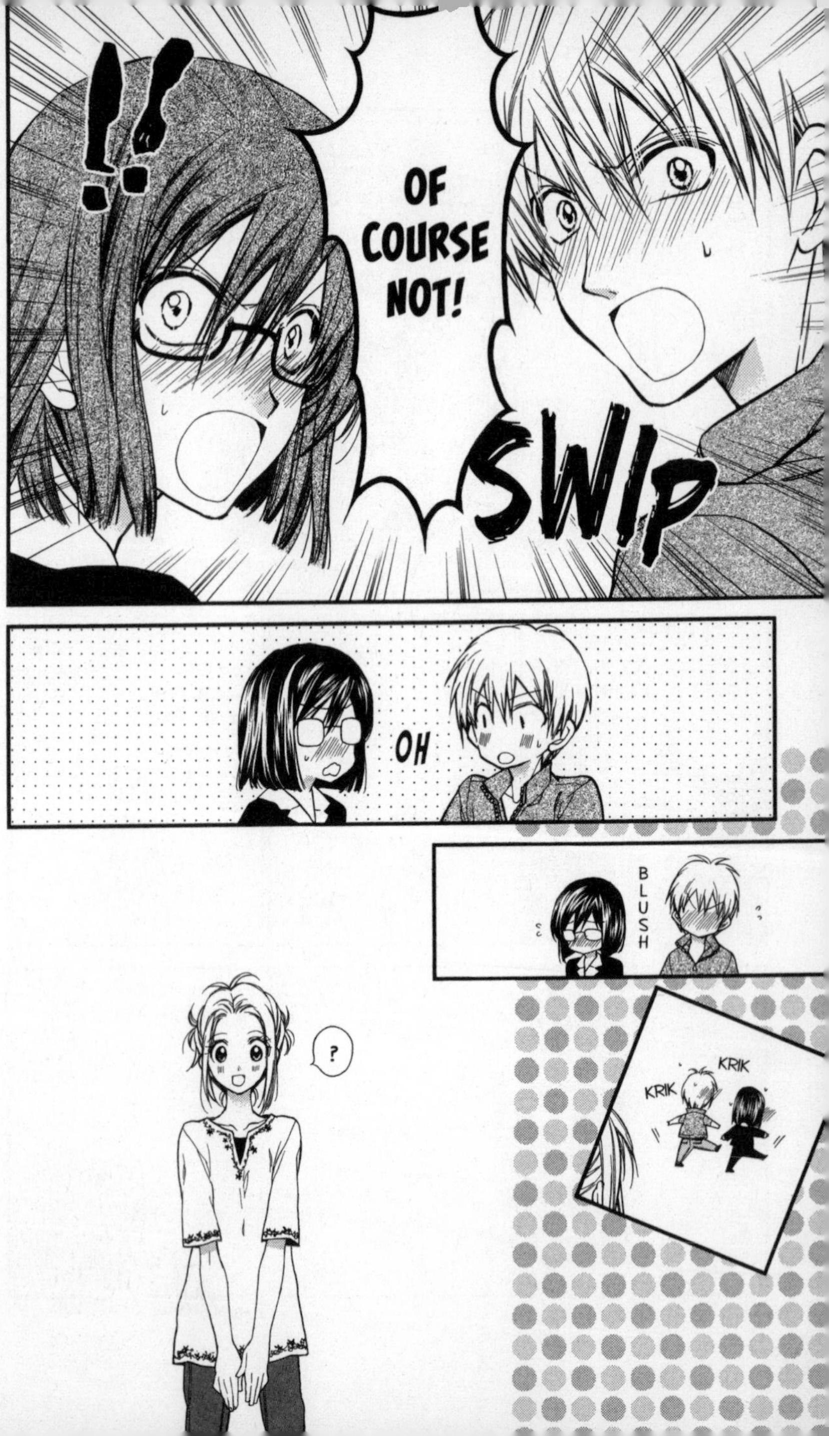
!!
OF COURSE NOT!
SWIP
OH
BLUSH
?
KRIK
KRIK

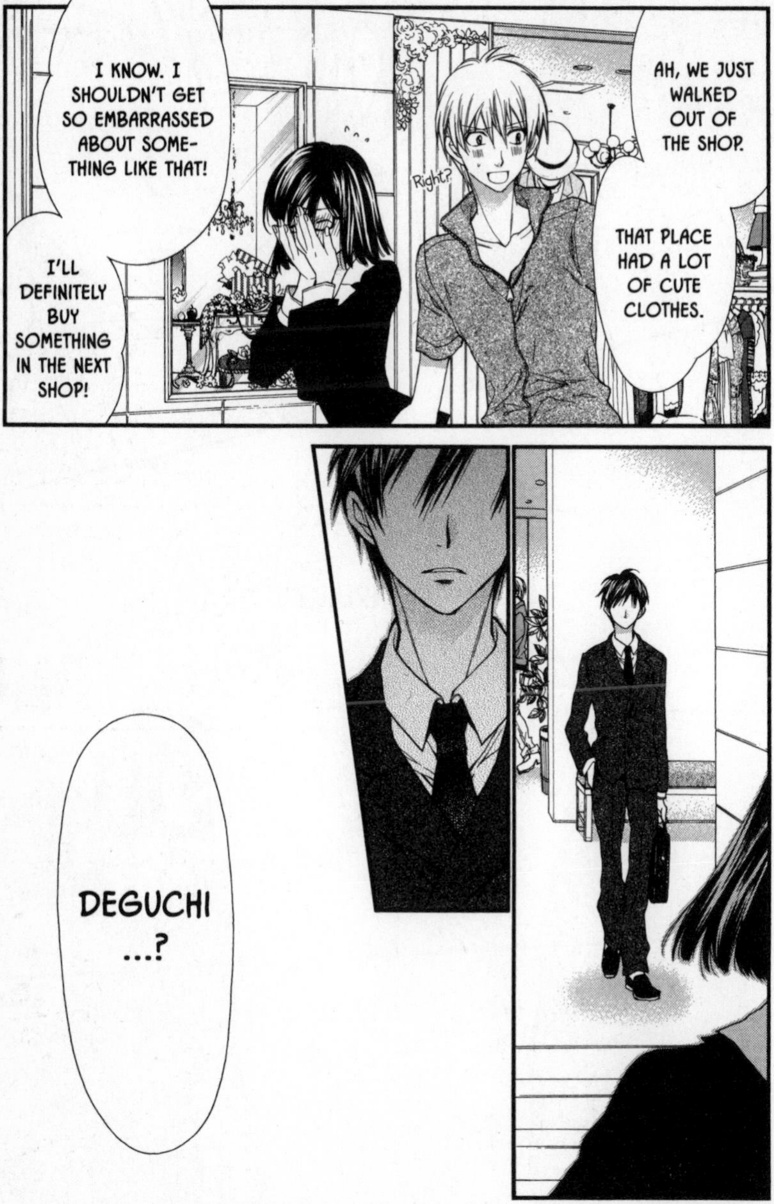
AH, WE JUST WALKED OUT OF THE SHOP.
THAT PLACE HAD A LOT OF CUTE CLOTHES.
Right?
I KNOW. I SHOULDN'T GET SO EMBARRASSED ABOUT SOME-THING LIKE THAT!
I'LL DEFINITELY BUY SOMETHING IN THE NEXT SHOP!
DEGUCHI ...?

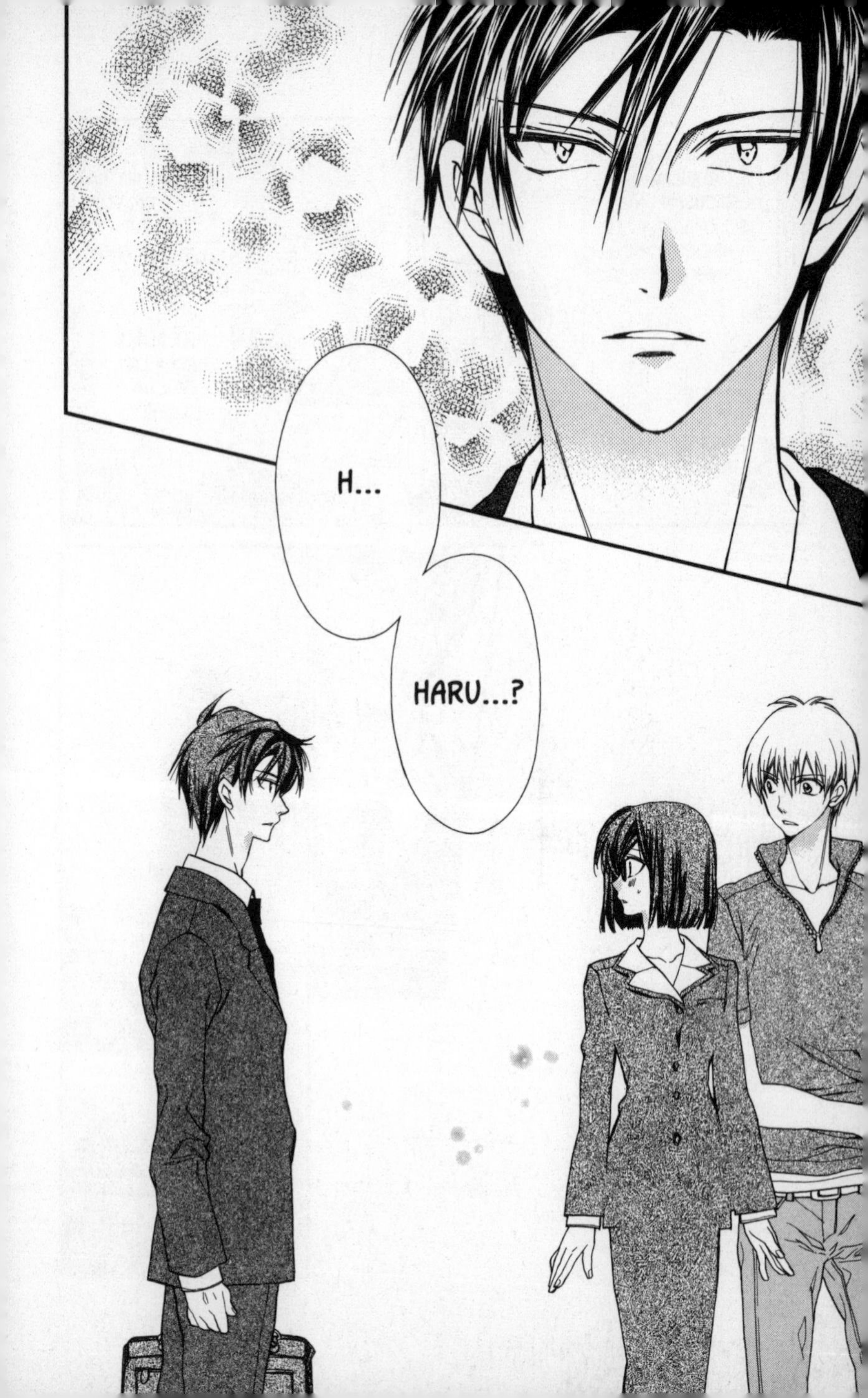
H...
HARU...?

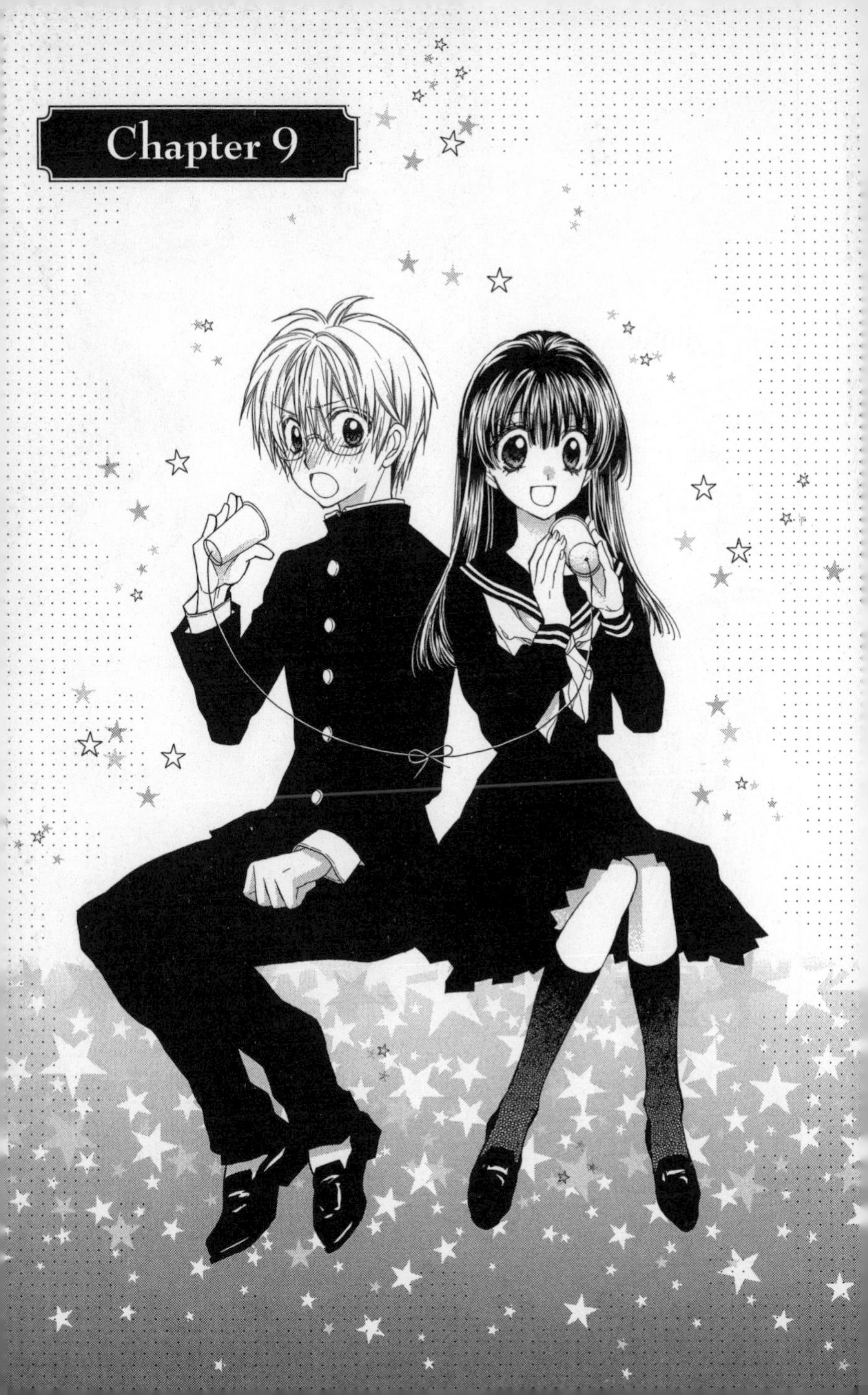
Chapter 9

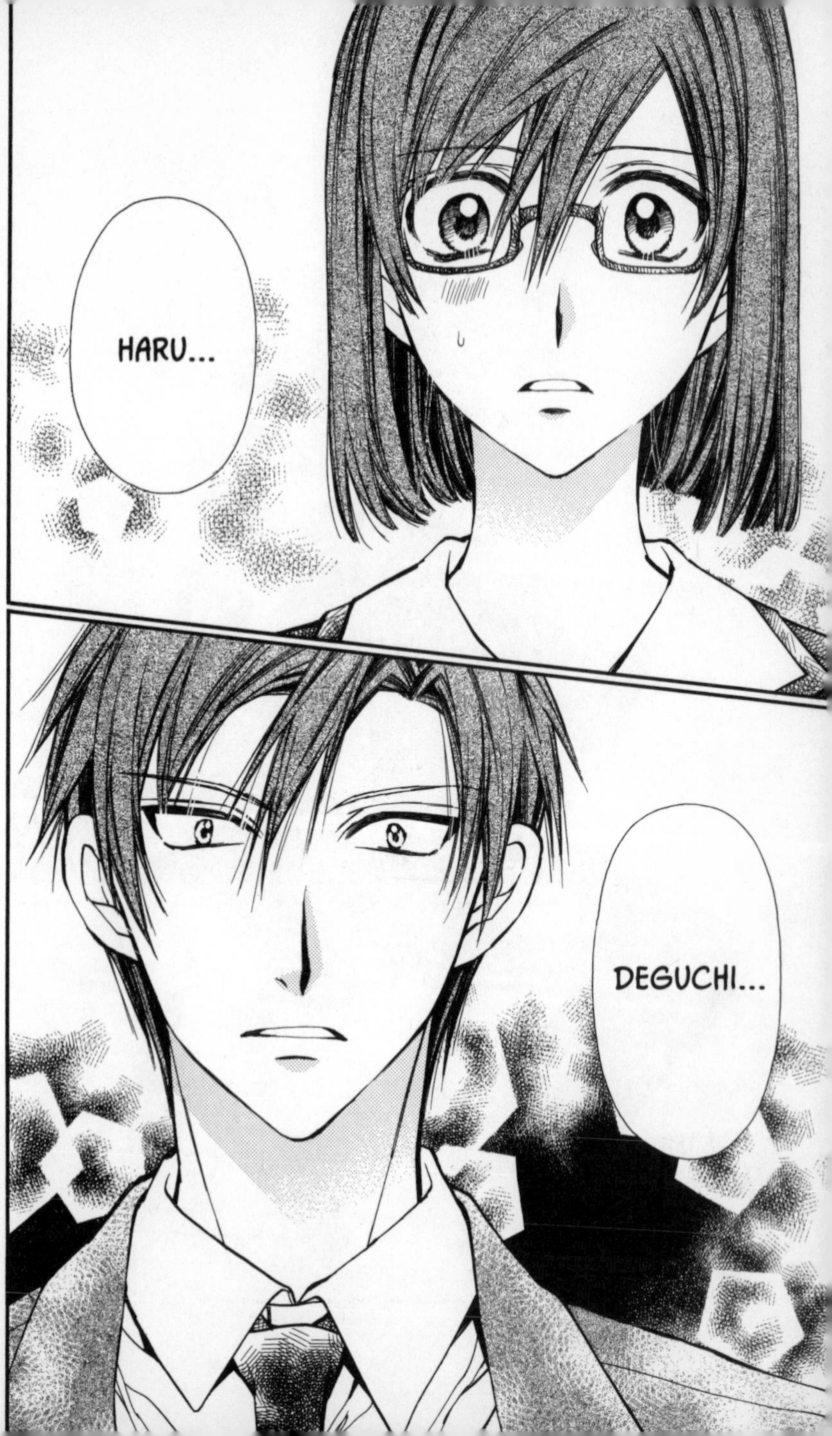
HARU...
DEGUCHI...

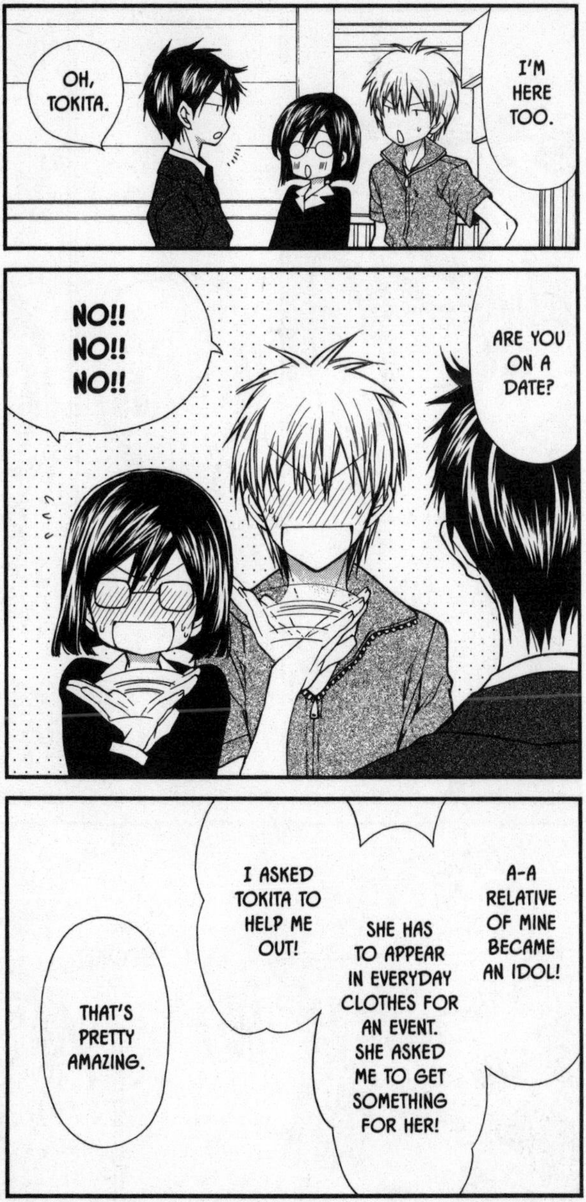
I'M HERE TOO.
OH, TOKITA.
ARE YOU ON A DATE?
NO!! NO!! NO!!
A-A RELATIVE OF MINE BECAME AN IDOL!
SHE HAS TO APPEAR IN EVERYDAY CLOTHES FOR AN EVENT. SHE ASKED ME TO GET SOMETHING FOR HER!
I ASKED TOKITA TO HELP ME OUT!
THAT'S PRETTY AMAZING.

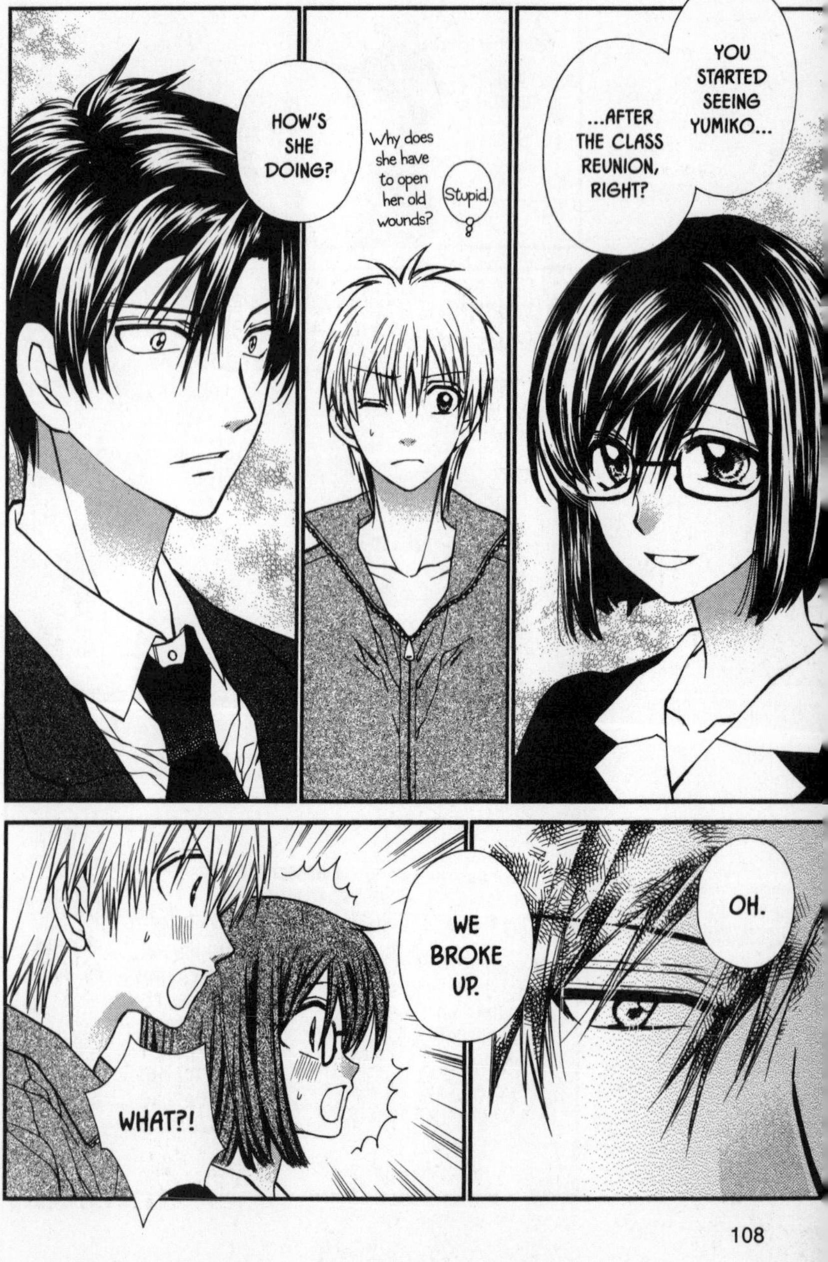
YOU STARTED SEEING YUMIKO...
...AFTER THE CLASS REUNION, RIGHT?
Why does she have to open her old wounds?
Stupid.
HOW'S SHE DOING?
OH.
WE BROKE UP.
WHAT?!

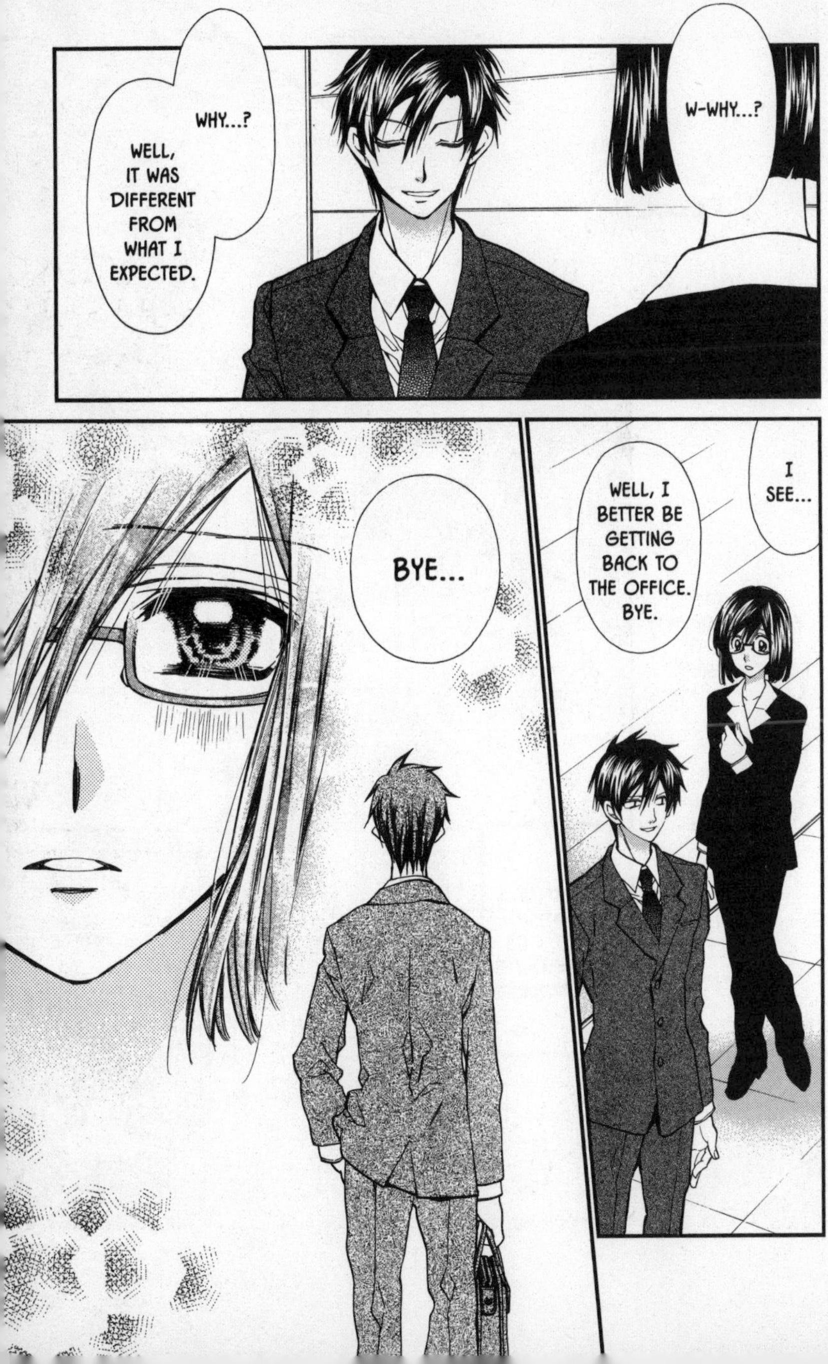
W-WHY...?
WHY...? WELL, IT WAS DIFFERENT FROM WHAT I EXPECTED.
I SEE...
WELL, I BETTER BE GETTING BACK TO THE OFFICE. BYE.
BYE...

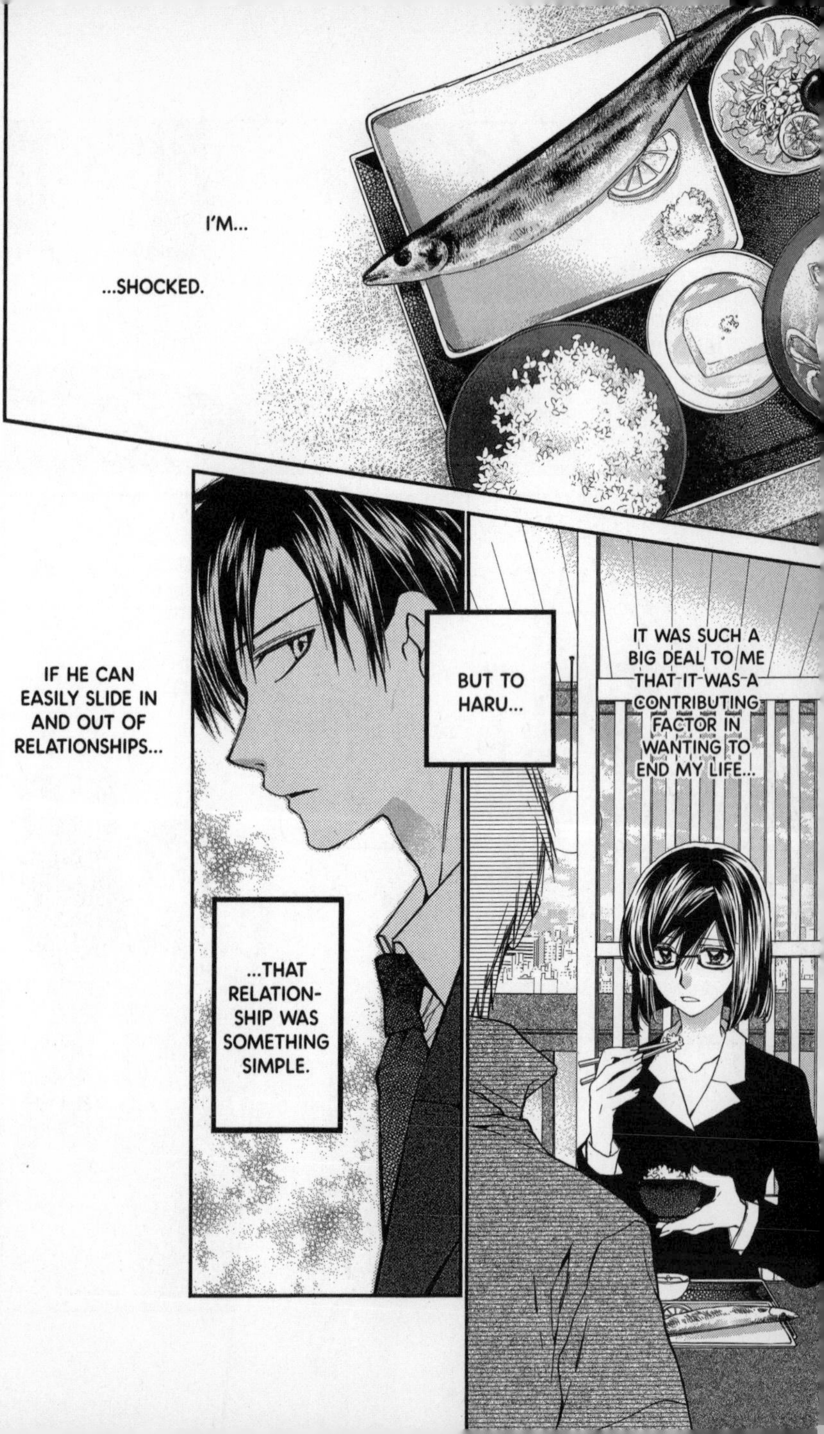
I'M...
...SHOCKED.
IT WAS SUCH A BIG DEAL TO ME THAT IT WAS A CONTRIBUTING FACTOR IN WANTING TO END MY LIFE...
BUT TO HARU...
...THAT RELATION-SHIP WAS SOMETHING SIMPLE.
IF HE CAN EASILY SLIDE IN AND OUT OF RELATIONSHIPS...

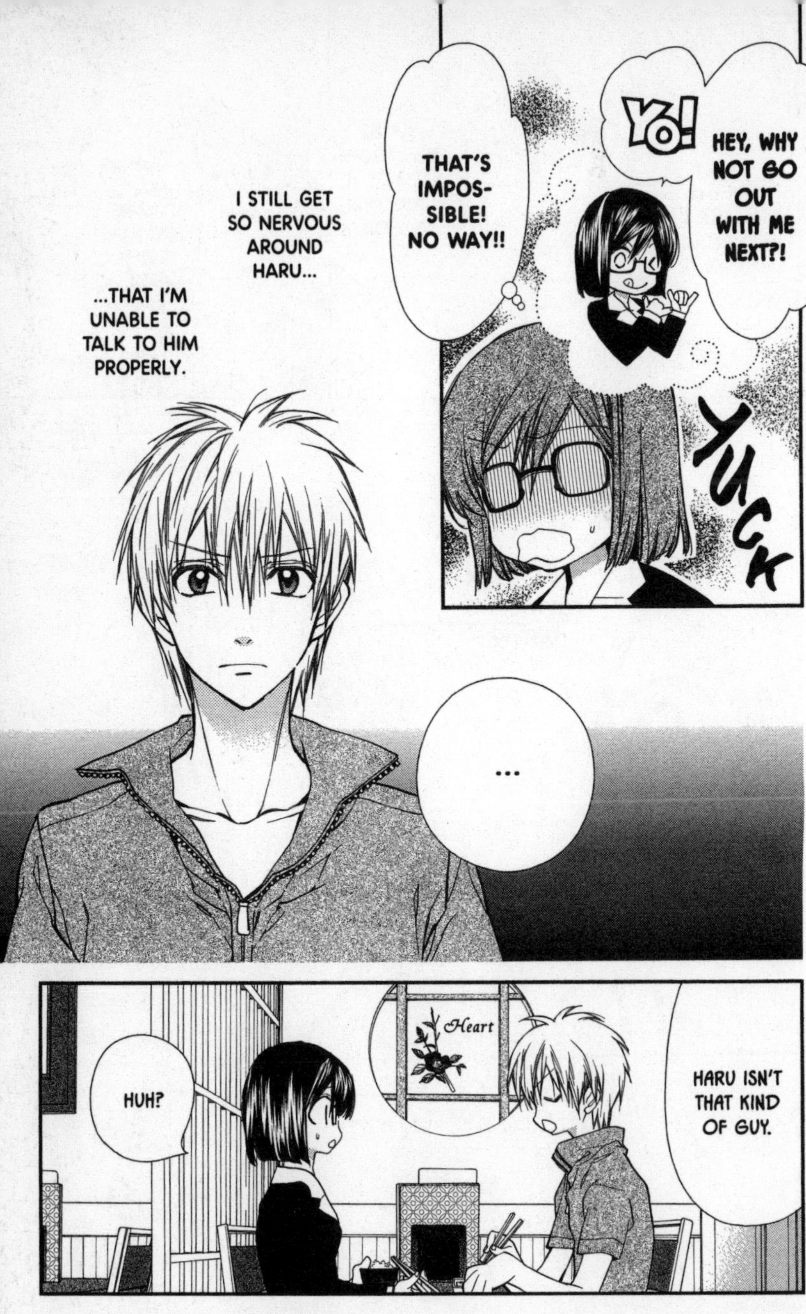
YO!
HEY, WHY NOT GO OUT WITH ME NEXT?!
THAT'S IMPOS-SIBLE! NO WAY!!
YUCK
I STILL GET SO NERVOUS AROUND HARU...
...THAT I'M UNABLE TO TALK TO HIM PROPERLY.
...
HARU ISN'T THAT KIND OF GUY.
Heart
HUH?

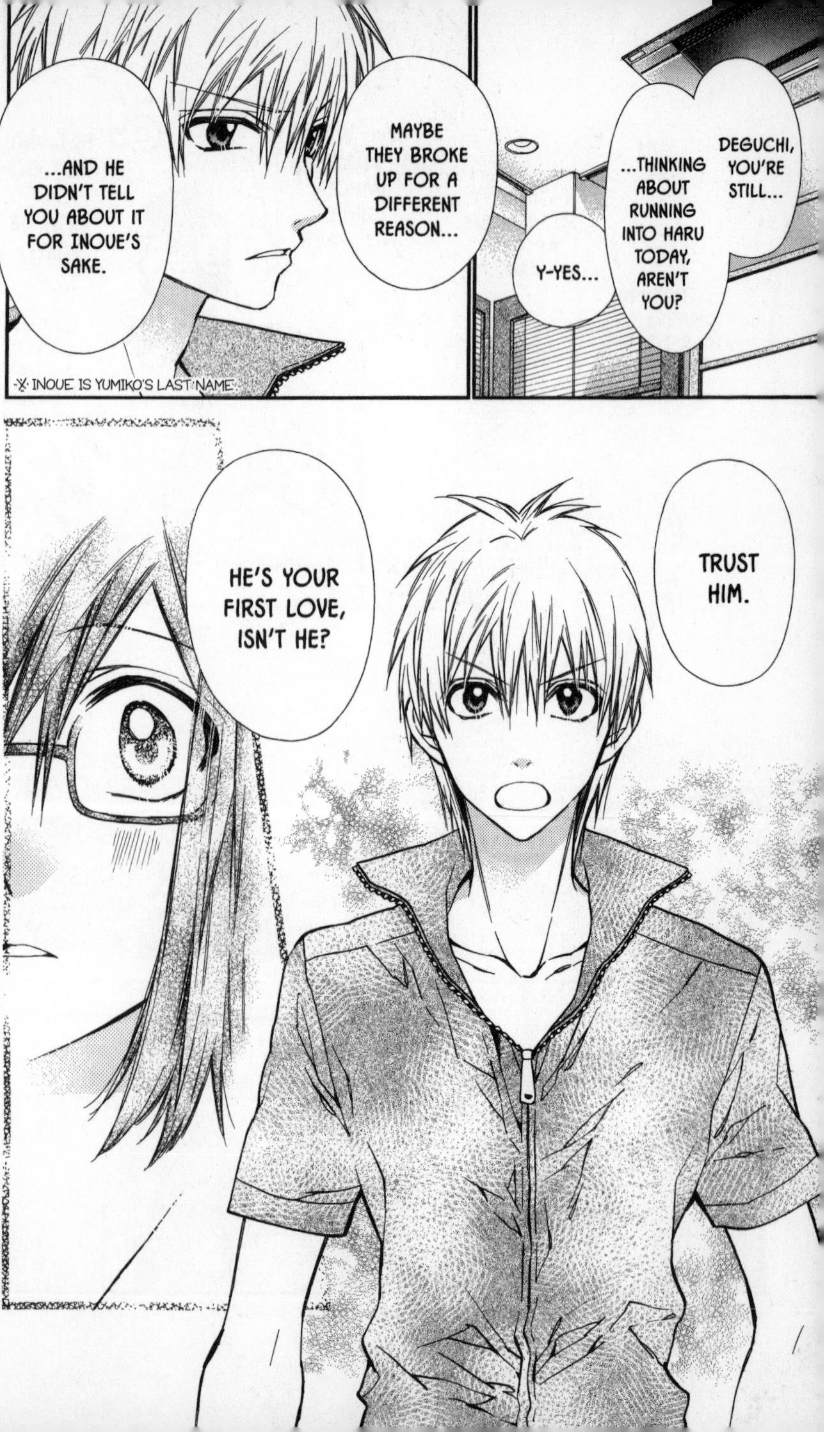
DEGUCHI, YOU'RE STILL...
...THINKING ABOUT RUNNING INTO HARU TODAY, AREN'T YOU?
Y-YES...
MAYBE THEY BROKE UP FOR A DIFFERENT REASON...
...AND HE DIDN'T TELL YOU ABOUT IT FOR INOUE'S SAKE.
※ INOUE IS YUMIKO'S LAST NAME.
TRUST HIM.
HE'S YOUR FIRST LOVE, ISN'T HE?

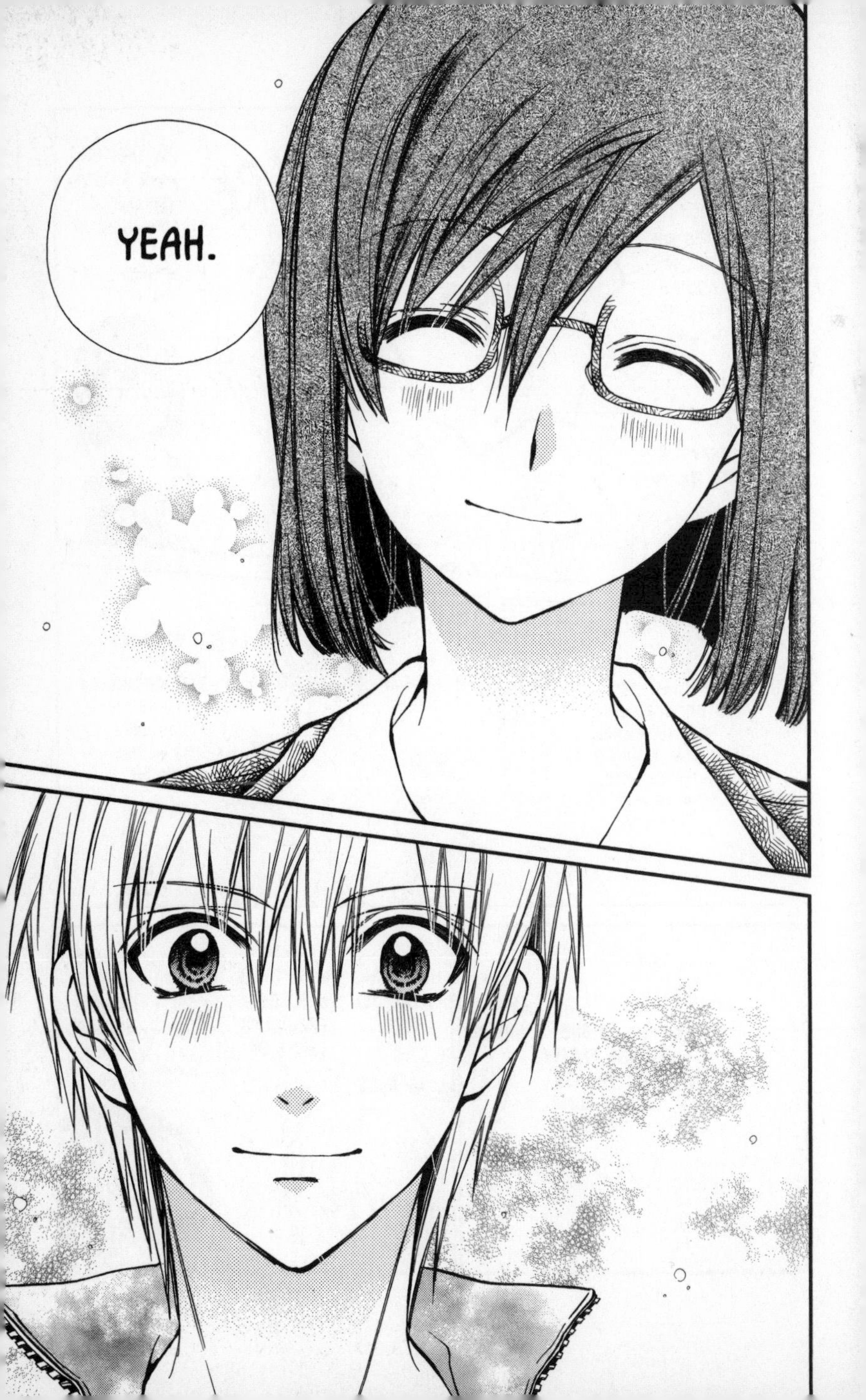
YEAH.

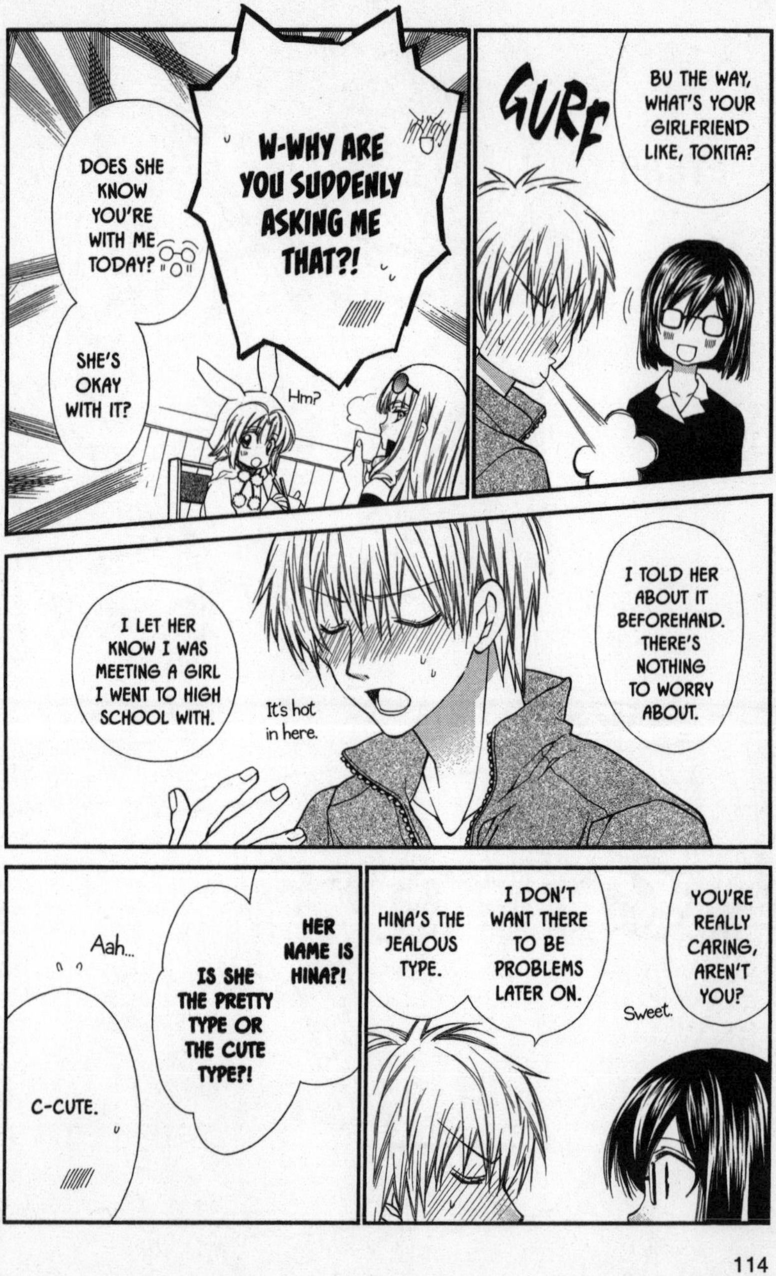
GURF
BU THE WAY, WHAT'S YOUR GIRLFRIEND LIKE, TOKITA?
W-WHY ARE YOU SUDDENLY ASKING ME THAT?!
DOES SHE KNOW YOU'RE WITH ME TODAY?
SHE'S OKAY WITH IT?
Hm?
I TOLD HER ABOUT IT BEFOREHAND. THERE'S NOTHING TO WORRY ABOUT.
I LET HER KNOW I WAS MEETING A GIRL I WENT TO HIGH SCHOOL WITH.
It's hot in here.
YOU'RE REALLY CARING, AREN'T YOU?
I DON'T WANT THERE TO BE PROBLEMS LATER ON.
HINA'S THE JEALOUS TYPE.
Sweet.
HER NAME IS HINA?!
IS SHE THE PRETTY TYPE OR THE CUTE TYPE?!
Aah...
C-CUTE.

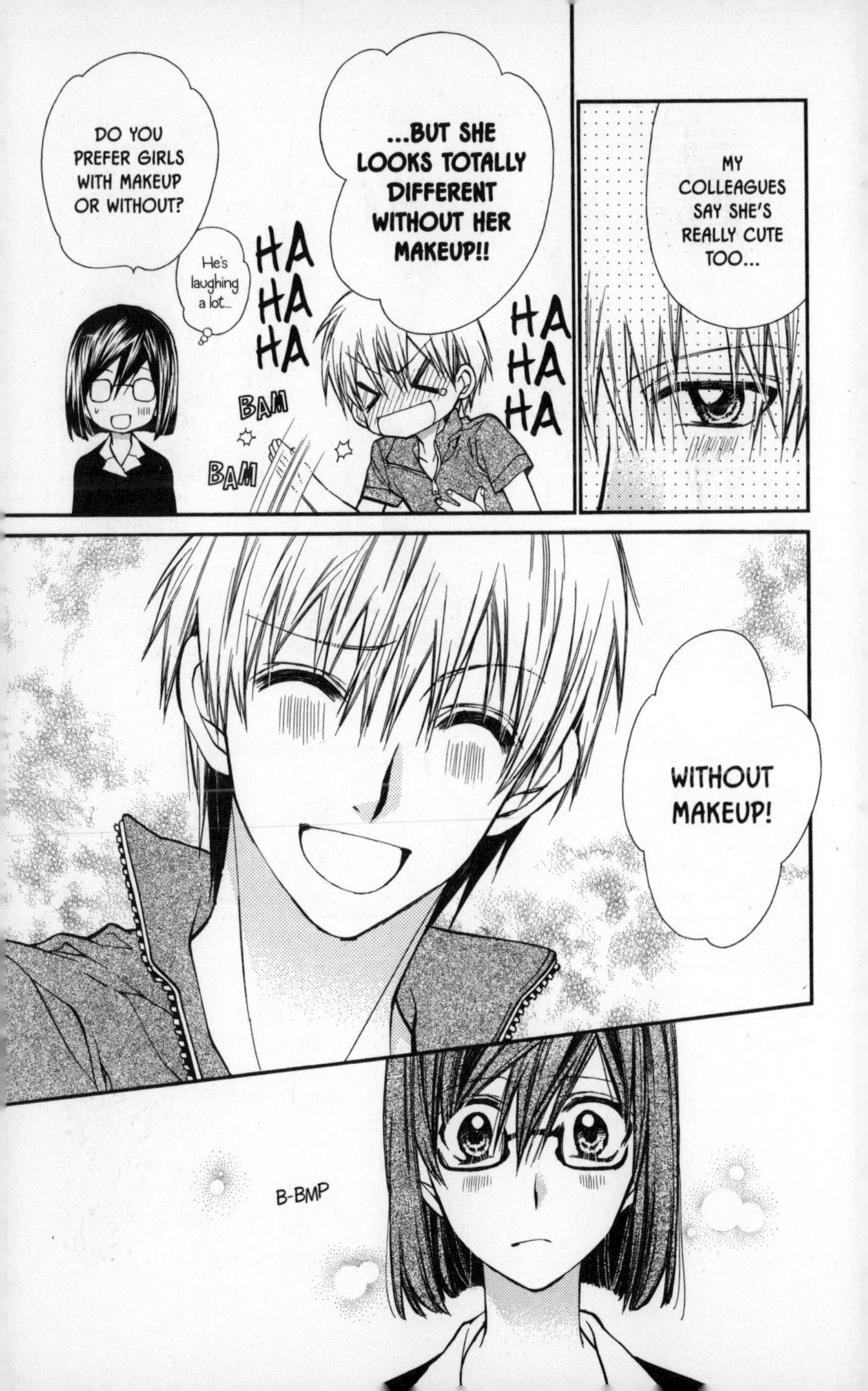
MY COLLEAGUES SAY SHE'S REALLY CUTE TOO...
...BUT SHE LOOKS TOTALLY DIFFERENT WITHOUT HER MAKEUP!!
HA HA HA
HA HA HA
BAM
BAM
He's laughing a lot...
DO YOU PREFER GIRLS WITH MAKEUP OR WITHOUT?
WITHOUT MAKEUP!
B-BMP

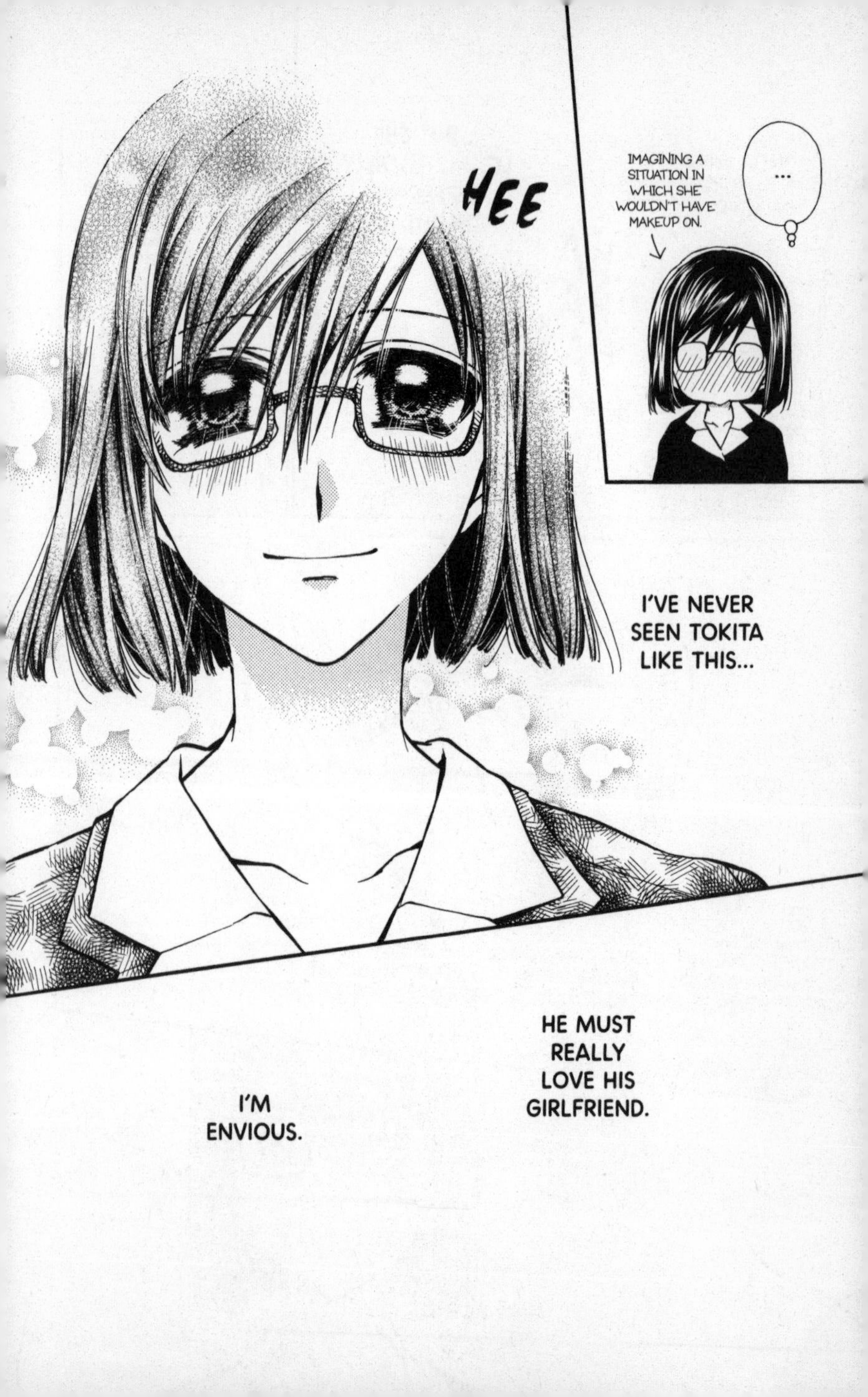
...
IMAGINING A SITUATION IN WHICH SHE WOULDN'T HAVE MAKEUP ON.
HEE
I'VE NEVER SEEN TOKITA LIKE THIS...
HE MUST REALLY LOVE HIS GIRLFRIEND.
I'M ENVIOUS.

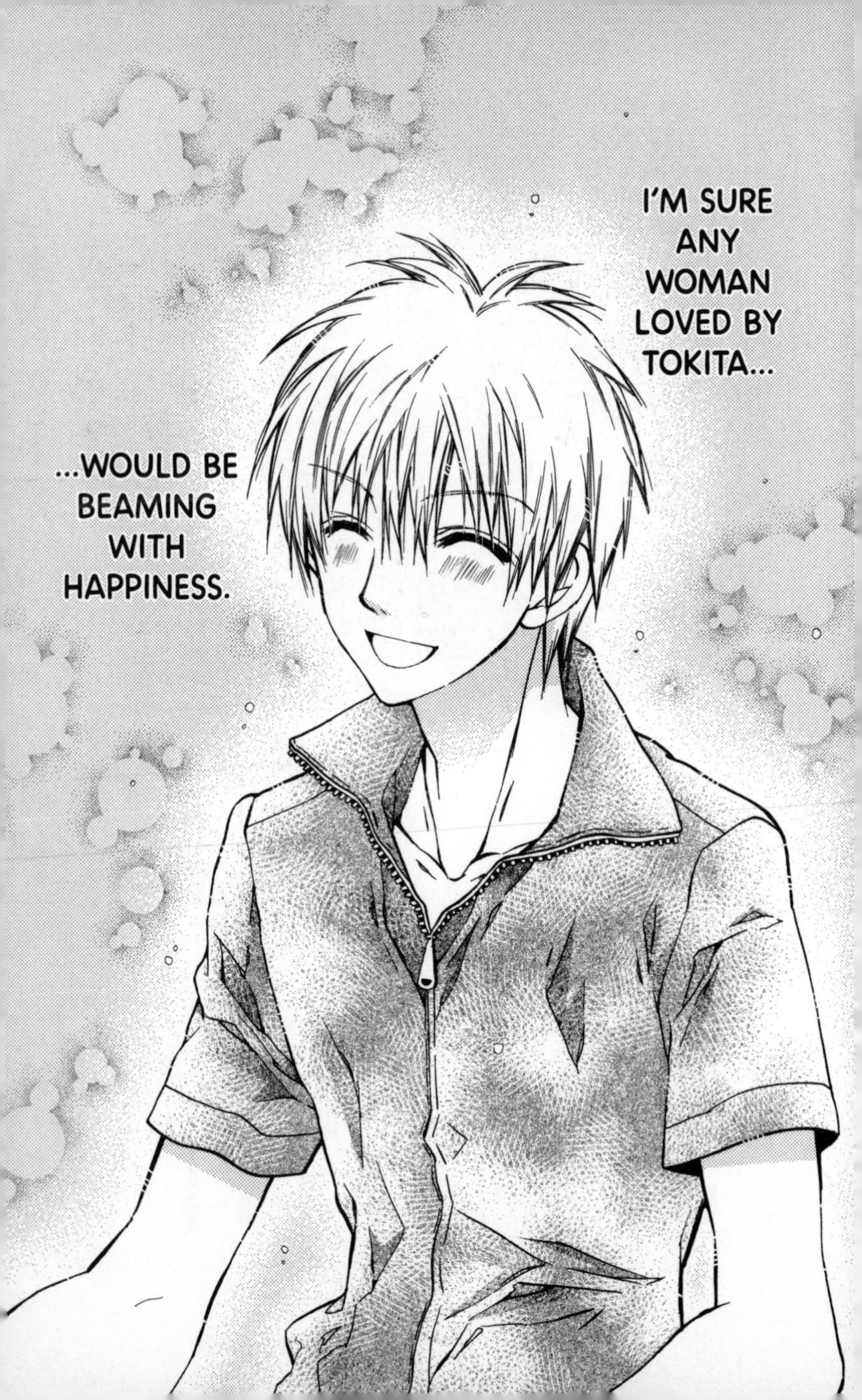
I'M SURE ANY WOMAN LOVED BY TOKITA...
...WOULD BE BEAMING WITH HAPPINESS.

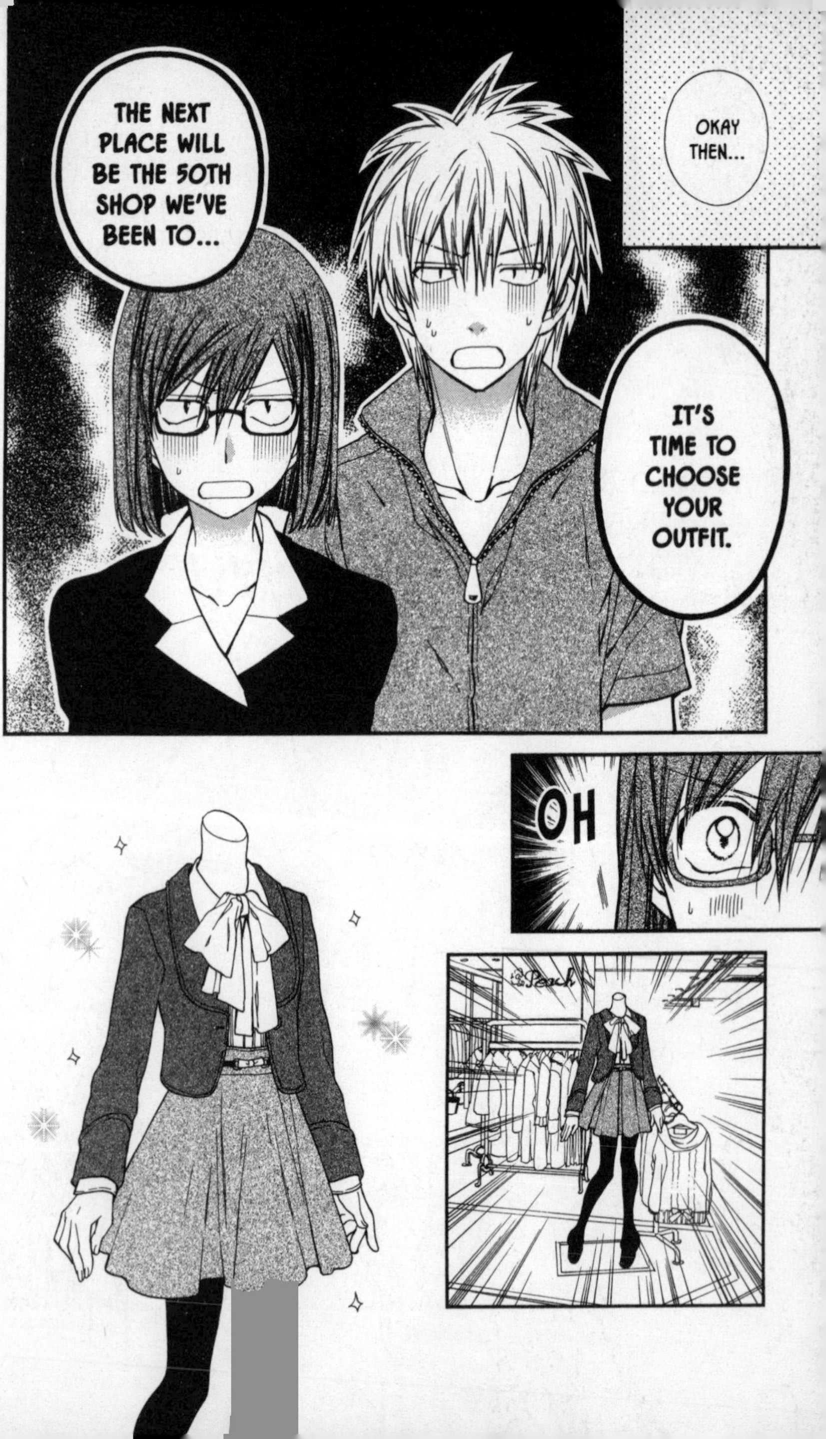
OKAY THEN...
IT'S TIME TO CHOOSE YOUR OUTFIT.
THE NEXT PLACE WILL BE THE 50TH SHOP WE'VE BEEN TO...
OH
Peach

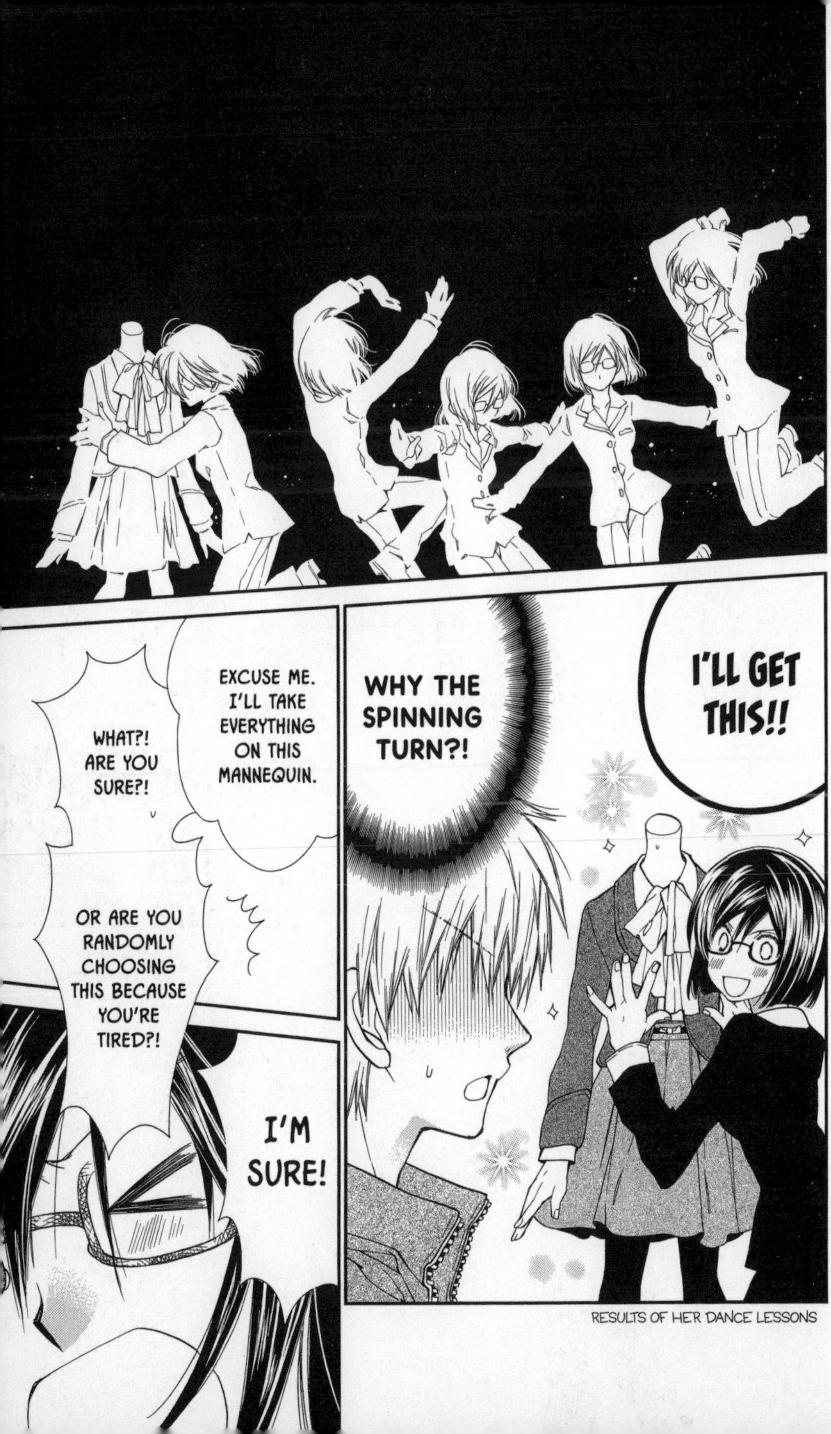
I'LL GET THIS!!
WHY THE SPINNING TURN?!
EXCUSE ME. I'LL TAKE EVERYTHING ON THIS MANNEQUIN.
WHAT?! ARE YOU SURE?!
OR ARE YOU RANDOMLY CHOOSING THIS BECAUSE YOU'RE TIRED?!
I'M SURE!

RESULTS OF HER DANCE LESSONS

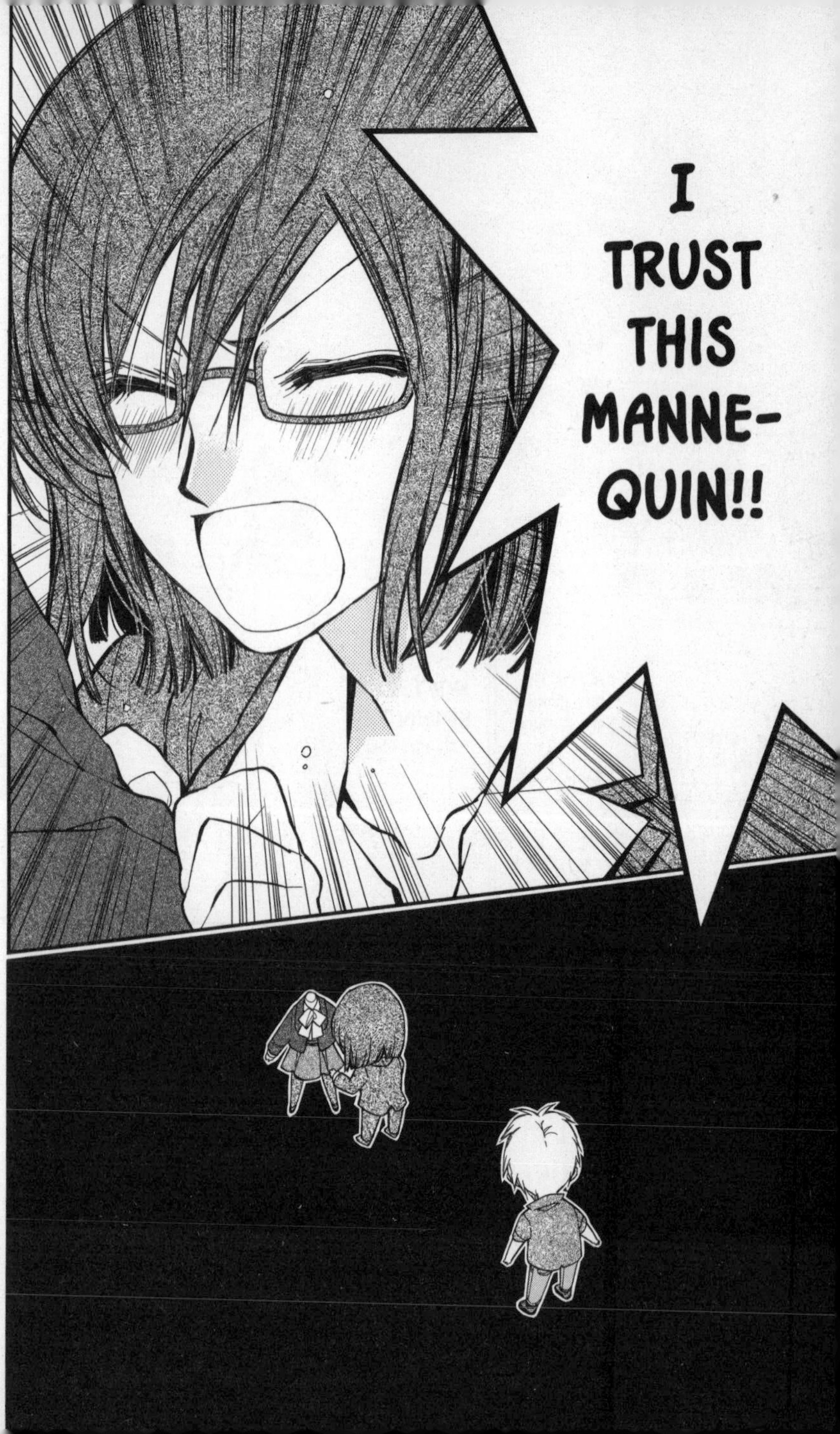
I TRUST THIS MANNE-QUIN!!

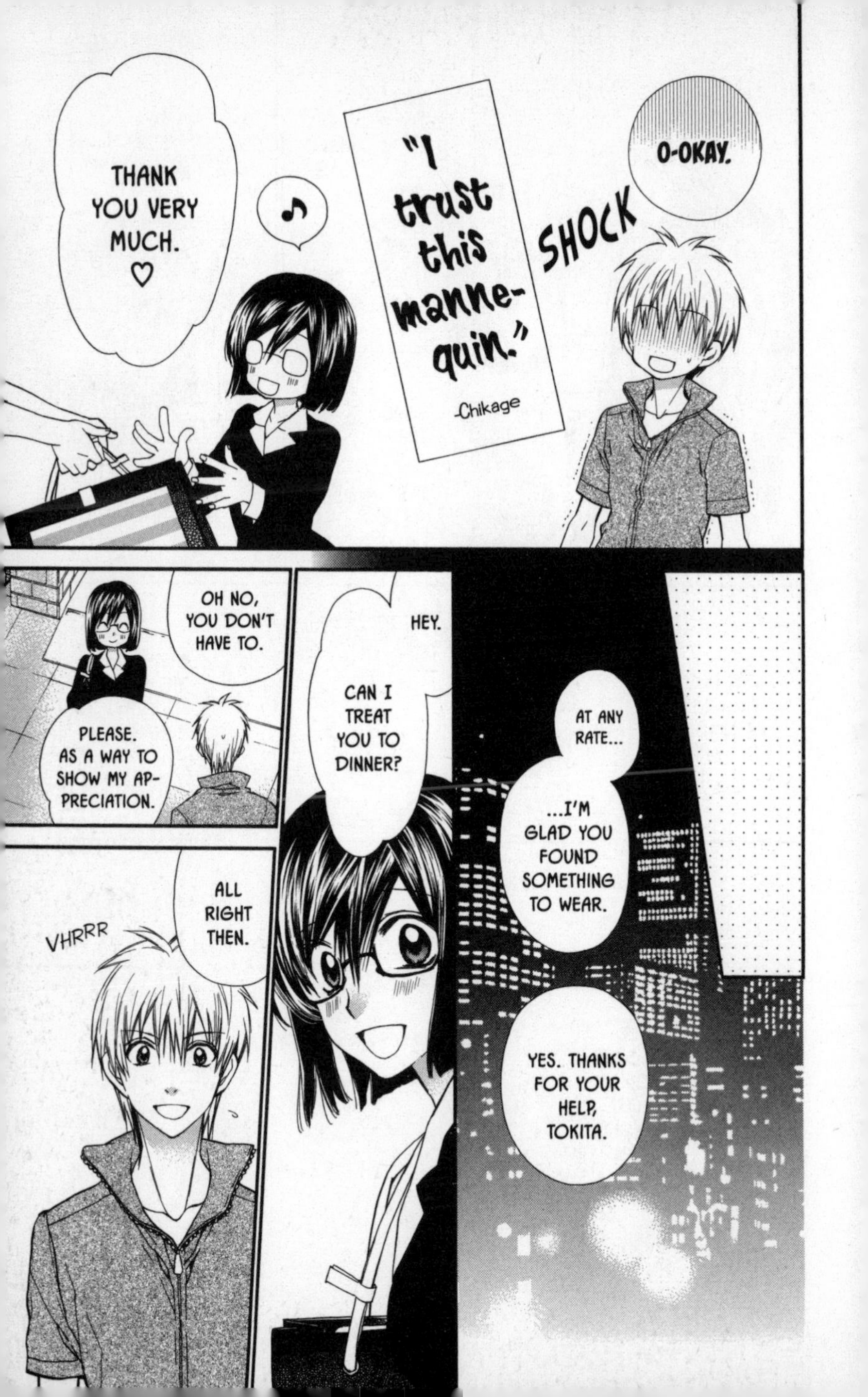
O-OKAY.
SHOCK
"I trust this manne-quin."
-Chikage
♪
THANK YOU VERY MUCH. ♡
AT ANY RATE...
...I'M GLAD YOU FOUND SOMETHING TO WEAR.
YES. THANKS FOR YOUR HELP, TOKITA.
HEY.
CAN I TREAT YOU TO DINNER?
OH NO, YOU DON'T HAVE TO.
PLEASE. AS A WAY TO SHOW MY AP-PRECIATION.
ALL RIGHT THEN.
VHRRR

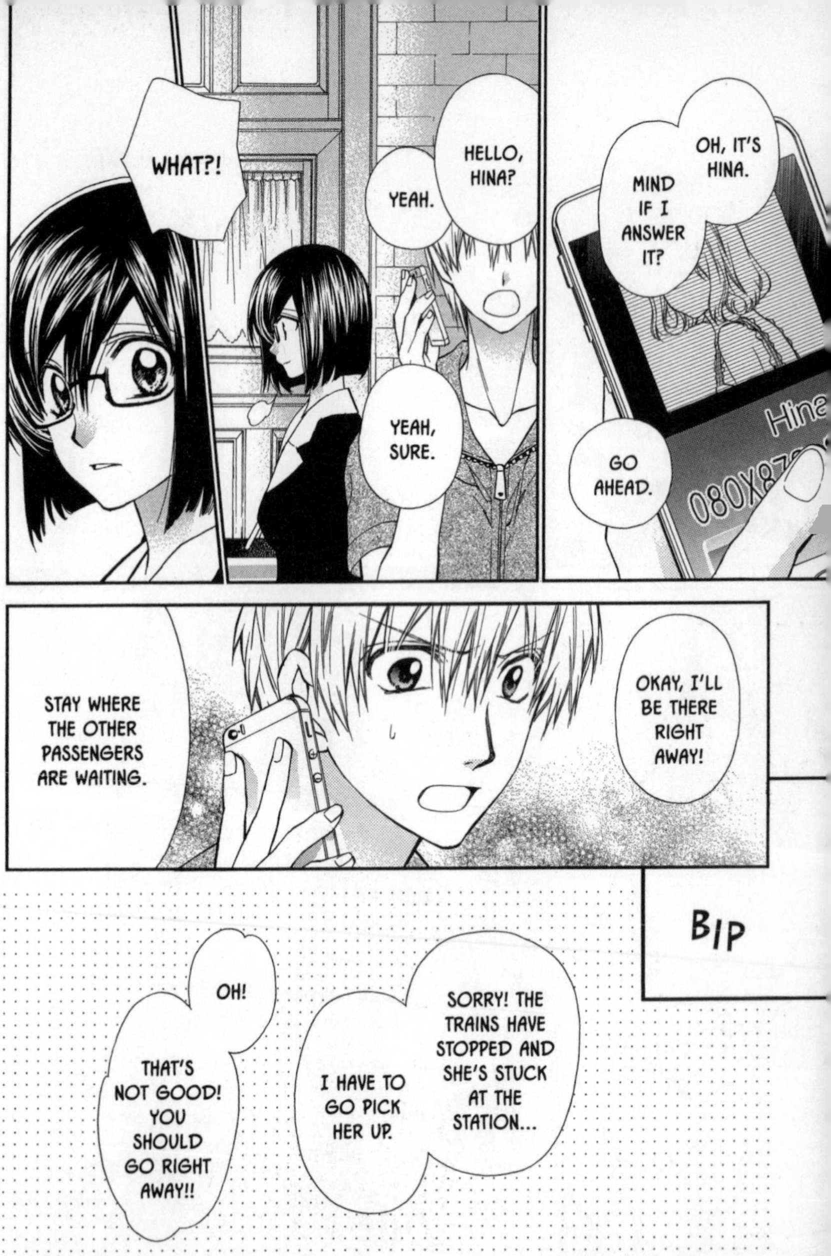
OH, IT'S HINA.
MIND IF I ANSWER IT?
Hina
GO AHEAD.
HELLO, HINA?
YEAH.
YEAH, SURE.
WHAT?!
OKAY, I'LL BE THERE RIGHT AWAY!
STAY WHERE THE OTHER PASSENGERS ARE WAITING.
BIP
SORRY! THE TRAINS HAVE STOPPED AND SHE'S STUCK AT THE STATION...
I HAVE TO GO PICK HER UP.
OH!
THAT'S NOT GOOD! YOU SHOULD GO RIGHT AWAY!!

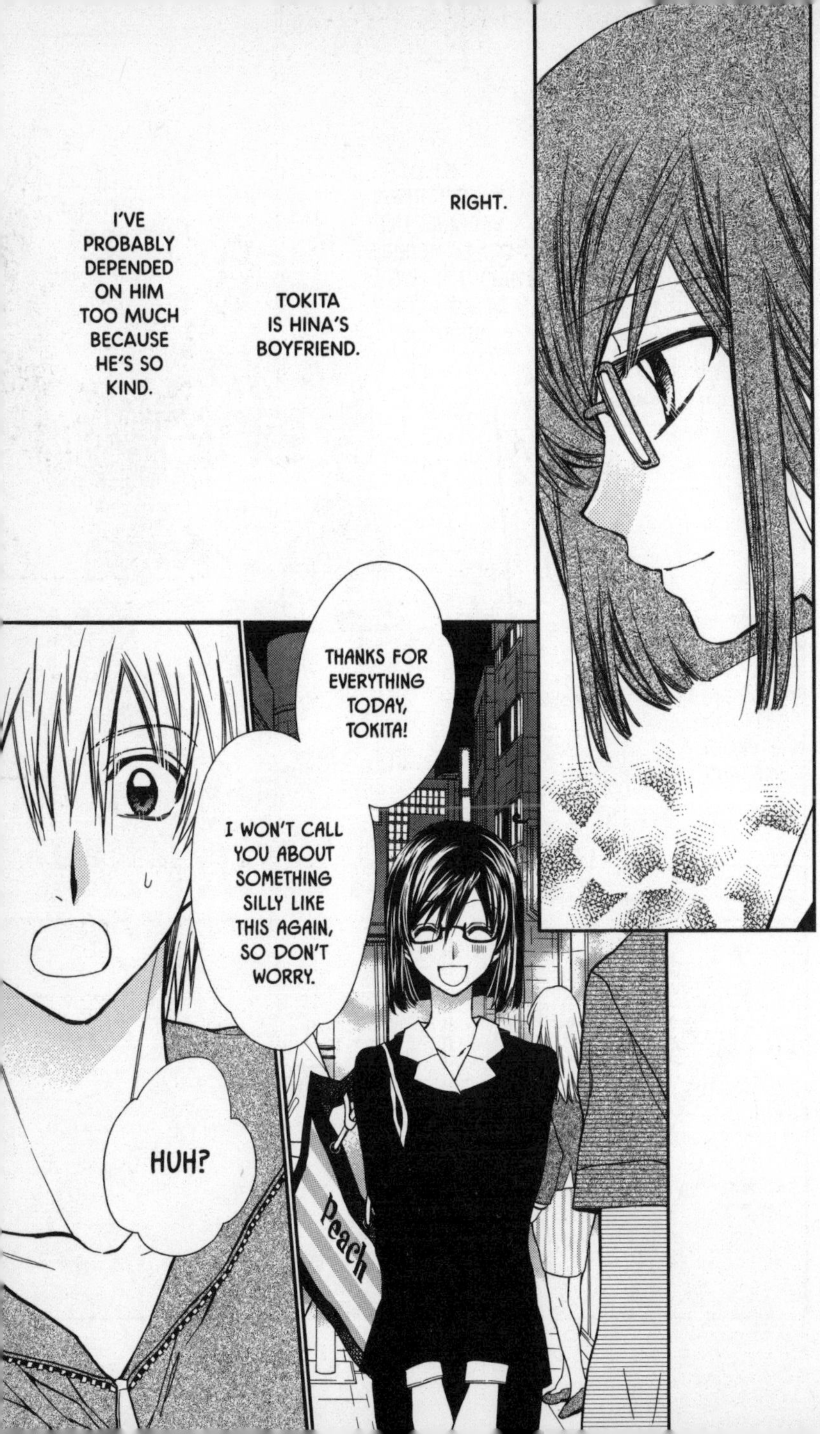
RIGHT.
TOKITA IS HINA'S BOYFRIEND.
I'VE PROBABLY DEPENDED ON HIM TOO MUCH BECAUSE HE'S SO KIND.
THANKS FOR EVERYTHING TODAY, TOKITA!
I WON'T CALL YOU ABOUT SOMETHING SILLY LIKE THIS AGAIN, SO DON'T WORRY.
Peach
HUH?

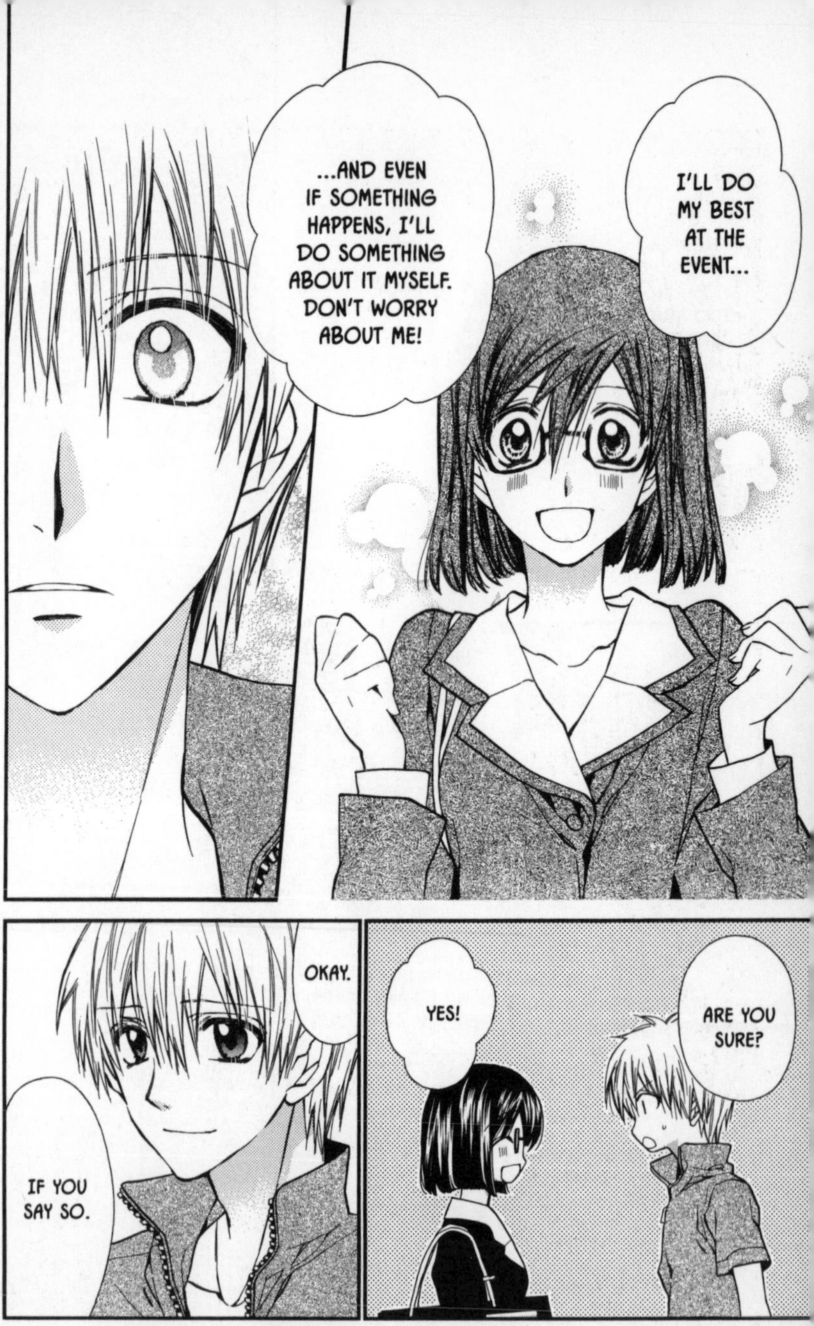
I'LL DO MY BEST AT THE EVENT...
...AND EVEN IF SOMETHING HAPPENS, I'LL DO SOMETHING ABOUT IT MYSELF. DON'T WORRY ABOUT ME!
ARE YOU SURE?
YES!
OKAY.
IF YOU SAY SO.

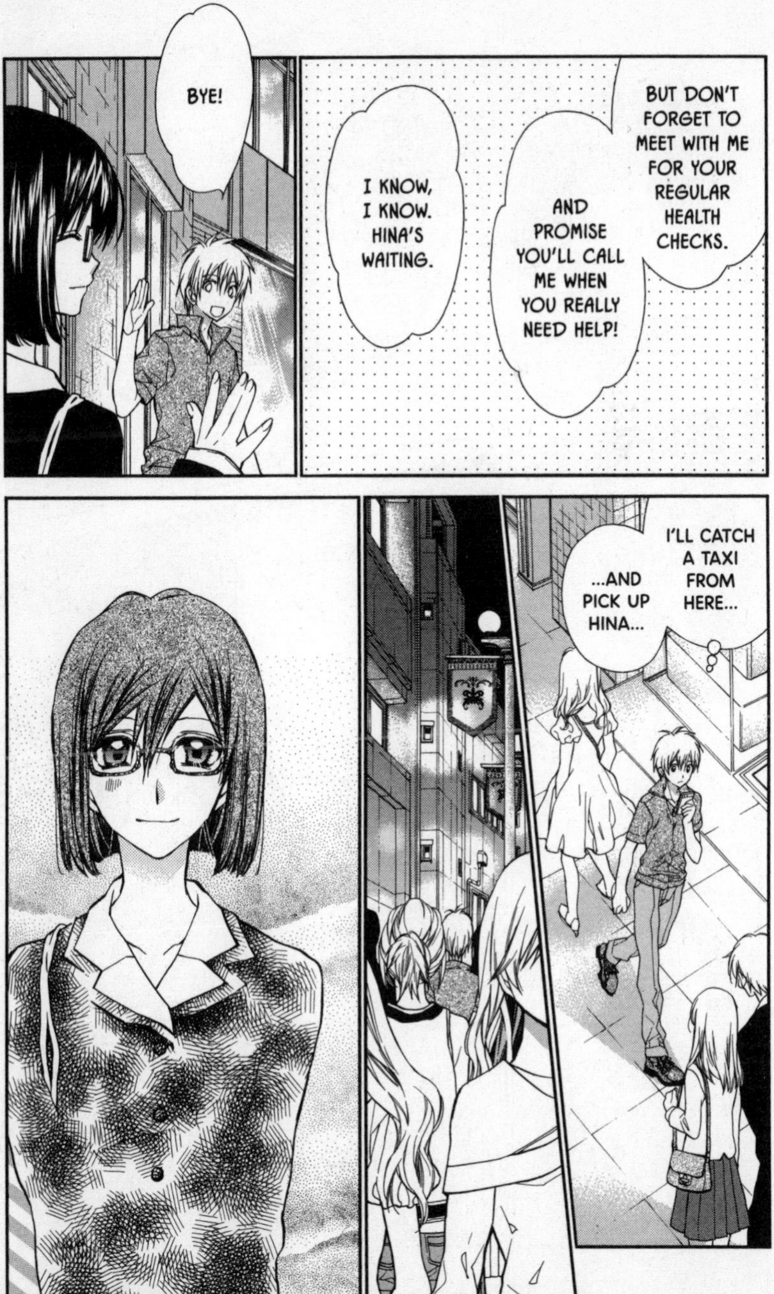
BUT DON'T FORGET TO MEET WITH ME FOR YOUR REGULAR HEALTH CHECKS.
AND PROMISE YOU'LL CALL ME WHEN YOU REALLY NEED HELP!
I KNOW, I KNOW. HINA'S WAITING.
BYE!
I'LL CATCH A TAXI FROM HERE...
...AND PICK UP HINA...

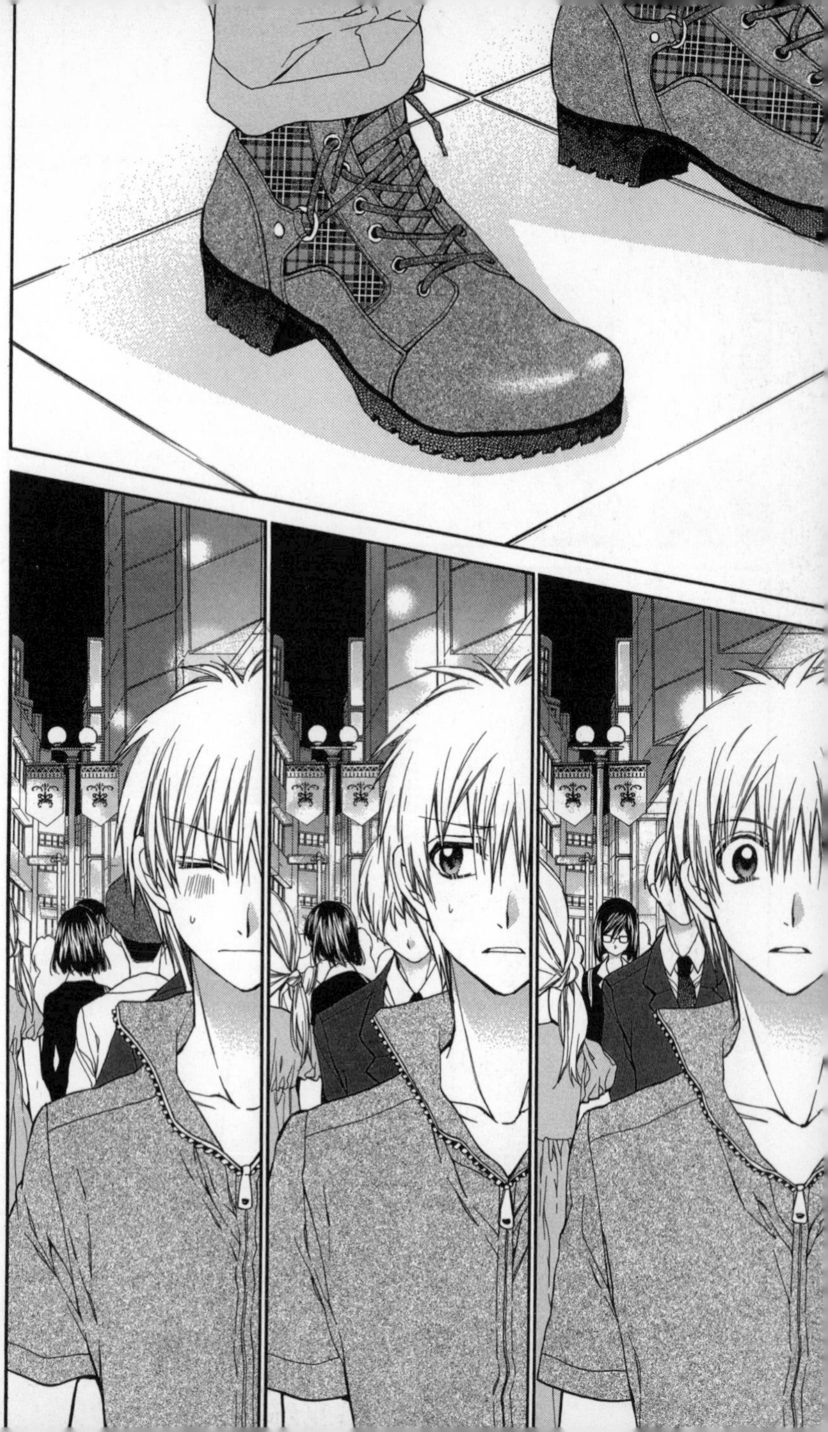

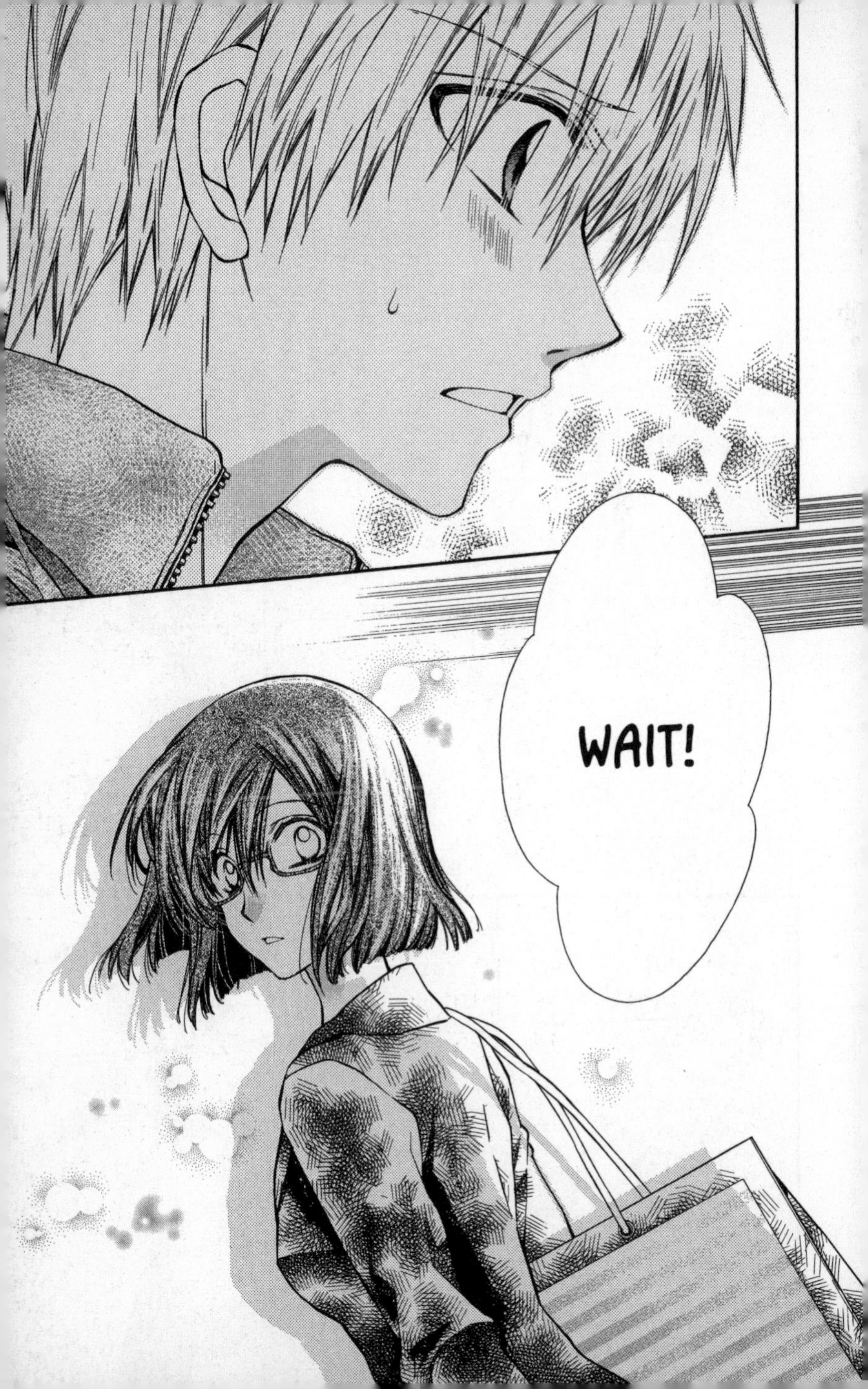
WAIT!

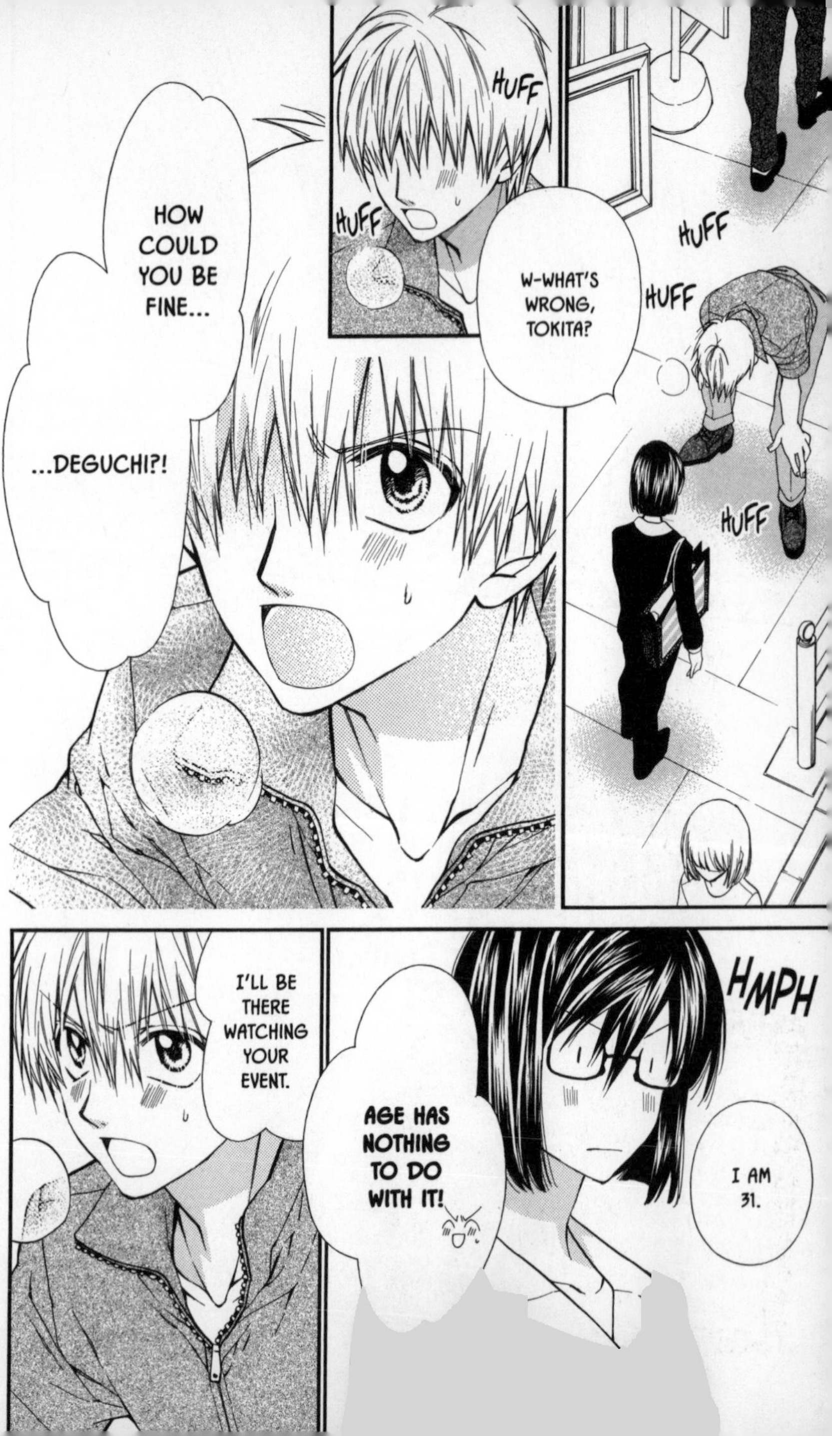
HUFF
HUFF
HUFF
W-WHAT'S WRONG, TOKITA?
HUFF
HUFF
HOW COULD YOU BE FINE...
...DEGUCHI?!
HMPH
I AM 31.
AGE HAS NOTHING TO DO WITH IT!
I'LL BE THERE WATCHING YOUR EVENT.

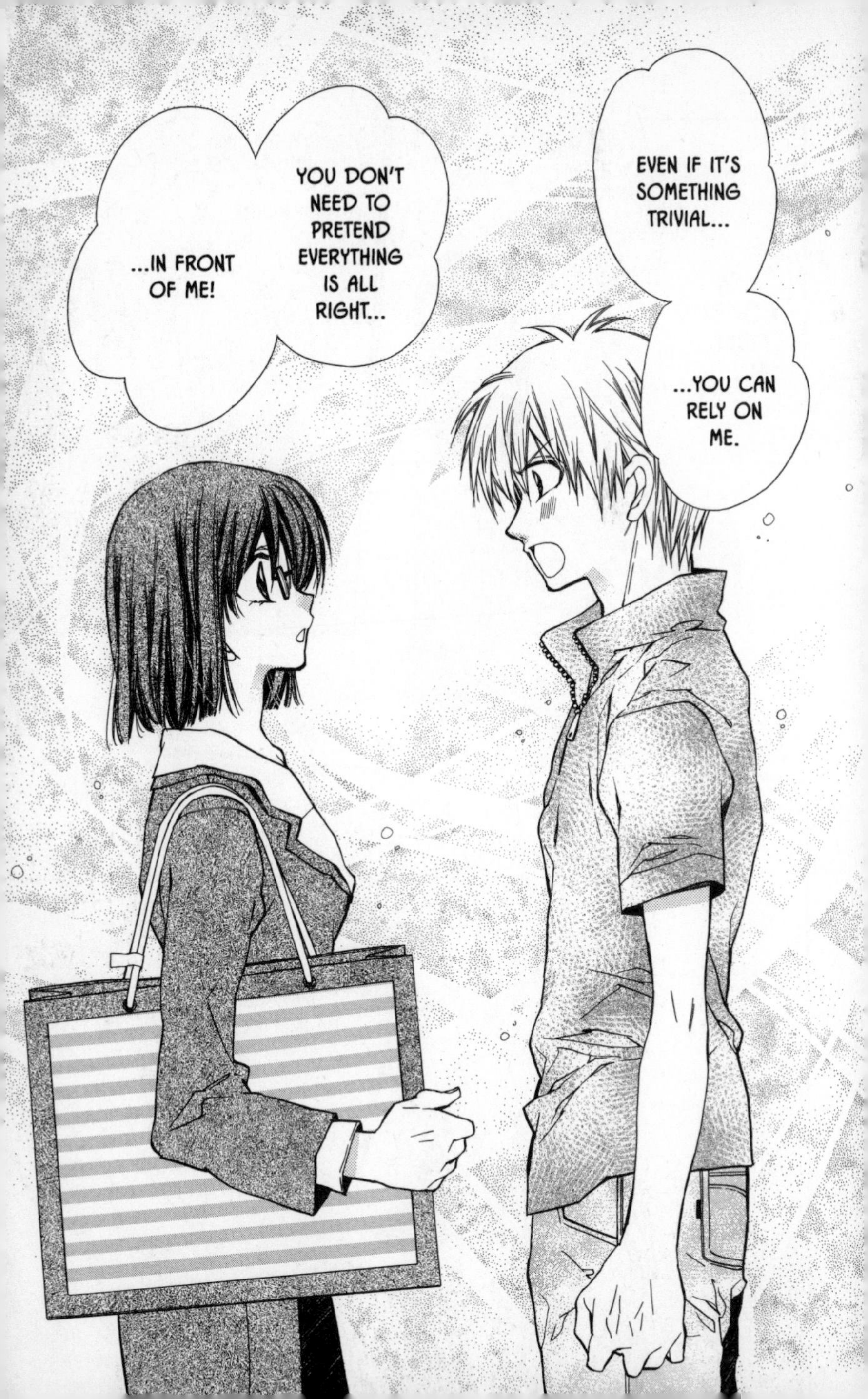
EVEN IF IT'S SOMETHING TRIVIAL...
...YOU CAN RELY ON ME.
YOU DON'T NEED TO PRETEND EVERYTHING IS ALL RIGHT...
...IN FRONT OF ME!

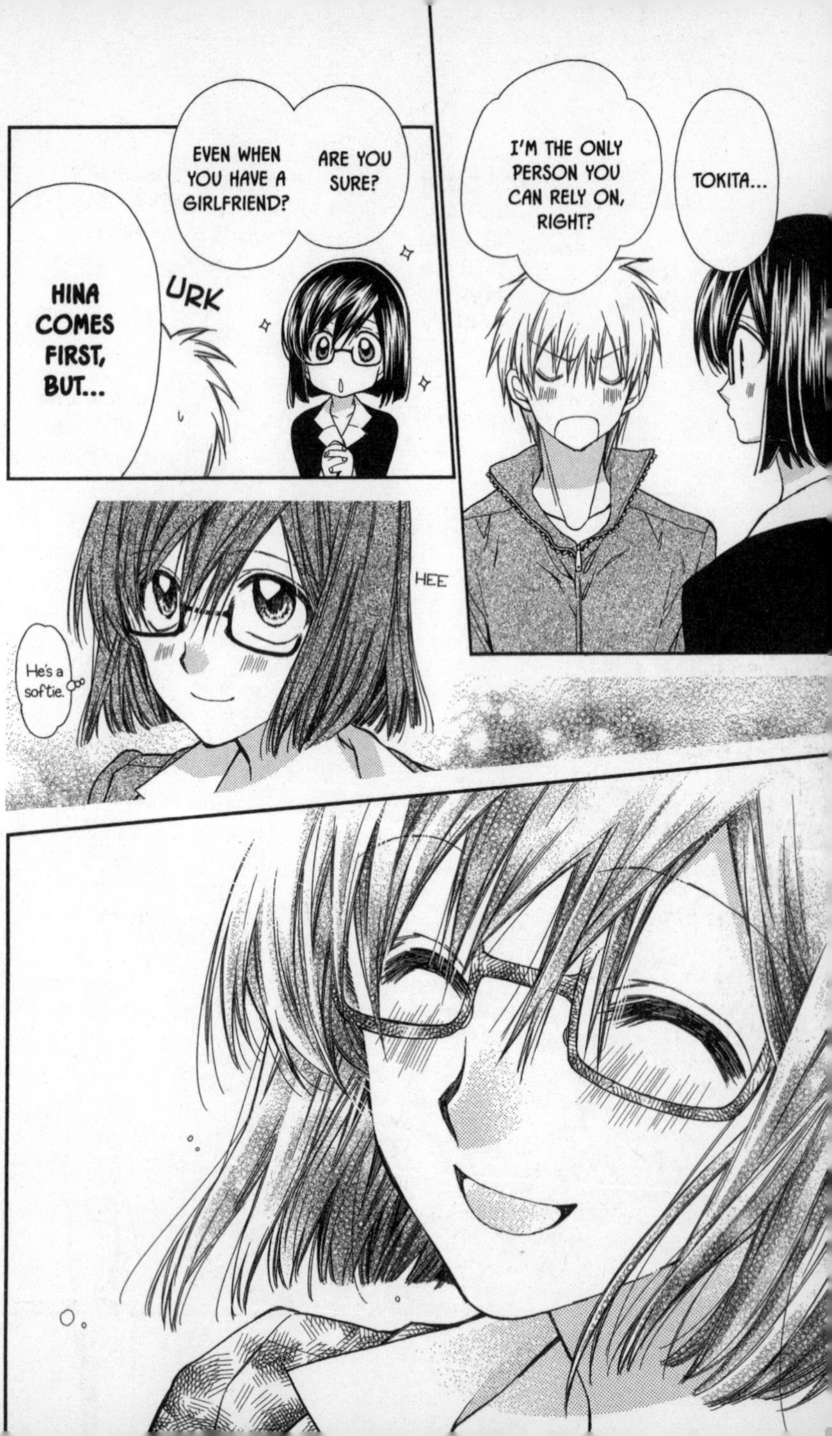
TOKITA...
I'M THE ONLY PERSON YOU CAN RELY ON, RIGHT?
ARE YOU SURE?
EVEN WHEN YOU HAVE A GIRLFRIEND?
URK
HINA COMES FIRST, BUT...
HEE
He's a softie.

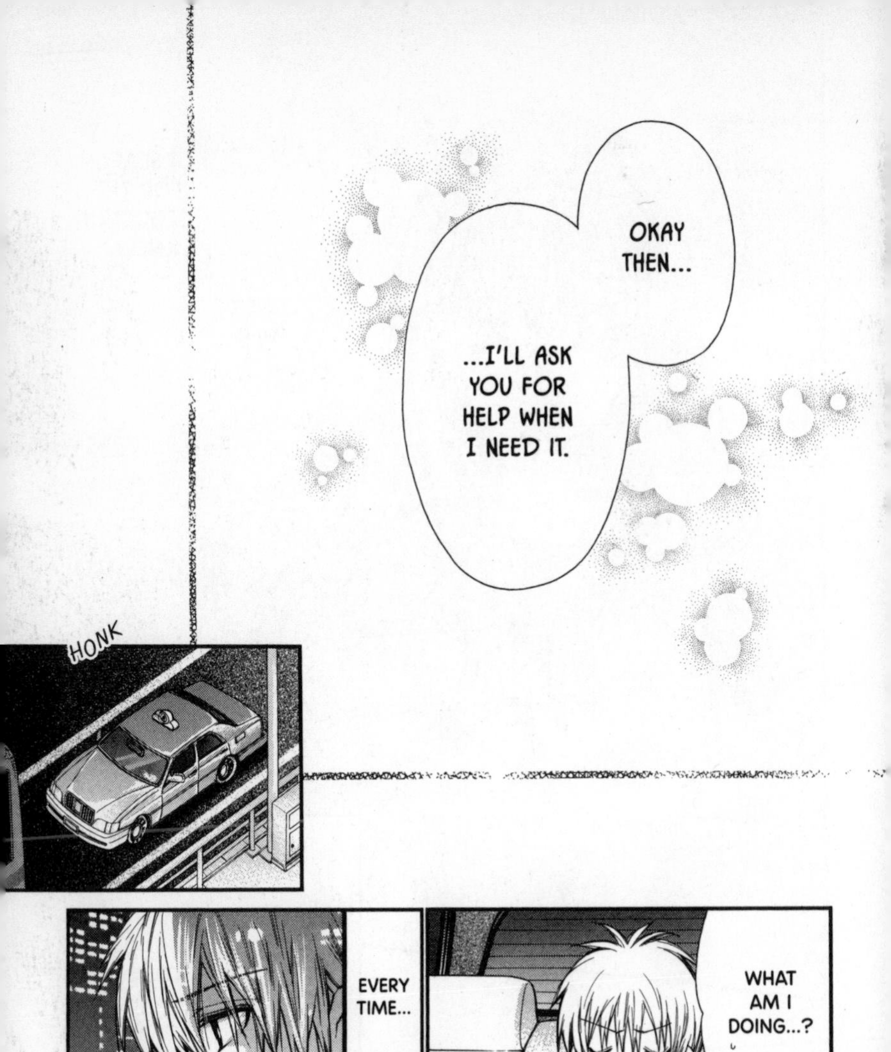
OKAY THEN...
...I'LL ASK YOU FOR HELP WHEN I NEED IT.
HONK
WHAT AM I DOING...?
EVERY TIME...
...I SEE HER...

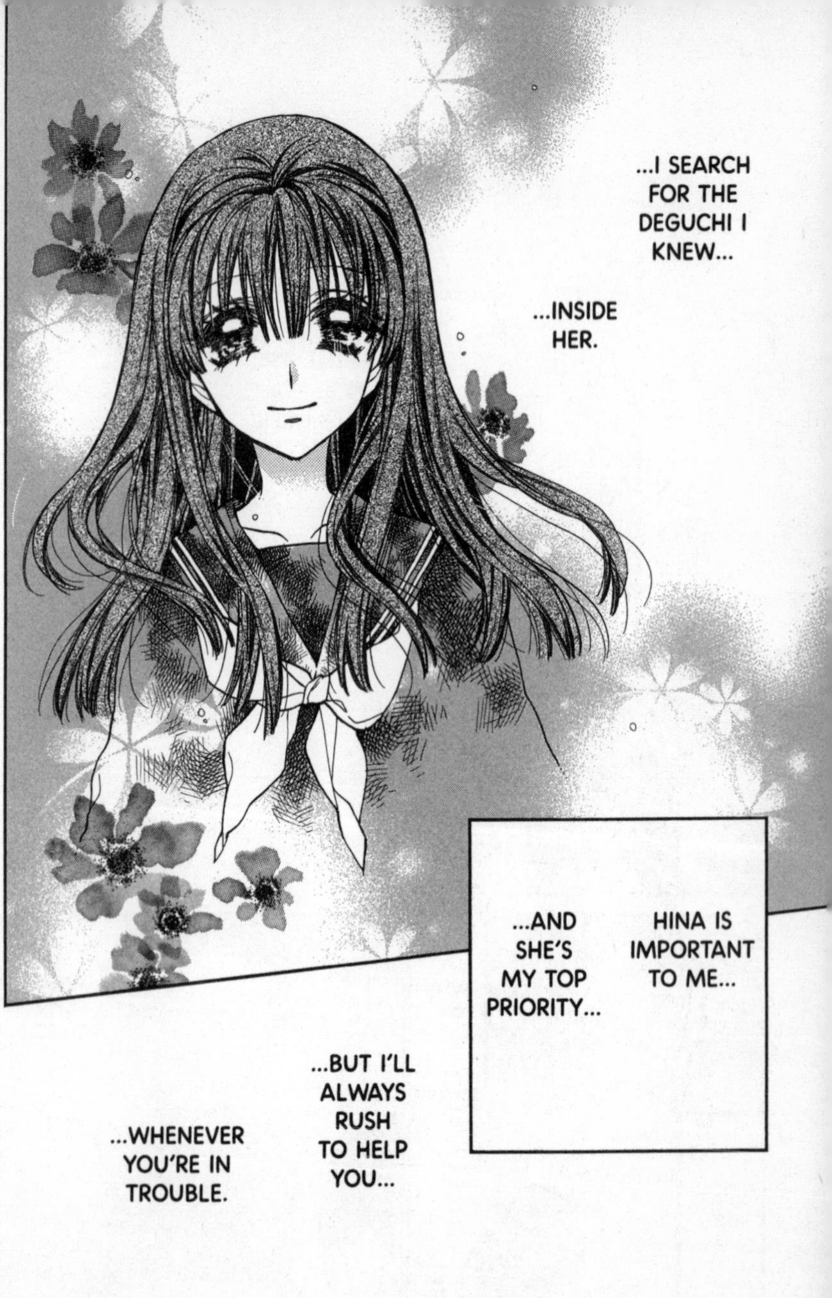
...I SEARCH FOR THE DEGUCHI I KNEW...
...INSIDE HER.
HINA IS IMPORTANT TO ME...
...AND SHE'S MY TOP PRIORITY...
...BUT I'LL ALWAYS RUSH TO HELP YOU...
...WHENEVER YOU'RE IN TROUBLE.

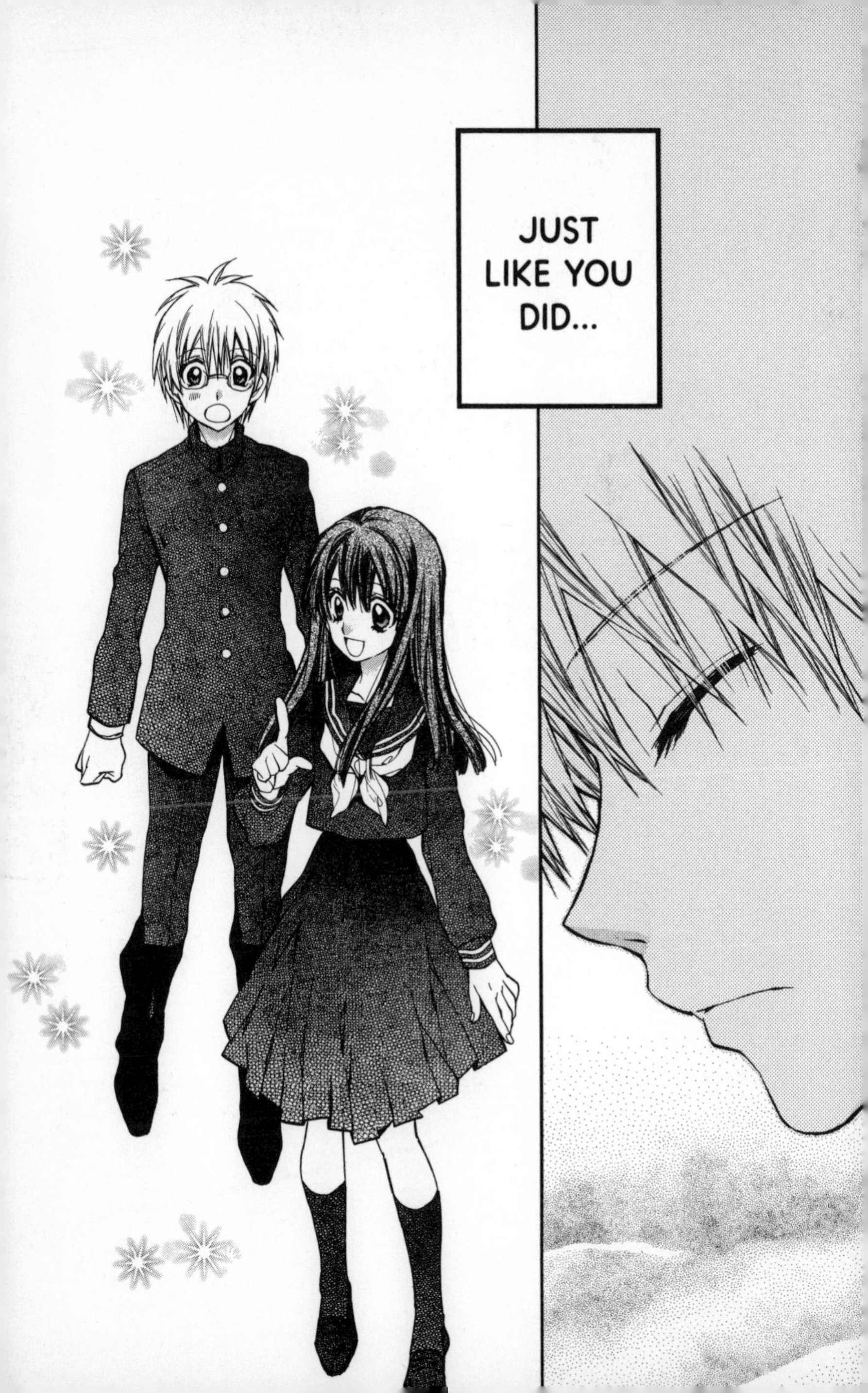
JUST
LIKE YOU
DID...

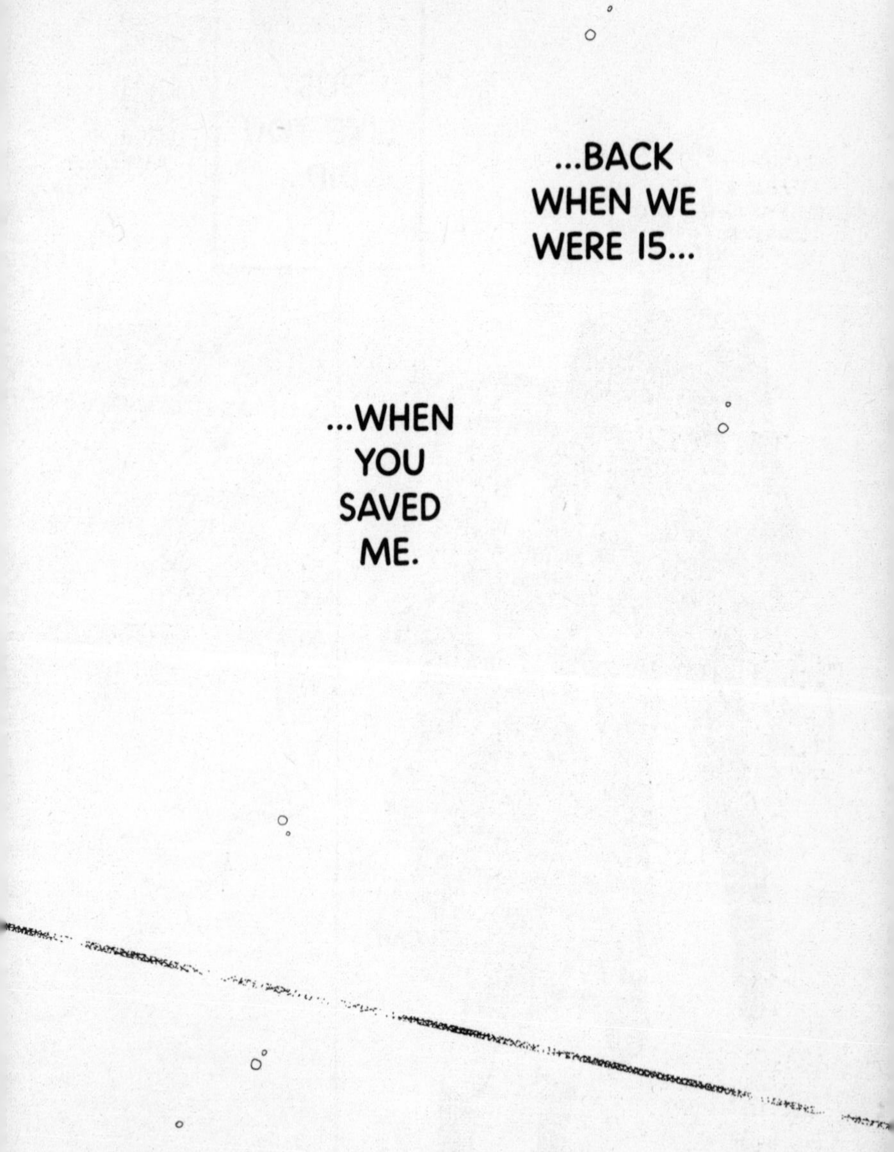
...BACK WHEN WE WERE 15...
...WHEN YOU SAVED ME.

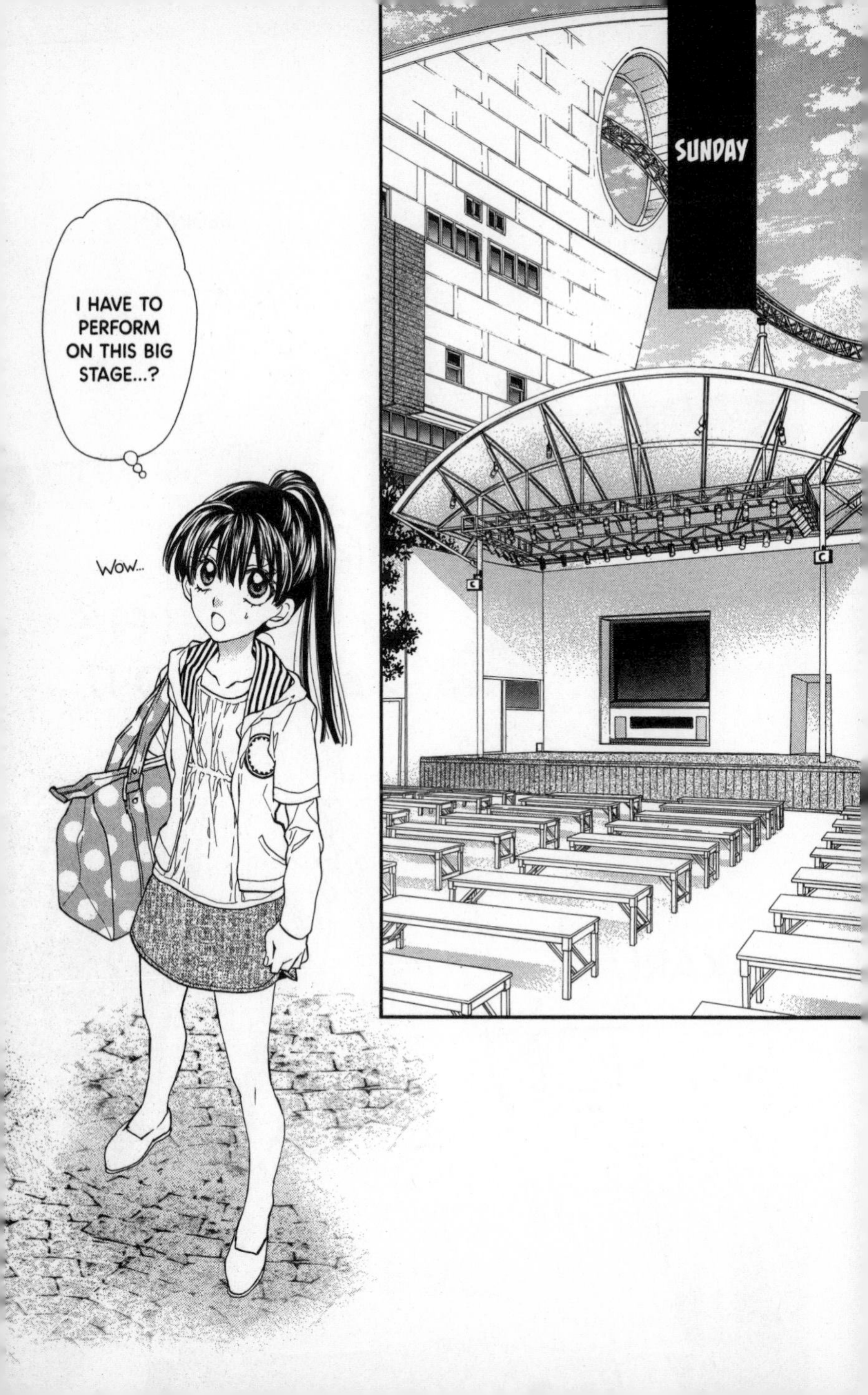
SUNDAY
I HAVE TO PERFORM ON THIS BIG STAGE...?
WOW...

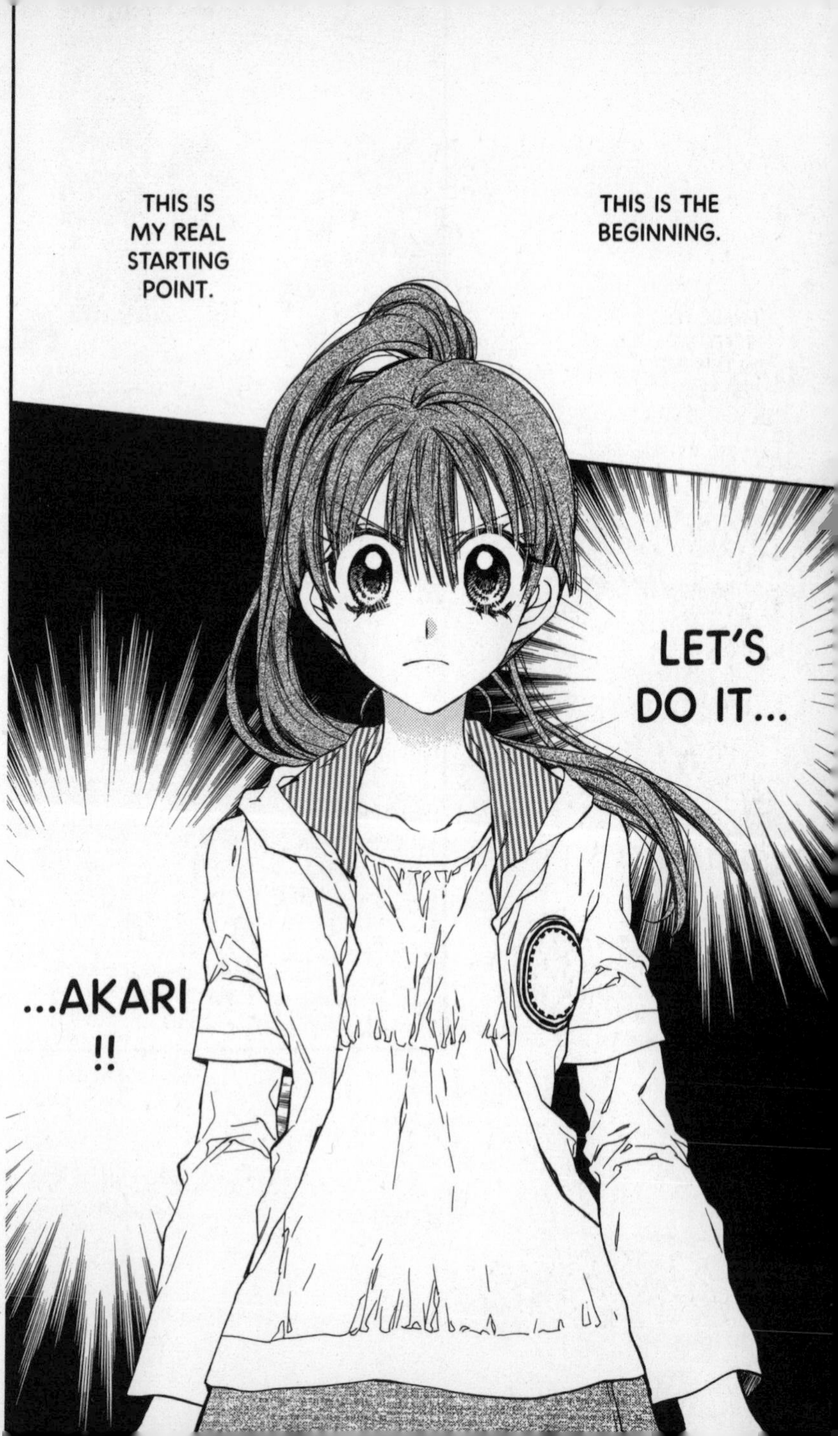
THIS IS THE BEGINNING.
THIS IS MY REAL STARTING POINT.
LET'S DO IT...
...AKARI !!

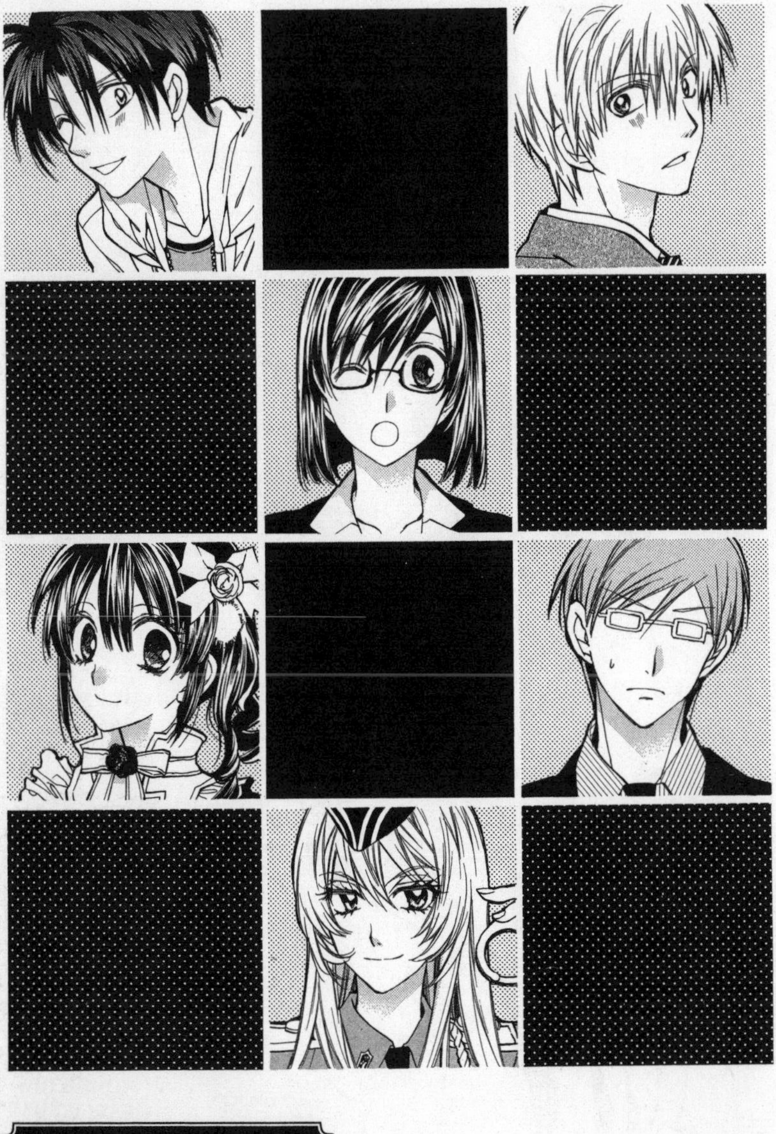

Chapter 10

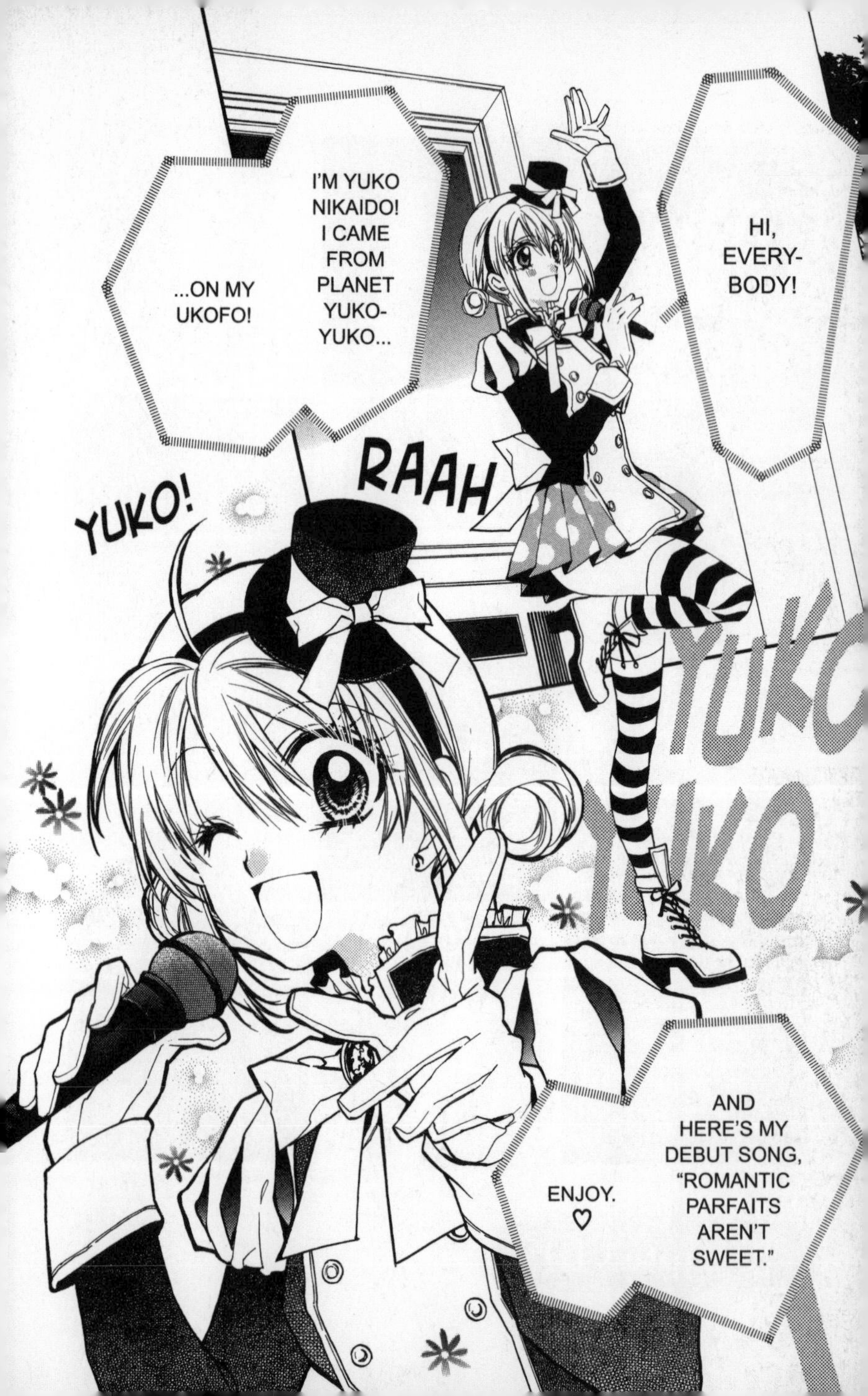
HI, EVERYBODY!
I'M YUKO NIKAIDO! I CAME FROM PLANET YUKO-YUKO...
...ON MY UKOFO!
RAAH
YUKO!
YUKO YUKO
AND HERE'S MY DEBUT SONG, "ROMANTIC PARFAITS AREN'T SWEET."
ENJOY. ♡

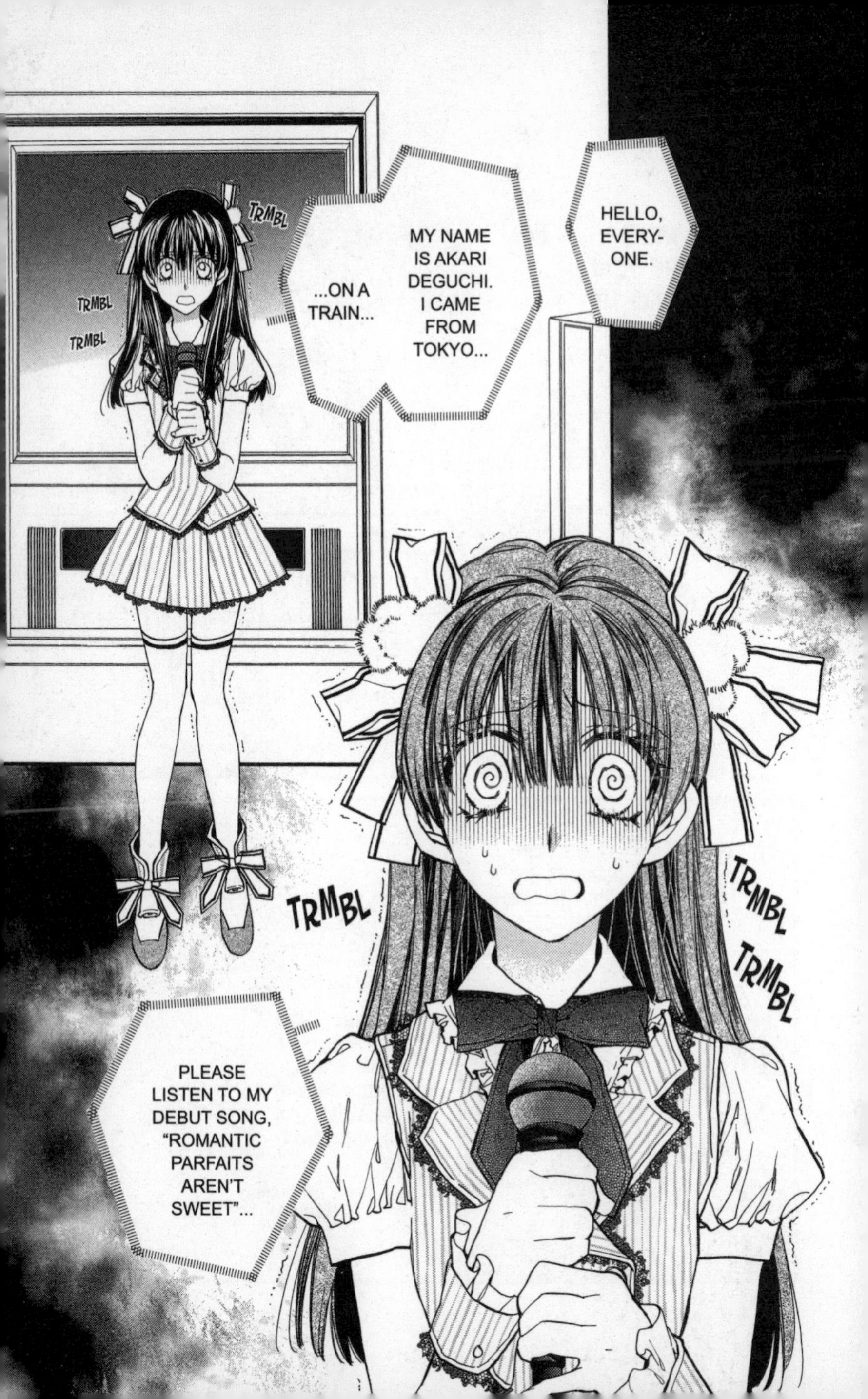
HELLO, EVERYONE.
MY NAME IS AKARI DEGUCHI. I CAME FROM TOKYO...
...ON A TRAIN...
TRMBL
TRMBL
TRMBL
TRMBL
TRMBL
TRMBL
PLEASE LISTEN TO MY DEBUT SONG, "ROMANTIC PARFAITS AREN'T SWEET"...

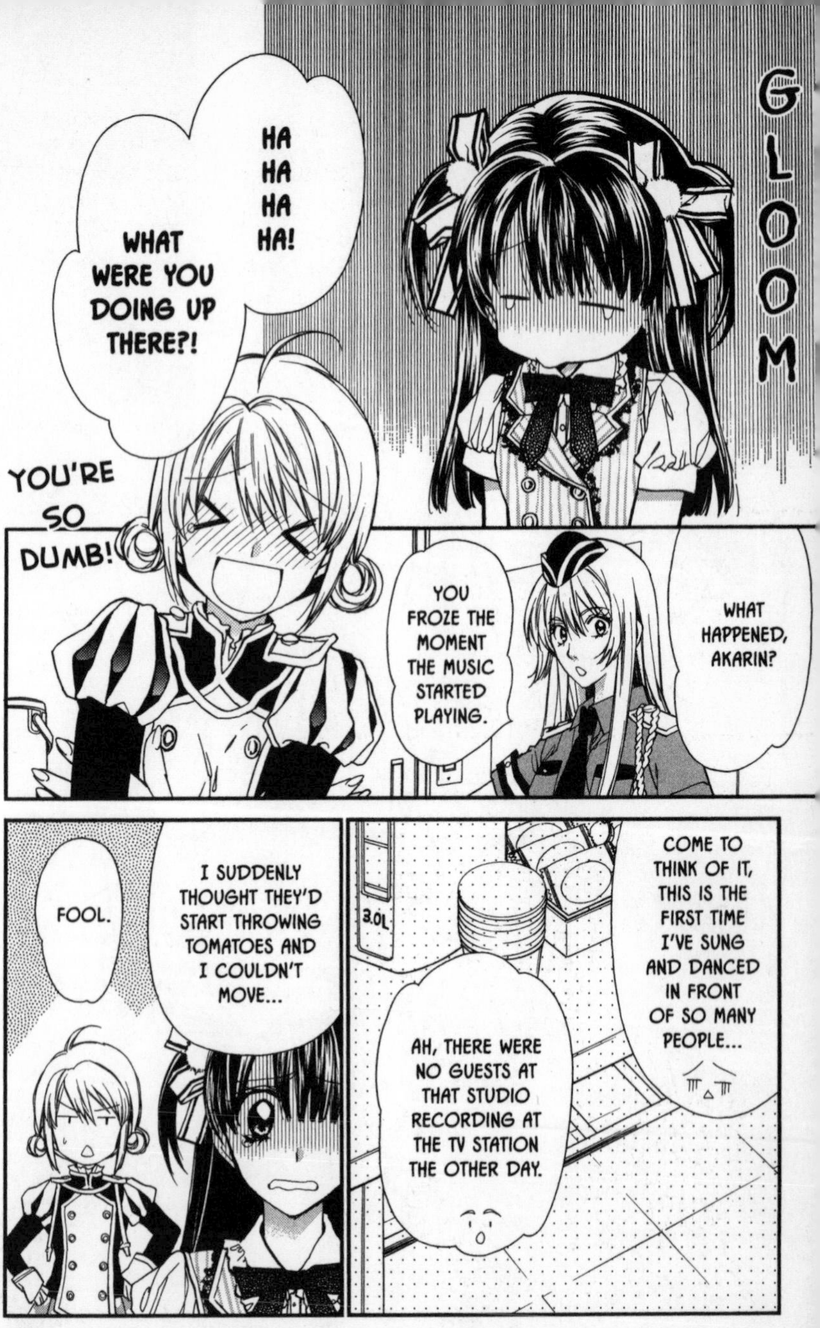
GLOOM
HA HA HA HA!
WHAT WERE YOU DOING UP THERE?!
YOU'RE SO DUMB!
WHAT HAPPENED, AKARIN?
YOU FROZE THE MOMENT THE MUSIC STARTED PLAYING.
COME TO THINK OF IT, THIS IS THE FIRST TIME I'VE SUNG AND DANCED IN FRONT OF SO MANY PEOPLE...
AH, THERE WERE NO GUESTS AT THAT STUDIO RECORDING AT THE TV STATION THE OTHER DAY.
I SUDDENLY THOUGHT THEY'D START THROWING TOMATOES AND I COULDN'T MOVE...
FOOL.

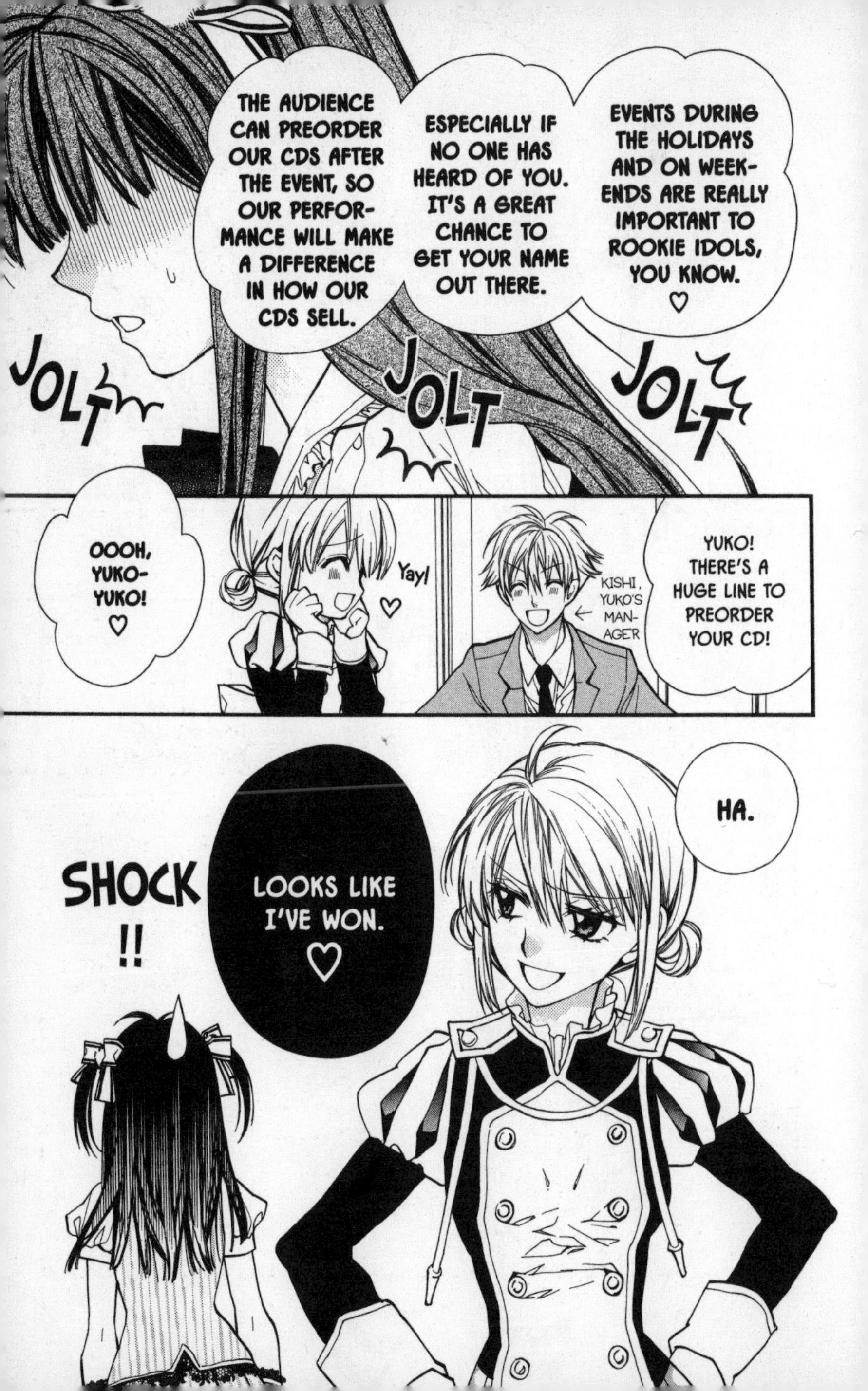
EVENTS DURING THE HOLIDAYS AND ON WEEK-ENDS ARE REALLY IMPORTANT TO ROOKIE IDOLS, YOU KNOW. ♡
ESPECIALLY IF NO ONE HAS HEARD OF YOU. IT'S A GREAT CHANCE TO GET YOUR NAME OUT THERE.
THE AUDIENCE CAN PREORDER OUR CDS AFTER THE EVENT, SO OUR PERFOR-MANCE WILL MAKE A DIFFERENCE IN HOW OUR CDS SELL.
JOLT
JOLT
JOLT
YUKO! THERE'S A HUGE LINE TO PREORDER YOUR CD!
KISHI, YUKO'S MAN-AGER
Yay! ♡
OOOH, YUKO-YUKO! ♡
HA.
LOOKS LIKE I'VE WON. ♡
SHOCK !!

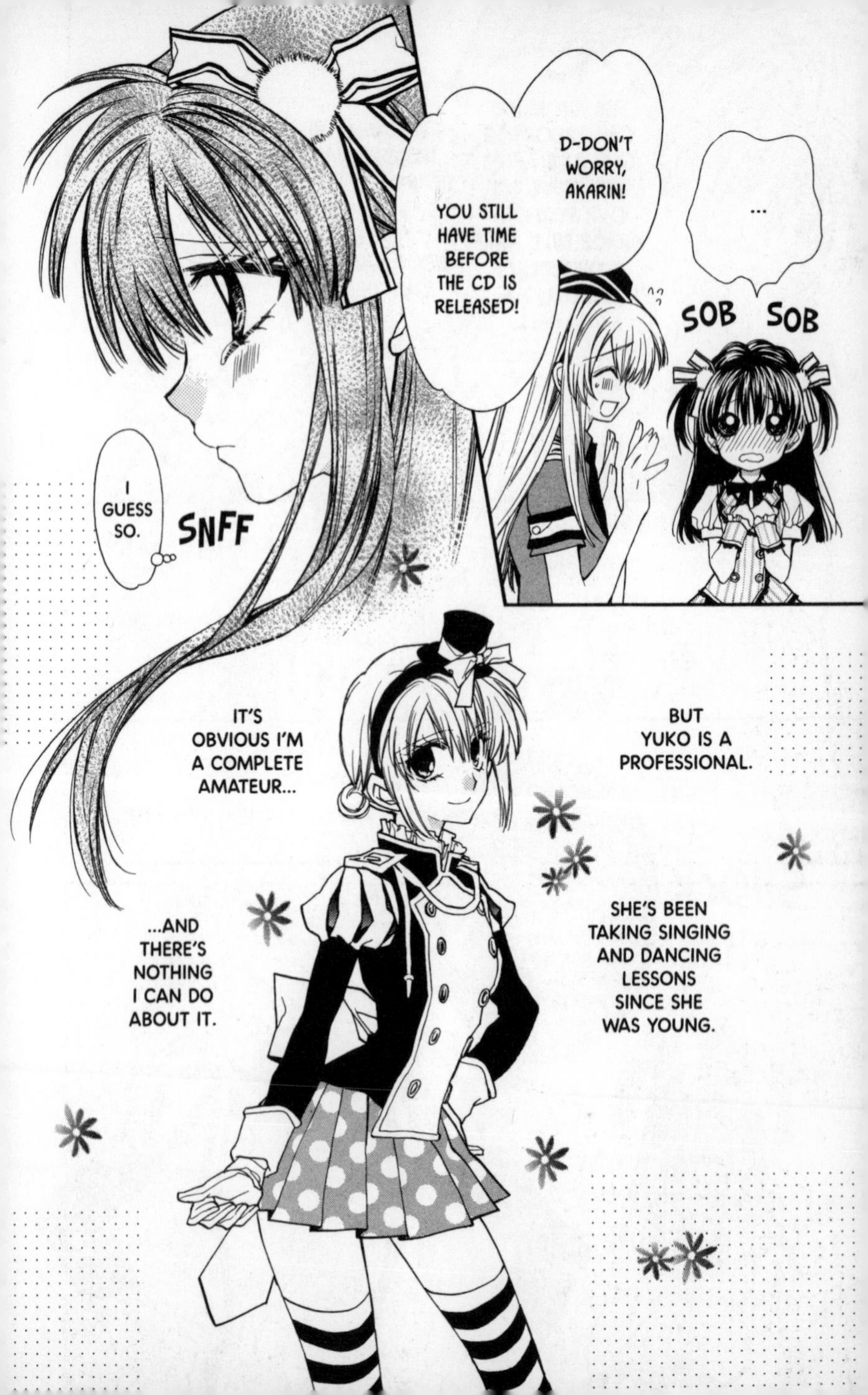
...
SOB SOB
D-DON'T WORRY, AKARIN!
YOU STILL HAVE TIME BEFORE THE CD IS RELEASED!
I GUESS SO.
SNFF
BUT YUKO IS A PROFESSIONAL.
SHE'S BEEN TAKING SINGING AND DANCING LESSONS SINCE SHE WAS YOUNG.
IT'S OBVIOUS I'M A COMPLETE AMATEUR...
...AND THERE'S NOTHING I CAN DO ABOUT IT.

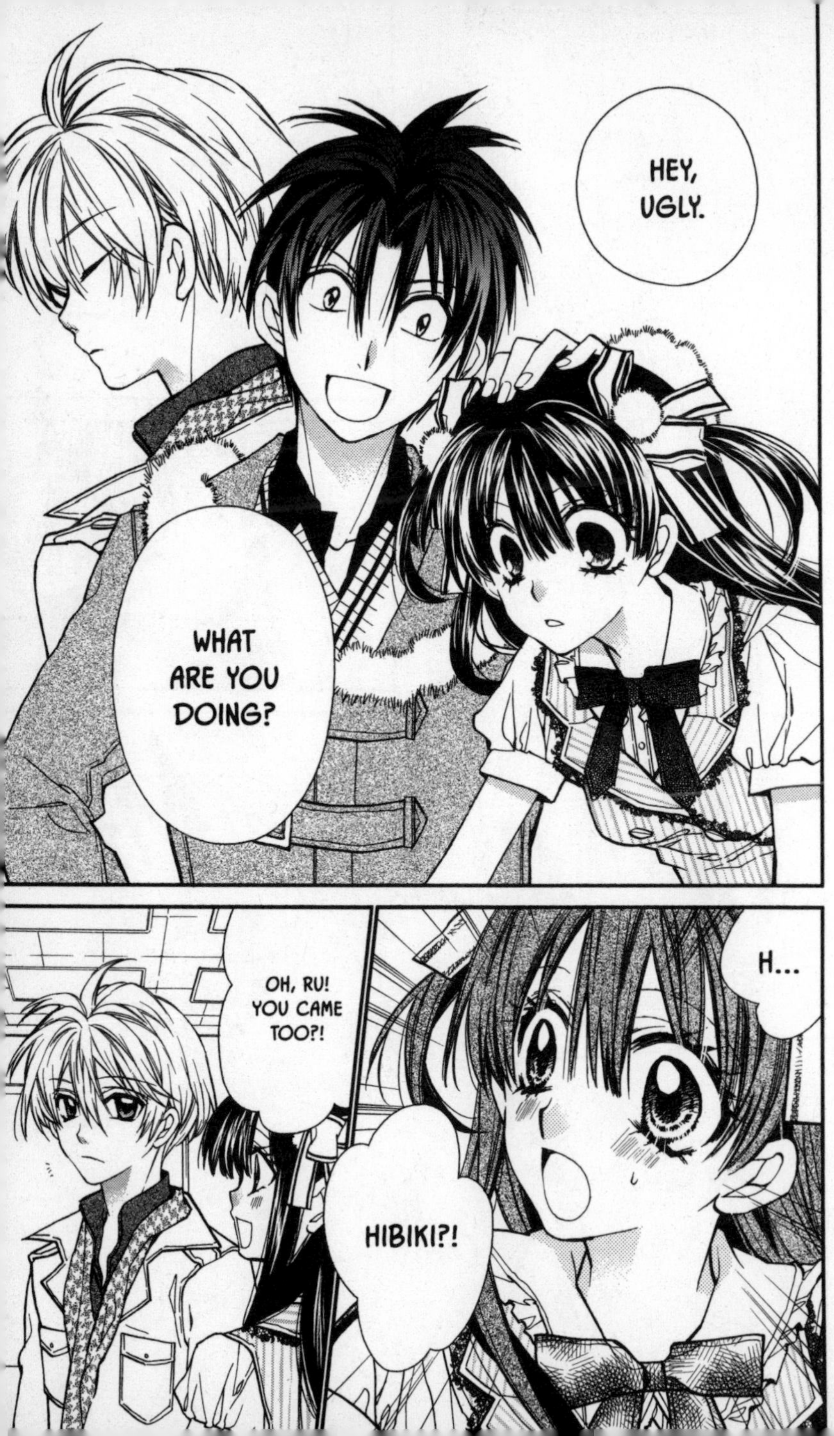
HEY, UGLY.
WHAT ARE YOU DOING?
H...
HIBIKI?!
OH, RU! YOU CAME TOO?!

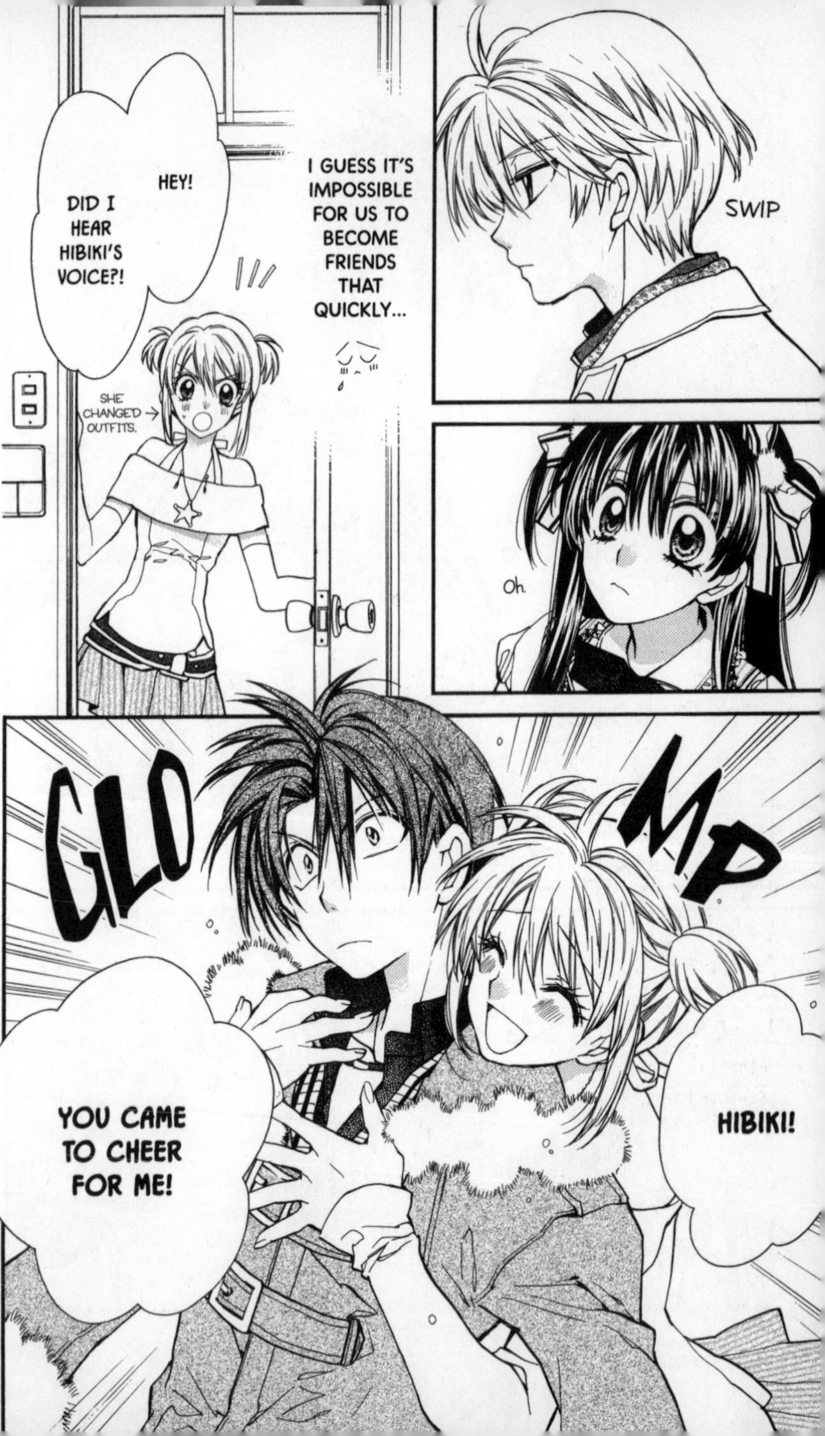
SWIP
Oh.
I GUESS IT'S IMPOSSIBLE FOR US TO BECOME FRIENDS THAT QUICKLY...
HEY! DID I HEAR HIBIKI'S VOICE?!
SHE CHANGED OUTFITS.
HIBIKI!
GLOMP
YOU CAME TO CHEER FOR ME!

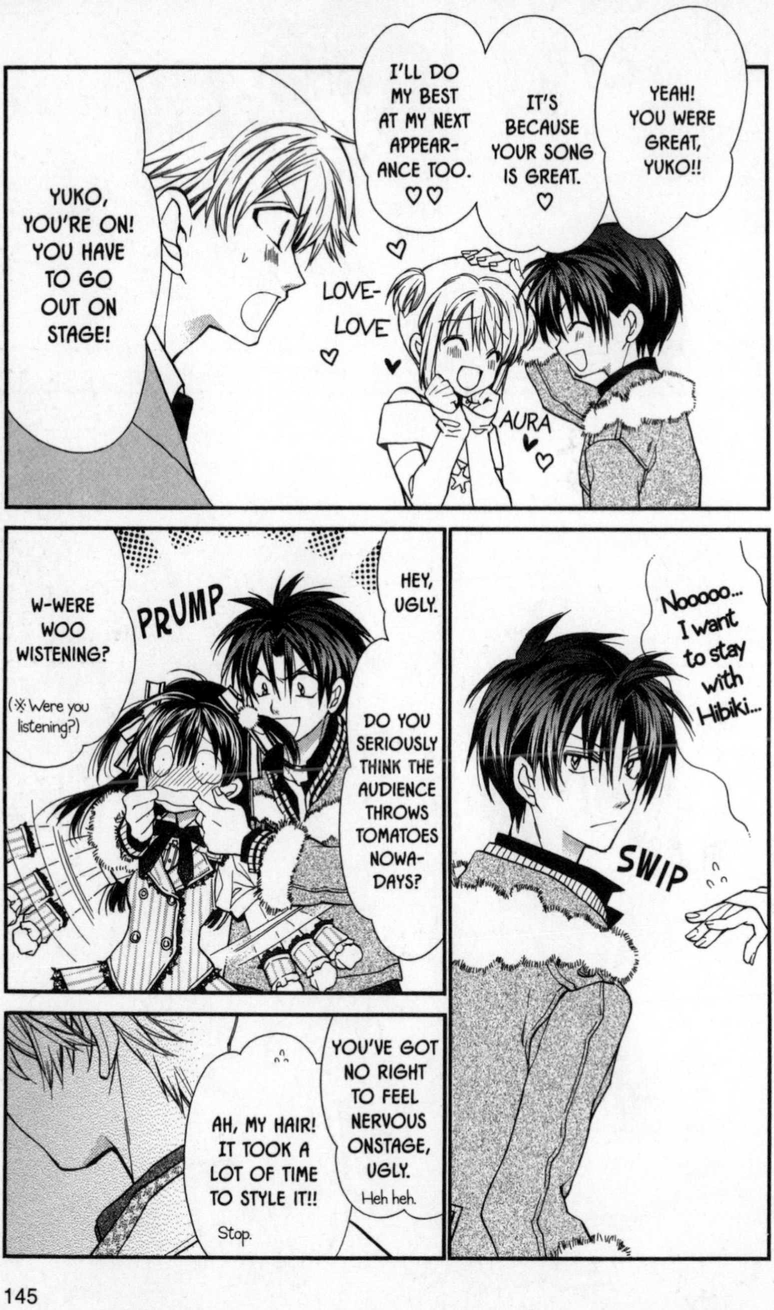
YEAH! YOU WERE GREAT, YUKO!!
IT'S BECAUSE YOUR SONG IS GREAT. ♡
I'LL DO MY BEST AT MY NEXT APPEARANCE TOO. ♡♡
LOVE-LOVE
AURA
YUKO, YOU'RE ON! YOU HAVE TO GO OUT ON STAGE!
Nooooo... I want to stay with Hibiki...
SWIP
HEY, UGLY.
DO YOU SERIOUSLY THINK THE AUDIENCE THROWS TOMATOES NOWADAYS?
PRUMP
W-WERE WOO WISTENING?
(※ Were you listening?)
YOU'VE GOT NO RIGHT TO FEEL NERVOUS ONSTAGE, UGLY.
Heh heh.
AH, MY HAIR! IT TOOK A LOT OF TIME TO STYLE IT!!
Stop.

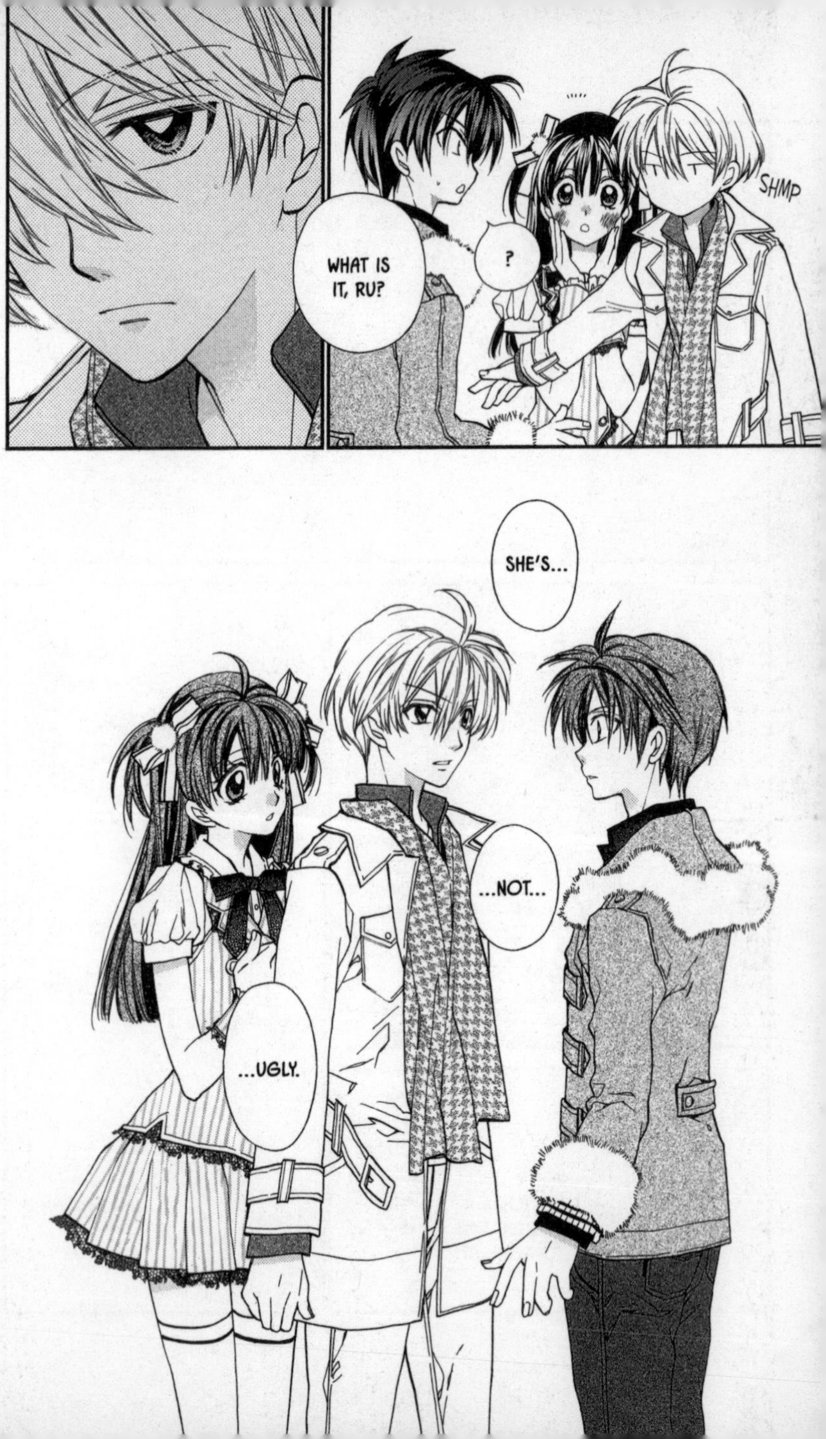
SHMP
?
WHAT IS IT, RU?
SHE'S...
...NOT...
...UGLY.

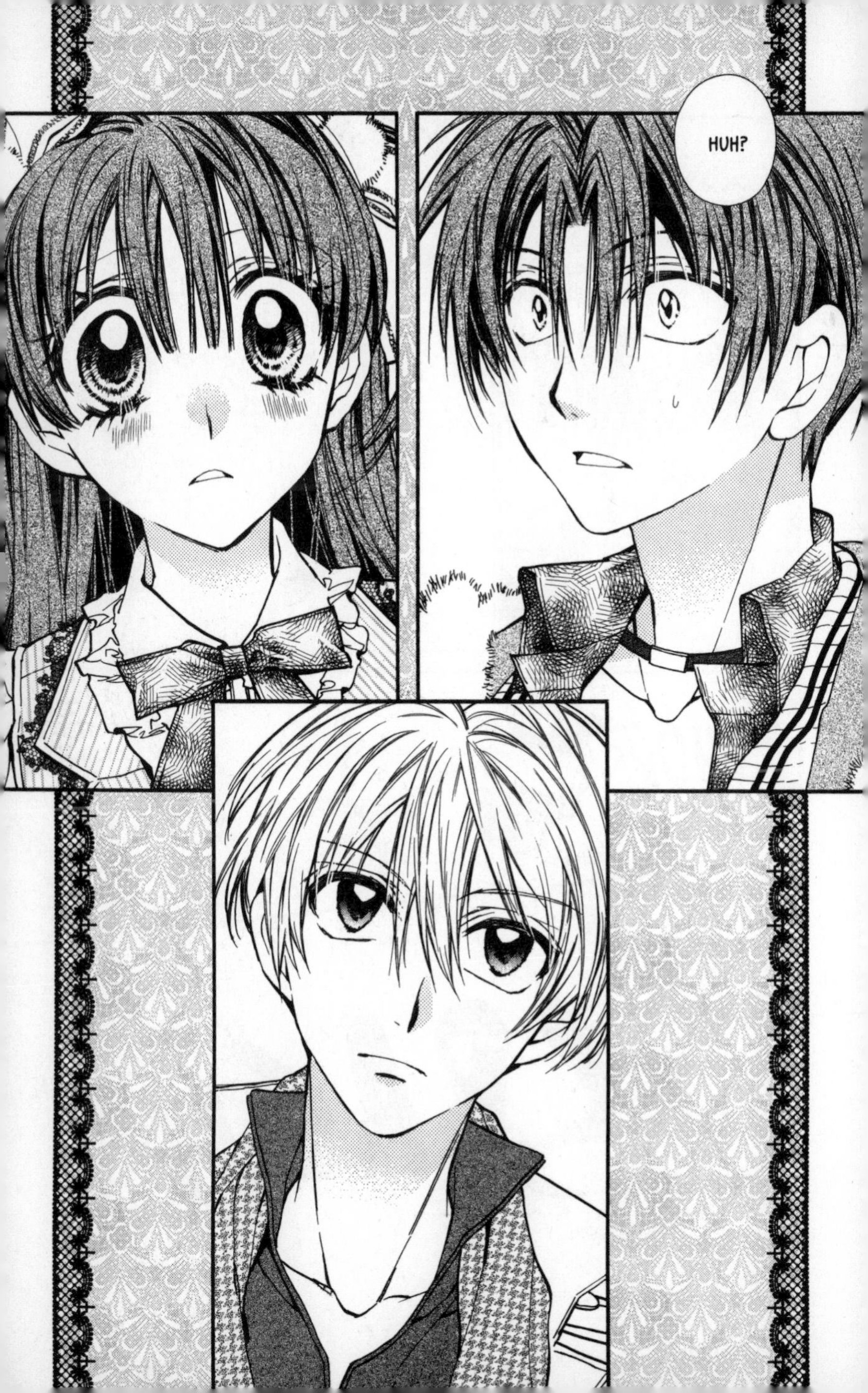
HUH?

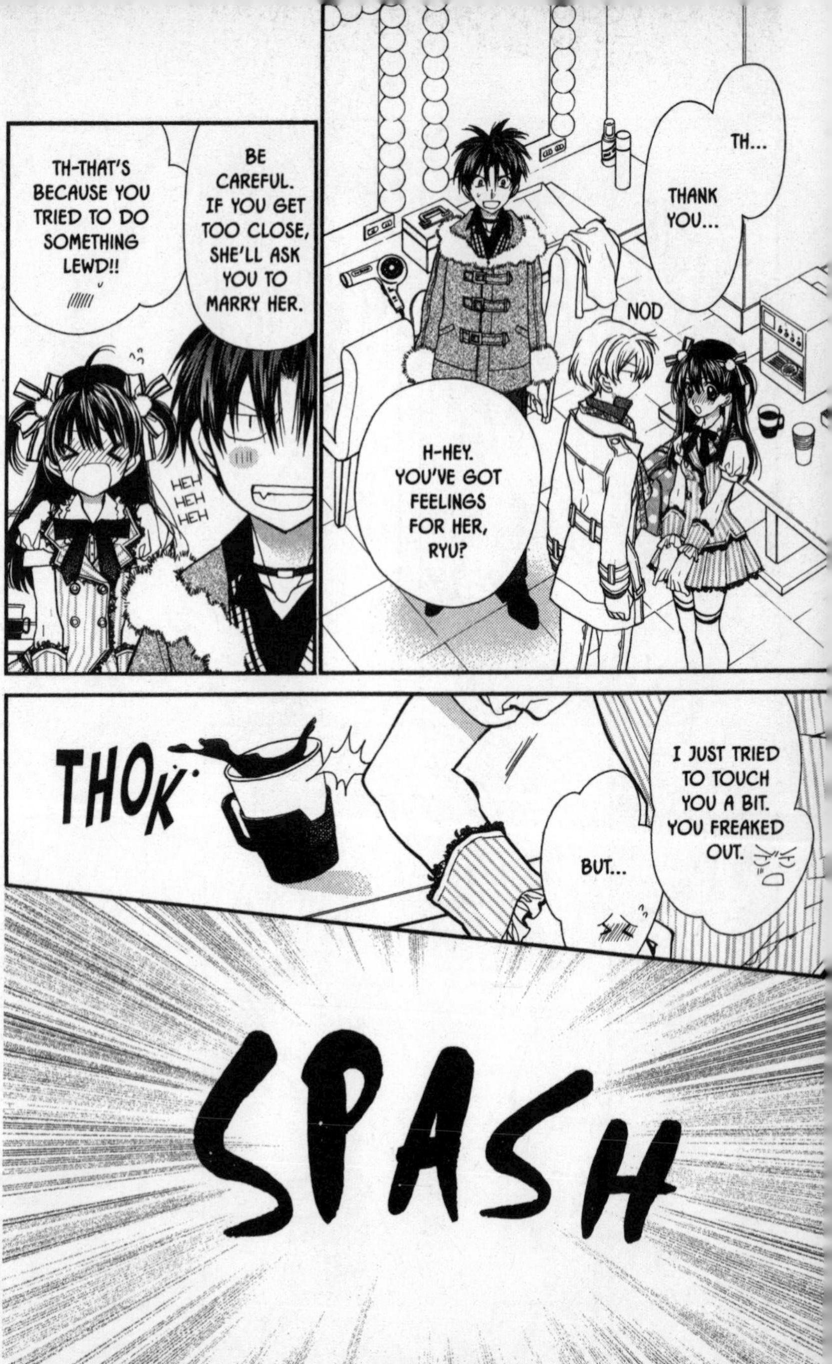
TH...
THANK YOU...
NOD
H-HEY. YOU'VE GOT FEELINGS FOR HER, RYU?
BE CAREFUL. IF YOU GET TOO CLOSE, SHE'LL ASK YOU TO MARRY HER.
TH-THAT'S BECAUSE YOU TRIED TO DO SOMETHING LEWD!!
HEH HEH HEH
I JUST TRIED TO TOUCH YOU A BIT. YOU FREAKED OUT.
BUT...
THOK
SPASH

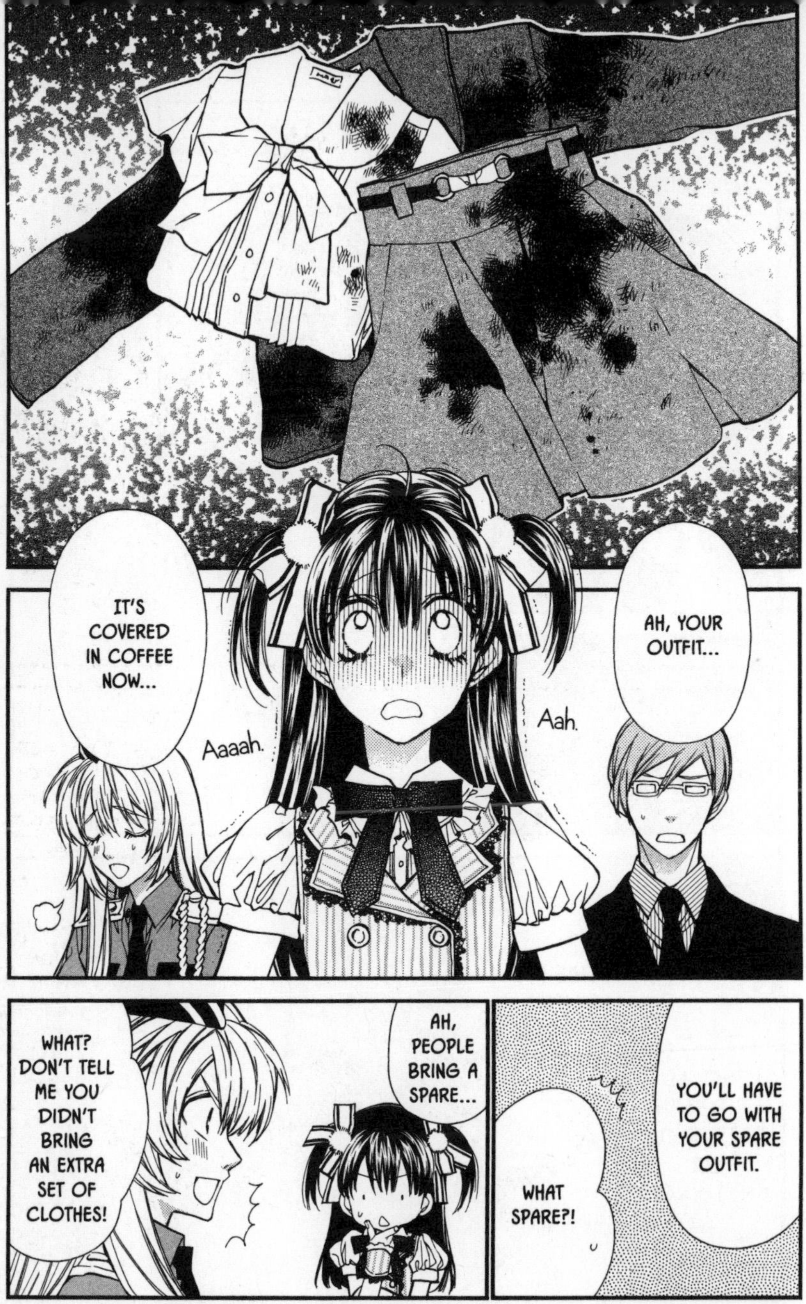
AH, YOUR OUTFIT...
Aah.
IT'S COVERED IN COFFEE NOW...
Aaaah.
YOU'LL HAVE TO GO WITH YOUR SPARE OUTFIT.
WHAT SPARE?!
AH, PEOPLE BRING A SPARE...
WHAT? DON'T TELL ME YOU DIDN'T BRING AN EXTRA SET OF CLOTHES!

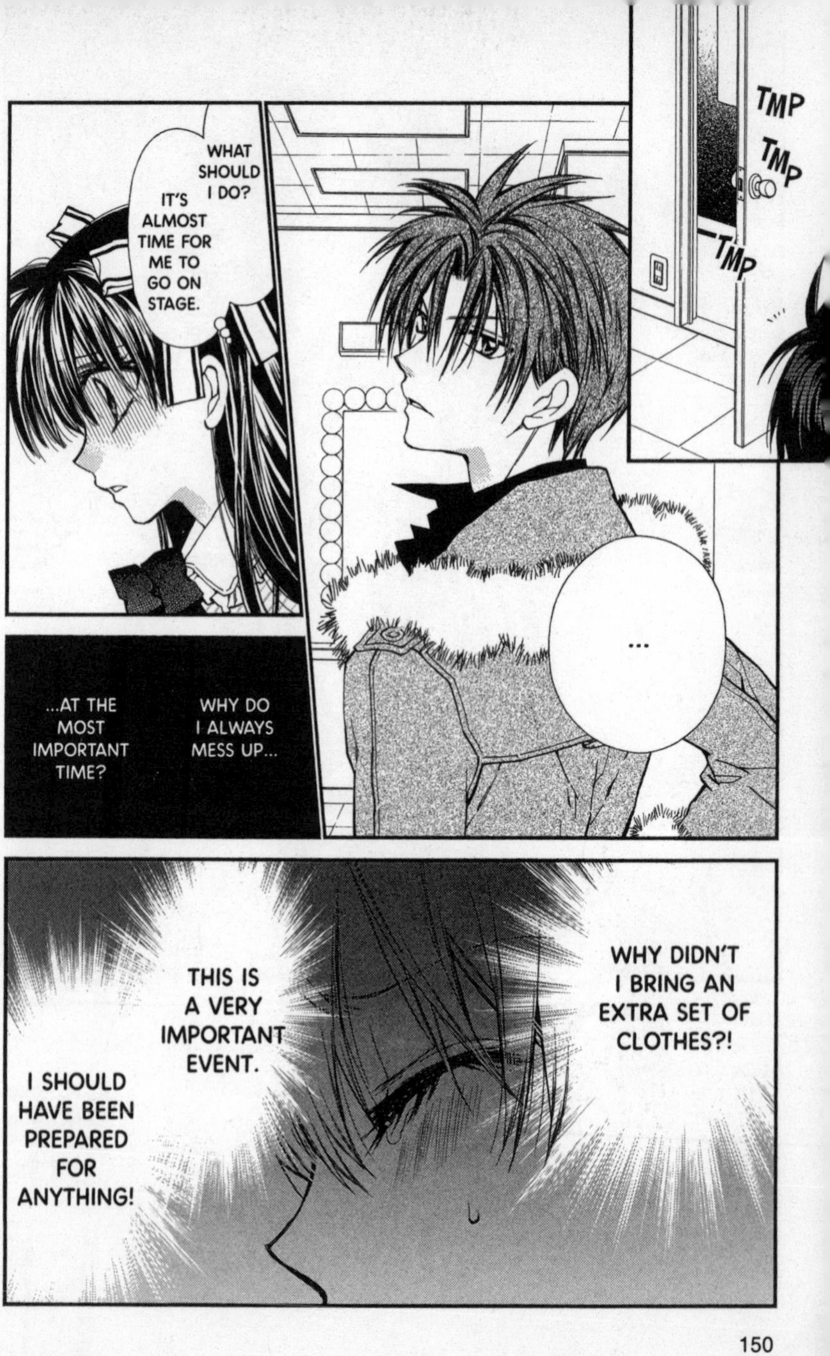
TMP
TMP
TMP
...
WHAT SHOULD I DO?
IT'S ALMOST TIME FOR ME TO GO ON STAGE.
WHY DO I ALWAYS MESS UP...
...AT THE MOST IMPORTANT TIME?
WHY DIDN'T I BRING AN EXTRA SET OF CLOTHES?!
THIS IS A VERY IMPORTANT EVENT.
I SHOULD HAVE BEEN PREPARED FOR ANYTHING!

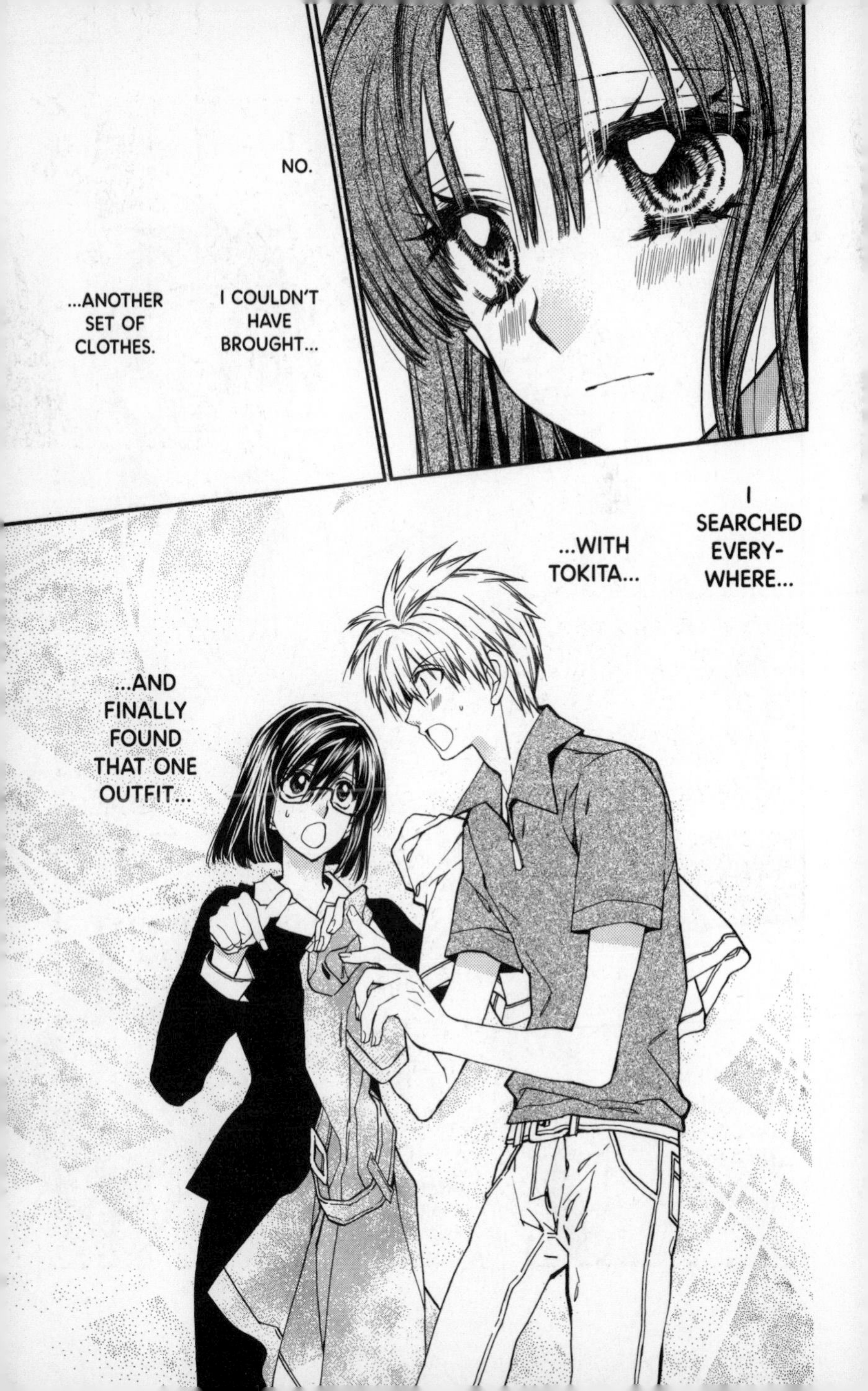
NO.
I COULDN'T HAVE BROUGHT...
...ANOTHER SET OF CLOTHES.
I SEARCHED EVERY-WHERE...
...WITH TOKITA...
...AND FINALLY FOUND THAT ONE OUTFIT...

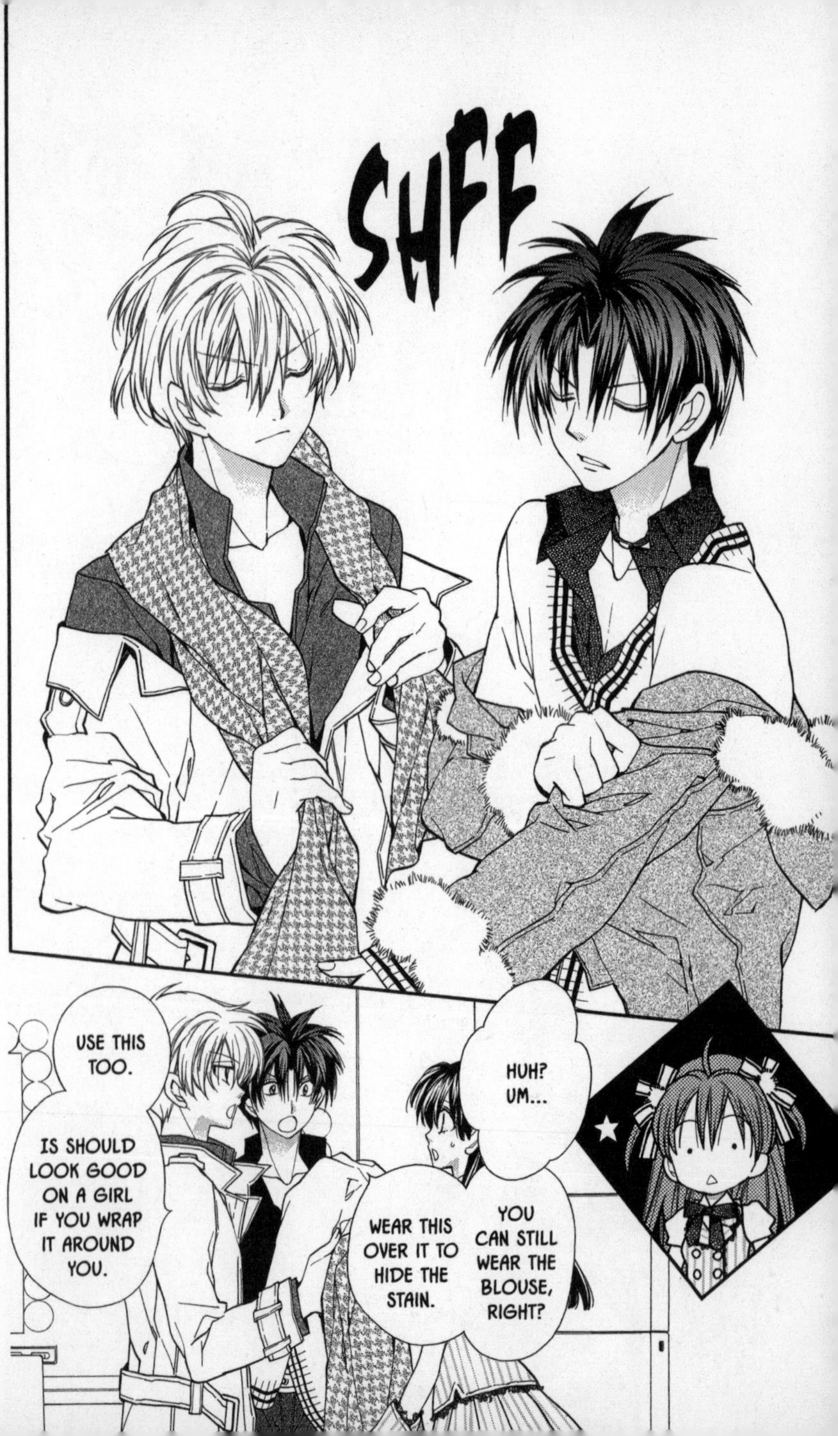
SHFF
HUH? UM...
YOU CAN STILL WEAR THE BLOUSE, RIGHT?
WEAR THIS OVER IT TO HIDE THE STAIN.
USE THIS TOO.
IS SHOULD LOOK GOOD ON A GIRL IF YOU WRAP IT AROUND YOU.

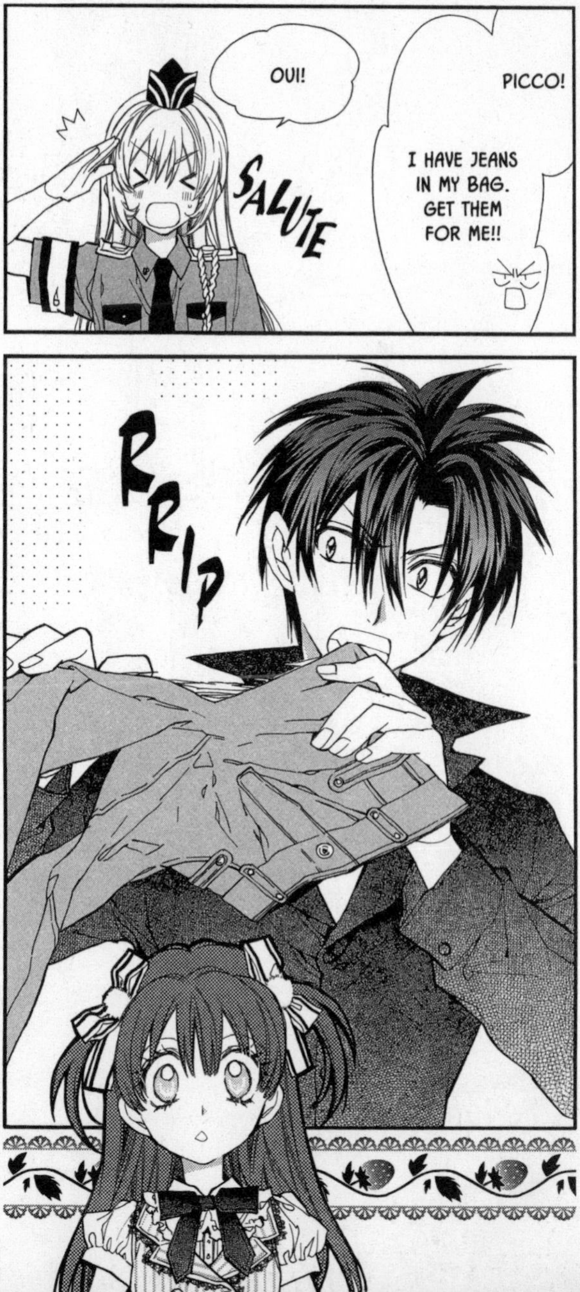
PICCO!
I HAVE JEANS IN MY BAG. GET THEM FOR ME!!
OUI!
SALUTE
RRIP

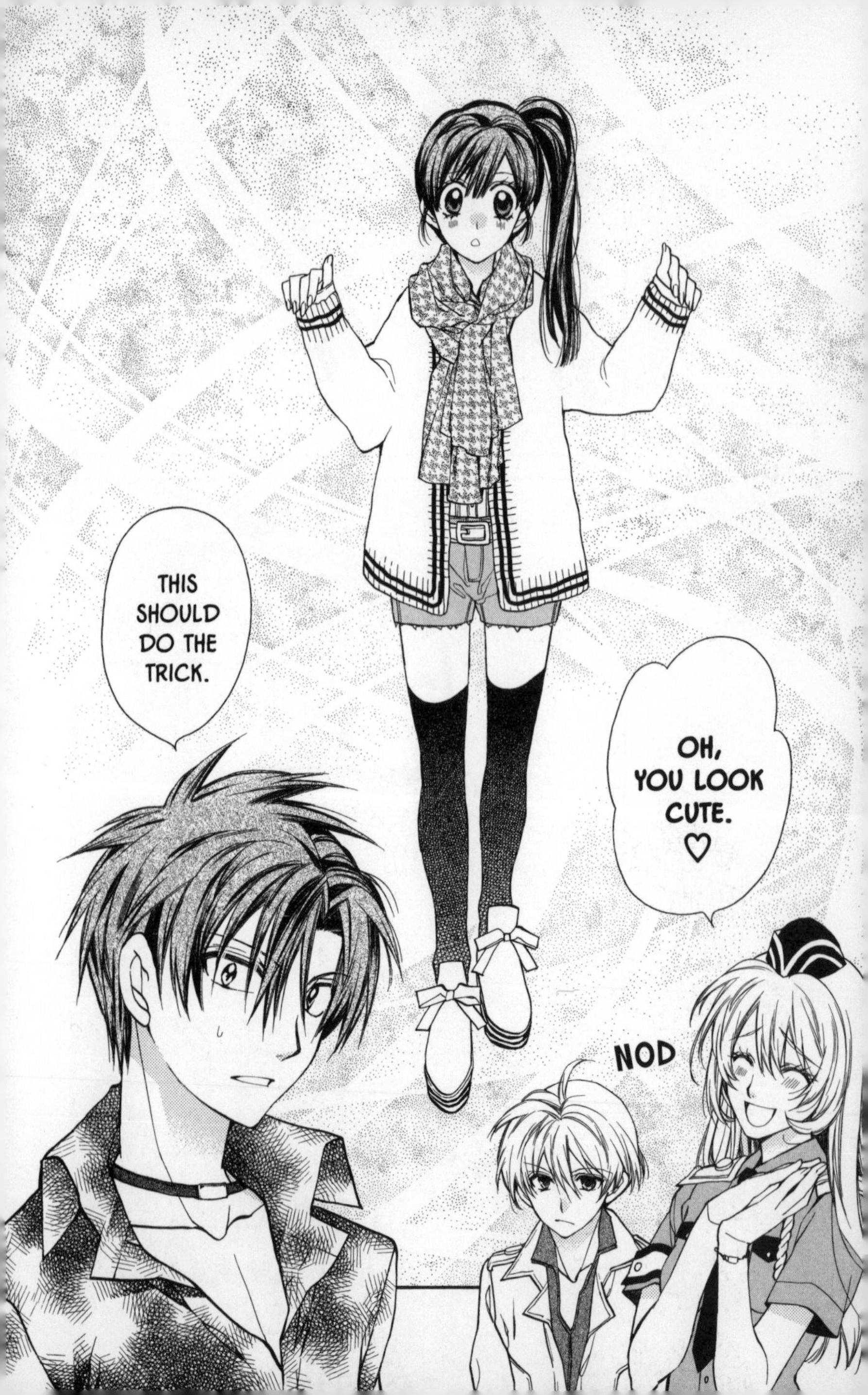
OH, YOU LOOK CUTE. ♡
THIS SHOULD DO THE TRICK.
NOD

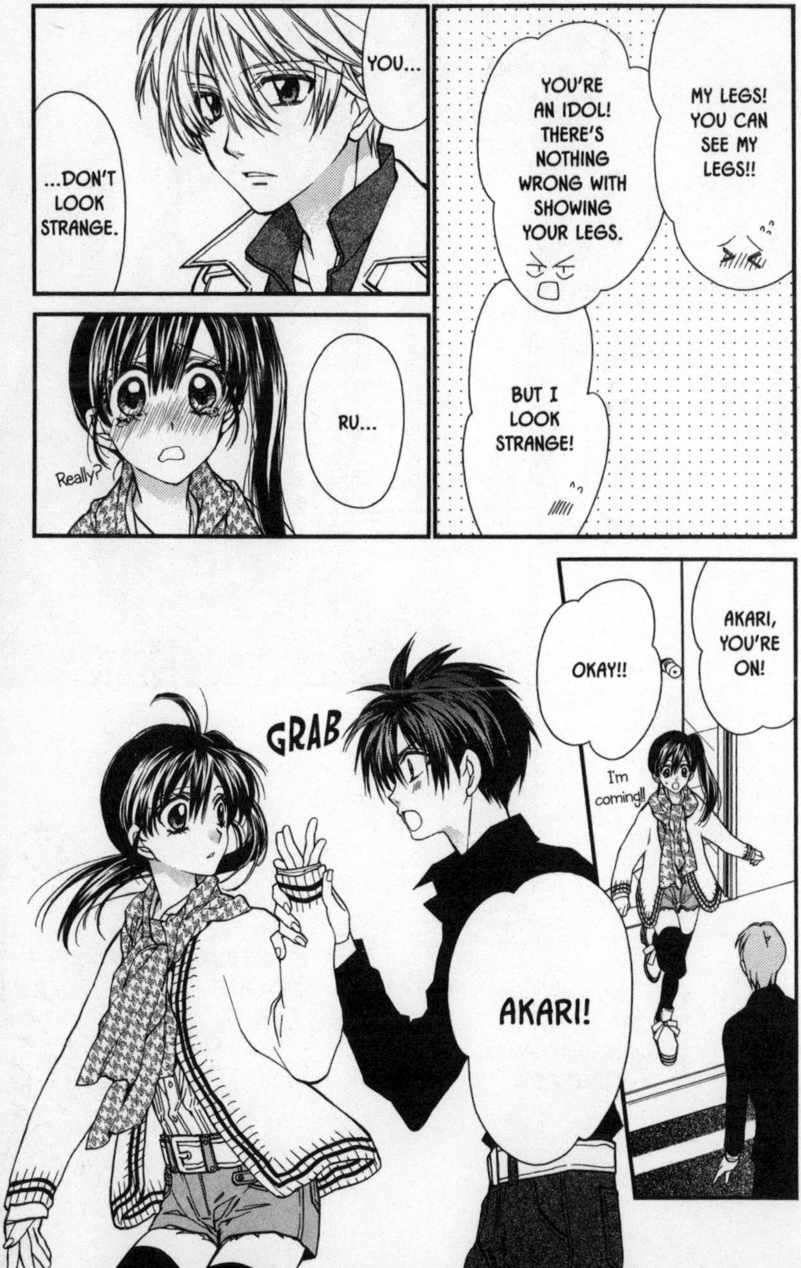
MY LEGS! YOU CAN SEE MY LEGS!!
YOU'RE AN IDOL! THERE'S NOTHING WRONG WITH SHOWING YOUR LEGS.
BUT I LOOK STRANGE!
YOU...
...DON'T LOOK STRANGE.
RU...
Really?
AKARI, YOU'RE ON!
OKAY!!
I'm coming!!
GRAB
AKARI!

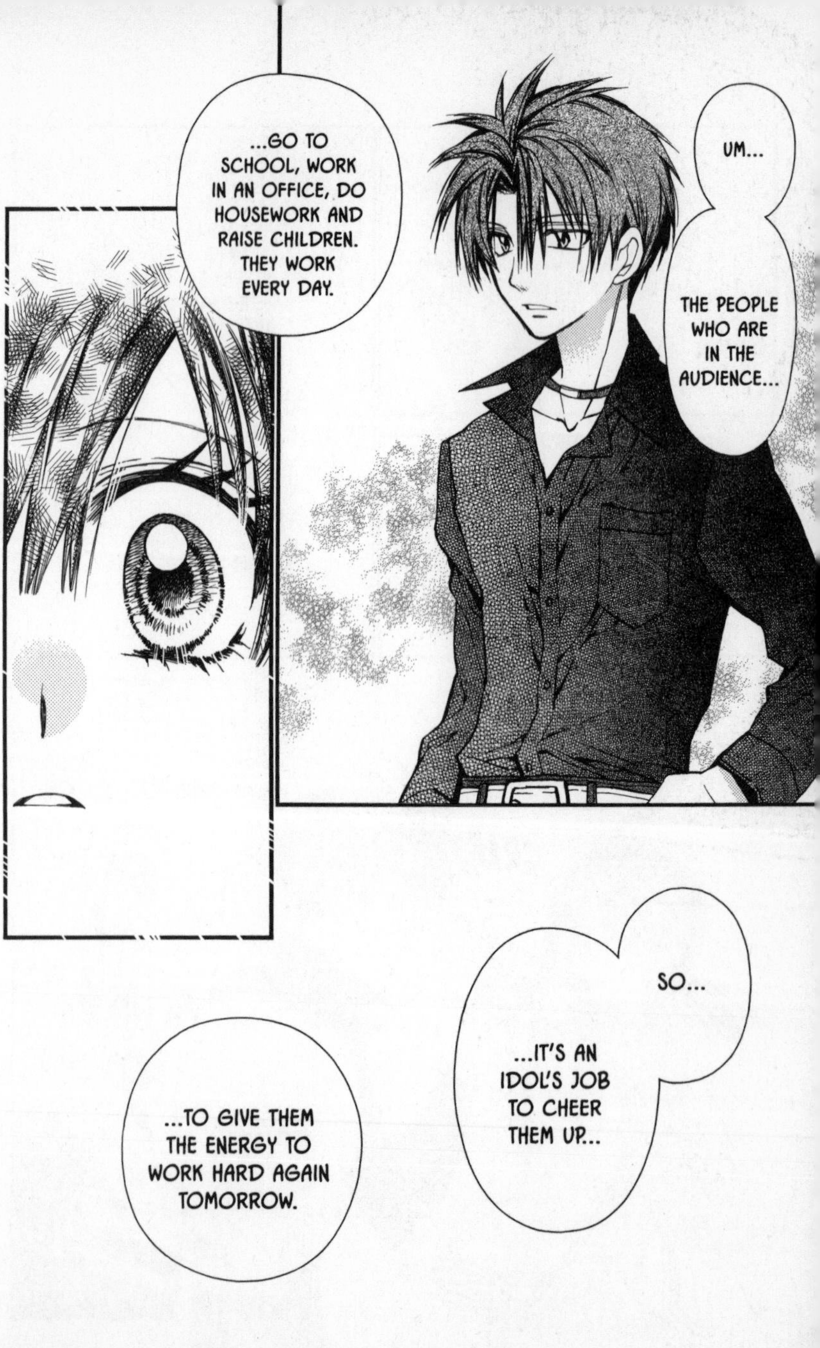
UM...
THE PEOPLE WHO ARE IN THE AUDIENCE...
...GO TO SCHOOL, WORK IN AN OFFICE, DO HOUSEWORK AND RAISE CHILDREN. THEY WORK EVERY DAY.
SO...
...IT'S AN IDOL'S JOB TO CHEER THEM UP...
...TO GIVE THEM THE ENERGY TO WORK HARD AGAIN TOMORROW.

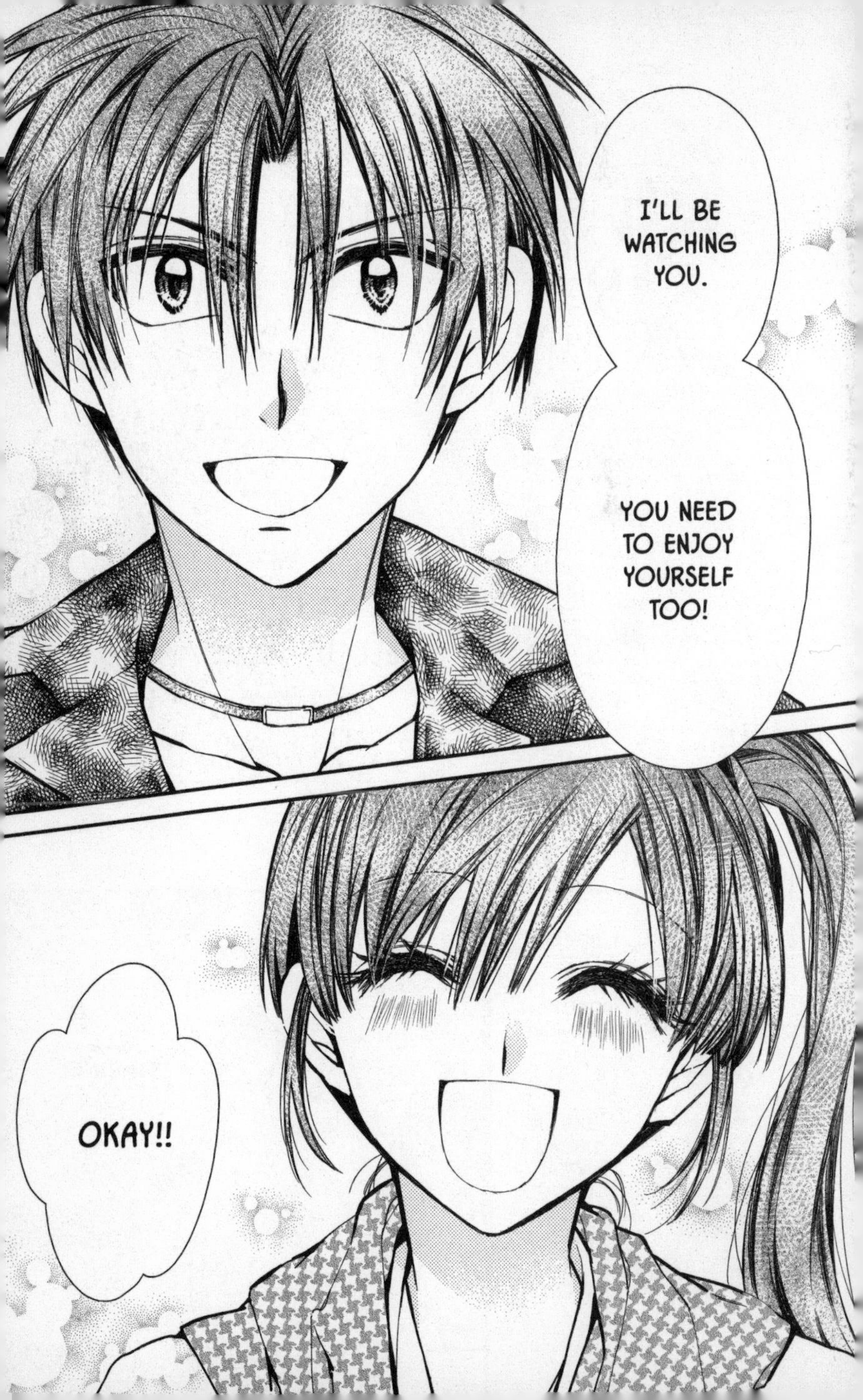
I'LL BE WATCHING YOU.
YOU NEED TO ENJOY YOURSELF TOO!
OKAY!!

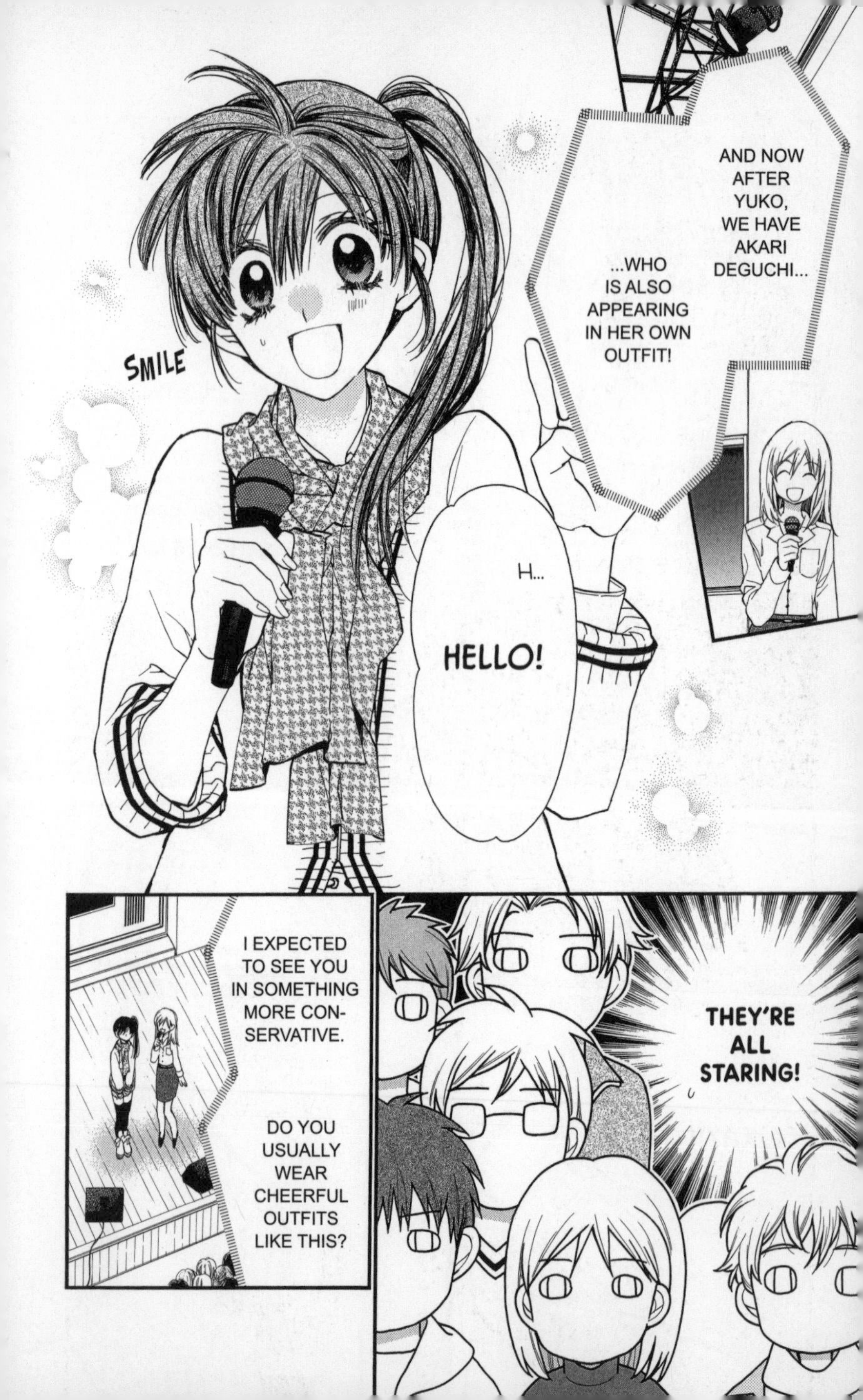
AND NOW AFTER YUKO, WE HAVE AKARI DEGUCHI...
...WHO IS ALSO APPEARING IN HER OWN OUTFIT!
H...
HELLO!
SMILE
THEY'RE ALL STARING!
I EXPECTED TO SEE YOU IN SOMETHING MORE CON- SERVATIVE.
DO YOU USUALLY WEAR CHEERFUL OUTFITS LIKE THIS?

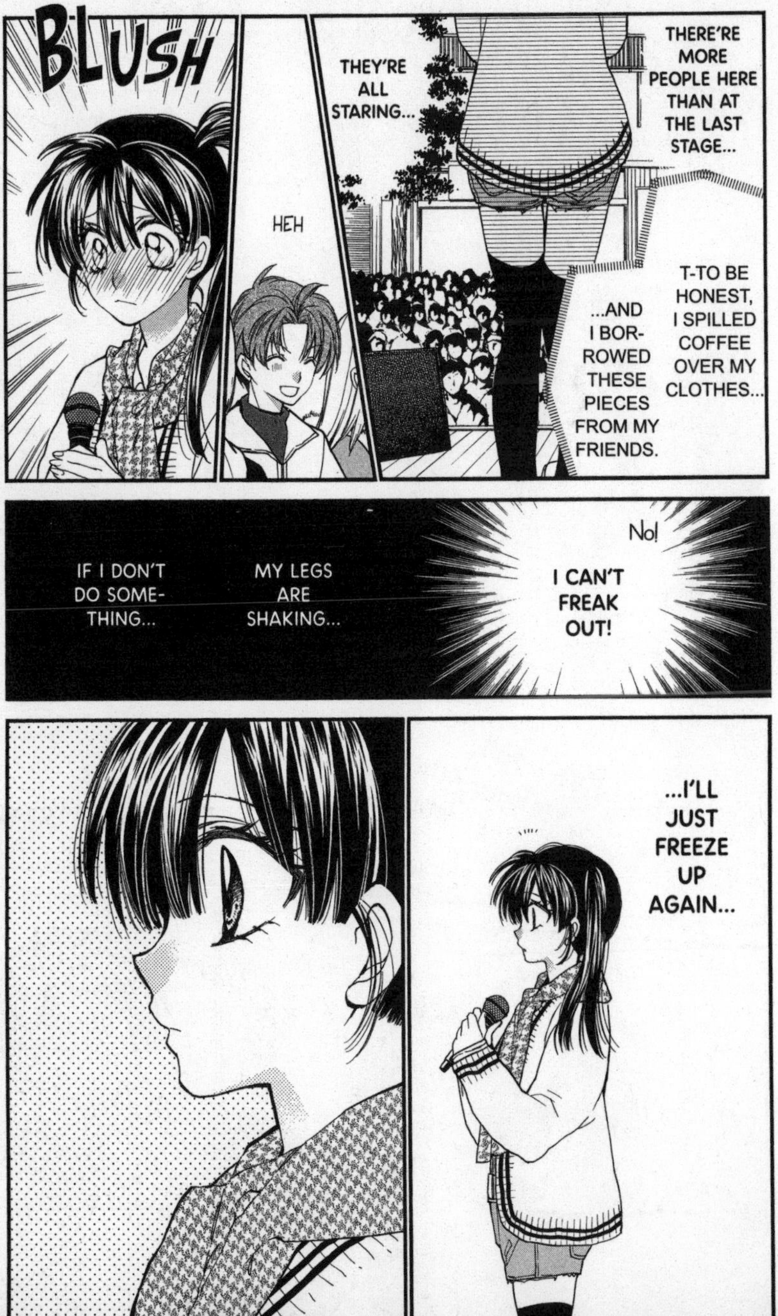
THERE'RE MORE PEOPLE HERE THAN AT THE LAST STAGE...
T-TO BE HONEST, I SPILLED COFFEE OVER MY CLOTHES...
...AND I BOR-ROWED THESE PIECES FROM MY FRIENDS.
THEY'RE ALL STARING...
HEH
BLUSH
No!
I CAN'T FREAK OUT!
MY LEGS ARE SHAKING...
IF I DON'T DO SOME-THING...
...I'LL JUST FREEZE UP AGAIN...

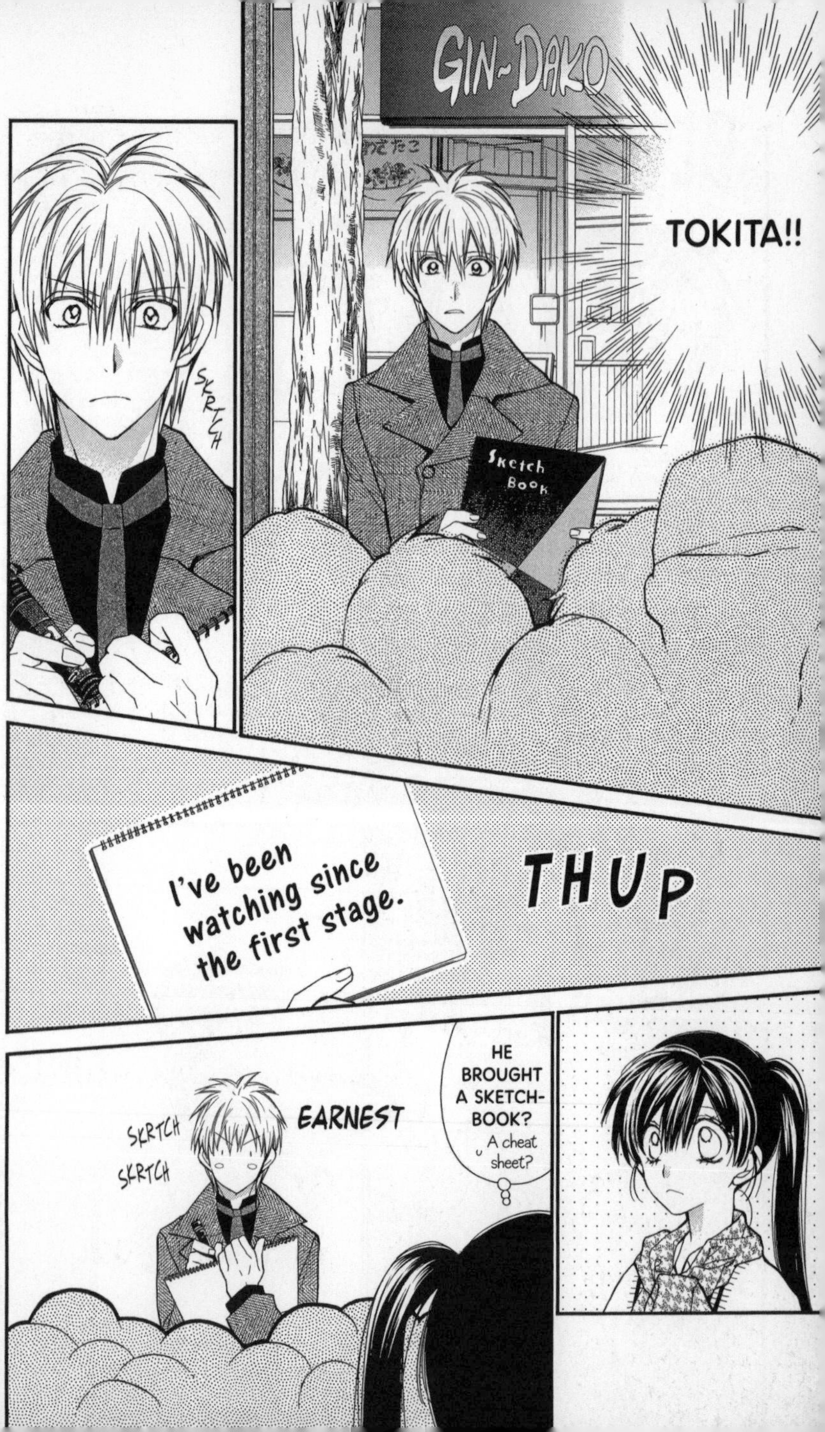
GIN-DAKO
TOKITA!!
SKRTCH
THUP
I've been watching since the first stage.
HE BROUGHT A SKETCH-BOOK?
A cheat sheet?
EARNEST
SKRTCH
SKRTCH

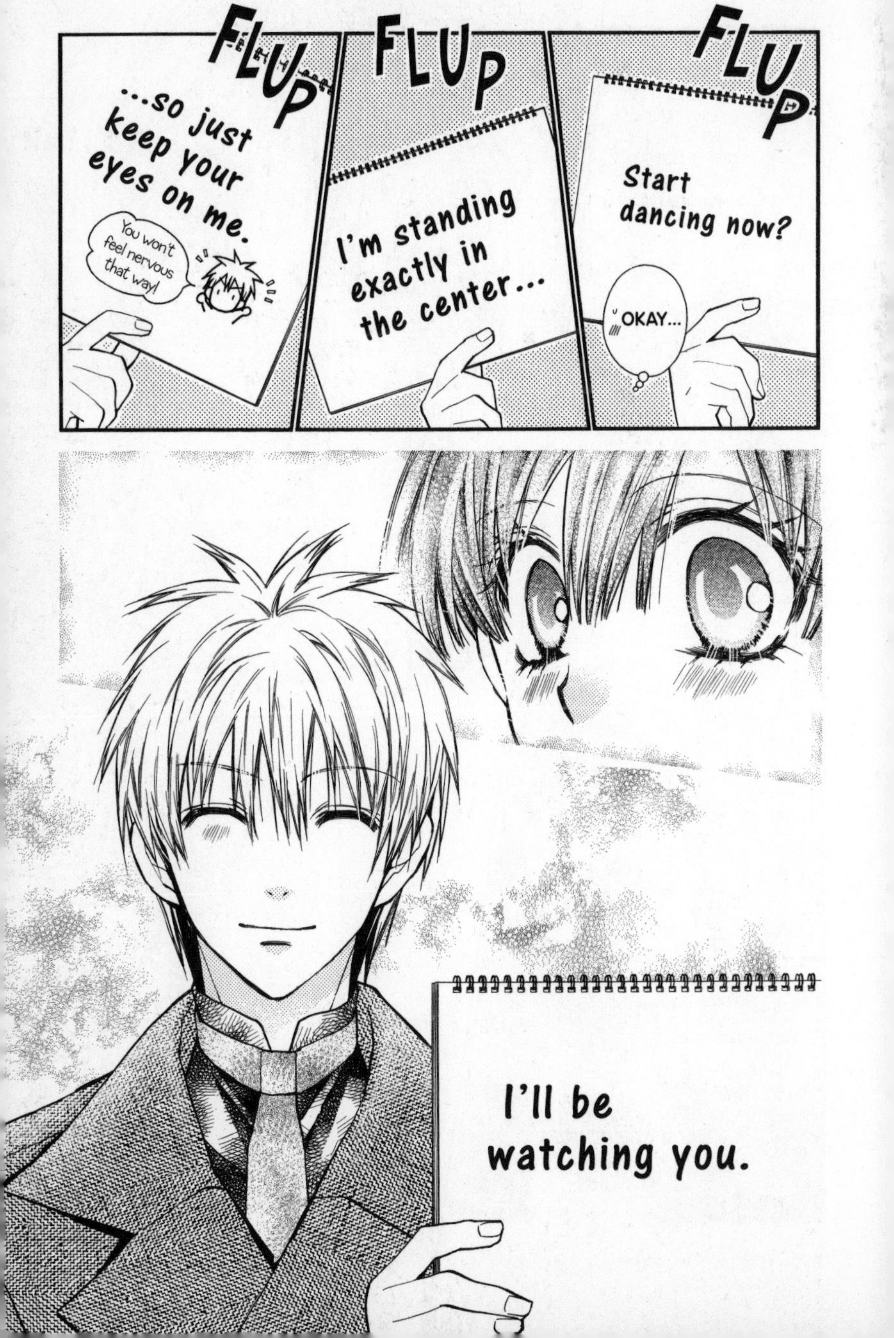
FLUP
Start dancing now?
OKAY...
FLUP
I'm standing exactly in the center...
FLUP
...so just keep your eyes on me.
You won't feel nervous that way!
I'll be watching you.

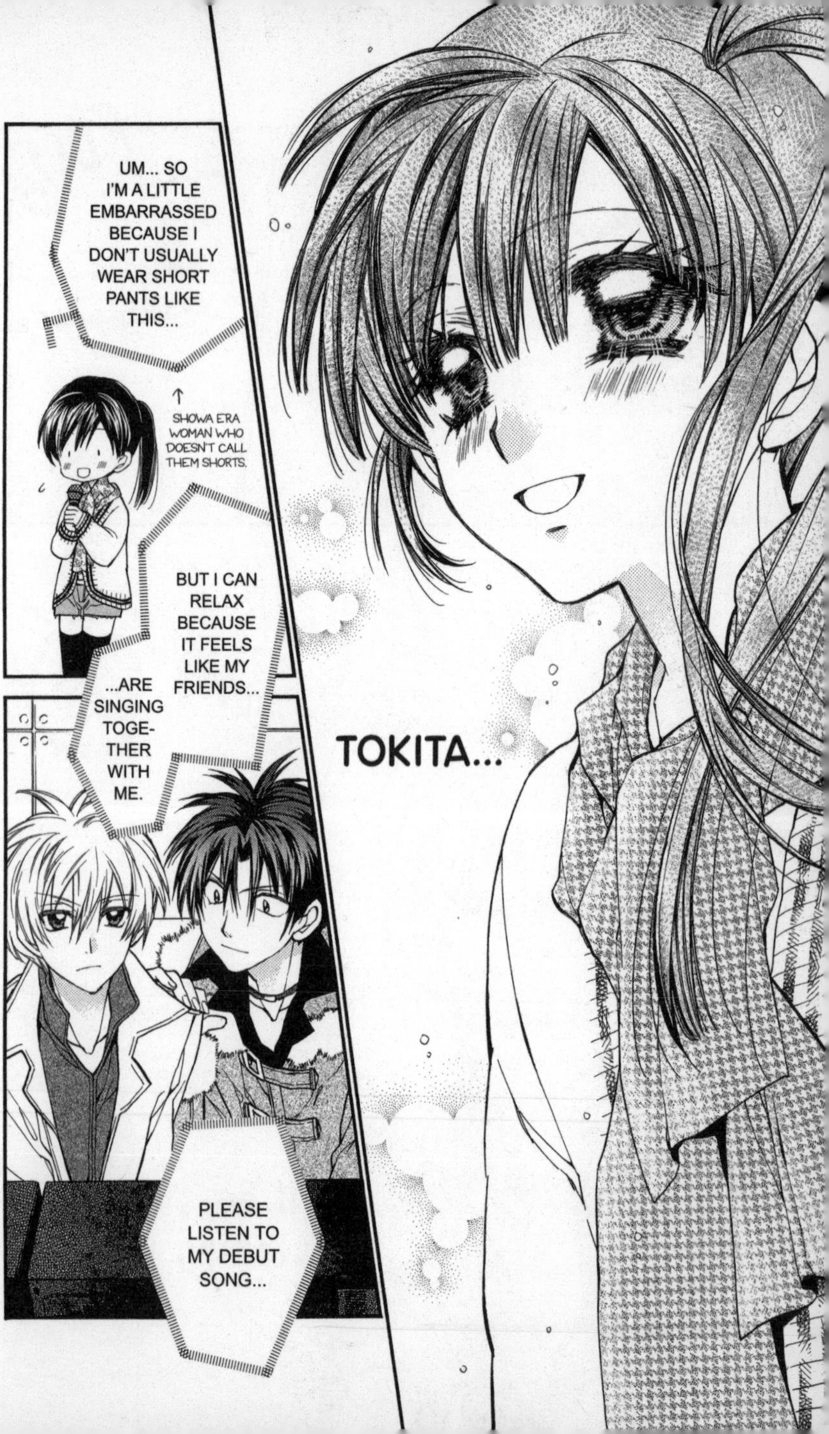
TOKITA...
UM... SO I'M A LITTLE EMBARRASSED BECAUSE I DON'T USUALLY WEAR SHORT PANTS LIKE THIS...
↑ SHOWA ERA WOMAN WHO DOESN'T CALL THEM SHORTS.
BUT I CAN RELAX BECAUSE IT FEELS LIKE MY FRIENDS...
...ARE SINGING TOGE-THER WITH ME.
PLEASE LISTEN TO MY DEBUT SONG...

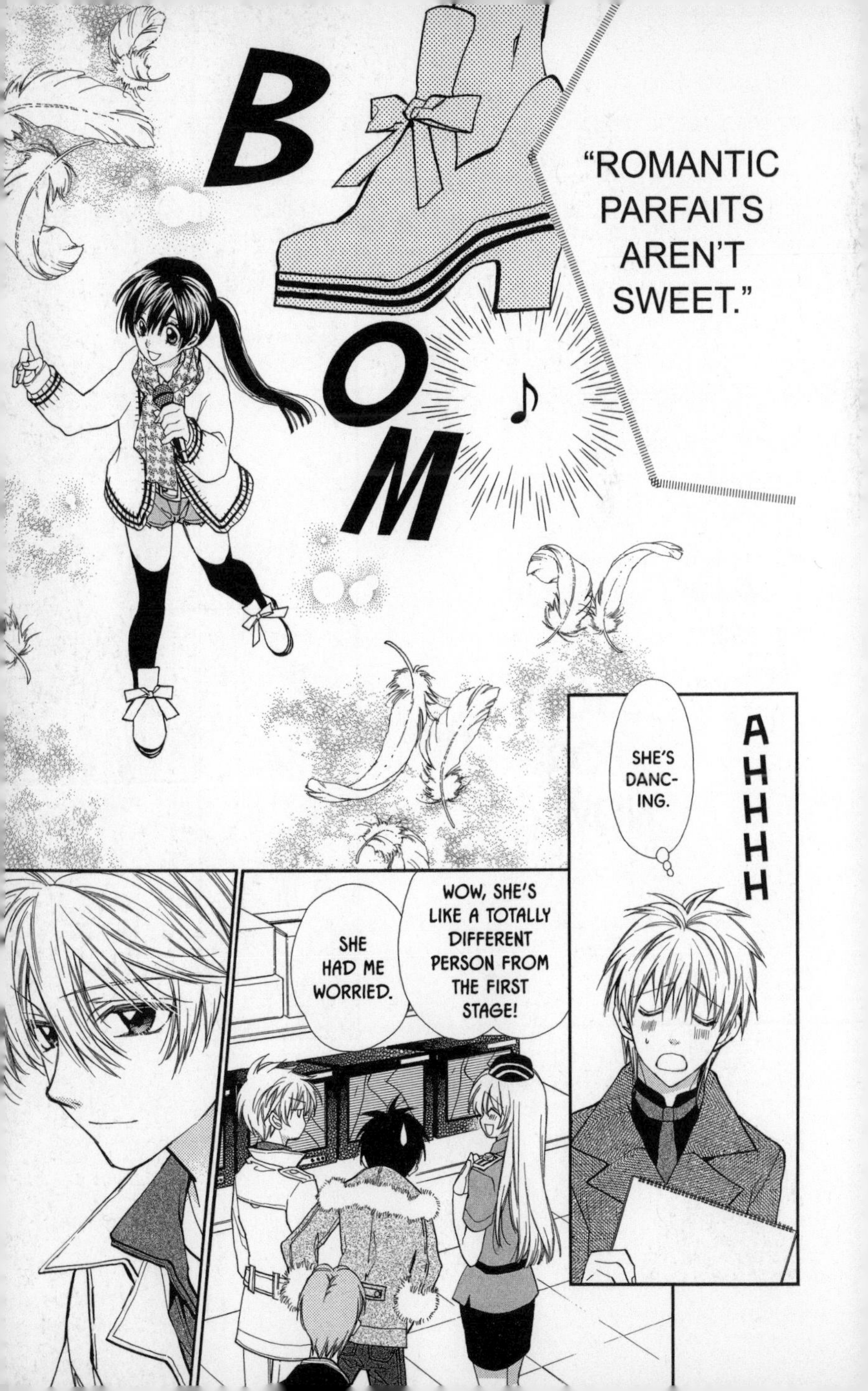
"ROMANTIC PARFAITS AREN'T SWEET."
BOOM
♪
AHHHH
SHE'S DANC-ING.
WOW, SHE'S LIKE A TOTALLY DIFFERENT PERSON FROM THE FIRST STAGE!
SHE HAD ME WORRIED.

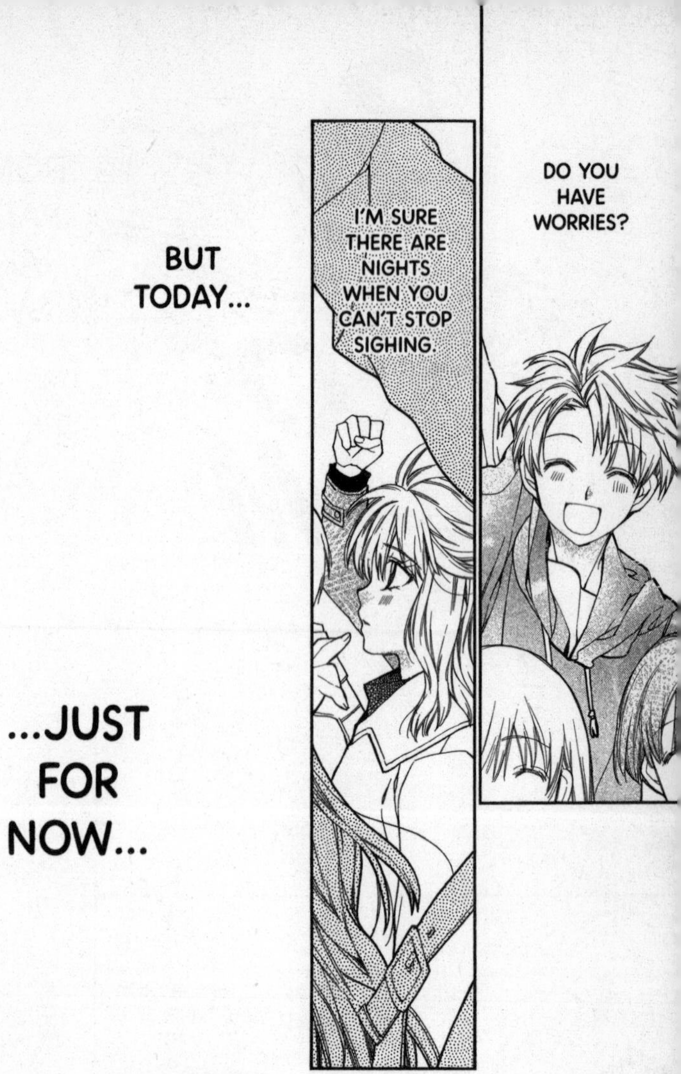
DO YOU HAVE WORRIES?
I'M SURE THERE ARE NIGHTS WHEN YOU CAN'T STOP SIGHING.
BUT TODAY...
...JUST FOR NOW...

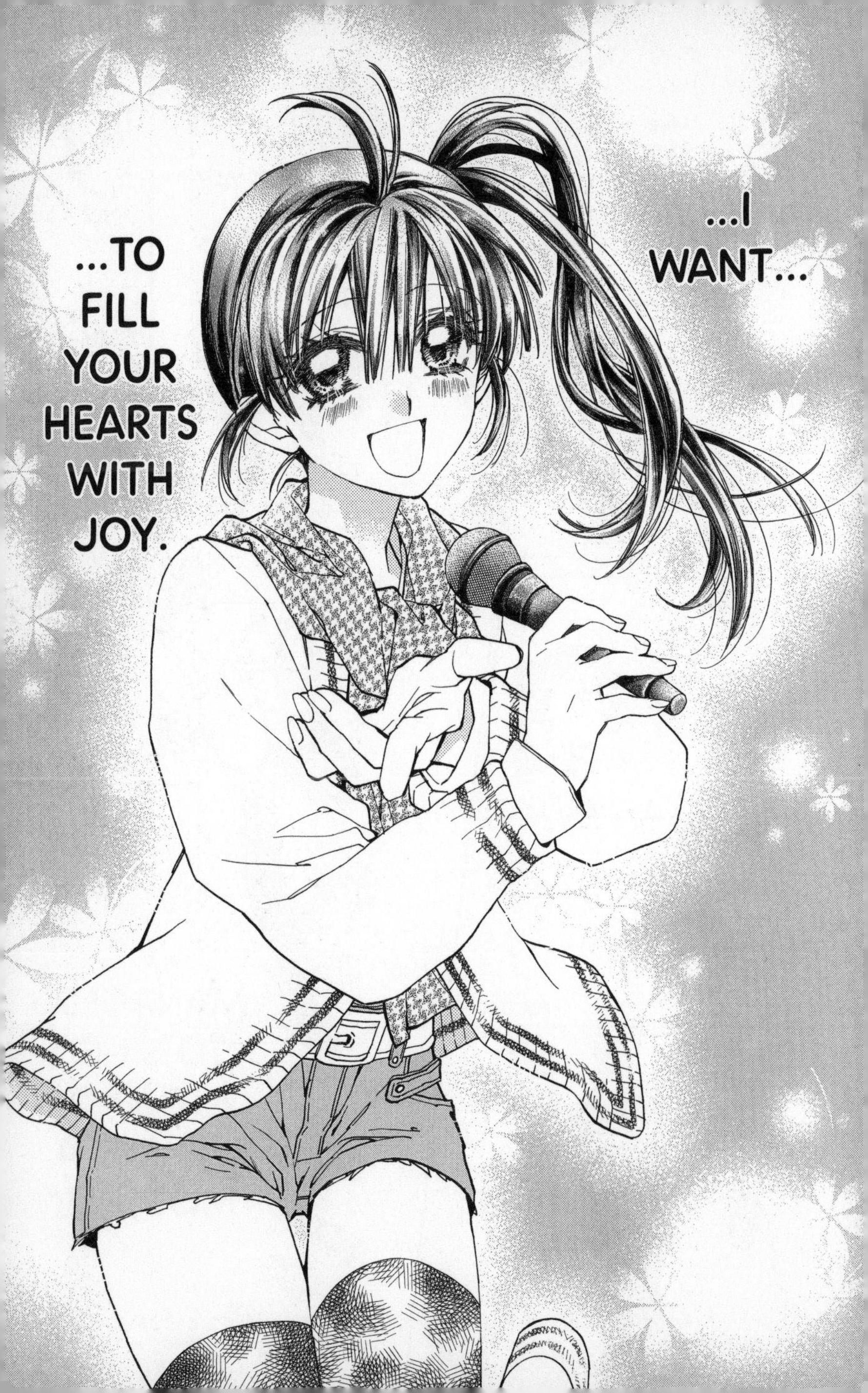
...I WANT...
...TO FILL YOUR HEARTS WITH JOY.

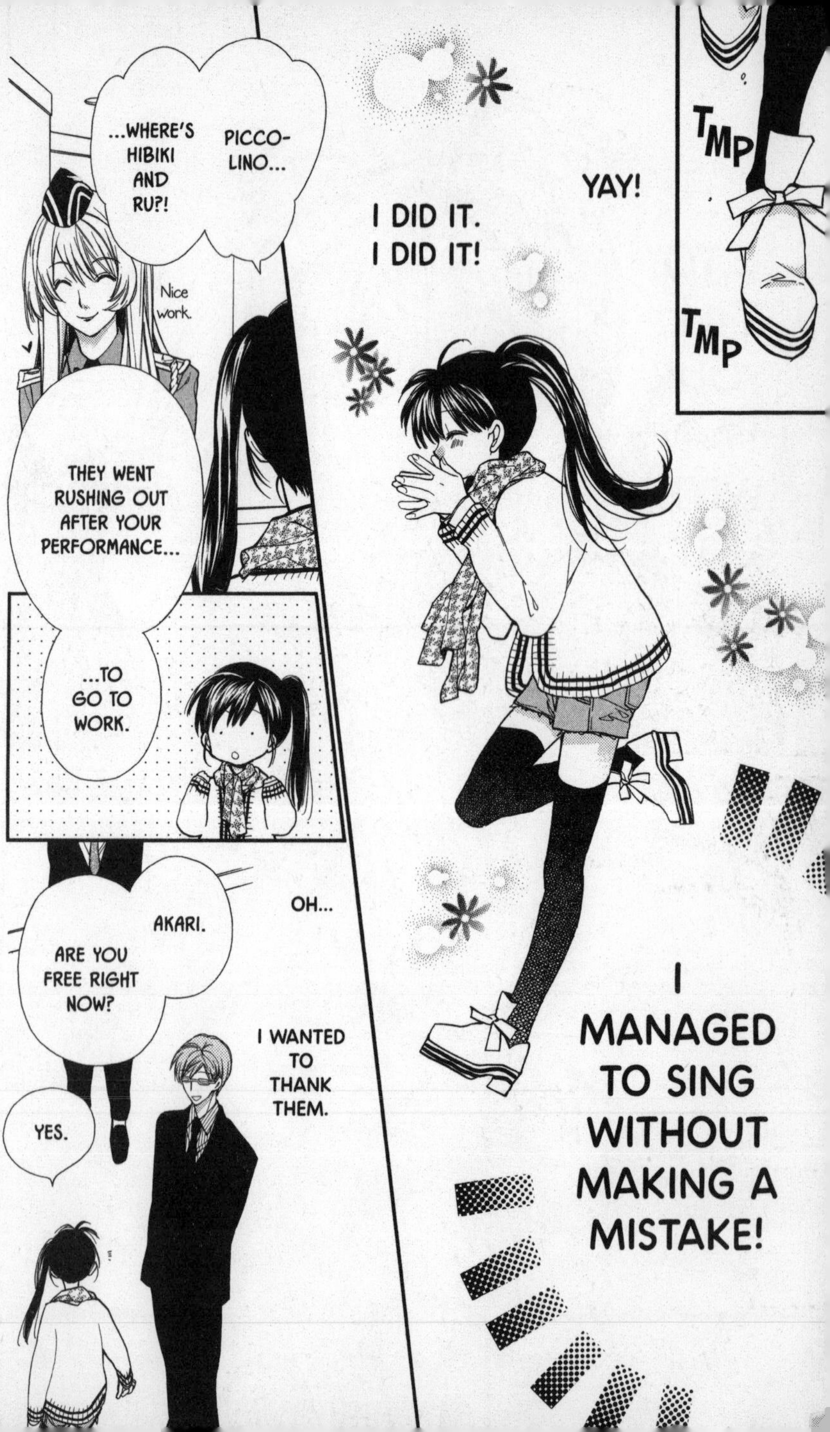
TMP
TMP
YAY!
I DID IT.
I DID IT!
I MANAGED TO SING WITHOUT MAKING A MISTAKE!
PICCO-LINO...
...WHERE'S HIBIKI AND RU?!
Nice work.
THEY WENT RUSHING OUT AFTER YOUR PERFORMANCE...
...TO GO TO WORK.
OH...
I WANTED TO THANK THEM.
AKARI.
ARE YOU FREE RIGHT NOW?
YES.

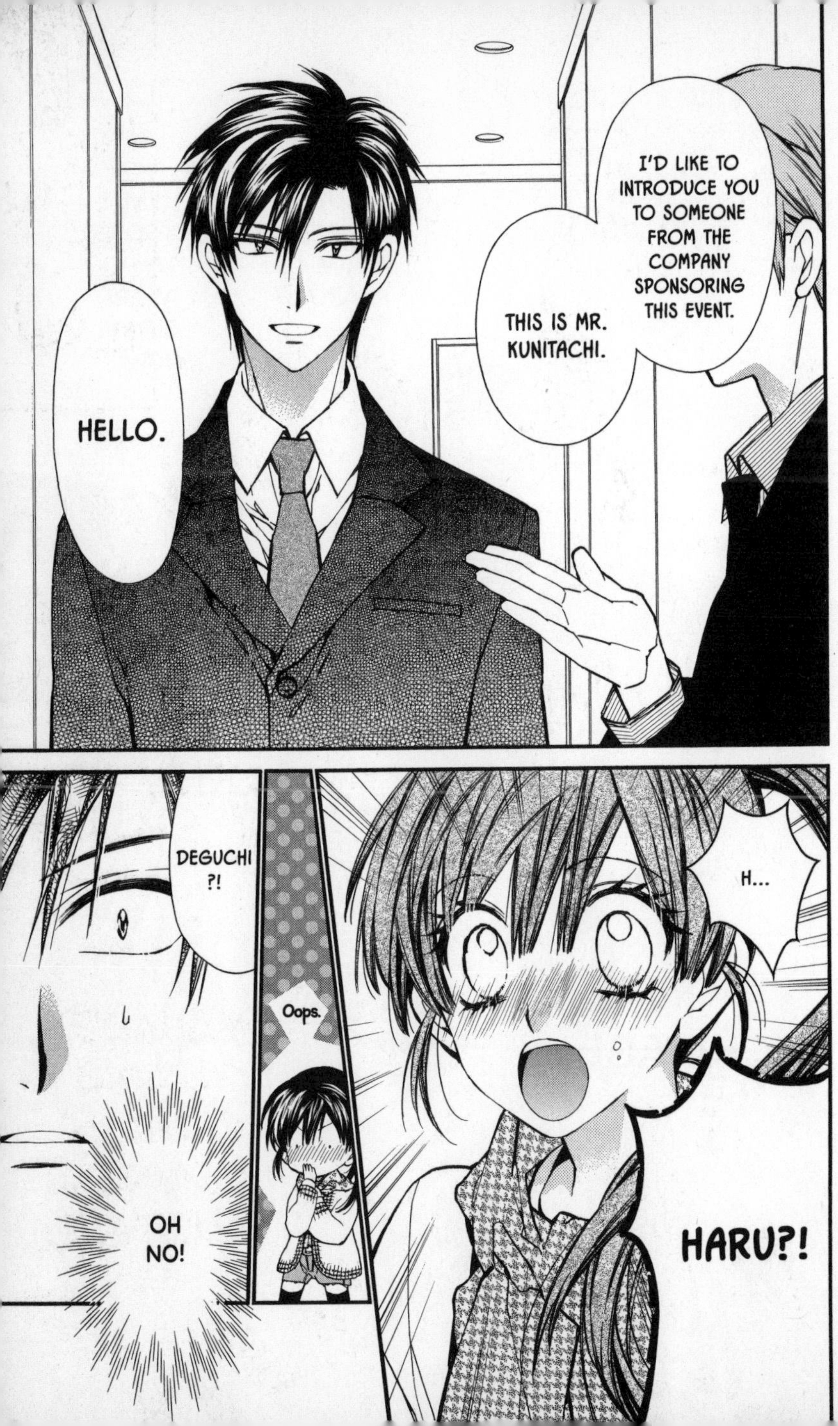
I'D LIKE TO INTRODUCE YOU TO SOMEONE FROM THE COMPANY SPONSORING THIS EVENT.
THIS IS MR. KUNITACHI.
HELLO.
H...
HARU?!
Oops.
DEGUCHI ?!
OH NO!

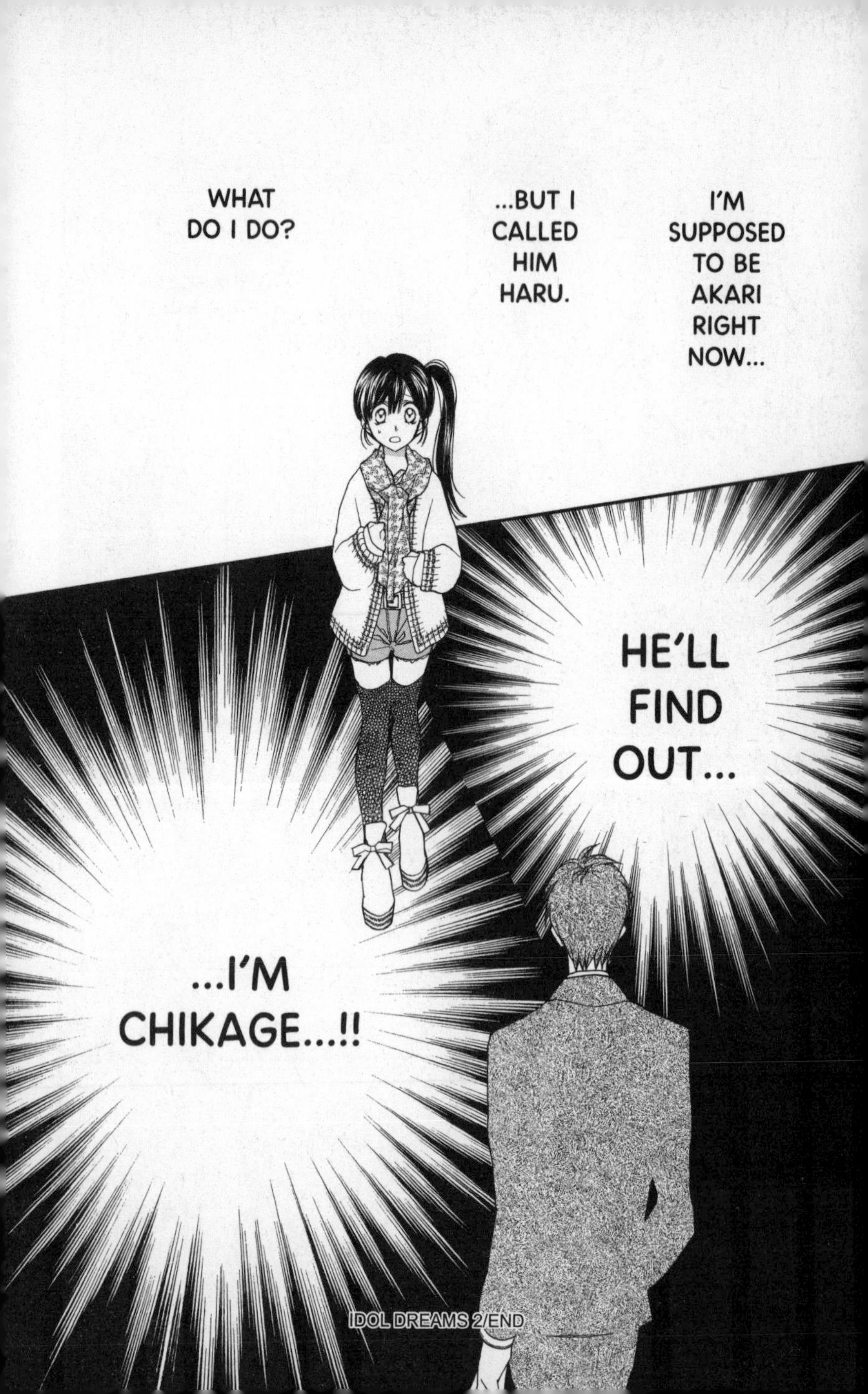
I'M SUPPOSED TO BE AKARI RIGHT NOW...
...BUT I CALLED HIM HARU.
WHAT DO I DO?
HE'LL FIND OUT...
...I'M CHIKAGE...!!
IDOL DREAMS 2/END

dreams

IDOL

SHOJO MANGA ARTIST INTERVIEW

ARINA TANEMURA

This interview appeared on *Lala Melody Online*. ☆
We asked Arina Sensei about *Idol Dreams* and her other
currently running series, *Neko to Watashi no Kinyobi* (The
Cat's and My Friday)!

A Magical-Girl Manga for Adults!

Idol Dreams, currently serialized in *Melody* magazine, is a
story about 31-year-old Chikage transforming back into
her 15-year-old self to become an idol named Akari. Her
romance with the 15-year-old idol Hibiki and her 31-year-old
classmate Tokita is also a major part of the story.

You've been creating manga with young girls as the main
character in *Ribon* until now, but the main character of this
series is a lot more grown-up, isn't she?

Tanemura: The readers who have been my fans since I
made my debut are currently in their late twenties and
thirties, so my editor proposed I create a magical-girl
manga for adults my adult fans could enjoy. Magical-girl
works tend to be about battles or becoming idols, but I had
been working on a manga with a lot of action scenes, so
I wanted to create something different this time. *Neko to
Watashi no Kinyobi*, which I'm also currently working on,
is about the world of show business as well, so I thought I
could create a new series with a similar atmosphere.

Full Moon o Sagashite was about the world of show
business, so it's a subject the readers are used to seeing.

Tanemura: *Full Moon* was about idols, but the story leaned more toward fantasy. The theme of that manga was "*shinigami* (death reapers) and an idol" but it was more shinigami. So I decided to place more emphasis on the idol this time.

The 15-year-old Akari is very cute. The 31-year-old Chikage is cute too, but...

Tanemura: She used to be really cute when she was young, after all. She is the first main character in my manga on whom I haven't drawn eyelashes. (*laugh*)

Because she doesn't wear makeup?

Tanemura: She probably wears some makeup, but she never gets around to applying mascara. She has only black underwear too. (*laugh*) I enjoy drawing rather tacky-looking clothes for the 15-year-old Akari—modest clothes that would look pretty ordinary on a 31-year-old. Of course another reason behind that is because she has just become 15 again and hasn't had time to get any suitable clothes.

I guess Chikage is wearing outfits she would normally wear. Like you said, the main characters of your previous manga would never wear anything like Chikage does.

Tanemura: Right. (*laugh*) But I really enjoy that. I had been working with *Ribon* for a long time, so my mind was always caught up with adding something fancy and cute. But I don't need to do that for this series, so I'm working on it in a very relaxed mood. To be honest, I'm not thinking much about winning the popularity of the readers. The people who read *Melody* are probably not familiar with my work. I'm a new manga creator to this magazine, and I don't expect my work to become popular quickly, so I'm taking things easy.

You've created enough chapters for one volume now, but how do you feel about the series so far?

Tanemura: I really enjoy working on it. I'm not thinking about creating a fast-paced series or doing this and that with it. I'm just concentrating on creating what I truly want to, so even I don't know how the story will turn out.

The manga is about a woman who becomes young again with the aid of a drug, and I thought age 15 was perfect. Age 18 is a bit too close to adulthood. [In Japan, one becomes a legal adult at age 20. -Ed.]

Tanemura: Age 18 is just a step away from becoming an adult. I wanted her to be at an age where she still had time before adulthood. An age with a fresh feeling to it, when teenagers aren't talking all that much about relationships and love. The last time she met Tokita was when she was fifteen, which is roughly half of 31, so I thought it was just the right age.

The main character transforms from 12 to 16 in *Full Moon*. And your other current series, *Neko to Watashi no Kinyobi*, is about a romantic relationship between an elementary school boy and a high school girl. I get the feeling you often use age as an important factor in your manga.

Tanemura: Personally, I don't really give age that much thought, but it seems to be an important factor to many people. For example, many of the early magical-girl series were often about a young girl transforming into a woman because of her adoration of the adult world. That's how I came up with the idea for a "transformation in reverse" shojo manga.

Reverse?

Tanemura: I feel that adults nowadays would watch idols like AKB and think, "If only I were ten years younger..." and feel adoration for them. So I came up with the idea of an adult transforming back into her young self.

I see. The interesting thing is that she's still a 31-year-old inside. If you could become young again with the knowledge you have as an adult, you could do all sorts of things with it.

Tanemura: That's right! If I could become a high school student again, I'm sure I'd be able to do better in my relationships and my school studies. (*laugh*)

SEXINESS...
TWO ORDERS OF THE COLD SOBA SET.
...URGENTLY NEEDED!!

***Idol Dreams* volume 1, page 85. Tokita is shocked to see how unpopular Chikage is with men now...**

I like how Chikage is absolutely gauche and unpopular as a 31-year-old. I really enjoyed the scene in which she took Tokita to a classic soba restaurant, and Tokita thinks to himself, "Sexiness...urgently needed!!"

Tanemura: Sexiness is something she doesn't have.

But the restaurant itself was good.

Tanemura: Chikage's in for the authentic stuff. (*laugh*) Tokita feels there's nothing sexy about having a meal at a soba restaurant, but he still says, "The soba here is really good!!" Tokita is the one acting more like a popular girl. (*laugh*) And Chikage is happy to hear him say that, you know? She's blushing a bit. But she doesn't say, "Really? That's great!" ...Ahh, no wonder she's unpopular.

Unpopular...

Tanemura: Being unpopular with men is something I share with Chikage, so I've included personal experience when writing about her. But there are times when I can't help thinking, "Keep at it, Chikage!" and "Why can't you do it differently?"

What should she do...?

Tanemura: First of all, she should take her glasses off. And she should stop wearing black all the time. How she reacts is a problem. Chikage doesn't know how to react to others in a cute way. She doesn't even so much as smile when Tokita takes her out for a cream soda, which she loves to drink. If she enjoyed it, she should at least smile. The characters from my previous work would have said, "It's delicious. ♡," but all Chikage does is just nod in agreement to the fact that she's enjoying it. (*laugh*) I'm sure men would like it if the girl told them the food is good. But she can't even do that! (*laugh*) He came to pick her up, but she doesn't thank him for that either. She's too self-involved...

I'm sure there are many women who—even if they wanted to—can't act in ways that would make them popular with men, so there must be people who sympathize with her. I also thought it was interesting that she doesn't drink. Adult female characters like her tend to love liquor.

Tanemura: I don't drink. I'm not good at drawing scenes like that, so I thought I'd make her a non-drinker too. That way it makes it even harder for her to be popular with men. Getting drunk so men will relax around her is not an option. I'm sure there are readers who can't drink, so they probably understand that non-drinkers have their own set of problems too. (*laugh*)

NOD
NOD NOD
DOES THAT MEAN SHE'S ENJOYING IT?
Hmm...

Idol Dreams **volume 2, page 8. Chikage drinking her favorite cream soda...**

It's also in line with her love of cream soda.

Tanemura: Cream soda is a Showa era soft drink, isn't it? You don't see it being served in cafés. The green beverage, the ice cream, and the bright red cherry on top! But there are people who have an ardent love for it. It'd be great if the readers would think "this is the drink Chikage loves" whenever they have a cream soda.

Is there anything to be careful of when you're drawing Akari, the 15-year-old Chikage?

Tanemura: She is young and cute, so I want to draw cute girly actions like an ordinary girl. Then I stop for a moment to remind myself that she is actually 31-year-old Chikage! Usually my characters look people in the eye when talking to them, but Akari keeps looking away, you know. (*laugh*) The reason she is able to speak with Hibiki and Ru (also idols) is because they are much younger than she is.

To someone who is 31, 15-year-olds seem like little children.

Tanemura: That's why she has that firm attitude with them. The first time Chikage meets Hibiki, she says, "He's a blunt boy." I used "boy" on purpose. A 31-year-old will not see a 15-year-old as a man. I used "boy" to make it sound like she's observing him. But she still can't look him in the eye when they're alone. (*laugh*)

Chikage also said, "I don't have trouble talking to men who have girlfriends or wives. It feels like I'm talking to my father or brother, so I'm not nervous at all." I understand what she means.

Tanemura: That's from personal experience. (*laugh*) I spent three years in high school with only girls, so I still have a slight problem when talking to men. But if they're married or have a girlfriend, I can easily open up to them as if I'm talking to my brother or father. It makes it a lot easier once I realize I don't have to think about anything romantic.

I understand. It's not about whether I like them or not. It's just that I feel more comfortable after knowing that's not part of the equation.

Tanemura: But when I told a male friend that, he said, "I think men who have girlfriends or wives are more dangerous."

Tokita said that too. Chikage says it and Tokita disagrees. I thought that was a very grown-up scene.

Tanemura: I thought, "Hey, I'll use that," and decided to include it in the manga. My previous works were either fantasy or the main characters were very young, so I was unable to put in my personal experience. But I would have the emotions from those personal experiences in the characters' monologues. Now I can use my personal experience directly in *Idol Dreams*. That's something new for me.

I have a feeling that the popularity of Tokita and Hibiki will be divided equally among the readers. The kind Tokita versus the gorgeous and assertive idol Hibiki.

Tanemura: Hibiki makes an effort at being on top too. I think the young readers will like Hibiki, but the adult readers will choose Tokita.

You haven't decided which one Chikage will eventually get together with, right?

Tanemura: No, I haven't made up my mind yet. I'm thinking about going with the most popular character, so I've been considering both possibilities—Chikage with Tokita and Chikage with Hibiki.

A 31-year-old male character is pretty rare in a Tanemura manga.

Tanemura: A man in his thirties won't be taken over by his emotions. There's a scene in which Tokita tries to kiss the drunk and sleeping Chikage, but he holds himself back. I bet Hibiki would have kissed her. People in their thirties have many other problems they have to deal with, so they're more rational. *(laugh)* Also, even if he feels that Chikage is reacting in the wrong way, Tokita doesn't actually tell her so. That's how an adult in their thirties would act too.

Sometimes in My Mind I Read the Manga I Am Going to Create in the Future.

This is a manga about an adult woman, but it doesn't get too serious, so I enjoy reading it.

Tanemura: It might be because I'm working on *Neko to Watashi no Kinyobi* at the same time. For that series I am trying to create a work that is happy and cheerful without any depressing scenes. It probably has had a positive effect on this series too. The ideas in my head aren't leaning toward the dark side right now.

So it's good to work on two series at once? Don't you have trouble switching from one series to the other?

Tanemura: Oh, there are times when they get jumbled up in my head. I often enter my manga when I'm taking a bath. At the beginning I'll be inside *Neko to Watashi no Kinyobi*, but the next moment I'll be in *Idol Dreams*, so I'll be like, "Aaah! No, no!" to pull myself back to where I was.

What do you mean by "entering your manga"?

Tanemura: It's kind of like reading the manga I am going to create in the future... In my mind I flip through the pages and read it.

So there's an already completed manga in your head?

Tanemura: Yes, in my head. But it all depends on the current mood of the manga. There are times when I have to make little changes or change the story completely when I transfer the manga in my head to a sheet of paper.

Is there anything you have deliberately changed in *Idol Dreams* from your previous series?

Tanemura: This was at the request of my editor, but I'm holding back from using too much screentone to give the manga a simple look. And I've reduced the number of humorous scenes. I want to include gags that have nothing to do with the actual scene (*laugh*), but the manga ends up looking childish if I do that. Also I'm only concentrating on stories about the main character just like in *Neko to Watashi no Kinyobi*. In my previous series I often created story arcs about the supporting characters, but I'm only going to work with the main character this time. I think I'll do some chapters on Tokita and Hibiki for *Idol Dreams*, but I'll keep my hands off the other characters.

Unlike Chikage, Ai, the main character of *Neko to Watashi no Kinyobi*, is a cute and fashionable high school student. She was so cute when she whispered, "Hello? I love you," when Nekota was asleep.

IDOL dreams

Tanemura: When I draw girl heroines, it's always about creating a girl whom I would want for my girlfriend if I were a guy. Ai would be so cute if she were my girlfriend. But she'll get whisked away from me by an elementary school boy. (*laugh*)

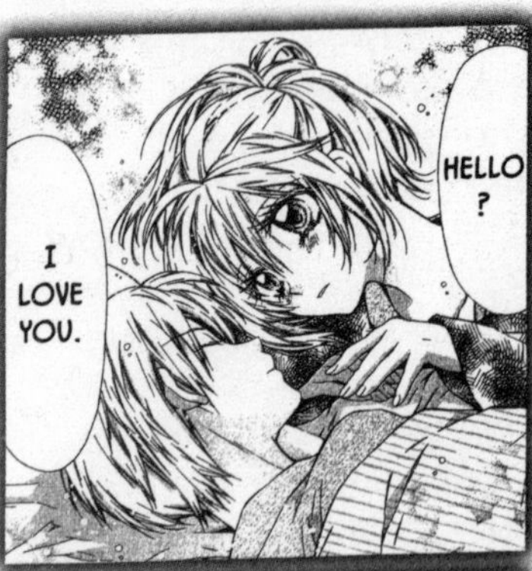

HELLO ?
I LOVE YOU.

Neko to Watashi no Kinyobi © Arina Tanemura/Shueisha Margaret Comics.

They're a May and December couple. Ai is a freshman in high school and her cousin Nekota is a fifth-grader in elementary school. They have a lot of things to overcome in order to have a relationship, don't they?

Tanemura: Nekota doesn't have a cell phone, so she can't text or call him. They're cousins, and Ai is Nekota's tutor, so there's nothing wrong with her calling his house, but people might get suspicious if she calls too many times. They can't call each other to decide when to meet, so the only possibility of seeing each other is by pure coincidence. (*laugh*) The only time they can see each other is on Friday when she goes to tutor him. They have a rather agonizing relationship, but I think romantic relationships are more passionate when there's an obstacle. It also makes it easier for me to come up with the story.

Their relationship make a huge advancement in volume 4 of *Neko to Watashi no Kinyobi*, right...?

Tanemura: It's basically a kissfest. I read over the volume and it was kisses from start to finish. (*laugh*)

You once said it was a "kiss scene" if the characters tried to kiss each other—it didn't matter if they actually kissed or not. That was an eye-opener for me.

Tanemura: They hardly kiss in volume 4, but it's still a kissfest by my standards.

I can't wait to read it. Do you enjoy drawing love scenes?

Tanemura: I could probably work on love scenes...forever. I blush and grin while I'm working on them. But every now and then I get annoyed and think, "I've had enough of you happy people! Be gone with you!" while I toss the storyboard aside. But I still have to turn in that storyboard, so in agony I eventually pick it up from the floor. (*laugh*)

(Conducted February 2014 at Tanemura Sensei's office. Interview & Text by Shima Kadokura.)

IDOL dreams

*This article is a re-edited version of the "Shojo Manga Artist Interview" series from *Lala Melody* online.

I like the middle school chapter about Tokita, Haru and Chikage—especially the way it shows Tokita and Chikage, whose personalities and relationship are quite opposite from how they are now. The person wearing the glasses has changed too. Maybe they are two of a kind because of all those similarities.

ARINA TANEMURA

Arina Tanemura began her manga career in 1996 when her short stories debuted in *Ribon Original* magazine. She gained fame with the 1997 publication of *I•O•N*, and ever since her debut Tanemura has been a major force in shojo manga with popular series *Phantom Thief Jeanne, Time Stranger Kyoko, Full Moon, The Gentlemen's Alliance †* and *Sakura Hime: The Legend of Princess Sakura*. Both *Phantom Thief Jeanne* and *Full Moon* have been adapted into animated TV series.